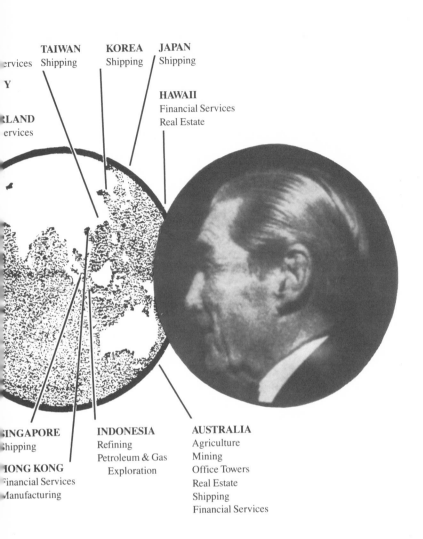

**TAIWAN**    **KOREA**    **JAPAN**
:rvices   Shipping    Shipping    Shipping

Y

**HAWAII**
Financial Services
:LAND    Real Estate
:rvices

:INGAPORE     **INDONESIA**     **AUSTRALIA**
:hipping      Refining      Agriculture
            Petroleum & Gas    Mining
**IONG KONG**    Exploration     Office Towers
:inancial Services                 Real Estate
Manufacturing                 Shipping
                                   Financial Services

*Daniel K. Ludwig and his world*

*The Invisible Billionaire*

By the same author

*Doctors on the New Frontier*
(with William Hoffman)

# The Invisible Billionaire

## Daniel Ludwig

BY

JERRY SHIELDS

Houghton Mifflin Company/Boston/1986

Library of Congress Cataloging-in-Publication Data

Shields, Jerry.
The invisible billionaire.

Bibliography: p.
Includes index.
1. Ludwig, Daniel Keith, 1897-    . 2. Merchant
marine — United States — Biography. 3. Capitalists
and financiers — United States — Biography.
4. Millionaires — United States — Biography. I. Title.
HE569.L84S55 1986      387.5′092′4 [B]      86-7519
ISBN 0-395-35402-1

Printed in the United States of America

V 10 9 8 7 6 5 4 3 2 1

*For Ted Keller,*
*who has more courage, integrity, and*
*human goodness than Ludwig has money,*
*and for environmentalists everywhere*

# Acknowledgments

During my research for this book, many people offered help in one form or another — information, suggestions, or services. Among those to whom I would like to say thanks are Shelton Davis and the staff of the Anthropology Resource Center, who provided many valuable sources on Ludwig's Brazilian activities; Mary Jane Harvey, Georgia Stamas, and Lennie Thomas of the Maritime Administration, who made my perusal of files there a lot easier; authors Charles Higham, Don Barlett, and Jim Steele, Michael Drosnin, and Jacqueline Thompson for their guidance and information; Professor Alan Block of Pennsylvania State University for his expertise on organized crime; attorney Jack Blum of Washington for a tip that led to a chapter; Joe Speer of Jack Anderson's staff for his help in deciphering some of Ludwig's Latin American activities; Matthew Rothschild and Russell Mokhiber, former editors of *Multinational Monitor,* for providing useful leads; Lee Gibson and Casey O'Connor of the Delaware Division of Libraries for answering countless requests for specific bits of information; R. W. Appleyard, historian of South Haven, Michigan, and a number of other South Haven residents who supplied information; Bill Hoffman for his encouragement and advice over the years; and especially my wife, Jane, without whose fortitude and support this book never would have been written.

# Contents

Preface            xi

1 The Richest Man Alive          1

2 South Haven          15

3 The *Mosher* Incident          31

4 The *Ulysses* Imbroglio          54

5 The Rockefeller Connection          88

6 D.K. Welshes on a Deal          100

7 The War Years          112

8 The Maritime Scandals          136

9 Going Japanese          154

10 Grand Bahama Island          181

11 Seadade          197

12 American-Hawaiian          203

13 Freeport          225

14 Whiteford          240

15 The Royal Commission of Inquiry          247

16 Hughes          253

17 Mercantile Bank          271

18 "Welcome to Brazil, Mr. Ludwig"          284

19 "A Gray Old Wolf and a Lean"          334

Sources          367

Notes          378

Index          392

# Preface

When I started this book four years ago, Daniel Keith Ludwig was generally conceded to be the wealthiest man in the world. This was reason enough to write a biography about him.

But besides being the richest, Ludwig was also reputed to be the most secretive man alive. One biographer of the late Howard Hughes had written, "Compared to Ludwig, Hughes was a press agent's dream."

The problem, then, was getting access to reliable information. A few articles had been written about this mysterious tycoon, but they were fragmentary, sometimes inaccurate, rarely incisive; they did not present a detailed portrait of the man and his financial empire. Ludwig had somehow managed to elude the spotlight that made billionaires like Hughes, J. Paul Getty, and H. L. Hunt widely known figures.

When I first broached the idea for a Ludwig biography, many people thought it couldn't be done, not, at least, by an outsider. But I felt it was time to strip away the veil that had surrounded this tycoon for so long — time to find out who he really was and how he operated.

It was not an easy task. Not only does Ludwig refuse to talk about himself, but others who know him well don't talk about him either. Unable to locate people willing to tell me about Ludwig, and dissatisfied with what the media had published about him, I began digging through government records. It was when I was sorting through thousands upon thousands of memos, letters, and documents that I felt I was finally on the trail of the real Daniel Ludwig.

Correlating these records with information from other sources, I compiled what appears on the following pages. I wish I could say it is a definitive picture of the man, but I cannot. His worldwide empire is too extensive, and too many details of his life are still hidden behind the veil.

This book is to be regarded not as the final word on Ludwig but as a beginning from which other researchers can launch their own investigations.

Curiosity is a healthful thing. Secrecy is the enemy of democracy, not its protector. Men as rich and powerful as Ludwig have an effect on all of us, and it is in our best interests to keep a watchful eye on their activities.

*The Invisible Billionaire*

*One*

# The Richest Man Alive

The photographer from *New York* magazine stood stamping his feet
and blowing on his fingers at the entrance of mid-Manhattan's fifty-
story Burlington House office tower. The wind sweeping off Central
Park and down the Avenue of the Americas this November morning
in 1977, ruffling the overcoats of pedestrians rushing to jobs in the
gleaming skyscrapers flanking the street, was damp and chill.

The cameraman, Morris Warman, was excited and more than a
little nervous. In a matter of moments, by his calculation, he would
enjoy a unique opportunity: the chance to snap the first unposed
picture ever taken of the richest man in the world.

The strange thing was that most Americans had never even heard
of Daniel Keith Ludwig. Even these sophisticated New Yorkers,
who fancied themselves the smartest, best-informed people on the
face of the planet, had not the least glimmering that the old man
who'd soon come striding purposefully up the street was the world's
only living multibillionaire.

It was hard to figure. How could a man — any man — in these days
of mass media coverage and public obsession with world records,
manage to accumulate a $3 billion fortune with hardly anyone
becoming aware of it?

If it takes a sixteen-inch stack of hundred-dollar bills to make a
million, then a stack equaling a billion would tower over the Empire

State Building. Ludwig's riches would be three times as tall.

Most of the man's wealth, of course, was not in hundred-dollar bills, but in ships and minerals and real estate. Initially he had made most of his money building tankers and hauling oil in them. This, at least, was comprehensible. Nearly all the acknowledged American billionaires had made the bulk of their fortunes in oil-related activities.

Rockefeller, Hunt, Getty, Hughes — names that have already become legends in the history of American enterprise. John D. Rockefeller, founder of the Standard Oil Company, built an empire that, two generations later, still controls most of the earth's energy and mineral resources. H. L. Hunt, a pugnacious Western wildcatter, left a fortune that enabled two of his sons to get within whispering distance of cornering the world market in silver. J. Paul Getty, inheriting millions from his oilman-father, shrewdly turned them into billions. And Howard Hughes, heir to a company holding virtual monopoly rights on oil-drilling equipment, used the money to branch into aircraft manufacture and vastly increase his wealth.

Each of these oil billionaires had enjoyed fame as well as fortune. Rockefeller was known for tipping his caddies and others with shiny new dimes. Hunt was notorious for his fanatic espousal of right-wing causes. Getty wrote business-advice columns for *Playboy* magazine and built a superb art collection. Hughes, after dazzling the public with record-breaking flight exploits and risqué movies, bought up most of Las Vegas and became well known just for being mysterious.

But Ludwig, richer than Hughes, is so enigmatic as to remain almost unknown; he has managed to amass his fortune while avoiding the fame. Obsessed with privacy, he reportedly pays a major public relations firm fat fees to keep his name *out* of the papers. From time to time, of course, stories have crept into the media, even — very rarely — with Ludwig's cooperation. It was from such pieces that the *New York* magazine photographer had learned that the world's richest man was living, almost anonymously, right in the middle of Manhattan and that he was in the habit of walking to work every day, unrecognized by his fellow pedestrians. It was a good story, one the magazine's readers should get a kick out of. Now, if he could only get a picture of the old man to run with the article . . .

Standing in front of Burlington House (the skyscraper Ludwig, in joint venture with Fisher Brothers Construction Company, had built to house his flagship corporation, National Bulk Carriers), the photographer waited for the billionaire to walk the few blocks from his penthouse apartment on East Sixtieth Street. The story behind his assignment was a long one.

Ludwig had first come into the news in 1956 because of an event taking place nearly halfway around the globe. In the summer of that year, President Gamal Abdel Nasser of Egypt had startled the world by nationalizing the Suez Canal, setting up the Egyptian Canal Authority in place of the international private Suez Canal Company. He intended to keep all of the proceeds from the tolls to finance the Aswan High Dam, an ambitious project he had planned for his poverty-stricken country. Since its opening, in 1869, the canal had been used to cut the time and expense of shipping goods between Europe and Asia, but Egypt — though the isthmus lay in its territory — had never received a large share of the profits.

Nasser's move was obviously not popular with other nations. Late in October, Israel, quickly followed by Britain and France, invaded Egypt to retake the canal. By the time the United Nations intervened, the waterway was blocked by sunken and damaged ships, and it remained that way for over six months. Oil tankers and other merchant vessels were forced to haul their cargoes along the old route, around South Africa. Winter was approaching in the Northern Hemisphere, and the added distance was creating a severe oil shortage. With more vessels needed to haul petroleum, anyone with tankers to lease could just about name his own price, but only a handful of shippers were in position to take advantage of the opportunity.

The media were full of news about the oil crisis and of stories about the few lucky devils who were getting fabulously rich from it. Much of the attention focused on the "Golden Greeks," a New York–based coterie of Greek Americans who owned and operated a majority of the world's independent merchant ships.

For decades, the acknowledged leader of this little fraternity had been a canny old ex-skipper, Stavros Livanos. In recent years, challenges to his supremacy had been mounted within his own family. His two daughters had married a couple of eager young entrepreneurs named Aristotle Onassis and Stavros Niarchos, and the competition between these brothers-in-law was threatening to put Livanos in the shade.

When people talked about the Golden Greeks, they usually meant

Onassis and Niarchos. Not only were they making money hand over fist from the oil crisis; they were spending it almost as fast in a rivalry to see who could make the bigger splash among the international set. If Niarchos built a huge, expensive yacht for himself and his guests, Onassis would start a bigger, costlier one. If Onassis hung his yacht's staterooms with priceless old masters, Niarchos would have art experts combing European auction houses to bid on even more valuable masterpieces.

Both entertained lavishly, holding parties at the finest restaurants in Paris, Rome, London, New York, Hollywood, Rio, and becoming the darlings of café society. Both shamelessly courted royalty: Niarchos wooed Queen Elizabeth and Prince Philip at Ascot; Onassis (after buying control of Monte Carlo) fêted Princess Grace and Prince Rainier in Monaco.

Gossip columnists loved them, and celebrity worshipers everywhere clamored for more stories about these modern sons of Midas who were throwing money around like confetti. It was natural, then, that *Time* magazine in 1956 should run an article, "The New Argonauts," about the incredible Greeks. The story centered on Niarchos, but midway through was a curious sentence: "Customarily included among 'the Greeks' is Midwestern-born Daniel K. Ludwig, 58, whose fleet (estimated at 1.5 million tons) is second only to Niarchos'."

*Time* went on to note that the fleet of Onassis ranked third behind the ships of Niarchos and Ludwig, that Ludwig had started the race to build bigger and bigger supertankers with the 30,000-ton *Bulkpetrol* in 1948, and that, in the very week the article ran, "Ludwig's 84,730-ton *Universe Leader* [the world's largest tanker to date] will go down the ways at Kure, Japan, where Ludwig has turned out more than half a million tons of shipping since he leased the former Imperial Navy Yard in 1951. Six feet wider than the *Queen Elizabeth,* the *Universe Leader* will be able to haul more than enough gasoline in one trip to fill the tanks of every General Motors car produced in the first six months of 1956."

What the world had perceived as a two-man race between the Livanos sons-in-law to build the largest ship, the largest fleet, and the largest fortune was, the *Time* article pointed out, really a three-man contest in which a little-known American was very much in the running.

So it was that a *Business Week* writer, after reading the *Time* story, became eager to learn more about this mysterious shipper from the Midwest and do a feature article on him. The task was not easy. Learning that Ludwig operated a shipping concern called National Bulk Carriers, then located at 380 Madison Avenue in Manhattan, the writer went to the office to try to obtain an interview. He got no farther than what he described as an "unadorned and nameless reception room" before being turned away by a polite but distinctly unhelpful employee.

Not only did he fail to get an interview, the *Business Week* reporter couldn't even find a picture of the elusive shipper. Daniel K. Ludwig was not listed in any *Who's Who,* and a search through various newspaper- and magazine-clipping files failed to turn up any previous stories. It was as though the man had been wearing a cloak of invisibility all these years.

Undaunted, the writer kept digging, reading shipping records and talking to people in the industry. Out of the research, he began to form a picture of this invisible magnate. In March 1957, *Business Week* ran an article, "Tanker King Who Shuns Crown," summing up what the author had learned.

"Limelight-shy Daniel K. Ludwig," it began, "is a 'man nobody knows' — yet his tanker fleet rivals those of the fabulous Greeks whose names are symbols of wealth. His empire began with shipping, grew big with shipbuilding, is branching out now into other fields. Here's the story of its little-known ramifications — and the quiet American who runs it and has amassed a half-billion-dollar fortune in the process."

The four-page article went on to list visible parts of Ludwig's corporate holdings: ship-operating companies (National Bulk Carriers, Seatankers, Inc., Universe Tankships) with a combined 3.3 million deadweight tons* of vessels in operation, under construction, or scheduled to be built; shipping affiliates (American Petroleum Transport Company, National Petroleum Transport Company, American Tankers Corporation of Delaware, National Tankships, Oceanic

---

*Ship size is normally measured in three ways: in deadweight, gross, or net tons. Only deadweight tonnage is a measure of weight, or displacement of water, referring to the difference between the displacement of a light (empty) ship and a fully loaded one. Gross tonnage is a measure of volume capacity (one ton equaling 100 cubic feet of interior space) for an entire vessel, and net tonnage measures the volume of the cargo area.

Tankships, International Tankers, High Seas Tankships); shipbuilding and ship-repair yards at Norfolk, Virginia, Kure, Japan, and Freeport, Grand Bahama Island; majority interest in a roll-on-roll-off intercoastal shipping operation, American-Hawaiian Steamship Company (the only company or project on the list that Ludwig didn't own entirely and outright); plus a host of other ventures scattered around the world, including a refinery and petrochemical complex in Colón, Panama, oil properties in South America, the world's largest salt evaporation plant on the Baja California peninsula of Mexico, a giant cattle ranch and rice plantation in Venezuela, huge timber tracts in Venezuela and Brazil, a marine insurance company in Bermuda, and a bank in Liberia.

All these companies and ventures (except American-Hawaiian, a public corporation whose shares he was buying up) had been started by Ludwig himself, qualifying him as a one-man multinational operation. But he was also a flesh-and-blood human, and the *Business Week* writer gave as much about Ludwig the man as he had learned through research:

> D.K. — as Ludwig's close associates call him — isn't the tycoon type that bowls people over with an aggressive personality. Nearly six feet tall, with black, slightly graying hair, he's described by friends as a quiet, rather relaxed businessman who doesn't talk much. With his family, Ludwig lives in Darien, Connecticut, has an apartment in New York, too. He travels extensively, often aboard his swank yacht, *Danginn*. His long-time second-in-command is William W. Wagner, National Bulk's executive vice president and treasurer.

The writer concluded that D.K. was all business.

> With Ludwig, work is almost an obsession. A non-smoker, only a moderate drinker, Spartan in personal habits, business gets almost 100% of his attention. If he's retiring in outside life, in company operations he is stage front most of the time, a one-man director who relies on assistants and in-betweens to clean up the details. On a project, his greatest gift is seeing the big picture. Once a project begins, Ludwig doesn't rest easy until completion date. There's no lack of projects — an associate speaks of his unlimited ingenuity in dreaming up new ways of doing things. He willingly gambles on an idea that looks good — but his formula is to add a large dose of hard work to the gamble.

The reporter found it hard to get a fix on Ludwig the man.

In rising to the top he has made hardly any arch enemies — among shipping people, his reputation varies from "not too well-liked" to "a damn nice guy." But few really know him, for he keeps deliberately to himself.

The word portrait *Business Week* drew of the hitherto-invisible tycoon showed him as a no-nonsense, nose-to-the-grindstone, rather colorless man who, though his ships and money rivaled theirs, stood in somber contrast to the vivid Greeks. Seemingly, the only concession D.K. had made to the social demands incurred by wealth was in building his yacht, the *Danginn* — a 190-foot, 381-ton luxury vessel constructed at Ludwig's Norfolk shipyard in 1950 at a cost of over $2 million, including $25,000 worth of plush carpeting. The article quoted a business acquaintance of D.K.'s who had been aboard: "The maid's room looks like the finest hotel suite you ever saw."

Yet Ludwig seems to have built the boat to impress celebrities and people with whom he did business, rather than for his own pleasure. As *Business Week* noted, "He has entertained Saudi Arabia's King Ibn Saud aboard the *Danginn* in the Persian Gulf, has taken Clark Gable along on a trip to Venezuela to hunt jaguar. In a typical year, the *Danginn* logs some 40,000 miles — much of it with Ludwig's friends, but not Ludwig himself, aboard."

With the publication of the *Business Week* article, Ludwig's veil of secrecy was rent. He was now, at least to the magazine's readers, a public figure, something of a known quantity. The story, despite his lack of cooperation, had been fair and objective, saying nothing derogatory. He had finally gotten the publicity he had so long avoided and had suffered no real damage as a result.

Perhaps this encouraged him. Or perhaps he figured that, as long as the cat was at least partway out of the bag and people were going to write about him, with or without his consent, he might as well have control over what was said. In any case, soon after the *Business Week* piece appeared, Ludwig consented to have *Fortune* magazine, well known for its upbeat treatment of business executives, send over a writer and a photographer for a personal interview.

Soon the *Fortune* reporter, Dero Saunders, found himself sitting in National Bulk's reception room on the twenty-second floor of 380 Madison Avenue. On his way to the office, Saunders had seen little to remind him of the grandeur that had once adorned this site. Not many years earlier, the legendary Ritz-Carlton, one of the world's great hotels and the locale of New York's finest hospitality, had stood on the spot. Now a "glassy new building, looking much like a number of others going up around the city," stood in its place.

Saunders was no more impressed with National Bulk's reception area than the *Business Week* writer had been; he characterized it as a "tiny green-drab waiting room with one nondescript table and two leather chairs," hardly the furnishings a visitor would expect in the office of so rich a man. But this was as far as the other journalist had gotten. Now Saunders was about to become the first writer ever to penetrate Ludwig's *sanctum sanctorum* for a personal chat with the great man himself.

Saunders had boned up as well as he could for the interview, but except for the *Business Week* piece, there was almost nothing in print about the shipper or his holdings. After a short wait, the writer was greeted by a National Bulk staffer and ushered in to meet the subject of his story.

"A long corridor leads past congested rows of well-worn desks," he wrote, "to an unexpectedly spacious office done in shades of brown and beige. There, flanked by an aneroid barometer and several minutely detailed ship models, Daniel K. Ludwig can be found gazing at the ceiling, head cocked and mouth slightly ajar, thinking . . ."

Saunders's first impression was of "a handsome man of trim build and iron-gray hair, who often wears a half-smile, as though seriously contemplating a practical joke. . . .

"Perhaps," the writer speculated, "it amuses him that he is one of the outstanding business figures of the age and almost nobody knows it."

The *Fortune* reporter was keenly conscious of the honor being accorded him. "Until he was interviewed for this article," he wrote with a touch of awe, "Ludwig had never talked to the press, a circumstance that has led to some imaginative journalism."

As examples of what he meant, Saunders cited two reports he had gleaned from foreign press sources: "One Italian paper, denied an interview, wrote that Ludwig loved to shoot seagulls from his yacht and eat them raw; a 1950 Reuters dispatch from Cannes spread the weird rumor that he had Hitler aboard."

In dismissing these stories as "imaginative," Saunders ignored the implication that perhaps Europeans were more familiar than Americans with Ludwig's name, and that they regarded the shipper as something of an ogre. The writer was, however, struck by the fact that D.K. was a mystery even in the town where he lived: "In Darien, Connecticut, few of the neighbors who see him irritably looking for crabgrass on the lawn around his unostentatious house have more than an inkling of his business stature. . . . Ludwig's most notable characteristic, besides his imagination and pertinacity, is a lifelong penchant for keeping his mouth shut."

Saunders attributed this to the shipbuilder's single-minded absorption with getting things done: "He is interested in achievement, not fame. . . .

" 'I'm in this business because I like it,' " he quoted Ludwig as saying. " 'I have no hobbies.' "

To the interviewer, D.K. was strictly a solo act: "His zest for these operations is that of the lone wolf. He shares neither the rewards nor the risks with anyone."

Yet it seems not to have struck Saunders as contradictory that here was Ludwig, whose legendary silence made Trappist monks seem garrulous by comparison, chatting amiably about his early life and career, and even showing the writer snapshots in an old family album.

What D.K. was doing was what Jay Gatsby had done in F. Scott Fitzgerald's classic novel of the Jazz Age: constructing a myth of self around a few skeletal facts and bits of tangible evidence. The account included the stuff of which Horatio Alger stories were made — hard work, thrift, ingenuity, luck and pluck, and a driving desire to succeed — and how all this had brought Ludwig from a childhood of limited means in South Haven, Michigan, to possession of one of the world's great fortunes.

The tycoon was sketching for his interviewer a typical portrait of the self-made man, the sort of success story so popular in late-nineteenth-century fiction and biography. Saunders, an uncritical listener, asked few questions and faithfully jotted down details as Ludwig told them.

The narrative revealed a boy interested in boats and a young man who struck out on his own as a ship owner and operator before the age of twenty. After struggling through several lean years during the shipping slump that followed World War I, Ludwig said, he had just started making money as an oil hauler when the Depression hit, wiping out nearly everything he had.

But he had persevered, and during the mid-1930s had developed an ingenious ship-financing scheme that would make his fortune. The idea was to use other people's credit. First he would go to an oil company and persuade it to grant him a long-term charter to haul its petroleum. This done, he would go to a bank, where, using the charter as collateral, he'd take out a loan to obtain a ship to haul the petroleum. Instead of paying D.K., each oil company would make the charter payments directly to the bank, which would deduct the loan payment and put whatever was left into Ludwig's account.

The beauty of the scheme was that it allowed D.K. to build or renovate tankers without having to put up collateral or use his own credit. The oil companies were satisfied, because they were getting their petroleum hauled at bargain rates. The banks were satisfied, because oil companies were a much better credit risk than a small shipper like Ludwig. And D.K. was more than satisfied. As long as he took care to fulfill his charter contracts, he had a small but steady income, and, more important, by the time the contract expired he was the owner of a paid-up ship without having invested any of his own money.

This mutually beneficial financing arrangement, Ludwig confided to Saunders, was the foundation of his shipping empire. Once he got things rolling in the late 1930s, it was simply a matter of hard work and efficiency — plus a genius for innovative ship design — to become one of the world's largest ship owners. In his rise to the top, D.K. had been responsible for several major changes in shipbuilding. Some were design and structural modifications to eliminate nonessentials while increasing a ship's cargo-carrying capacity. His main contribution, though, was the supertanker.

By the time he had stopped renovating old ships and started building his own, D.K. told his interviewer, he had figured out that one large ship could haul oil a lot more cheaply than two small ones. Therefore, as demand increased, it made sense to build bigger and bigger tankers so that he could cut his own hauling costs and underbid his competitors, who were still using small ships. Of course he was taking a gamble that demand for foreign oil would continue to increase, but so far it had paid off.

After several years of renovating old tankers, Ludwig said, he set up his own shipbuilding operation, Welding Shipyard, Inc., in Nor-folk in 1939. When World War II started, he was able to procure government contracts to build tankers capable of carrying large supplies of oil to Europe and the Far East to sustain the military efforts of the Allies.

Once the war was over, the government, having no further use for the tankers Ludwig had built, let him have them back. Suddenly he was the fifth largest private ship owner in America and well on his way to becoming number one. With the Marshall Plan and other postwar efforts to rebuild the shattered economies of Europe and Asia, a shipping boom was created, and Ludwig was quick to take advantage of it.

But his shipyard at Norfolk was becoming too cramped for the large ships Ludwig planned to build. In 1951 he was able to make a deal with the occupation government in Japan to lease the former Imperial Navy Shipyard at Kure, where many of the largest war vessels had been built, and move most of his shipbuilding operation there. There were plenty of workers eager for jobs at any wage.

While he built tankers, he was also experimenting with other kinds of vessels, mainly self-unloading vessels for hauling dry cargo — iron ore, coal, and other minerals — or versatile bulk carriers able to haul either ore or petroleum. To help provide cargo for his ships, he diversified into other activities — mining, ranching, timber grow-ing, oil refining, salt production — and became a major supplier of many commodities to Japan, producing as well as hauling raw materials from South America, Australia, and other areas where he had established projects.

With such a variety of activities, he was able to ride out short-term slumps in the oil market and could afford to let a few tankers sit idle while he concentrated on producing and transporting other cargoes. When the 1956 Suez crisis came along, Ludwig had been able to lease these idle vessels at high spot-charter prices and increase his already considerable fortune. By this time, just short of his sixtieth birthday, he was sitting very comfortably; he was one of the world's largest ship owners, with a diverse portfolio of other interests.

As he listened to Ludwig relate his success story, Saunders developed an almost unqualified admiration for the man he was writing about. The only negative aspect the *Fortune* writer would mention was

D.K.'s monumental stinginess. Cutting out all frills was fine to a point, Saunders felt, but if the practice was applied to management, it might cause problems for D.K. in the future.

> Ludwig's organization is staffed with competent men — but not one man too many. As he proceeds almost to triple his tonnage, more men must be added; and sheer numbers of staff have a way of upsetting organizational structures. The present setup allows him to step into any decision anywhere in the organization. True, he frequently delegates decisions, even some major ones. But it will be a severe strain on him either to make or to delegate any more decisions than he already does.

Ludwig's frugality, Saunders concluded, made him almost an ascetic, despite his great wealth.

> Loving his work to the ultimate degree, Ludwig is unable to take much pleasure from anything else. . . . He counts calories religiously, and occasionally brings a new diet book into the office to show some subordinate who is betraying expansive tendencies. He likes martinis, but in recent years he has leaned toward milder substitutes such as buttermilk and soda. As one friend summed him up, "Ludwig doesn't drink much, he doesn't smoke at all, he doesn't entertain lavishly. His only bad habit is work — and that he can't stop."

This was Saunders's final word on Ludwig. It became the definitive one. As the only in-depth interview of the shipper ever done — the only record of his openly discussing his life and career with a journalist — the *Fortune* article remained the chief source of information for later researchers on D.K.'s background. Six years would pass before Ludwig talked to another writer for publication, and in that interview — with a *Business Week* reporter doing a piece called "A Shipping King Comes Ashore" — he seemed only to have contributed a few sentences about his business methods.

As time went on, Ludwig, though keeping his hand in shipping, turned more toward land-based ventures: real estate speculation, house building, hotel construction, banking, and financial services. At times he even built entire towns, both in the United States and abroad.

In 1967, Ludwig launched his biggest enterprise ever — an attempt to turn nearly four million acres of Amazon rain forest into productive forestry operations, rice paddies, cattle ranches, and mines. This project was so vast that even Ludwig couldn't keep it a secret. As a battle in the continuing struggle between man and nature, this Brazilian venture was the heavyweight championship of the world. It was the ultimate exploiter — Ludwig — against the earth's largest jungle.

Forty years earlier, Henry Ford had tackled the same jungle and had come out poorer and wiser. But Ludwig was richer than Ford, and bolder. Ford had merely tried to domesticate a native species of rubber tree. Ludwig was leveling the existing forests with tractors and bulldozers, fire and explosives, airplanes and herbicides, chain saws and axes, in order to grow a tree brought from Asia by way of Africa. Within a few years he had turned thousands of square miles of tropical forest into a charred, blackened battlefield littered with stumps.

By 1976 he started constructing two huge factories in a Japanese shipyard — a power plant and a pulp mill — to be towed halfway around the world and set in place in the midst of the Amazon jungle. "Why, man, he doth bestride the narrow world like a Colossus," Shakespeare's Cassius said of Julius Caesar, who had conquered Gaul and Britain. But the sun never set on Ludwig's empire, which he had extended into areas Caesar never would have dared to go.

The year of the American bicentennial also marked other important events. Howard Hughes died while being flown from a Ludwig-owned hotel in Acapulco to Houston. Two months later, on June 6, J. Paul Getty died of a heart attack at his mansion in Surrey, England. Getty had been considered the world's richest man, with Hughes a close second.

Looking around for a successor, the *Sunday Telegraph* of London, after evaluating the claims of a number of contenders, concluded, "According to the experts, the man upon whose elderly and seemingly reluctant shoulders the mantle of Richest Man in the World must fall is the almost completely unknown American tycoon, Daniel K. Ludwig."

This was the person the *New York* magazine cameraman, standing impatiently in front of Ludwig's Burlington House, had come to photograph. He had learned that, several years earlier, D.K. had given up the commuter life and his Darien house and had adopted as his primary residence the penthouse of the apartment building he had constructed on Sixtieth Street and Fifth Avenue, overlooking the Pond in Central Park.

Just as Warman was starting to think something had gone wrong and Ludwig wasn't coming, he spied a slightly stooped, gray-haired figure in a black overcoat, walking briskly but with a slight limp toward the Burlington House entrance. As the old man drew close, the photographer raised his camera and aimed. Ludwig, surprised, turned his head and looked up warily from beneath bushy brows. The shutter clicked. The next instant the world's richest man — eighty years old but still fit and trim from the daily swims he took in his private pool in the basement of Burlington House — charged the startled newsman and grabbed him in a half nelson, presumably to wrestle him to the sidewalk and take the camera. But Warman, recovering from this unexpected attack, twisted out of Ludwig's grasp and ran down the street with his prize picture, leaving D.K. glaring angrily at his retreating back.

*New York* magazine ran the photo, with an accompanying article, "The Richest Man in America Walks to Work," in its November 28, 1977, issue. What effect it had on Ludwig's morning strolls is not certain. At the time he was having much more serious problems: his Brazilian empire was falling apart and taking much of his wealth with it.

At this writing, Daniel Ludwig is still alive and still one of the world's richest men, despite his Amazon debacle and his having turned over much of his fortune to two foundations — one in Zürich, the other in New York — set up ostensibly to find cures for cancer but more probably as preventive medicine against paying a sizable fraction of his wealth in taxes.

Notwithstanding the publicity surrounding his Brazilian misadventure, he remains very much a mystery figure. Yet he has played an important, if largely hidden, role in some of the major stories of modern history — stories that one cannot fully understand without some knowledge of his participation in them.

*Two*

# South Haven

The winter of 1896–1897 had been a long, cold, bitter one in the Midwest. Now, in early summer, the big sidewheel steamer *Idle-wylde,* stacks belching black smoke and heavy wooden paddles beating the water, was making fine time eastward across the seventy-five-mile stretch of lake separating Chicago from South Haven, Michigan.

South Haven . . . The very name conjured up visions of a warm, happy, friendly community. To be sure, the "South" part was a bit misleading. On about the same latitude as Chicago, the resort was south mainly in relation to the rest of the Michigan peninsula.

But a haven it was. Since its founding in the early 1850s, the village had become a popular vacation spot for thousands of Chicagoans seeking to escape the crowded streets of the city for a day, a week, or — for those who could afford it — a month or sometimes an entire summer in a quiet seaside atmosphere.

By 1897, South Haven had grown from a village to a town. Its year-round population of seven thousand swelled to ten times that number during the height of the tourist season. Fine, large hotels, enticing shops, comfortable boarding houses, rows of neat cottages, and an abundance of clean restaurants serving tasty, wholesome food awaited visitors.

Beef and seafood were plentiful and cheap. Also, South Haven was an important shipping port for Michigan's justly famed fruit. To the north, east, and south of the town were orchards, vineyards, brambles, and bushes yielding some of the finest apples, pears, peaches, plums, cherries, grapes, and berries to be found in the world. Most of the fruit was grown for export, but some of the choicest got no farther than South Haven, where it was included in the fare available at local markets and eating places.

The resort's best-known hotel was the Avery Beach. Built during the early years of the village, and run hospitably by Mrs. H. M. Avery for many years after her husband died, the big frame structure trimmed with gingerbread eaves remained South Haven's premier hostelry for two generations of tourists before a fire leveled it in 1907.

Running a close second was Fidelman's, another large wooden hotel, famed for its kosher cooking. Many of the tourists who came to South Haven were Jews. The resort was fast becoming to Chicago what the Catskills were to New York City — a summer vacation spot for prosperous Jewish merchants and their families. Occasionally, arguments would flare between tourists and the natives, many of whom were of German stock with a strain of anti-Semitism in their heritage. But in the main South Haven residents welcomed the flow of tourists and money from the other side of Lake Michigan, and many a steamer, schooner, or smaller vessel plied a busy and lucrative trade ferrying goods and people back and forth across the waters.

The boom economy would not last many years longer. On the other side of the peninsula, in a little shed behind his house at 58 Bagley Avenue in Detroit, a young inventor named Henry Ford was spending his spare hours tinkering with a horseless carriage, which was to change the nature of American mass transportation and put an end to much of the water travel that kept places like South Haven thriving.

But now — on June 24, 1897 — the sun was shining, a warm breeze was blowing, and the passengers aboard the *Idlewylde* were crowding against the starboard rail to get a first glimpse of their destination. Men with black derbies and handlebar mustaches, women in white lawn dresses and broad-brimmed hats, laughing children in Buster Browns and pinafores — all peered eagerly toward the coastline for a glimpse of the South Haven dock.

Just south of town, a long pier jutted out toward the passing steamer. This, the passengers were informed by an *Idlewylde* guide, was Ludwig's Pier — not a landing spot for tourists but a commercial facility for loading cargo vessels with the products of local industry: fruit, lumber, and furniture.

Had any of the passengers been curious enough to inquire, they might have been told that Ludwig's Pier had been built by Charles Palman Ludwig, Sr., one of South Haven's most prosperous citizens since he came to the region in 1866. Born in Pennsylvania in 1821, he was the grandson of a Hessian soldier who had served as a British mercenary during the American Revolution and stayed on afterward.

Charles Sr. married Mary Groff, also Pennsylvania-born but with maternal roots in Virginia, and the young couple, like many others at the time, migrated westward across northern Ohio and settled in Michigan. Typically Victorian, they raised a large family; of their thirteen children, ten survived infancy. Only one was a girl, named after her mother. The boys were Charles Jr., John, Samuel, Franklin, Lancaster, Ben, Herman, William, and Daniel F. At the beginning of the Civil War, the two oldest boys, then in their teens, enlisted and served with honor in the Union Army.

The war over and the pair safely home, Charles Sr. sold off a number of successful investment properties and moved his large family to Michigan's lake region. There he purchased nearly a section of land — over six hundred acres — in South Haven Township on the lake just below the village and, with the help of the older boys, began clearing it.

He evidently had considerable money, for in 1869 he was one of the chief founders of the First National Bank of South Haven. At around the same time, he invested in other local commercial ventures, including a bakery, a furniture store, a restaurant, and a music store. In connection with this last enterprise, he had all his sons learn to play at least one instrument, and soon the Ludwigs were entertaining visitors and providing music for dances and concerts with a family-based brass band and a string orchestra.

Much of the time, though, was spent in harder work. Charles Ludwig was a patriarch of great energy and ambition who kept himself and his family busy with numerous projects. One of these, Ludwig's Pier, was started in 1870. The following year he opened the first of several sawmills, which would provide lumber, bark, and other wood products to be shipped from the pier. In the space of a few years, using the money from his previous investments and the labor of himself and his family, he was able to build in South Haven what one present-day historian of the area refers to as "Charles P. Ludwig's Little Empire."

In 1873 he embarked on still another venture: shipbuilding. After bringing in timber from his sawmills and setting up a keel-laying area near the pier, he put a crew of carpenters to work on one of the first vessels to be constructed in the region. The *Mary Ludwig* (named for his wife) was soon ready for launching. A letter in the *South Haven Sentinel* at the time describes the event:

The New Boat

Ludwig's Pier<br>April 21st, 1874

Mr. Editor:

We have been passing through a gala day at the "Pier," and are so unselfish as to wish our neighbors at the "Haven" to share our enjoyment. Our winter's labors have been crowned with success unparalleled in the history of boat building. And even before "the time for launching birds had come" we were ready for our grand launch, but like all sojourners by the sea we were obliged to wait for the wind and waves to be propitious.

The elements smiled upon us on Saturday; and under the able directions of Mr. Lovelace, assisted by Mr. J. Stanton, who worked on the boat from the commencement, our craft was fairly launched.

All that was promised by her builder, Mr. Otis Shaw, seems to have been effected, and "she walked the water like a thing of life." She is schooner built, 19½-foot beam and 85-foot keel overall, and cost $6,500. She will sail under command of the able and trustworthy young seaman, Capt. William Erkenbeck.

I think we have demonstrated that for a shipyard Ludwig's Pier is unsurpassed if equalled by any place on the eastern shore of Lake Michigan, having all the advantages of oak timber of the first quality, which can be transported by Packard's horse railroad, and every facility for launching.

Too much credit cannot be given to the able and energetic proprietor, C. P. Ludwig, and his estimable lady for whom the vessel is appropriately named.

Yours truly,<br>A Looker On

Allowing for the exaggeration typical of the period, the *Mary Ludwig* nonetheless seems to have justified the letter writer's pride. A photograph taken of her many years later shows a sturdy two-master, somewhat broad in the beam and built more for capacity

than speed, but essentially a well-constructed vessel that could
— and would — give several decades of reliable service.

The boosterism in the letter suggests that "Looker On" may have
been more than a casual observer — may even have had a vested
interest in the project. And the next-to-last paragraph indicates that
Charles Ludwig, Sr., had plans to build other boats at the pier,
perhaps even to turn it into a major regional shipbuilding center. But
economic adversity intervened.

The year before the *Mary Ludwig* was launched — the first year
of Grant's second term — had brought the Panic of '73. In the
aftershock, property values across the United States plummeted. By
the middle of the decade things were so bad in South Haven that
Charles Sr. decided to cut his losses, sell off most of his local enterprises, and try elsewhere. Years earlier he had acquired substantial
acreage around Saginaw and in nearby Gratiot County in central
Michigan. It was there he decided to move and take as many members of the family as were willing to go.

Several of the older boys, having become sailors on Lake Michigan, chose to stay in South Haven, but in 1877 Charles, Mary, and
the younger children went to the Saginaw area, where they spent the
next thirteen years "cleaning up four or five farms."

By 1890, with most of the children grown and gone, the parents
found themselves nearly alone in a big house. Charles was now
seventy; his wife, sixty-nine. They were still healthy and vigorous,
but they missed their family. Several of the younger boys, as they
came of age, had returned to South Haven to join their older brothers
in the lake trade, and the elder Ludwigs decided to go back, too.
Charles had retained a sizable tract of land there — 166 acres
— where they could retire.

So, "retaining . . . one beautiful farm along Pine River," which
they leased out, the Ludwigs sold off the rest of their central Michigan properties and moved back to South Haven Township. Living
in temporary quarters, they built a house, barn, sheds, and other
outbuildings, with the help of some of their sons. The structures were
completed by the winter of 1890, and they were able to spend Christmas in their new residence.

Settled in, with some of the boys and their families living nearby,
the old couple spent their remaining years doing the necessary farm
chores, giving advice, and enjoying their grandchildren. Several sons

had become captains of boats and, among them, owned three vessels. The youngest of the brothers, Daniel F., soon joined them. Ambitious and precocious, at the age of seventeen he married a local girl, Flora, three years his junior. Three years later, in 1895, after a short apprenticeship on the lake, he received his master's certificate, making him the youngest ship's captain on Lake Michigan, "for which," Charles Sr. noted proudly in an extant family record, "it seems he did not miss his calling, for he has been very successful."

Successful enough, apparently, to start a family of his own; on June 24, 1897, just as the *Idlewylde*'s passengers were disembarking at the South Haven dock, Flora Ludwig gave birth to a son, who would be christened Daniel Keith.

Little is known about Daniel F., his wife, and young son over the next several years. It is recorded that he took over as skipper of the *Mary Ludwig* for a time. And the 1898 *South Haven Directory*, published during his son's first year, lists him as a resident of the town, occupation: sailor. The 1900 census, however, failed to enumerate the Daniel F. Ludwig family. It did mention Charles Sr., listing him as a seventy-nine-year-old retired farmer living in South Haven Township. Mary had apparently died, but Charles Sr. survived another seven years. He died at the home of his daughter on April 18, 1907, just a few days short of his eighty-sixth birthday.

Daniel Keith would have been nearly ten then. Whether or not he knew his grandfather is not clear from the sparse records. Probably only D.K. himself can answer that for sure, and the one time he ever talked about his early life for publication — to Dero Saunders — he referred to his parents only in passing and mentioned no other relative.

It is a safe bet, though, that the boy did know Charles Sr., and that the older man was held up to him as an example. Since they were living in the same community, it is likely that Daniel F. brought his family over at least occasionally to visit the old man. And Charles Sr.'s proud mention of his youngest son's accomplishments, plus the fact that Daniel F. was captain of the *Mary Ludwig*, point toward strong bonds between the generations. Certainly D.K. can be said to have inherited his grandfather's entrepreneurial streak and to share his ambition to make a fortune through a variety of profitable activities.

Even as a boy in South Haven, young Daniel K. exhibited a strong drive toward the acquisition of money. During the interview with Saunders he showed the writer a snapshot of himself as a youngster in a baseball uniform, explaining that he had never been much of an athlete but had been made manager of the local team because of his ability to raise money for uniforms.

During the summers, he told the *Fortune* reporter, he had worked at a South Haven dance pavilion of which his father was treasurer. Mostly he had shined shoes and sold peanuts and popcorn, and he saved much of what he made. Some of this money he invested in what he termed his first venture into shipping.

As Saunders related the episode: "At nine, he scraped together $75 to buy a sunken twenty-six-foot boat that seemed beyond salvaging. But he raised her, slaved all winter on repairs, and chartered her out the following summer for more than twice her cost. He did not act as crew, since he was too small to crank the massive one-cylinder engine."

Of such stuff are legends made. Later writers looking for background material on Ludwig have picked up this little anecdote — almost the only human interest detail available about Ludwig's boyhood — and repeated it (sometimes getting the figures wrong) in their own stories.

But the *Fortune* version is misleading; it portrays young Daniel K. as some sort of superchild. At no time does it seem to have occurred to Saunders (or any of those who repeated the story) to ask how a nine-year-old child, too small to crank a one-cylinder engine, could have managed to raise a sunken twenty-six-foot boat, weighing at least a few tons, out of several feet of water, get her to dry dock, and make the repairs necessary to return her to operating condition.

The written account smacks more of myth than of fact. Not that there was a calculated attempt to deceive; Ludwig was hardly the first old man to try to impress a younger listener by exaggerating his boyhood exploits. And Saunders, not wanting to offend his host and eager to portray D.K. as a shining example of the rags-to-riches, Horatio Alger, classic American success story, can certainly be pardoned for accepting uncritically his subject's version of the incident.

But for the sake of accuracy it should be recorded that the boy had a father, a grandfather, and several uncles who were experienced sailors or shipbuilders, and that the feat of raising and renovating a twenty-six-foot boat clearly required more than the efforts of a child.

Still, it is not difficult to believe that young Daniel, given his later reputation for stinginess, was able to save up the $75 to buy (or have his father or another relative help him buy) the sunken boat. Whether it was on his initiative is another question. Fathers often encourage their sons in such projects to teach lessons of thrift and hard work.

Let's assume, then, that Captain Daniel F. Ludwig worked out the deal whereby his young son invested in salvage rights the $75 he had hoarded. Then the two, perhaps accompanied by several crewmen, went out on Captain Ludwig's boat, raised the vessel, and towed it to Ludwig's Pier, where it could be fixed. Young Daniel probably helped with the repair work. It's likely that he spent some of his early years around the shipyard, doing little jobs and storing up knowledge. It's also likely that when the job was finished and the renovated boat was chartered out, he was told by his proud father that *he* had done it all and was allowed to keep the profits. D.K.'s selective memory and his desire to portray himself to Saunders as a self-made man can account for the rest.

The fact is that D.K. was following in the footsteps of his male relatives. In building an empire based on shipping, shipbuilding, lumbering, farming, and other commercial activities, he was essentially emulating his grandfather, though on a much grander scale — being "a ship off the old dock," as it were. Had Charles Sr. decided to stay in South Haven and weather out the Panic of '73 instead of selling out and going to Saginaw, he might have reaped the same kind of financial rewards his grandson did later by staying at the helm during the Depression.

But the figure mainly responsible for D.K.'s success, and the person who, up to now, has been even more invisible than the billionaire himself, was his father, Captain Daniel F. Ludwig. South Haven historians are aware of Charles P.'s place as a prominent citizen of the community. They also report that, in modern times, D.K. returned to the town of his birth and was spotted in a local barbershop, where he became annoyed at being recognized and departed in a huff. But information about Daniel F. is extremely hard to locate and is sometimes contradictory.

There is even some question about how long he stayed in South Haven. A local librarian believes that Daniel F. and his family moved up to Saugatuck, a smaller community some fifteen miles north on the Michigan shore, shortly after D.K.'s birth. If that is true, then the boy did not go to school in South Haven. There is no documented source for this information, though, and a local Chamber of Commerce official has said that the family never lived in Saugatuck. Confusion reigns.

If the boat-repair anecdote has any validity, D.K. as a nine-year-old in 1906 or 1907 was in South Haven then — if Ludwig's Pier was used for the dry dock. Also, the dance pavilion of which Daniel F. was treasurer for a time was in South Haven. None is known to have existed during the period in Saugatuck.

However, the U.S. Census report for 1910 showed a Daniel F. Ludwig, his wife Flora B., and their son, listed as "D. Keith," living in Saugatuck. Daniel F. was thirty-five, Flora thirty-two, and the boy twelve. The couple was listed as having been married eighteen years and producing two children, one of whom died in infancy.

Daniel F. gave his occupation as "real estate," a business he operated out of his "own office." This indicates that, for a while at least, he had stopped being a boat captain. It also confirms D.K.'s statement to Saunders that his father was a real estate agent.

No occupation was listed for Flora outside the home. Like nearly all the women in D.K.'s life, his mother is an unknown quantity. The only mention of her, other than in the census, is in the *Fortune* article, where Saunders reported that D.K.'s parents were separated when the boy was fifteen. Even her maiden name is not known.

Like almost everyone else in the Saugatuck census report, she gave the name of the state where she was born: Michigan. But Flora's responses about her parents' birthplaces were vague. Under "Father's Birthplace," the enumerator wrote "In English." (Throughout, the enumerator's writing is legible, with no evident carelessness, but this response leads one to conclude that he did transcribe incorrectly at least once.) Given that Flora cited "United States" as her mother's place of birth, she probably said "In England" in reply to the query about her father. Both responses indicate that she knew little about her parents. Perhaps she was orphaned when very young. Certainly her marriage at fourteen makes one wonder whether she had a nest to leave, even at so early an age.

But there is a more disturbing question about Flora: Why, around 1912, did Daniel F. Ludwig leave his wife, taking their fifteen-year-old son with him? The question remains unanswered. But according to D.K.'s own testimony, the event left a mark on him. Some writers even speculate that this traumatic occurrence was the chief causative factor in Ludwig's becoming a billionaire. One such analyst, Max Gunther, in his book *The Very, Very Rich and How They Got That Way,* includes a chapter entitled "The Psychology of the Rich." In it he passes quickly over such Freudian theories as anal retention and castration anxiety to focus on a few basic characteristics the very rich have in common.

One immediately apparent trait is that all the very rich — at least the ones who have not inherited their wealth — are male. According to Gunther, "There are no women among the great self-made rich."

Why not? The author cites an unnamed psychiatrist who believes that, although women are often fond of luxury and comfort, once they reach the point of having enough money to buy whatever they want, they stop striving. "Many men, on the other hand," he says, "go on furiously piling up wealth long after they've got more than they can possibly spend."

The main reason, Gunther suggests, may be that most of these rich, compulsive men suffered the agony of a broken home when they were young. He comments, "It's remarkable how many of these stupendously successful men lost one or both parents early in life through death or divorce. More than half of them, in fact, went through that wounding experience."

He substantiates his correlation by quoting from a university study in which psychologists interviewed the "founding entrepreneurs" of 110 successful companies. One conclusion:

> The theme of parental death crops up repeatedly. The picture that comes through from the interviews is one of the lonely child, grubby fists in tear-filled eyes, accepting the loss and facing a dangerous future. . . . The bereaved child, from then on, has a massive sense of insecurity. He sets out to get so much money that he can never be left stranded again.
>
> Another possibility is that the loss of a parent makes him more than usually self-reliant. In trying to heal his emotional wound, he convinces himself that he doesn't really need the parent; he can hack it on his own. While most of us meekly bumble through life working for other people (the company becoming our "parent"), an orphaned or half-orphaned youngster may try instead to climb the economic ladder by himself, as head of his own business.

How closely does this apply to Ludwig? In some ways he seems to fit neatly into the pattern. The insecurity and the obsessive drive to make money are certainly present. Yet the little evidence we have suggests he was motivated to make money even before the breakup of his parents' marriage. It may be that the schism served to reinforce tendencies already present. Or possibly the insecurity started earlier, since the union between Daniel F. and Flora Ludwig may have been an unhappy one even before the split. D.K.'s father seems not to have been content selling real estate. It is perhaps significant that as soon as the marriage broke up, the former skipper took his son and headed down the Mississippi to Port Arthur, Texas, a major oil port on the Gulf Coast, where he presumably got a job connected with shipping. Dero Saunders, listening to D.K. tell about this part of his life some forty-five years after the fact, got the impression that the boy was intensely lonely.

Gunther quotes Dr. Alfred E. Messer, professor of psychiatry at Emory University and an authority on the psychology of wealth: " 'The [self-made rich] man's childhood is likely to have been rough. The typical story is that of a parent dying or going away or — what amounts to the same thing — rejecting the child, abandoning him emotionally.' "

In Ludwig's case, of course, we would know more about the man if we knew more of the circumstances relating to his parents' separation. It seems curious that Daniel F. took his son along to Texas. A man making a break of this sort and starting a new career elsewhere could be expected not to want the burden of caring for a teenager. That Daniel F. *did* take on the responsibility suggests a strong bond between father and son. How did D.K. get along with his mother before the split? We have no way of knowing.

Other questions come to mind. Did Daniel F. consider Flora an unfit mother? Did D.K. have any choice in deciding which parent he would go with? We can assume, if we wish, that Daniel F., a former boat captain and a man used to command, took the initiative and made the decisions. But this is only speculation.

Once in Texas, if the *Fortune* article is accurate, D.K. found himself more or less on his own. His father probably still cared about him, but he had other things to do and could spend little time with the boy. A thousand miles from home, taken away from family, from school, from friends, the fifteen-year-old must have felt miserable and frightened.

Gunther quotes Messer again: " 'The child grows up with the understandable feeling that he can't rely on other people; he must prove himself worthy *by himself.* He seeks to prove it with money. In one typical case, I had a patient who habitually carried $4,000 around in his pocket: his way of showing he'd made it on his own; he didn't need anybody.' "

In later years, D.K. exhibited the same compulsion, but he boasted of bigger amounts. When other businessmen would question the wisdom of his Amazon venture, according to *Fortune* writer Gwen Kinkead, he'd often ask how much money *they* had in the bank, then gloat, "*I* have $300 million. I'm a banker's banker. Banks come to *me* for deposits."

But in 1912, there was no basis for such arrogance. First he had to get a job, which, for a boy who knew a little about boats, wasn't very hard in a busy shipping town. "For a year or so in Port Arthur," Saunders wrote, "D.K. was a runner for a firm of ship chandlers [dealers in marine equipment], going out in small boats to sell supplies to the sailing ships and steamers that anchored in Port Arthur waters; at the same time he went to night school, to get the math he needed for a marine engineer's degree."

The youngster had finished only eighth grade in Michigan before being taken to Texas. No records are available to show what kind of student he had been, but his letters in later life show a good grasp of the language and a bright mind. Being a ship chandler's assistant was an education in itself, and the boy was learning much that he was to use later.

As for his taking night school math, one suspects the hand of Daniel F. in that decision. A marine engineer's papers would provide the youth with a marketable skill and perhaps enable him to get a master's certificate in a few years and become captain of a vessel, as his father had been.

After the "year or so" in Port Arthur, D.K., according to Saunders, returned to Michigan, but the article gives no details of the move, nor says whether his father returned with him. Chances are that he did. It is not likely that the boy did a reverse Huck Finn and headed up the Mississippi on his own. And a couple of years later Daniel F. was co-signer on a loan note enabling D.K. to purchase his first steamer, so obviously there had been no rupture in the father-son relationship.

Saunders wrote of D.K.'s working for twenty cents an hour at a Fairbanks, Morse marine engine plant at Three Rivers, Michigan, some forty-five miles away from his home town. Published with the *Fortune* article was a picture of a darkly handsome, rather cocky-looking seventeen-year-old dressed in dark trousers, white shirt with sleeves rolled to the elbow, and wide polka-dot tie, one arm akimbo, the other propped against a "hot-bulb" semidiesel engine in the Fairbanks, Morse plant.

The job at the engine plant was another educational experience; it gave D.K. a thorough knowledge of marine mechanics and helped him to complete the work requirements for his engineer's certificate. He was evidently a fast learner and a good worker; after a little more than a year at Three Rivers he was considered competent enough by company officials to be sent to the Pacific Northwest and Alaska to do installation work.

But Fairbanks, Morse soon lost him. D.K. told Saunders that shortly after his arrival in the Northwest, he started moonlighting, installing ship's engines on his own time as well as for the company. "He found the work so profitable," wrote Saunders, "that he soon drew his last wages and, at nineteen, went permanently into business for himself."

It was a profitable time to do so. The year was 1916, and the shipping industry was booming. Much of Europe was engaged in a world war. Woodrow Wilson was campaigning for a second term on the slogan "He Kept Us Out of War," but anyone who thought that record would be continued was in for a disappointment. Officially, America was still neutral, but war matériel was secretly being shipped from New York ports to Britain.

A year earlier, there had been a bitter argument on the subject of such contraband, inflaming war passions in the United States. In May 1915, a German submarine sank the British liner *Lusitania* en route from New York. Nearly 1200 people had gone down with the ship, among them 128 Americans, including the author-publisher Elbert Hubbard and the capitalist Alfred Gwynne Vanderbilt.

President Wilson fired off an angry dispatch, demanding reparations, but the Germans defended the sinking, charging that the ship was carrying arms and ammunition to the British. Wilson heatedly denied the charge, starting a chain of events that led to the United States entry into the war in 1917. But history proved the German charge correct. Decades later, documents showed that the *Lusitania* had indeed been carrying war matériel, in violation of American neutrality.

The war news in 1916, though, had to vie for front-page space in American newspapers with a domestic issue nearly as hot as the trench warfare in France. *Prohibition* was the word on everyone's lips. Not since the abolition of slavery had there been a controversy that so divided the public. The Anti-Saloon League, bolstered by a coalition of other religious, temperance, and women's organizations, had succeeded in persuading several state legislatures to ban the manufacture, importation, and sale of liquor. Now the push was for a constitutional amendment and a national law to rid the United States once and for all of the evils of demon rum. The temperance groups cited the European war as a reason for halting the manufacture of liquor in America, on the grounds that the grain used in the production of alcohol should be conserved to alleviate food shortages abroad.

Much to his dismay, President Wilson was caught in the middle. On the one hand, he favored the reformers' intentions and backed the general goals of the Anti-Saloon League. On the other, he felt that the imposition of a sudden and total ban on all alcoholic beverages would be too extreme and doomed to failure.

When the Eighteenth Amendment, empowering Congress to write a law making it illegal to sell, make, or import intoxicating liquors within the United States, was submitted to the states for ratification, the term "intoxicating liquors" was left deliberately vague. It would be up to Congress to determine precisely what percentage of alcohol in a beverage was intoxicating.

Wilson favored a moderate interpretation, setting the permissible limit at around 5 or 6 percent, which would exempt beer and light wines, and soften the blow for Americans who liked to drink. The more radical of the Prohibitionists were pushing for a level of only .5 percent, which would outlaw virtually every alcoholic beverage. These extremists, joining forces with isolationist congressmen who were attacking Wilson's war policies and his attempts to start the League of Nations, managed to carry the day.

By 1919, when the National Prohibition Act — also called the Volstead Act, after its chief sponsor — came to the president's desk for his signature, Wilson was a pathetic figure. Harassed by enemies, exhausted by his efforts to get the United States to join the League of Nations, the president only a few days earlier had collapsed with a massive stroke. Now partly paralyzed, barely able to speak or move, he could not even hold a pen to carry out his intention of vetoing the legislation. His wife, Edith Bolling Wilson, held a pen in his hand and guided it to write his name. The result was so shaky that several Prohibitionists in Congress proclaimed the signature a forgery. Not that it mattered. Within weeks, Congress passed the Volstead Act over the presidential veto, making it law. Prohibition went into effect at midnight on January 16, 1920, and set off the greatest crime spree in the nation's history.

This sequence of events had a notable effect on the career of the young marine engineer Daniel Keith Ludwig. He was about to become the owner of a vessel for the first time since his salvage effort at the age of nine. He was a decade older now, and much better equipped to handle the responsibility. Still, he had to turn to his father for help.

The old sidewheel lake steamer *Idlewylde* was now idle and up for sale through a Detroit bank, which had gotten her through foreclosure. She could be bought for a mere $5000 — less than what it had cost D.K.'s grandfather to build the *Mary Ludwig* thirty-five years earlier.

The money he borrowed to buy her, Ludwig later told Saunders, was raised mostly on his father's signature, but he almost immediately recovered the purchase price by gutting the once-proud excursion vessel, selling off her machinery and boilers, and turning her into an iron-hulled barge. Then, according to the *Fortune* story, he "boldly advertised in a New York paper for a charterer."

Why "boldly"? Did it take more chutzpah to advertise in a New York paper than in a Chicago or Detroit one? Yet the choice was significant. In Manhattan beat the heart of the world of commerce. Goods and money flowed in and out of New York Harbor like lifeblood for the rest of the globe. This was where it all began, where it all ended. It was a long way from the Midwest, but it would become home to the boy from South Haven.

"The ad," wrote Saunders, "drew a response from A. I. Kaplan, a New Yorker who had virtually cornered the market in blackstrap molasses. Kaplan chartered the *Idlewylde,* as well as some wooden barges and tugboats that Ludwig bought on the Great Lakes; and for a couple of years during World War I Ludwig hauled Kaplan's molasses up the Hudson, through the Barge Canal, and across Lake Ontario to a Canadian distillery."

What Saunders failed to note is that Kaplan was the chief supplier for a major bootlegging operation. The molasses D.K. was hauling was not intended to go on biscuits. At the Toronto distillery, it was turned into rum and brought back across the border into those states which had already outlawed the importation and sale of liquor. Kaplan had seen the handwriting on the wall; it was a foregone conclusion that the entire country would go dry in a matter of a few months or years. When that happened, he wanted to be in a position to get rich from it. Liquor made in Canada could be smuggled across the border with ease, and there would be — already was, in fact — a tremendous demand from Canadian distilleries for West Indian molasses to refine into hooch.

Since he was merely hauling molasses to Canada, D.K. was doing nothing illegal, but he was an important part of the process and stood to make money from it. Then something happened. After two years, the charter agreement was broken off. Ludwig would not tell Saunders the reason for the split; he called it simply a "misunderstanding."

But the *Fortune* piece says, "He ruefully credits Kaplan with giving him 'a sort of postgraduate course' in shrewd trading. The relationship was terminated, though the two men do business in friendly fashion to this day. Ludwig sold his barges to Kaplan and did general hauling with his broken-down tugs until the bottom fell out of the shipping market."

This, at least, is the version D.K. gave his interviewer. There was, however, another episode in the young shipper's life at that time which has never been noticed until now.

*Three*

# The *Mosher* Incident

Just before one o'clock on the morning of January 17, 1920 — less than an hour after the Volstead Act went into effect — a truck pulled into a railway switchyard in Chicago. Six masked gunmen, pistols in hand, leaped out, overpowered the watchman, and bound and gagged him. Then, moving swiftly to the yard office, they surprised six on-duty engineers, herded them into a shed, and padlocked the door. After breaking open two freight cars, the bandits loaded the contents onto their truck and drove away with more than $100,-000 worth of whiskey in bottles labeled FOR MEDICINAL USE ONLY. The great liquor war had begun.

Government stocks were the first target. Prohibition had ushered in almost a total ban on booze in America. U.S. officials, yielding to the claims of many doctors that whiskey had legitimate medicinal uses, had stocked several warehouses around the nation with well-known brands of liquor, and physicians were able to requisition these supplies by filling out the proper forms. But certain criminal elements found these stocks an irresistible temptation. Some used deception, forging requisition forms or paying off a doctor to sign correct ones. Others, like the Chicago railyard gang, preferred more direct methods.

As a result, warehouses that had been stocked with enough medicinal spirits to last for several years were emptied within a few months. As these supplies dwindled, truckloads were brought in from Canada, usually under cover of darkness. At first, rumrunners were a lot more worried about being hijacked by rival gangs than being nailed by the Feds. Although there were not nearly enough border patrolmen to police the long boundary between the United States and Canada, there were plenty of "pirates" waiting along the roads to waylay convoys from Canadian distilleries and make off with their cargoes. Trucks leaving from Toronto had toughs riding shotgun, and many a battle was fought along dark highways. Local morgues soon filled up with unidentified, unclaimed, bullet-riddled bodies.

Eventually Prohibition enforcement officers — those who weren't on the take — got their border patrols beefed up enough to slow the flow of contraband liquor from Canada. But by then the bootleggers had started bringing it in by sea from Great Britain. Many thirsty Americans were learning to get by on homemade hooch — home brew, moonshine, and bathtub gin — but those who could afford better wanted name brands: fine Scotches, gins, and Irish whiskeys made in the British Isles. The trick was to get them across the Atlantic and into the United States past Customs agents, Prohibition men, and pirates.

To do this on a scale large enough to be profitable — to buy, transport, protect, wholesale, and retail millions of cases of liquor — was a major operation requiring the coordination of many people. Bootleggers needed freighters to haul large cargoes of liquor across the ocean and smaller vessels to offload and take it to shore. They needed crews who could be trusted. They needed contacts on both sides of the Atlantic. And this was tricky. Selling liquor in Britain was not against the law, but selling it in large quantities to buyers who were going to carry it to America and break the laws there was considered unethical. Still, there were enough businessmen who were willing to stoop a bit for several thousand pounds' profit. Because of the financial opportunities it offered, the "bootlegger armada" was welcome in Britain, unlike the Spanish one sent in 1588.

Once the liquor crossed the Atlantic, things got really complicated. Fishermen and other small-boat operators had to go out and get it off the bigger ships and bring it to shore, where trucks could pick it up and haul it to warehouses. There it would often — though not always — be cut with grain alcohol and distilled water, one bottle being turned into four, each labeled to look like the genuine article. After this it would be wholesaled and then retailed to speakeasies and small clubs and bootleggers across the country.

The men involved in the American phases of the operation required protection, in part from thugs, in part from paid-off public officials. But in spite of risks and losses of cargo, the profits were enormous. A case of good Scotch could be bought in Britain for $8.00. By the time it was shipped over to the United States, brought ashore, cut, rebottled and relabeled, and sold to a retailer, it might bring as much as $400. With that kind of markup, rumrunners could afford to take some chances and spread a little money around.

Finding officials willing to take bribes wasn't hard. What was amazing was that so many stayed honest. The average Prohibition enforcement agent was then making about $30 a week to do a dangerous, highly unpopular job. By simply agreeing to look the other way at the right time and place, an agent could make several years' salary in a few minutes. There was little incentive for him to stay honest. Much of the public held the "revenuers" in contempt, and any liquor raid in a big city might draw a crowd to cheer the arrested bootleggers and hoot "Pirates!" at the officers making the pinch. Even when a raid was successful, the agents often saw their hard work go for nothing when their superiors, paid off by the rumrunners, freed the accused on some technicality.

The liquor war, then, was an unequal struggle between a handful of honest, dedicated officers trying to enforce a widely despised law, and ruthless opportunists, who became richer, more sophisticated, and better organized with each venture.

One of the shrewdest of the opportunists was a young Italian American from New York's Lower East Side. He once had been Francisco Castiglia, but after noting the advantages of having an Irish-sounding name in New York's political circles, he changed his own to Frank Costello.

While the big American Mafia chiefs — Giuseppe (Joe the Boss) Masseria and Salvatore Maranzano — were fighting it out for control of the rackets in Little Italy, Costello allied himself with a younger, more diverse gang that was making plans to kill off these old "mustache Petes" and mold the feuding gangs into an organized crime syndicate run along the lines of big business.

Several members of this younger group, like Charles (Lucky) Luciano, Vito Genovese, and Costello himself, were Italian. Others, like Arthur (Dutch Schultz) Flegenheimer, Benjamin (Bugsy) Siegel, and Meyer Lansky, were Jewish. Costello's own mentor — the man who had taught him nearly everything worth knowing — was a Jew, Arnold Rothstein. Historians of criminal activity in America later accorded Rothstein the title of Father of Organized Crime; apparently he was the first to realize that the rackets — prostitution, gambling, drugs, bootlegging — could be run much more profitably as large-scale, businesslike enterprises than as small, independent undertakings. And Fitzgerald gave the gangster a measure of literary fame by using him as the model for the sinister Meyer Wolfsheim — he of the hairy nostrils and human-molar cufflinks — in *The Great Gatsby*.

Costello, having learned much about Rothstein's methods, was, by the age of thirty, running a major bootlegging operation and supplying a large number of New York speakeasies with contraband liquor. Siegel and Lansky ran his escort service, and their "Bugs and Meyer" gang rapidly became the most feared bunch of gunmen in Manhattan. It would eventually win national notoriety as the nucleus of Murder Incorporated.

In 1921, Costello took a step that was to expand his rumrunning capabilities enormously. He boarded an ancient freighter in New York Harbor bound for St. John's, Newfoundland, but as the creaky old tub passed Nova Scotia, the young bootlegger prepared to disembark. He had not intended to go all the way to St. John's. His destination was a tiny fishing village, St. Pierre, on an island of the same name tucked under Newfoundland.

Along with two small neighbors — Great Miquelon and Little Miquelon — St. Pierre belonged to France; the islands were almost the only New World possessions retained by the French after the British conquered all of Canada in 1763. Since that time, France had shown little interest in the Miquelons and St. Pierre, which had become virtually self-governing.

Not that there was much to govern. The islands were little more than rocky protuberances on which scant vegetation grew. The few hundred human inhabitants all fished for a living, expected little, and got less. But the islands' independence intrigued Costello. Neither Canadian nor United States law applied to them. Moreover, St. Pierre was a convenient stopping place for vessels traveling from Britain to Canada and the northern United States. Scotland, noted for its fine, smooth whiskeys, was just twenty-seven hundred miles across the ocean, and major American cities like Boston, New York, and Philadelphia were a few hundred miles down the continental coast.

So Costello made the islanders of St. Pierre an offer they couldn't refuse. If they were willing to cooperate, he would make them richer than they had ever dreamed of being. His plan was simple. Large vessels, each capable of carrying several thousand cases of liquor, would transport the booze from Britain to St. Pierre in the North Atlantic and to Bermuda, the Bahamas, and other British-owned islands in the Caribbean. There the ships would be unloaded and the cargo stored in warehouses. Then smaller vessels would run a shuttle service up and down the East Coast of the United States. Picking up a load in St. Pierre, a ship could sail down to a U.S. port and offload its cargo onto fishing smacks and other boats that would sail to shore as time and the presence of the authorities permitted. Once empty, the shuttle vessel could continue to Bermuda or Nassau, pick up another load, unload that one on the way back, return empty to St. Pierre, and start the triangle again.

Arrangements had already been made in the Caribbean. Now, if the islanders on St. Pierre would only listen to reason . . .

They did. After huddling with the mayor and aldermen of the little fishing village for several hours, Costello walked out with the deal he wanted. St. Pierre would become the major transshipment center in northeastern North America for liquor being brought from Britain to the United States. Wharves, docking facilities, warehouses, and other structures would be built or improved to handle the increased traffic. In return, the inhabitants of St. Pierre would get $2.00 for every case that passed through the port, in addition to a number of well-paying jobs. The village officials liked the sound of it. For them it would be a windfall — good money with almost no risk. The French government, busy repairing the ravages of World War I, was unlikely to cause any trouble, and no other country had the authority to do so.

Soon the population increased dramatically with the arrival of boatloads of immigrants — carpenters, seamen, thugs, prostitutes. But the natives didn't mind. They were getting rich. By the time Prohibition was repealed, over a decade later, more than two million cases of liquor had passed through this little village on their way to the United States. And the people of St. Pierre had come to regard bootleggers like Frank Costello and Al Capone as heroes, benefactors, and patron saints.

In the United States, Prohibition agents and Customs officials had no way of knowing about that agreement between Costello and the people of St. Pierre. All they knew was that, around the beginning of 1922, liquor-laden vessels flying the British flag started showing up in numbers along the coast near populous cities. These ships — mainly medium-sized steamers and schooners — would anchor just outside the limit of U.S. territorial waters and wait. Eventually, smaller boats would come from shore, offload part of the larger ships' cargoes, and make a mad dash back to land.

The small craft had the risky part of the operation. As long as the seagoing vessels stayed outside territorial limits, they were safe. Enforcement officials could only watch helplessly as bootleg ships lined up at anchor just beyond the invisible barrier. In New York, the newspapers soon gave the name Rum Row to the area twelve miles below the south coast of Long Island.

Actually, the law was somewhat ambiguous regarding the extent of territorial waters. At an earlier period, international custom had come to accept one league (three statute miles) as within a country's watery boundary. This was the distance a cannonball could carry from the shore and was therefore defensible. Any ship outside this three-mile limit was considered to be under the jurisdiction of its country of registry, not the country whose coast it was near.

But another, even older, custom held that a country's territorial waters extended four leagues (twelve miles) from its shore at mean low tide. During the early 1920s, this issue became a matter of hot debate in the United States. Those lawyers and politicians who were soft on Prohibition insisted that the three-mile limit was the correct one; officials arguing for stricter enforcement favored the twelve-mile figure.

Customs officials and Prohibition agents usually followed the rule of thumb that any vessel found carrying liquor within three miles of the U.S. coast could be seized and impounded, and her crew and officers arrested. A vessel more than three but less than twelve miles offshore could be stopped and searched if suspected of carrying contraband. But only if she was known to be engaged in an activity (such as offloading liquor) illegal in the proximal country could she be seized and her crew placed under arrest. Merely having liquor on board beyond the three-mile limit was not illegal.

Even so, the captains of rumrunning ships, knowing the law to be unevenly enforced, usually stayed at least twelve miles out, where they would wait for small boats — fishing smacks or swift speedboats like the "Jersey skiffs" — to come out under cover of darkness or fog and offload their alcoholic cargoes.

There was a chance that these small boats might be seized, but the odds were long. For one thing, they could pick their own times and conditions for making a run. For another, many enforcement officials were being paid under the table *not* to catch them. For a third, the bootleggers maintained an elaborate spy network, which usually kept them well informed of police activities. And for a fourth, many of the Jersey skiffs and other rumrunning speedboats were equipped with such powerful engines that they could leave patrol boats and Coast Guard cutters wallowing in their wakes.

Federal agents in New York — the honest ones — were getting more than a little tired of being laughingstocks of the cocky rumrunners. To even the odds a little, they secretly had the *Hansen* made ready. Designed during the World War for sub-chasing duty, this sleek vessel was built for speed. Now, fresh out of the nation's mothball fleet, she became part of the Treasury Department's "Prohibition navy," ready to chase bootleggers instead of submarines.

In the early morning of July 27, 1922, the *Hansen* set out on the first voyage of her new assignment. At the helm was Captain J. H. Dizer, an experienced naval officer. On board, besides her crew, were three Customs agents, Inspectors Lynch, Thropp, and Hartman. Little did they know, as they cruised out of New York Harbor toward the south Long Island shoreline and Rum Row, that they were about to make the biggest catch so far in the Prohibition war, nor that their raid would nail a young marine engineer named Dan Ludwig, who would someday be the richest man in the world.

The night before, Inspector James J. Lynch, sitting at his desk in the Barge Office of the U.S. Custom House in New York, had received a call from a man who identified himself as a Coast Guardsman named Baker at the Bay Shore station on south Long Island. A small boat called the *J.H.B.,* Baker told Lynch, had just put out toward a schooner lying off Fire Island in Rum Row. The previous night, the *J.H.B.* had come in with a load of liquor from the same schooner.

After taking the call, Lynch had alerted two fellow inspectors, and the three had gone down to the harbor and boarded the *Hansen* to go out and investigate. At about 4:00 A.M. they arrived at Rum Row, where they observed a two-masted schooner anchored near the Fire Island Light Ship. Surprisingly, the schooner was well within the twelve-mile limit. The Customs agents decided to board and search her.

Approaching closer, they could make out the schooner's name: *Marion Mosher.* As the *Hansen* drew alongside, a man stuck his head out of the *Mosher*'s cabin door. The agents shouted over to him, asking where the captain and mate were. The man replied that they had gone ashore to enter their ship in the Custom House (a requirement for vessels planning to dock and unload cargo). When asked if anyone else was in charge, the man ducked back inside the cabin.

Almost immediately, another man emerged from the forecastle, yelling to the *Hansen:* "For God's sake, take me off this ship! I am an American citizen and I have been shanghaied and beaten and kicked!"

Still another man then came on deck, saying that he too had been shanghaied. These two sailors (later found to be named Cox and Meier) were asked what the *Mosher* was carrying. They replied, "Rum."

The water was too rough for the *Hansen* to come close enough alongside to permit boarding, so a small boat was lowered, and Inspectors Lynch and Thropp, accompanied by two sailors, pulled over to the *Mosher.* Once aboard, they found a man in the cabin who identified himself as Jacob Gushue, the schooner's mate. Asked whom the cargo belonged to, Gushue professed ignorance, but Cox, the man who had first proclaimed himself a shanghai victim, identified the owner as a Captain Mart Gilbert.

This was all Lynch and Thropp needed to hear. Gilbert was already under indictment in New York on several counts of rumrunning. He was a partner in the Globe Steamship Line, which had had eight or nine ships seized by government agents for illegally landing liquor. The other partner, the Customs officials now learned from Cox, was a man they had never heard of: Captain Daniel Ludwig. He had not been seen recently, Cox told the agents, but his son, also named Daniel, was aboard the *Mosher* as engineer.

Lynch and Thropp soon rounded up the eight-man crew and placed them under arrest. They also noted that in the *Mosher*'s hold were 1208 cases of whiskey and 20 barrels of gin, which they impounded, along with the ship itself.

The *Mosher*, its crew, and contents would have to be towed into New York Harbor; the ship had apparently encountered some rough weather, which had disabled both its engine and mainsail. While preparing the ship to be taken in, Lynch asked Cox to cover up the donkey engine used to hoist the anchor. Cox, feeling brave now that he had been freed by the agents, replied, "I am not going to do it. Let the owner," and pointed to the engineer, Ludwig, who obediently placed the cover over the engine.

On the way in, one of the prisoners who had identified himself as Frank Patten, a checker for the Globe Line, reportedly offered Lynch and Thropp a bribe of $25,000 to let the *Mosher* go, but the agents were having none of it. Patten, trying to be friendly, told his captors that this was the first load the *Mosher* had brought up from the Bahamas, and that other cargoes were being brought from England, Scotland, and islands off the Canadian mainland. He also confided that the Globe Line had recently acquired the *Mosher* for $10,000. The owners, he said, were selling the ship's cargo from on board at $85 per case.

While Lynch and Thropp were bringing in the *Mosher*, another Customs agent was seizing the *J.H.B.*, which had run aground near Point o' Woods on the Long Island shore with 100 cases of whiskey and 39 barrels of gin it had unloaded from the schooner the previous night.

The combined value of the cargoes was estimated at a quarter of a million dollars, a fact duly noted in a *New York Times* article the day after the capture and headlined PROHIBITION NAVY MAKES BIGGEST HAUL HERE SINCE THE VOLSTEAD ACT PASSED. The story gave a brief account of the seizure and arrests from the facts the Customs agents had radioed back to the Barge Office. Most of the article was correct, but there were numerous minor mistakes, due probably to hastily scribbled notes taken from the wireless message. One of the crewmen aboard the *Mosher*, for example, was listed as "Daniel Ludwig, 28, of 25 South Street, who said he was the son of a member of the firm of Ludwig & Gilbert of the Globe Line, Inc., of 150 Broadway." Ludwig's age and his street address had evidently been transposed. In testimony later before a New York grand jury,

Cox said that he had been recruited to serve on the *Mosher* by a Captain Ludwig — an older man — in front of a clothing store at 28 South Street, where the Ludwigs had an upstairs apartment. And the younger Daniel Ludwig had just turned twenty-five a month before the *Mosher* was captured.

Cox's grand jury testimony was not pretty. A sailor by profession, he had been signed on by Captain Ludwig to go down to Nassau on a "pleasure trip." Later he had met the other partner, Captain Gilbert, who gave him money to take a train to Greenport, Long Island, where he was put aboard the *J.H.B.* and told to stay out of sight. After dark the smaller boat took him out to the *Mosher,* anchored off Montauk Point.

According to this testimony, Captain Ludwig had told Cox he would be shipping aboard the *Mosher* as mate, but when Cox got aboard, he found that the schooner already had a mate and he would have to ship as a common seaman. When he refused, he was ordered to the forward area, where the seamen's quarters were. He was threatened, he said, so he went, but he refused to stand watch. The cook was then ordered to give him no food until he obeyed.

Cox related how he had gone below and discovered hundreds of cases of whiskey in the hold. He again asked to leave the ship but was told, "You are not going to leave. You're going to stay here. Captain Gilbert will be aboard in two or three days and he will let you know whether you are going or not."

When Gilbert came aboard, he ordered Cox to turn to and stand watch like an ordinary seaman. Again Cox refused. Gilbert and another man gave Cox a savage beating and kicking, blacking both of his eyes and breaking several ribs. Cox still refused and was finally told to go to the forecastle and lie down.

A few days later, Cox said, the *Mosher* sailed from Montauk Point to a spot off Fire Island. It was at this time that the ship ran into the rough weather that disabled its engine and mainsail. Captain Gilbert and the young Dan Ludwig, reported Cox, went ashore and returned with some stores. Gilbert went ashore again, came back with a gang of men in the *J.H.B.,* and proceeded to load that vessel with liquor from the *Mosher*'s hold. The smaller boat landed its cargo, returned for another load, and had just left with that when the *Hansen* came alongside and hailed the *Mosher.*

Inspector Lynch then took up the story, giving his account of the capture. Several other witnesses testified after him. Following the hearing, the grand jury retired and soon returned indictments against the officers and crews of the *Mosher* and *J.H.B.* and also against Captains Ludwig and Gilbert of the Globe Line for violations of the Volstead Act.

Immediately after the two vessels were captured, Customs agents had been dispatched to the Globe Line offices on Broadway (just a few blocks' walk from the Ludwigs' rooms in lower Manhattan) to arrest the ships' owners. By the time they got there, though, business hours were over and the offices were locked and deserted. Returning early next morning, the agents were met by an unidentified man who claimed to work for another company and told them: "The Globe Line left here more than a week ago, and their telephone service was disconnected. Where they went, or what became of their office staff or the boats the line claims to operate, are mysteries to us."

The agents took the statement at face value, though it was probable that Ludwig and Gilbert had been tipped off about the capture the previous day and had fled, leaving someone to tell a phony story.

What exactly *was* the Globe Line? There was no listing for either a Globe Steamship Line or a Ludwig & Gilbert in the Manhattan directory or New York corporate records. Yet the firm did exist, because several bootleg vessels belonging to it had previously been seized by Prohibition enforcement officials. The evidence suggests that the company was one of several firms established as covers for ships tied to the bootleg network set up by Frank Costello and friends and operated out of a central headquarters at 405 Lexington Avenue in mid-Manhattan. This was the nerve center for rumrunning operations along the East Coast, and it was being run like a gigantic multinational business (which in fact it was), with departments for purchasing, shipping, distribution, marketing, and security. It also had elaborate files on hundreds of elected and appointed officials, with information on who could be bought and for how much. These files were only part of a complex system that told the bootleggers far more about the enforcement agents than the enforcement agents knew about the bootleggers.

The agents, for example, never seemed able to find out more about the "Captain Daniel Ludwig, Sr.,"* who was one of the partners of Ludwig & Gilbert and the father of the young *Mosher* engineer. This

*The federal agents never learned the middle initials of either Daniel F. or Daniel K. Ludwig, and referred to them instead as Daniel Ludwig, Sr., and Daniel Ludwig, Jr.

mystery man was never apprehended, never seen at any of the court hearings, and tied to the operation only through his son's arrest and Cox's testimony. Even Cox, who had been on the New York shipping scene for forty years and recalled knowing Captain Gilbert from fifteen years back, knew nothing about Captain Ludwig other than that the man had recruited him to sail aboard the *Mosher*.

Gilbert was much better known locally. During the war he had been employed by the Morse Steamship Line. But once Prohibition started, he became familiar to agents as a ship operator heavily engaged in smuggling into the United States much of the liquor that had been taken out of the country just before Prohibition went into effect. During the grand jury hearing for the *Mosher* defendants, Inspector Lynch, asked what he knew about Gilbert, had responded: "Now this Mart Gilbert is . . . one of the leading men in the Globe Steamship Line, and he is also under indictment in New York. They had a habit of exporting liquor from the United States to foreign ports and, instead of going outside, they lay off the shore and bring it back in lighters, tug boats, and other vessels. However, the Government has seized about eight or nine vessels belonging to the Globe Line."

All of this suggests that when young Daniel Keith Ludwig came to New York in 1916 or 1917 to haul molasses for Kaplan up the Hudson to a Toronto distillery, his father came with him. It also suggests that, rather than being on his own at age nineteen, as he later told Saunders, D.K. may have been working with and for his father. Daniel F., who probably moved to New York during the war years, may have owned most or all of the barges that were chartered to Kaplan. Perhaps he had co-signed the loan to let his son buy the *Idlewylde* in order to teach him about the business.

Sometime between 1916 and 1920, Daniel F. had evidently gone into partnership with Gilbert, who was more experienced in New York shipping, and the two had combined resources to form the Globe Line, using their vessels to bootleg whiskey into the city. Young Daniel K. may have been getting experience on the Globe Line's rumrunning ships.

Given the times, this is hardly surprising. Nearly everyone along the coast who had any knowledge of boats or ships was invited to join a bootleg operation, and many succumbed to the temptation. The impulsive Captain Daniel F. Ludwig, having seen his career as the youngest skipper on Lake Michigan dashed by hard times, and having run away from a wife and a real estate office, was apparently one of those attracted by the lure of easy money. Moreover, it is clear, in the interview years later, that D.K. misled Saunders about his early career in shipping by exaggerating the degree of his own independence and playing down his father's influence.

After the *Mosher* indictments were handed down, Captain Ludwig managed to avoid being caught. Captain Gilbert was not so lucky. On August 17, less than a week after the grand jury returned its true bill against the defendants, the *New York Times* carried the following story:

> Captain Mark* L. Gilbert of 461 West 148th Street was arrested yesterday by Federal agents on a charge of being connected with a gigantic rum-running plot. Agents have sought him ever since the capture, on July 27, of the auxiliary schooner *Marion Mosher* [and] the sloop *J.H.B.* . . . off Fire Island with $250,000 worth of whiskey.
>
> Federal Judge Chatfield issued a bench warrant for the arrest of Captain Gilbert, who was found yesterday at Seventh Avenue and 51st Street. He is charged with being one of the principals in the rum-running plot, and with participation in the shanghaiing of one of the crew of the *Marion Mosher*. He was held in $25,000 bail by Judge Chatfield for examination before a U.S. Commissioner. In default of the bail, Captain Gilbert was locked up in Raymond Street Jail. The arrest was made by Special Agent Barron, Inspector James J. Lynch and Inspector Frank Thropp.

Lynch and Thropp could take pride in a job well done. Not only had they made the biggest bust of the liquor war; they had also managed to track down and nail Gilbert. Captain Ludwig was still at large, as were two of the other principals in the case. But thirteen of the sixteen defendants indicted had been taken into custody, and two vessels, plus a quarter of a million dollars' worth of bootleg whiskey, were being held in government security. What's more, there were witnesses and a shanghaiing charge. The case seemed just about ready to be wrapped up.

*Court records refer to Gilbert as "Mart." Newspaper accounts call him "Mark." It is not certain which is correct.

Elsewhere, however, wheels were starting to turn to reverse everything Lynch and Thropp had accomplished.

Paul Zizelman was one of New York's sharpest lawyers. The word was that if you were guilty, Zizelman was a good man to handle your case. He was smart at figuring angles and had contacts in the highest and lowest places. When Captain Gilbert called him for legal help, the attorney was already familiar with the *Mosher* case; he had represented another of the defendants, Frank Patten, at the arraignment. For the past two years he had been making a substantial living extricating bootleggers from federal raps. He was ready for the challenge of getting Gilbert off, too.

His first task was to put together a version of the events surrounding the *Mosher* capture that would explain the facts — some of them, at least — while making his client appear innocent. For starters, the *Mosher* was a British vessel. At least that's what her registry papers said. Her owner of record (though not the actual owner) was a Canadian citizen, Captain Joseph Pettipas, who had left the ship shortly before she was seized.

These facts could be documented. Now, what was she doing at the Fire Island Light Ship with a load of liquor on board? Well, Zizelman thought, as a vessel engaged in intracoastal trade, she might have been hauling a cargo of whiskey from Bermuda to St. John, New Brunswick — nothing illegal in that — and staying close to shore when she was hit by a storm just off Long Island. Her engine was disabled and her mainsail spar damaged so badly that she could not continue her journey without repairs. In distress, she had hailed a passing fishing boat, the *J.H.B.,* and asked that it help lighten her by taking off part of her cargo temporarily and carrying her captain and some of her crew to shore for stores and assistance. She had planned to reload the cargo after the repairs were done and resume her voyage to Canada.

The story sounded plausible. Certainly the *Mosher* had sustained some storm damage off Long Island; Cox, Lynch, and others had said as much at the grand jury hearing. But Zizelman's version flew in the face of much of the other testimony. Cox had stated, for instance, that part of the *Mosher*'s cargo had already been landed at Greenport before the schooner moved on to Fire Island. None of this liquor, though, had been apprehended by government agents, so there was no evidence to back the assertion. For the rest, if he could shake up Cox and Lynch enough at the trial to create doubt in the jury's mind about the accuracy of their testimony, Zizelman thought he had a fighting chance.

Even so, it was a long shot. He might rattle Cox, but Lynch and the other Customs agents were too experienced to be thrown off. A much better gambit would be to prevent the case from coming to trial. To achieve this, he had to pull strings at high levels. *Very* high levels.

Putting together a package of material that seemed to document the version he had concocted, Zizelman sent one set to Sir Auckland Geddes, the British ambassador to the United States, and another to U.S. Secretary of State Charles Evans Hughes.

As the official representative in the United States of His Majesty George V, Sir Auckland would be concerned with the fate of three of the Crown's subjects, namely, Captain Pettipas, *Mosher* mate Jacob Gushue, and another seaman, Zedadok Baker, all of whom were Canadian citizens. The *Mosher* itself was apparently under British registry, and its cargo, allegedly belonging to Canadian subjects, was under the protection of the British flag.

More important, Zizelman knew that Geddes was connected with certain interests in Britain which were reaping fortunes from the illegal liquor trade to America, and that the ambassador might be just as well pleased if the *Mosher* case never got to court. The attorney had judged his man correctly. Immediately after receiving Zizelman's package, Sir Auckland threw himself tirelessly into getting the charges dropped and the men, ships, and cargoes freed.

Charles Evans Hughes was even more helpful. Well before his Cabinet appointment as administrator of President Warren Gamaliel Harding's foreign policy, he had been a powerful figure in New York and national Republican politics. In 1910, he was elected to the first of his two terms as governor of New York. He resigned in 1916, in the middle of his second term, to accept his party's nomination to run against Woodrow Wilson for the presidency. The race was a squeaker. Hughes thought he had won, and Wilson was almost ready to concede, when the news was flashed that Hughes had lost California by a mere four thousand ballots, giving the state's electoral votes — and the national election — to Wilson.

Out of public office for a few years, Hughes set up a successful private law practice in which he used his knowledge and influence to help corporate clients sidestep government regulations. In 1921 the newly elected Harding called him back to public life to serve as secretary of state. He would remain in that post until 1925, when he returned to private practice until 1930, when another president, Herbert Hoover, appointed him chief justice of the U.S. Supreme Court. Tall, patrician, handsome, and distinguished, looking like a whiskered eagle, with his white hair, neatly trimmed beard, and black robes, Hughes ruled the Court during the Depression years with an iron fist, voiding much of Democratic President Franklin Delano Roosevelt's New Deal legislation by declaring it unconstitutional.

Now, as his first contribution to Zizelman's defense of Captain Gilbert, the aristocratic secretary of state contacted President Harding and set up a Cabinet meeting to discuss the *Mosher* case and several similar actions being brought by the government against rumrunners. Although sworn to uphold the law of the land, Harding was notoriously soft on nearly all forms of moral restraint, including enforcement of the ban on liquor. Unknown to the American public, he maintained a well-stocked bar on the second floor of the White House and even had his own personal bootlegger, a shady character named Elias Mortimer, to keep it supplied.

Presiding at the Cabinet meeting, and armed with Zizelman's brief, his own legal acumen, and some juridical razzle-dazzle from the State Department's chief solicitor, Hughes had little difficulty convincing the other Cabinet members and the president they should endorse a policy of enforcing Prohibition laws no more stringently than absolutely necessary. Granting the dubious wisdom of these laws, it is clear that, in adopting this policy of softness, Harding, Hughes, and the other Cabinet officers were undercutting the entire law enforcement mechanism of the nation and playing into the hands of the criminals.

Insofar as the *Mosher* case was concerned, Hughes argued for a strict interpretation of the three-mile limit to territorial waters. Only if a vessel was caught using its own boats to transport liquor to shore from beyond three miles would it be liable to seizure. Simply transferring liquor to another boat outside the three-mile limit, under this reasoning, would not constitute a violation of U.S. law.

After Harding and the Cabinet had agreed to this interpretation,

Hughes sent a formal request through Attorney General Harry M. Daugherty (whose chief qualification for the office was that he was a crony of Harding's) to New York enforcement officials for information pertaining to the government's case against the *Mosher* defendants.

The request came to the desk of Mabel Walker Willebrandt, assistant attorney general in charge of Prohibition enforcement for the New York area. An honest, dedicated official, Mrs. Willebrandt did her best to back up the agents under her and shield them from political influence. From the letter she wrote in response to Hughes's query, marked *Confidential* and dated September 26, 1922, it is apparent that she knew what he was up to and was trying to head him off.

Two of the *Mosher* defendants, she wrote, had already pleaded guilty to the charges. (Gushue and Baker, both from Halifax, Nova Scotia, had posted bail and been released, but the bonding company, fearing they would skip to Canada, had brought them back in and turned them over to a U.S. marshal. On the suggestion of an assistant district attorney, they were held as material witnesses. Soon after, they agreed to change their plea from not guilty to guilty. Sentencing was postponed until the other defendants, including young Daniel Ludwig, could be tried.)

In her letter to Hughes, Mrs. Willebrandt gave a summary of the allegations in the government's case. Captain Pettipas (whom she designated as the owner of the *Mosher*) had sailed the schooner from Halifax to Newfoundland* and then to New York, where he had conspired with certain Americans to violate the Volstead Act. Then he had taken the *Mosher* to Bermuda,† picked up a load of liquor, and returned with it to New York. There the *Mosher* had been met by the *J.H.B.*, also operated by the conspirators, at Greenport, where part of the contraband was offloaded and landed. Pettipas accompanied the liquor to shore aboard the *J.H.B.* and headed back to Canada, leaving the *Mosher* under the command of a Captain Larsen.

After landing the whiskey and putting Pettipas ashore (Mrs. Wil-

---

*Probably to St. Pierre, but Mrs. Willebrandt did not seem to have been aware of this bootlegger depot at the time.
†Sometimes she wrote Bermuda, sometimes the Bahamas. Both were bootlegger supply depots for the East Coast shuttles.

lebrandt's letter continued), the *J.H.B.* returned to the *Mosher,*\* which towed it some forty to seventy miles to a point near the Fire Island Light Ship and offloaded another portion of the liquor for landing near Bay Shore, Long Island.†

Writing as a representative of the U.S. Department of Justice, Mrs. Willebrandt firmly rejected Zizelman's contention that the *Mosher* was merely a Canadian vessel blown off course and so badly damaged by a storm that it was forced to offload part of its liquor cargo temporarily to keep from sinking. She was also intent on convincing Hughes that Zizelman's claims about the *Mosher*'s being an innocent Canadian vessel were patently false and contrary to known facts. In order to get around Hughes's restrictive interpretation of the law (which he may have devised to create a loophole the *Mosher* could escape through), Mrs. Willebrandt stretched the law a bit herself, arguing that the *Mosher*'s act of towing the *J.H.B.* from Greenport to Fire Island for the purpose of landing liquor made the smaller vessel part of the schooner's equipment and gave the Customs agents the right to seize both vessels and their cargoes.

To back up her position, Mrs. Willebrandt cited as precedent the recent case of *The United States v. the "Grace and Ruby,"* in which a bootlegger vessel had been seized outside the three-mile limit after government agents on shore had captured a lighter carrying part of the *Grace and Ruby*'s cargo. A federal judge in Boston had deemed that seizure proper.

From the tone and substance of her letter to Hughes, it is evident that Assistant Attorney General Willebrandt thought she had a strong case against the *Mosher* participants — if the people in Washington would just leave her alone to pursue it. Although she felt handicapped by the narrow interpretation of the law just handed down to her, she made plans to argue around that point to obtain convictions. Certainly there seems to have been no doubt in her mind that the defendants in the case were guilty and that the Customs agents had been well within their rights in seizing the vessels and arresting their crews.

But Hughes was every bit as committed to getting the bootleggers

---

\*This would have been when Cox, having been told by Captain Ludwig that he was signing on as the *Mosher*'s new mate, was taken out to the schooner.

†This was when the Bay Shore Coast Guard, having observed the *J.H.B.* land a load of liquor and head back out toward the *Mosher,* called the Custom House Barge Office.

off as Mrs. Willebrandt was to putting them behind bars, and the details in her letter told him the thing he needed to know: exactly how she planned to argue the government's case. Now that he knew, he could try to prevent her getting the matter into court.

Early in October the secretary of state wrote to Attorney General Daugherty, Mrs. Willebrandt's boss, "I have the honor to state that this Department does not concur in the view that, in towing the *J.H.B.* in the circumstances mentioned, the *Marion Mosher* made the *J.H.B.* a part of the equipment of the vessel."

He added that the principles cited in Mrs. Willebrandt's letter were not valid under international law and that the *Mosher* should be considered as having been seized improperly outside U.S. territorial waters. He reminded Daugherty that the Cabinet had determined that no foreign vessel should be seized outside the three-mile limit unless her own boats and other equipment were involved in carrying contraband to shore. "In a communication received by this Department from a representative of the owners," Hughes concluded, "it is stated that if the ship and cargo are released promptly, a stipulation will be furnished on behalf of the owners to the effect that no claim shall be made for damages resulting from the detention of the ship and cargo, and a bond will be deposited for the faithful completion of the voyage and the delivery of the cargo to its original destination in St. John, New Brunswick."

The implied threat that the *Mosher* owners might sue the government for damages and the offer to post a performance bond were clever moves by Zizelman to give Hughes more leverage for getting the Justice Department to quash the case. They would not have worked if used directly against Mrs. Willebrandt, but they were powerful inducements to top officials looking for excuses not to enforce the law.

On October 28, 1922, after receiving Hughes's letter, Attorney General Daugherty sent a curt note to New York District Attorney Ralph C. Greene ordering him to drop the efforts to retain custody of the *Mosher* and her cargo: "You are hereby directed to dismiss all libel* proceedings of the United States against said vessel and said liquors, and to deliver said vessel to the owners

---

*Libel as used here simply means an action brought under admiralty law and has nothing to do with defamation.

thereof, and to discharge said liquors insofar as the United States is concerned."

Thus Zizelman, working through the British ambassador and the U.S. secretary of state and attorney general, had seemingly accomplished a good part of what he had set out to do — freeing the *Mosher* and its cargo of liquor — which he probably would not have managed by going through the courts.

But Hughes had neglected to keep Geddes informed, and the British ambassador was getting a bit worried. On November 2, he wrote to remind the secretary that he had previously asked a question about the Cabinet's new three-mile ruling: Would it apply retroactively to vessels already seized — specifically, the *Marion Mosher*? He noted that the case was being pushed in the courts "with the apparent intention of securing a conviction under that section of the Tariff Act which extends the territorial limit to four leagues from the coast of the United States." He added, "It appears to have been proved that this vessel did not use her own boats in communicating with the shore, the captain having been taken ashore in an American fishing boat."

In fact, Sir Auckland did have reason for concern. A memo dated November 4, 1922, from the State Department solicitor to Hughes, noted that "Mrs. Willebrandt was of the opinion that the government should not release the *Marion Mosher.*" He added that a Mr. Pell, attorney for the ship, had complained about the difficulties he was having in getting her released.

Shortly afterward came the following sequence of events: Pell went to the British embassy and complained. Geddes wrote to Hughes again. Hughes called the State Department solicitor into his office and demanded to know what progress had been made. When he learned there had been none, he telephoned Daugherty and ordered him to release the ship.

Mrs. Willebrandt had run out of maneuvering room. To hold off longer would probably have cost her her job, so, on November 6, she wrote to Hughes, saying that the charges were being dismissed.

Sir Auckland was grateful — momentarily. When the owners' lawyers went down to claim the *Mosher* and her cargo, they were told that that liquor could not be released; it was needed as evidence in the trial of the *Mosher* and *J.B.H.* crews. Sir Auckland, distressed, sent Hughes a letter, and a reminder a week later, requesting the cargo's release. In due course, Hughes was able to assure him of this. The ambassador then busied himself in an attempt to get the crewmen released as well.

He was officially concerned with the two Canadians who had pleaded guilty, but their fate was closely tied to that of the American defendants. Geddes assumed, correctly, that once the ship and her liquor were released, the government would have little case against the bootleggers.

On December 7, Mrs. Willebrandt received a letter from Hughes demanding to know why the *Marion Mosher* was still in custody. She replied that the hitch was caused by some disagreement between the owners of the cargo and the ship's owners, and she told him that both owners were British subjects.

This, of course, was dubious. The probable owners of the *Mosher* were Captains Ludwig and Gilbert, both American. The cargo was almost certainly the property of the New York mob. That had been concealed, however, by the action of the Great Western Wine Company of Canada, which came forward to claim ownership after the seizure.

Gushue and Baker each served one day in prison for violating the Volstead Act and were freed on December 7. The *Marion Mosher* was released on the eighteenth and reportedly headed for St. Pierre. All charges were dropped against the Ludwigs and against Gilbert, who had shanghaied and savagely beaten Cox. Charles Evans Hughes and Ambassador Sir Auckland Geddes had flexed their muscles and won this ignoble little victory.

And what did the *Marion Mosher* do? Precisely what was to be expected of any bootlegging vessel. She sailed out of New York Harbor as far as Rum Row, anchored, and proceeded to dispatch her cases of liquor, via small boats, right back into the United States. The New York collector of customs, on January 20, 1923, had definite proof of this and reported it to the Treasury Department.

Two months later, the embarrassing news was passed on to Secretary Hughes. The owners of the *Mosher* had been forced to put up a bond as surety that the ship would deliver its cargo to St. John, and Hughes now ordered proceedings to obtain its forfeiture. He was still intervening, however, and took the trouble to warn the collector not to make any attempt to seize the rumrunner outside the three-mile limit. In August, Judge Woodrough and a jury of the Federal Court of the Eastern District of New York awarded the government the $20,000 surety bond.

An interesting aspect of the judge's charge to the jury was his interpretation of the law as it bore on federal agents' powers to pursue bootleggers beyond the three-mile limit. Citing a precedent from a Massachusetts case, he said that the ship "was hovering close to our shore for the purpose and intent of violating our law and that under such circumstances the seizure was justified by the usages of international law." He added that the decision to drop charges was a political one by the executive branch of the government and not a judicial one. His position was strongly supported in an editorial in the *Manchester Guardian* of August 16, 1923. The *Guardian* advised His Majesty's government to "put its foot down" and halt the illegal liquor traffic.

That was not very likely. Too many influential Englishmen and Americans were getting rich from smuggling liquor. There were not only the mobsters, like Costello, Luciano, and Lansky, but respectable establishment figures, too. One of them allegedly was Joseph Kennedy, later ambassador to Great Britain and the father of a president. Five decades afterward, Frank Costello would tell Peter Maas of the *New York Times* that he had been a partner with Kennedy in the illicit liquor business. Charles Evans Hughes — whatever his interest may have been — most surely intervened to see that Prohibition laws were not enforced and that violators were set free.

The bonding company appealed Judge Woodrough's decision, but it was upheld. Thus, there were now on the record two judicial affirmations of the stand Mabel Willebrandt and the Customs officials had taken. Consequently, there was a strong implication that Secretary Hughes had done violence to the law. This — if it had been publicized more — might have deterred Herbert Hoover from nominating Hughes as chief justice a few years later. And could Daniel Keith Ludwig, with a bootlegging conviction behind him, have gone on to become the world's richest man? It was fortunate for both of them that the *Mosher* incident sank out of sight almost at once.

As for the ship itself, she continued in the smuggling business through 1928, according to State Department reports. The remaining question of interest concerns the true ownership of the *Marion*

*Mosher.* Did she indeed belong to the elder Ludwig and Gilbert? Or were they fronting for others?

Mike San Antonio, the man in charge of the ship's cargo, had told Inspector Lynch that the real estate owners were "big people in New York." Frank Patten, the Globe Line checker, had said that "big men in New York" had an interest in the ship and cargo. The American vice-consul at St. John later reported to Washington that he was "informed that the schooner is owned by several parties of the Jewish race connected with the liquor trade."

Perhaps these clues pointed to Abner (Longie) Zwillman, Joe Reinfeld, Waxey Gordon, Max Greenberg, Al Lilien, Charles J. Steinberg, Dutch Schultz, Meyer Lansky, and Bugsy Siegel — all Jewish bootleggers and "big men" in New York.

As for the young Daniel Ludwig, he evidently learned a lesson from this close brush with the law and decided to get into another line of shipping. From now on, the liquid cargo he hauled would be oil, not spirits.

# Four

# The *Ulysses* Imbroglio

Not surprisingly, the version of his life story that Daniel Ludwig gave to *Fortune*'s Dero Saunders in 1957 omitted any mention of the *Mosher* incident. According to D.K., after his breakup with Kaplan, around the time of the Armistice, he did general hauling with a few broken-down tugboats until the bottom fell out of the shipping market in the early postwar years. Most of his cargoes, he said, had consisted of lumber and barrel staves before he decided to switch to oil transport. "I'd been getting ten or fifteen cents a hundredweight to haul a cargo of staves and lumber," he told Saunders. "I saw the tanker boys getting three or four times as much for oil."

His first experience in petroleum hauling, Ludwig said, came in 1921. He had heard of a small refinery in Fall River, Massachusetts, that had a contract to haul fuel oil for the Navy. If he could find any vessels, he would be able to charter them to the refinery. In a Long Island shipyard he'd found a little tanker that had been started under government contract during the war and was 98 percent complete when the Armistice was declared. Since then, there had been no incentive to finish her, but Ludwig could lease her cheaply if he was willing to put on the final few touches.

Selling some of his old tugs, he got enough money to complete the vessel, then talked the Coast Guard into giving him a certificate of seaworthiness. He wasn't even sure how to pronounce her name — the *Anahuac* — Ludwig told Saunders, but because it would have cost him $50 to paint it out and put on a new one, he decided to leave it as it was. Besides, he was just leasing the boat from the War Shipping Board, not buying it.

The *Anahuac,* only 473 tons, wasn't big enough to allow D.K. to fulfill the charter agreement he had made with the Fall River refinery. In 1923 (shortly after the *Mosher* incident), he found a larger ship in Baltimore. The *Wico* was already many years past her prime. In fact, she was the fourth or fifth oil tanker ever built and, since her maiden voyage in 1888, had hauled many a barrel of crude for Standard Oil. But now, after thirty-five years of service (the average life of an oil tanker was about twenty years), Standard had decided to scrap her and had sold her to a scrap dealer, Morris Schapiro, head of Baltimore's Boston Metals Company.

Learning of this, Ludwig traveled to Baltimore and, after looking her over, decided that the *Wico* was good for a few more trips. Schapiro (who over the years would become one of D.K.'s steadiest suppliers of used ship parts) was willing to let her go for $25,000 — $5000 up front and the rest on time. Even the down payment, according to Ludwig, was more money than he had on hand. In order to raise it, he had to take a partner.

William Tomlison, a shipper D.K. had met during the war, offered to put up the rest of the front money in exchange for a 51 percent share of the venture. Soon, though, Tomlison wanted it all, and asked his junior partner to get out. Ludwig settled for $40,000 in cash plus a few old tugs, and his greedy partner got the rest: sole ownership of the *Wico,* the *Anahuac* lease, and the Fall River refinery oil-hauling charter.

Relating this episode to Saunders, D.K. gave the impression that he had been squeezed out and cheated by Tomlison. At the time, however, he made no fuss. Accepting the settlement, he used the money to go into another partnership with a New England group that owned a chain of filling stations in Boston. His new partners were Marshall B. Hall and Francis T. Leahy. Hall was a Bostonian and a man of some substance. (Nothing has been learned about Leahy. A man by that name was deputy director of Customs of the Port of New York for many years, but it's not known whether this was the same person.) Together, the three formed a new company, American Tankers Corporation of Massachusetts, referred to as Amtankers. Hall was president, Ludwig vice-president and treasurer, and Leahy secretary. From the beginning of the company, around 1924, it was evident that D.K. was, for practical purposes, its chief executive officer. Neither Hall nor Leahy appears to have done much in the actual running of the corporation, and the job of keeping things going fell squarely on the shoulders of Ludwig.

The new company's first move was to arrange for the purchase of an unusual tanker from the War Shipping Board for a price of $57,000 — $14,000 put up by Amtankers, the rest borrowed from Grace National Bank. What made the *Phoenix* unusual was that she had been built as a dry-cargo vessel and converted to a tanker by a simple expedient: large cylindrical tanks were installed in her cargo hold. As matters turned out, this simple procedure was also dangerous.

One day in 1926, a year after Amtankers purchased her, the *Phoenix* was steaming into Boston Harbor with a load of gasoline when vapors started leaking through the seams into the cargo area. (The tanks consisted of curved panels of sheet steel riveted together. Through use and age, some of the rivets had begun to work loose.) Two crewmen working below on a balky pump were overcome by the fumes. Ludwig, who was then on board, went down to investigate. As he descended into the hold, a spark ignited the fumes and there was a powerful explosion that blew him upward through one deck and onto another — some twenty-five feet through the air — where he landed on his spine. Forever after, Ludwig was a proponent of welding, rather than riveting, ship seams.

The injury, though painful, did not seem serious at the time. A day or two later, Ludwig had recovered enough to return to the hold and bring up the bodies of the two crewmen. Not until several years later, when his back pains became unbearable, did he have x rays taken; they disclosed that three of his vertebrae had been cracked in the accident and had fused together as the new bone tissue formed.

D.K.'s bad back was to cause him many years of agony. At times the pain was so intense that he would black out or have to sit down suddenly, even in the middle of the street, unable to straighten up. Occasionally in later years he conducted business meetings lying flat on his office floor. Why he did not get help sooner is a mystery, but, despite his discomfort, he put off major corrective surgery until 1954, when he finally consented to an operation. He had to wear a knee-to-shoulder cast for nine months, but it did relieve much of the difficulty, though he was left with a slight limp and stoop.

Ludwig's long postponement of remedial surgery may have been caused by fear that a slip of the scalpel might kill him or leave him paralyzed for life, or by his compulsive drive for work which would not allow him to tolerate a long period of immobility. In 1926, at any rate, getting the *Phoenix* repaired and back in service seemed more urgent than nursing a bad back. The ship was losing money every day she was laid up, and, to make matters worse, the tanker business had gone into another slump and he could not find a local charterer. Amtankers was doing business out of 80 Boylston Street in Boston's Back Bay district — apparently Marshall B. Hall's office address. Most of Ludwig's contacts, though, were in New York's financial district, near the docks at the southern tip of Manhattan (and close to the Ludwigs' apartment at 28 South Street and the offices of Ludwig & Gilbert and the Globe Line).

Here, at 21 West Street, near the Battery, D.K. set up Amtankers' New York operation. The address was actually that of the David C. Reid Company, a small ship brokerage founded by a Scottish immigrant. Saunders gave the impression in the *Fortune* piece that Ludwig was too poor to be able to rent office space on his own. He quoted an old friend of D.K.'s: "In those days he didn't even have a desk. He was working from a windowsill."

Despite Saunders's claim (surely drawn from D.K. himself) that Amtankers was operating on a shoestring and could not afford office space, the company was able to buy two more ships shortly after Ludwig started operating out of the Reid office. The *Dannedaike,* a fairly large tanker, was sold a year later to a company that subsequently called itself the Dannedaike Steamship Company. The other vessel, the *Overbrook* (at 7400 deadweight tons about the same size as the *Phoenix*), was bought from the shippers M. & J. Tracy and sold back to them two years later.

During the mid-to-late-1920s, in fact, Ludwig was more involved in buying and selling ships than he was in operating them. In any case, he seems to have had time for a pursuit he had previously neglected: romance. There is no indication, from the little that is known, whether he had earlier had any appreciable contact with girls. But in 1927, at the age of thirty, he started dating, and the next year he got married.

As with the other women in his life, not much is known about his wife. A 1970 *Time* magazine article about his shipping activities made this passing mention: "Ludwig has been married twice. The first marriage broke up quickly, amid much bitterness. His daughter by that marriage admits to 'frustrating' relations with her father."

That was it. No names, no other details, were given to clarify the circumstances of Ludwig's first marriage. During the mid-1970s, though, an official at the South Haven Chamber of Commerce received a call that may throw a little light on the subject. The caller (an elderly man, from the sound of his voice) identified himself to the chamber official as an old friend of D.K.'s from the 1920s. Remembering that Ludwig was from South Haven, the man had called to see whether anyone there could tell him how to get in touch with the billionaire.

In the course of the conversation, Ludwig's former friend chatted at length about the old days and the good times he and D.K. had had together as young bachelors during the Roaring Twenties. According to the caller, Ludwig then had fallen madly in love with a "starlet" — actually a chorus girl named Gladys — and after a whirlwind courtship had married her.

The marriage, said the man on the telephone, had not been a happy one. Ludwig was gone a lot, traveling in connection with his shipping activities, and Gladys wasn't the type to sit patiently at home. When D.K. found out she had been playing around, he was devastated. There were stormy fights, and in 1937, shortly after Gladys gave birth to a daughter, Ludwig filed for and obtained a divorce.

The chamber official wasn't sure how much of the caller's story to believe. But in January of 1978, many of these details were confirmed. Half a century after she married him, and more than forty years after their divorce, Gladys Madeline Ludwig filed suit in a New York court against her former husband, now the world's richest man, for $10 million.

In her suit, Gladys claimed that soon after their marriage broke up, Ludwig had lied to her about the state of his finances and refused to provide money to support their daughter. She stated in the complaint that she had married Daniel Keith Ludwig in Florida on February 29, 1928, and that their daughter, Patricia Margaret, was born on October 8, 1936. A few months later, in April 1937, D.K. got a divorce. Under terms of the settlement, he was supposed to pay $200 a month in alimony and child support. But in 1939, Gladys alleged, Ludwig had fallen behind in these payments and come to her, saying he was in deep financial trouble and could no longer afford to honor the agreement. He had offered her a one-time, lump-sum settlement of $3000 if she would sign a paper freeing him from any future responsibility for alimony or child support.

Believing him, and needing the money, Gladys had consented. Why then, forty years after the fact, was she filing suit? Only recently, she said, had she become aware that he had deliberately misrepresented his true worth at the time and could easily have afforded the monthly payments.

Besides, she added, she was now old and sick; a patient at Columbia Presbyterian Medical Center in New York City, she was being treated for several illnesses, including breast cancer, and was in desperate need of money for her hospital bills. So, indigent and aware of how she had been misled, she was seeking to collect compensation for the money Ludwig had cheated her of all these many years.

She had waited too long. Ludwig's attorneys contested the claim, and before the matter could be brought to trial, Gladys died in the hospital, thus ending the suit.

Had Gladys indeed been cheated? A review of Ludwig's financial position in 1939 indicates that he was certainly prosperous enough to have kept up the alimony and support payments. On the other hand, if the man who telephoned the South Haven Chamber of Commerce was correct, Gladys may have gotten what she deserved. There is reason to surmise that Ludwig suspected the child wasn't his, since he got the divorce so quickly after her birth. D.K. himself, of course, has never said a word in public about the matter.

At the time of his marriage to Gladys, though, the young shipper had every reason for optimism. The shipping industry, after a brief slump, was on another upswing, and Amtankers was succeeding well enough for Ludwig and his partners to purchase three more surplus vessels from the War Shipping Board.

The sale of these ships was being handled through the Merchant Fleet Corporation, a branch of the Shipping Board, which, in turn, was a division of the U.S. Department of Commerce. The MFC's function was to act as liaison between the government and private ship owners in ship sales affecting the U.S. Merchant Marine. Long-standing government policy held that the country should maintain a large, modern fleet of merchant vessels available for the nation's use in times of war or other emergencies. The rest of the time, the American merchant fleet remained in private hands, to be operated for profit by individual owners and companies.

This policy created a particularly close relationship between private shippers and the government, and in many cases led to practices that amounted to government subsidies to the U.S. shipping industry. The reasoning was that it was in America's best interests to have a strong, privately owned merchant navy, and if a few shippers became rich in the process, so much the better.

Some clever shippers had learned to cash in on the policy, particularly after World War I, when large numbers of vessels built during the war were declared surplus and offered for sale to private investors to be renovated and maintained in good condition for regular use and future national emergencies.

This sale of surplus ships at bargain prices — much less than what it would have cost to build the vessels from scratch — had never really been authorized by Congress, but the practice, started almost as soon as the Armistice was declared, was never seriously questioned. The result was that hundreds of government-owned vessels, built at taxpayers' expense, were being sold off at well below cost both to legitimate shippers and to speculators who did the minimum required renovation work and then sold the ships for a quick profit.

Hall, Ludwig, and Leahy and their American Tankers Corporation of Massachusetts seem to have belonged to the latter category. They were primarily interested in buying surplus ships, doing the specified remodeling, and putting them up for sale. Of the ships they had bought so far, they retained only the *Phoenix,* possibly because its unusual and unsafe conversion to a tanker made finding a buyer difficult.

In 1929, Amtankers was interested in acquiring three more vessels to renovate. The *Terre Haute, John Jay,* and *James Otis* could be had from the U.S. mothball fleet for $35,000, $55,000, and $60,000 respectively. The Shipping Board would even finance the sale. In return, the purchasers had to agree to replace the old turbines in these vessels with modern diesel or reciprocating engines, and to spend a minimum of $100,000 on the *Terre Haute* and $120,000 each on the *Jay* and *Otis* to ensure good renovation work.

The total investment for the three ships was just under half a million dollars, but what made the deal attractive was that the Shipping Board required investors to put up only 10 percent of the purchase price and performance bond; the rest could be paid over time. Thus, by investing less than $50,000, Hall, Ludwig, and Leahy could buy three ships, remodel and sell them, use part of the proceeds to pay off the purchase price and renovation costs, and pocket the rest. If they managed to sell the three vessels for $1 million (a reasonable expectation at the time), they would reap over half a million dollars' profit on an investment of only $50,000.

To carry through this particular deal, the partners decided to set up a new company — American Steamship Corporation — which would be owned by American Tankers. The advantages of forming multiple companies to handle different projects were numerous. There were tax breaks to be gained, record keeping was simpler, and, most important, liability could be removed from the parent company. If for some reason the new project should fail, American Steamship could be dissolved and American Tankers would not be responsible for its debts.

American Steamship (Amsteam) was registered in Delaware on January 30, 1929. By now Ludwig had learned that there were distinct benefits to incorporating in Delaware, a bit of knowledge he would apply frequently in the future. In 1899, the state's legislature, traditionally controlled by the Du Pont family and company, had passed a law making Delaware a haven for corporate interests. This was evidently an attempt to compensate for the state's being small, not heavily populated, and nearly devoid of mineral resources. Small or sparsely populated states or countries not uncommonly take steps to make themselves attractive to people with money. Switzerland, for example, later established secrecy laws to protect bank depositors, and Nevada became a haven for divorce seekers and gamblers. So Delaware sought to attract corporations. By establishing a nominal corporate franchise tax and a minimum of regulations, and by displaying a decided lack of curiosity about corporate activities, the little state offered Hall, Ludwig, Leahy, and numerous other incorporators advantages not to be found in other states.

The records do not show that Leahy was an officer or director of American Steamship. Hall was again president, and Ludwig was vice-president and treasurer, but the secretary was a Frank J. Davidson, who has not been otherwise identified. The new company's business address was given as 52 Vanderbilt Avenue. This prestigious location near Grand Central Terminal was really the address of Ludwig's favorite insurance agents, Betts & Betts. Stuart Betts, one of the partners, was one of D.K.'s closest friends, and, as Ludwig would later say, he always preferred doing business with friends.

Having closed the deal to purchase the *Terre Haute, Jay,* and *Otis,* the Amsteam investors now had to get them renovated. That was Ludwig's job. As a marine engineer, he was responsible for supervising all mechanical work done on the vessels. Amsteam had no repair yard of its own, but D.K. had a close working relationship with, and possibly even a financial interest in, a Manhattan-based shipyard, United Dry Docks. It was there he brought the *Terre Haute* (the government had granted Amsteam the privilege of taking delivery of the vessels one at a time) for renovation.

While the work was going on, Ludwig got news of another possible deal. The *Ulysses,* a huge collier (coal-hauling vessel) was sitting down in the Panama Canal Zone, rusting away. The ship was the property of the Canal Office (a branch of the War Department) and could be bought reasonably. The government had this 14,000-ton white elephant on its hands and was eager to get rid of her before she fell apart completely. D.K., always thinking big, envisioned converting her into a tankship — the largest tanker afloat.

The asking price was substantial — $175,000 — but still cheap for a vessel of this size. The Canal Office was so eager to sell that it offered to lend most of the purchase money on an unsecured mortgage. The main cost would be in converting the ship from a collier to a tanker. Even here the government was helpful. The Shipping Board's Construction Loan Committee, Ludwig learned, would advance as much as three quarters of the renovation funds.

With these facts in mind, D.K. went to another shipyard — Bethlehem Shipbuilding and Dry Dock near Philadelphia — and obtained a bid for the remodeling. The figure was high: $589,000. But the Construction Loan Committee, without a blink, agreed to advance three fourths of the amount — $422,000. The loan was to be paid back over six years in annual installments of $70,000 plus semiannual interest.

For Ludwig the *Ulysses* deal looked very appealing. The government was not only lending him — unsecured — the money to buy the ship; it was also putting up most of the money to renovate it.

Once he had converted it into the world's largest tanker, he could pay back the loans out of the charter fees he charged for hauling petroleum. And all without risking much of his or his partners' money.

How had he managed to strike such a bargain? Obviously somebody must have been pulling the right strings — somebody with an insider's knowledge of how the federal bureaucracy worked, somebody with influence and contacts.

He was Robert W. Malone, a bright young former bureaucrat who knew his way around Washington. Until the summer of 1927 Malone had been the manager of the Merchant Fleet Corporation's Ship Sales Division. At the time, the MFC, an adjunct of the Shipping Board, was responsible for overseeing all vessels in the U.S. Merchant Marine, including some three hundred active ships and five hundred inactive ones. Malone's boss, J. Harry Philbin, was an MFC vice-president in charge of all the inactive vessels.

In mid-1927, an administrative shakeup at the MFC had resulted in Philbin's ouster. Malone, apparently disgruntled, had left with him. Now, on the outside looking in, Malone needed to turn his knowledge of the shipping bureaucracy into a way of making a living. The answer was simple: he would become a "Washington representative" for private investors trying to find their way through the mazes of government in search of profitable deals.

Somehow Malone met Ludwig, and the two young men hit it off. Malone was hired by D.K. to represent the interests of American Tankers (and, once it was set up in 1929, American Steamship) in Washington. The introduction may have come through United Dry Docks, where Ludwig was having renovation work done on the *Terre Haute*. Besides working for Amtankers, Malone was also working as United Dry Docks' Washington representative.

Six years later, in 1935, a Senate Munitions Committee investigation into the awarding of shipbuilding contracts threw some light on how Malone and United Dry Docks did business. The company was being charged with peddling influence and rigging bids in order to obtain U.S. Navy contracts to build warships during the early 1930s, and both Malone and United's president, Joseph W. Powell, were called before the committee to testify.

According to evidence presented at the hearings, Malone, representing Powell, had tried to strike a deal with President Herbert

Hoover to use his influence in persuading naval procurement officers to award United Dry Docks a contract to build three destroyers. Hoover had declined. A letter written by Malone to Powell at the time and introduced as evidence at the committee hearings reads, in part, "Any approach to Hoover invariably is found to be most disappointing. It is almost out of the question to expect anything of him via his secretaries. He will only yield if there is an advantage to be gained in political trading."

Failing to get action from the president, Malone wrote to Powell that he planned to work through other channels and was debating whether to go through Charles D. Hilles, a Republican National Committeeman from New York, or a friendly congressman, like Fred S. Britten of Illinois:

> It remains for determination whether the approach would be best through a contact such as Mr. Hilles or through a strong Congressional showing. Britten inclined to the latter belief and I do likewise, although quite possibly the approach could be made jointly with Congressional backing and with Mr. Hilles.
>
> What I am trying to convey is that any direct approach to Hoover, even through most personal channels, is almost sure to be unproductive. I will work with the New Jersey delegation.

Although Malone's attempt to get President Hoover to intervene with the Navy on United Dry Docks' behalf failed in this instance, it does indicate that the young Washington lobbyist Ludwig had employed had no hesitation about going directly to the top of the political structure, and that he and the interests he represented had powerful connections in the Republican Party. Malone's difficulty in getting the destroyer contract for United may have resulted from the government's financial problems as much as from anything else. In 1931, as the Depression deepened, Hoover postponed the project as a money-saving measure. But Malone and Powell persisted, turning their efforts toward making sure that the contract — if and when it was finally approved — would not be put out for competitive bidding. During the latter months of 1932, their hopes were buoyed by the possibility of war with Japan. On January 7, 1933 — a month short of eight years before Pearl Harbor — Powell wrote to a young naval engineer he was trying to woo away from government service, "Washington is all steamed up about the possibility of a Japanese war, and, if anything of that sort should eventuate, I may have something for you here in short order."

To a company like United Dry Docks, the impending war was regarded chiefly as another opportunity to make money. But four years earlier, the company had found another way to get nearly half a million dollars in government money. United was going to convert the *Ulysses* Daniel K. Ludwig had just bought into the world's biggest tanker.

Although D.K. had gotten the original conversion bid from Bethlehem Shipbuilding and Dry Dock, the Construction Loan Committee had obligingly written into the loan agreement a clause saying that he could use any shipyard he pleased without affecting the terms of the loan, even if the cost was lower than the original estimate. In other words, if he could get the work done for $200,000 at some shipyard besides Bethlehem, the government would still lend him $422,000 to complete the work.

In retrospect, Bethlehem's $589,000 conversion bid, on which the government loan was based, sounds grotesquely inflated. Half that amount seems more realistic. This may have been an instance of the bid rigging for which United Dry Docks was later investigated by the Senate Munitions Committee. If the government lent Ludwig $422,000 and United could do the renovation work for $300,000, D.K. and his friends would have $122,000 left over to invest in whatever activity they chose. Over the six-year loan period, they could pay off the principal and the interest and still, if they had invested wisely, show a profit, without having risked a penny of their own cash. And once the loans were paid off out of charter fees, they would own a giant tanker, again without having risked any of their own investment capital. Ludwig and his Amtankers and United associates would reap the profits; the government would take all the risks.

That, of course, would be so if all went as intended. But the best-laid plans, as Robert Burns wrote, have a way of going a-gley.

On September 11, 1929, Ludwig, through Malone, submitted a formal bid for a government loan of $422,000 to pay for converting the collier *Ulysses* into a tanker. A month and a half later (and just about the time Harding's former secretary of the interior, Albert B. Fall, was finally convicted for his role in helping private oil speculators plunder the Navy's Teapot Dome reserves), investors on Wall

Street, panicking in the face of falling stock prices, sent the market into its historic tailspin.

The Crash had no immediate effect on Ludwig's plans. With the bureaucratic wheels already in motion, the conversion loan rolled through without a hitch. The Shipping Board felt safe enough. Since the Canal Office had allowed D.K. to purchase the *Ulysses* with an unsecured loan, the board was able to hold a preferred mortgage on the vessel and insist that it be adequately insured at all times. Complying with this condition, Ludwig took out a million-dollar policy on the ship, giving the business, and a fat commission, to his friend Stuart Betts.

It was assumed by almost everyone that the stock market's sharp drop was a temporary phenomenon. But the expected upturn didn't happen. Stock prices sank lower and lower. World trade, including oil transportation, came to a virtual standstill. It suddenly dawned on Ludwig and his associates that they, too, might be hurt if things did not soon get better. Amtankers' single operating vessel, the *Phoenix*, was sitting idle, without a charter. The government loan was available to pay for converting the *Ulysses*, but after that, what? There was no strong prospect of her getting a charter either. The Depression had caught Ludwig smack in the middle of renovating his American Steamship vessels. The *Terre Haute* had been finished and sold for a profit. The *Jay* had a new engine and a fresh coat of paint, but no prospective buyer. The *Otis* had hardly been touched.

By spring of 1930, D.K. was forced to notify the Shipping Board that Amsteam could not meet the loan payments on the *Jay* and *Otis*. The board, all too aware by now of the dismal economic conditions, obligingly granted a six-month extension. Autumn came, but nothing had improved. Ludwig asked for, and got, another six-month extension — but the board was beginning to worry. By spring of 1931, four notes, totaling $20,000, would be due — and overdue — for payment, and Amsteam was still obligated to spend another $50,000 to renovate the *Otis*, which included replacement of its old, obsolete turbine engine.

There was ample reason for the board's nervousness. It had lent an inordinate amount of money to two small companies under the same basic ownership, and if these firms failed, the Shipping Board officials responsible for the loan might have a lot of explaining to do before a congressional investigating committee.

To prevent this frightening prospect from materializing, the Shipping Board, after granting Ludwig his second extension, sent one of its auditors to look over Amsteam's books. What the auditor discovered was not at all reassuring. Except for the *Jay* and *Otis,* American Steamship had no assets whatever. Half the company's stock was owned by Marshall B. Hall, who was also the major stockholder in American Tankers. The auditor's report continued: "Daniel K. Ludwig made a statement on January 31st, 1931, showing that he has one-half interest in American Steamship Corporation, and a substantial interest in American Tankers Corporation, but that he has no other property. He is also shown as a creditor of American Steamship Corporation, to the extent of $23,000."

Both Hall and Ludwig, it appeared, had gambled nearly every asset on selling or chartering the surplus ships they had bought from the government. Ludwig had even added $23,000 of his own money to his initial investment. The partners had managed to sell the *Terre Haute* before the Depression but they were saddled with four heavily mortgaged ships they had no idea what to do with: the *Jay,* the *Otis,* the *Phoenix,* and the *Ulysses.* Hall and Ludwig were not alone, of course. Many investors were stuck in situations as bad or worse. But that was no consolation. The loans still had to be paid back.

Because of the way the two corporations had been set up, neither was liable for the other's debts, and if one went, the other could stay afloat. Not that it mattered much. All Amtankers had to lose were its two ships, and it still owed Grace National Bank $35,000 on the *Phoenix* as well as the $422,000 plus interest due the Shipping Board for the *Ulysses* construction loan.

Even if the board foreclosed on both companies, it would get back only the *Jay,* the *Otis,* and the *Ulysses,* which together could probably not be sold for enough to cover the debt outstanding on the *Ulysses* alone. A Shipping Board functionary worried in a memo to his superior: "Our treasurer has made a report on Marshall B. Hall as of November 1st, 1930, and Mr. Hall has made a supplemental statement showing that his liability on the notes and on the bond of the American Steamship Corporation would be extremely embarrassing to him."

This was serious. The board had made the loans largely on the basis of Hall's reputation as a man of substance — "the only one of the sureties and endorsers," in one board official's words, "who could be considered financially responsible under the circumstances."

The implication was that the board did not consider Ludwig a man from whom it could get back the loans. The board was right. During the *Fortune* interview in 1957, D.K. told Saunders that in his early business years he was "always in hock." There may have been a good reason. As long as you're in hock, it's hard for a creditor to collect money from you.

It was Ludwig, though, who came up with a solution to the Amsteam debt problem. The suggestion was so outrageous that nobody else would have dared to put it forth. What he said to the Shipping Board was, in effect: "We at American Steamship bought three ships from you. We renovated one and sold it and paid off its indebtedness. We fixed up another one and want to keep that. Why don't you take back the one we haven't remodeled to pay for the two we still owe on?"

Incredibly, somebody at the Shipping Board bought the idea. This was J. Caldwell Jenkins, vice-president of the Merchant Fleet Corporation. A letter Jenkins wrote to the board arguing that Ludwig's proposal be accepted was almost certainly inspired by Malone. The reasoning was typically convoluted.

If we take the *Otis* back, said Jenkins in the letter, we can probably sell it for around $155,000. (This in itself was highly unlikely. Only two years earlier, and in a far more prosperous market, Amsteam had purchased the same ship for only $60,000 plus an unfulfilled promise to renovate it.) On the other hand, Jenkins continued, "if the *John Jay* and *James Otis* were sold under foreclosure proceedings, it is probably true that the Board would realize the amount of the mortgages now outstanding, but such amount would be far below the value of comparable tonnage and such a sale would tend to have a demoralizing effect on lines purchased from the Board at a price in excess of this amount."

What Jenkins was saying, though he was careful not to spell it out, was that the board could get back more by taking the *Otis,* as Ludwig suggested, than by foreclosing on and selling *both* ships. He justified this bit of sophistry with an implausibly low estimate of what the two vessels might bring if they were sold after foreclosure.

Jenkins ended by repeating Ludwig's proposal and recommending that Amsteam be allowed to return the *Otis* and transfer the *Jay* to Amtankers, giving that company more assets and thereby protecting the board's mortgage on the *Ulysses.*

Again the reasoning was specious. The board could hardly gain by giving the *Jay* to Amtankers rather than foreclosing on it. At best, Amtankers might be able to sell the *Jay* to help pay off the *Ulysses* loan, but this would be money due the board anyway, because it was owed on the *Jay.*

To its credit, the Committee on Ship Sales, after reviewing Jenkins's recommendations, rejected them out of hand as bad policy. But the matter was not to end here. Ludwig had another card up his sleeve. At the end of February he notified the Shipping Board that neither Amsteam nor Amtankers could afford to pay the insurance premiums due on the four mortgaged vessels.

The board, with its heavy investment, could not afford to let the insurance lapse. Instead of foreclosing on the *Jay* and *Otis,* it decided to override the Committee on Ship Sales and accept Ludwig's — and Jenkins's — proposal. The board would take back the *Otis;* the *Jay* could be transferred to Amtankers; and American Steamship, its two mortgages marked "paid in full," could slip quietly out of the picture. Everything was working out to D.K.'s satisfaction.

First, though, he had to sneak another bit of business past the Shipping Board. When the board agreed to take back the *Otis* as payment for both itself and the *Jay,* it did so stipulating that the ship be returned in operating condition. This meant it could not be returned as purchased, since the *Otis*'s old turbine engine had been inoperable at the time. But Ludwig did the next best — that is, cheapest — thing. When the *Otis* was returned, Shipping Board inspectors found it powered by the old turbine engine out of the *Jay.* He never liked spending money unless there was a good chance that it would make him more, and purchasing a decent engine to put in a ship he was giving back wouldn't earn him a penny.

Why, the board wanted to know, had the *Jay*'s old engine been returned in the *Otis?* Well, responded Ludwig glibly, at one point he had decided to replace the *Otis*'s old engine not with a diesel or reciprocating model but with a new, more powerful steam turbine. Before investing in the new turbine, he had simply transferred the *Jay*'s engine temporarily to see whether the *Otis*'s gear system was working properly.

The explanation was patently false. The loan agreement had clearly specified that Amsteam had to replace the old turbines with either diesel or reciprocating engines. Ludwig could not have made a unilateral decision to change types without the board's approval.

However lame the excuse, the board accepted it, along with the *Otis* powered by the *Jay*'s obsolete turbine. Once the transfers were effected and Amsteam had retired into corporate limbo, Amtankers had three ships instead of two. Only one was operating and earning income. While the *Jay* and *Phoenix* were still idle, Ludwig had gotten a charter for the *Ulysses* hauling crude for the Atlantic Refining Company from the Texas Gulf Coast to Philadelphia and clearing about $5000 per voyage.

This was enough to take care of some of the back interest on the giant tanker, but an annual payment of $70,000 was soon coming due on the principal. In August of 1931 Ludwig wrote another begging letter to the Shipping Board, saying that he was doing the best he could, but that Amtankers needed more time to make the payment. Malone followed with another written plea in September, asking the board for continued forbearance in holding off foreclosure. But D.K. and Malone had dragged things on for about as long as they could. The board had shown them Job's own patience, yet it was two years now since Amtankers had bought the *Ulysses,* and the company still hadn't paid off a penny of the loan.

Hall and Leahy were being no help at all. If the *Ulysses* was to be saved from foreclosure, Ludwig and Malone would have to do it. Up to now they had stalled, begged, cajoled, and wheedled for time. Now they needed outside help, preferably from someone higher up who could put real pressure on the board.

Malone turned to a man he knew he could count on: Charles Hilles, who had been helping him try to secure the Navy destroyer contract for United Dry Docks. Now, to help Ludwig, he wrote Admiral Hutchinson I. Cone, chairman of the Shipping Board, asking that the board look with kindness on the sad plight of American Tankers. Calling himself "a friend of some of the company's officers," Hilles professed "a personal, though not a financial, interest" in the matter of the *Ulysses* and expressed to Cone his feeling that the problem would be solved if only the Shipping Board would agree to re-amortize the construction loan over a period of twenty years instead of the original six.

Cone wrote back cordially and deferentially (a tacit acknowledgment of Hilles's political clout), saying: "I know two young gentlemen (Mr. Ludwig and Mr. Malone) who I believe hold high positions in the Corporation, and I have been much in sympathy with their efforts to work out a going company under the merchant marine.

They will undoubtedly explain to you the extent to which the Board has gone in trying to carry them along, by exchange of vessels and all other reasonable means."

The admiral was trying to tell Hilles in a nice way that the board had already bent over backward trying to bail out Ludwig and Malone and could do no more without arousing suspicion. He expressed regret that he had to turn down the Republican National Committeeman's suggestion to extend the loan over two decades, but such an extension would be poor policy. Granting a twenty-year loan on a ship that was already sixteen years old and could be expected to last only four or five more years was inviting financial disaster. Under the circumstances, Cone concluded, the Shipping Board had no choice but to foreclose on the *Ulysses.*

On September 17, 1931, the board moved forward with a suit to take the big ship back from Amtankers. Faced with losing his only vessel that was making any money, Ludwig suddenly came up with $5500 from somewhere to make a payment on the loan interest. He accompanied this with a promise to pay a like amount as soon as the *Ulysses* completed her next voyage, and said he would make regular payments of $5000 on the principal after every subsequent trip.

Dazzled by this miraculous display of fiscal responsibility, the Shipping Board's Loan Committee relented, voting to take no immediate action to foreclose and letting Amtankers retain possession of the ship until further notice. One Loan Committee member, more skeptical than the others, voted with the majority only after putting his opinion in the record: "I have little faith in the ability of the makers of this paper to keep their contract, but I think it best to adopt the recommendation of the Committee with the understanding that, on the failure of American Tankers Corporation to pay the $5,000 or more per voyage, legal proceedings be instituted."

Thus D.K., by sacrificing the profits of one voyage, managed to buy more time. And for a while he was true to his word. After the next three voyages he made another interest payment and paid two installments of $5000 each on the principal. By the end of 1931, following two years of procrastination, he had finally paid a total of $21,000 on the *Ulysses* construction loan. It wasn't much, but it was a start. And he even made a token payment of $3000 on the unsecured purchase loan from the Panama Canal Office. But Amtankers was still a long way from being out of the woods.

In February of 1932, Malone wrote to the board again, asking whether the per-voyage payment could be reduced from $5000 to $3000, since the company was having difficulty meeting its other expenses. Rather than saying yea or nay to the request, the board decided to send another auditor to examine Amtankers' books. What he found was a mess.

On March 1, the MFC president, Elmer Crowley, notified Admiral Cone that the "very unsatisfactory condition" of Ludwig's financial records made it impossible to get an accurate accounting in the limited time available, but enough had been learned to show that the voyage reports D.K. had been submitting with the loan payments were woefully incomplete. Many expenses were not shown at all. In order to hold off foreclosure, Ludwig had been painting a rosy picture despite Amtankers' gray financial situation.

Besides the Shipping Board loans, the auditor discovered, the company also owed debts of a few thousand dollars each to several other firms: the David C. Reid Company, United Dry Docks, and Alabama Dry Dock and Shipbuilding. None of these corporations, however, was pressing for payment.

What the government apparently did not know was that D.K. had very close connections with all three firms and possibly even a financial interest in some or all of them. It is also possible that his father was in some way connected with them, perhaps as an owner. In any case, they showed remarkable patience for creditors during these lean Depression years, so D.K. must have been more than just another customer.

The Shipping Board auditor also found that Amtankers owed $5000 to the insurance firm of Betts & Betts (suggesting that Stuart Betts had lent D.K. money to pay the insurance premiums) and another $51,000 to Grace National Bank on the *Phoenix* and *Jay* mortgages.

Several suspicious items showed up in the Amtankers books as well. Ludwig had siphoned $2000 out of the *Ulysses* account to repair one of his barges and had written off several thousand more in travel expenses. Then there was a substantial cash payment to Malone that nobody at D.K.'s office could account for.

The audit showed an unpromising financial picture, but the Shipping Board was still reluctant to foreclose on the *Ulysses*. Instead, it demanded that Amtankers turn over management of its finances to Grace National Bank. This seemed to reflect the board's feeling that, though there may have been some chicanery on the part of the shipping company, the main problem was inept management. Ludwig simply had not been doing a good job of handling money matters, and the other partners seemed uninterested. With an experienced hand from Grace National at the helm, the situation might well improve.

Ludwig was willing to agree to almost anything that would allow him to keep the *Ulysses*. Besides, there were some advantages to the Shipping Board's demand. It would relieve him of much responsibility and allow him to spend more time doing something he did well — keeping ships operating — and less on something he did not do well — managing money. Also, it would commit both the Shipping Board and Grace National to helping Amtankers succeed.

The help came just in time. The oil market, which had gradually been dragging itself up from the depths of the Depression, now took another nosedive. Over the next year, any business Ludwig could round up for his ships was on a short-term basis — mostly single-trip charters at low rates. Despite the very little money that was coming in, the Shipping Board, reassured that Grace National would manage Amtankers' affairs in a competent way, did not press for payment or foreclosure.

But now there were other problems. In the summer of 1933, Marshall B. Hall, evidently despairing of things getting better, sent word from Boston that he wanted to fold up Amtankers and call it quits. This was worrisome. For years D.K. and Malone had headed off one catastrophe after another to keep possession of the *Ulysses* and the other ships. If Hall threw in his hand, the effort would have been for nothing. Something had to be done, and quickly.

On June 20, 1933, a new company, named American Tankers Corporation, was set up in Delaware. It was not, however, the same company Hall was president of. All that Amtankers of Massachusetts had in common with this new Delaware Amtankers was the name and the same vice-president and treasurer, Daniel Keith Ludwig. The other officers of the new company were a secretary named Robert J. Schober (who was to be a chief functionary in D.K.'s organization for many years) and a president named Daniel F. Ludwig.

Daniel F. had been absent from — or at least not evidently involved in — his son's life since the *Mosher* incident in 1922. Now, eleven years later, he reappeared to lend a hand. Where he had been and what he had been doing in the interim are as mysterious as the man himself, but some reasonable assumptions can be made.

The Crash of 1929 and the following Depression had brought a virtual end to the traffic in illegal liquor. The bootleggers, already sitting atop mountains of money, suddenly found that few people had the cash to buy imported hooch. The Jazz Age was over, supplanted by a grimmer reality. By the time of the 1932 presidential campaign, Alfred E. Smith, who had lost as the 1928 Democratic candidate against Hoover, was telling his bootlegger friends, "Boys, you'd better start getting ready to go legit, because Prohibition will soon be a thing of the past."

And so it was. Shortly after Franklin D. Roosevelt took office in 1933, the Twenty-first Amendment was passed, repealing the Eighteenth, and liquor, for the first time since January 1920, was again legal in the United States. Those who had made fortunes in rumrunning now had to look for other sources of money. Many stayed in the profession they knew best, setting up legal distilleries and breweries and continuing to supply Americans with liquor and beer and wine. Others switched to activities that were still illegal: drug dealing, gambling, extortion, prostitution. Still others, finding themselves wealthy while men who had lost their shirts in the market were crying for investment capital, invested in various legitimate enterprises — banks, factories, insurance companies, hotels — and were soon in control of large segments of U.S. business activity.

With few facts to go on, we can only guess that Captain Daniel F. Ludwig stayed in the shipping end of the rumrunning trade until the end of Prohibition, then switched over, as his son had done a decade earlier, to oil transportation. One thing known from corporate records is that at the time he helped D.K. set up the new Amtankers in Delaware, Daniel F. was living in the prosperous commuter suburb of Stamford, Connecticut. D.K. may have been living there as well. All of the corporate records from the 1930s, with one exception, give only a Manhattan office address for him and no home address. That single exception, however, is a 1939 document listing his home address as 24 Pleasant Street, Stamford, Connecticut. It may be, then, that during the late 1920s and early-to-mid-thirties — the years of his marriage to Gladys and after — D.K. lived close to his father in Stamford.

The new American Tankers Corporation was almost certainly intended as a rescue operation. If Hall pulled out and Amtankers of Massachusetts became defunct, the new company would give D.K. a place to jump with the *Ulysses, Jay,* and *Phoenix.*

The Ludwigs were not the only ones anticipating the breakup of Amtankers. The Shipping Board was also worried that the Massachusetts company was getting ready to declare bankruptcy. This fear was increased when the board received a letter from D.K. asking that all future correspondence to American Tankers Corporation be addressed to 21 West Street in New York City rather than 80 Boylston Street in Boston. Four days after receiving D.K.'s letter, a Shipping Board solicitor wrote to the clerk of the Eastern U.S. District Court in New York:

> As I explained when I stopped in to see you this morning, I should appreciate your informing me immediately by telephone if any application is made for the appointment of a receiver either in bankruptcy or equity, for the Munson Line or the American Tankers Corporation. While I do not know that such proceedings are definitely contemplated, I am informed that there may be a possibility, and, as the government has very large amounts at stake in each case, I have been instructed to watch closely for any such development.

If the Ludwigs were planning to pull a fast one by switching the three ships from a defunct Massachusetts corporation to a new one of the same name in Delaware, one that had no contract — and no liability — with the government, the Shipping Board's alertness may have forestalled the move. It was in the government's interest to see that Amtankers of Massachusetts remained a viable company, so bankruptcy had to be blocked until the board could get its ships back. Once the vessels were transferred to the Delaware company, the government would have the devil's own time trying to recover any part of its loans.

The threat did not materialize. Amtankers of Massachusetts stayed in business, and the Delaware Amtankers remained on standby status as an inactive corporation. The financial picture, though, did not measurably improve. By the middle of 1934, five years after the board had granted the *Ulysses* construction loan, Amtankers owed more than it had originally borrowed: $460,000 ($410,000 on the principal plus $50,000 interest). Also, it still owed the Panama Canal Office $131,000 and had a number of outstanding debts to other creditors.

A Shipping Board auditor, reviewing the company's situation, came to an unavoidable conclusion: Amtankers was, for all practical purposes, insolvent. The firm had no securities left to borrow on, and virtually no chance remained that the massive liabilities could be paid off from the ships' small earnings.

Ludwig and Malone had been begging for more time, asking the board to extend the loan to 1940 — tacking another five years onto the original six-year loan period. But the *Ulysses* would be twenty-five years old by 1940, and the company would be required to make annual payments of $100,000 during the years 1935 to 1940. If the mortgages Grace National was holding on the *Jay* and *Phoenix* were figured in, the amount would be more like $150,000 a year.

The auditor frankly didn't think Amtankers could come up with that kind of money. Although it was true that both the *Phoenix* and *Ulysses* were currently under charter and earning money, the *Jay* was idle and too small and old to get work except as a tramp steamer at low rates. Looking at these facts, the auditor concluded that Amtankers' predicament was hopeless:

> All things considered, I do not believe that the debtor corporation will, saving war or emergency . . . be able to satisfy its stated obligations even within the extended time herein contemplated. . . . The corporation has not had good fortune during the present calendar year, and I think the time is at hand [to foreclose on the *Ulysses*]. . . . It would be advisable now to salvage what we can of our interest in the ship even though such action entail, as it probably will, the taking of a very substantial loss.

If the board continued to hold off on foreclosure, the loss would be even more substantial. Already the *Ulysses* was beginning to deteriorate. Ludwig, hard pressed for cash, was not doing the maintenance necessary to protect the ship from the weather. Her upper decks were rotting, and some of her machinery was breaking or wearing out. Unless a part was absolutely necessary for the vessel's continued operation, D.K. was unwilling to spend money to have it fixed. A structural survey by a Shipping Board inspector about this time estimated that it would take at least $26,000 worth of repairs to put the *Ulysses* back in acceptable condition.

The board itself was not willing to throw bad money after good by offering to lend Ludwig the funds for this repair work. Nor was Grace National eager to float another loan. And Ludwig would not let Amtankers spend money for the repairs. Although two of the company's ships were now busy, all three had shown operating losses for the first half of 1934.

Hoping to find a remedy, or even a reason for hope, the Shipping Board's Finance Committee called D.K. in for several conferences, but the shipper remained adamant in his refusal to spend money on the *Ulysses*. Finally, on September 11, after five years of being patient, the board approved the auditor's recommendation for foreclosure and served Amtankers with a default notice. Next day, Commerce Secretary Daniel Roper notified Grace National to close the joint account the government had maintained with Amtankers.

Evidently Ludwig had thought the Shipping Board would not carry out its threats. Now that it had, he panicked. On receiving the default notice, he fired off a four-page telegram to the board's director, James Craig Peacock, asking him to hold everything until D.K. could meet with him to discuss the matter. The wire concluded, WE ARE CONFIDENT WE CAN CONVINCE YOU AND SECRETARY THAT INTERESTS OF UNITED STATES AND OTHERS WILL BE BEST SERVED BY CONTINUED FORBEARANCE.

Reasons for holding off, Ludwig said, were that he now had a better charter for the *Ulysses* in the works and the sale of the *Jay* to a country in the Far East was being negotiated. He did not bother to explain why he hadn't told the board of these developments earlier.

But the gambit worked. Peacock obligingly set up a meeting with D.K. for the following Monday. During the conference, Ludwig requested a two-week grace period to prepare a proposal that would satisfy the board and let Amtankers retain the *Ulysses*. Again, Peacock consented. But when the proposition was submitted, it was anything but satisfying. It said nothing about a new charter for the *Ulysses* or sale of the *Jay;* all it offered was some of the necessary repair work. Ludwig's main argument was that the board should postpone foreclosure moves for several months while Congress was considering a bill that might create more demand and higher rates for tankers.

While Ludwig was playing for time, Robert Malone was busy

lining up allies who could bring pressure on the Commerce Department to delay foreclosure. He talked a Panama Canal Office official into writing a letter to Secretary Roper saying that if the Shipping Board foreclosed on the *Ulysses,* the unsecured mortgage the Canal Office held on the vessel would be wiped out, with no hope of repayment. The letter also asked Commerce to hold off until Secretary of War George Dern returned from a trip abroad to decide what action the War Department (of which the Canal Office was an agency) might want to take in the matter.

Replying for Roper, Peacock wrote that, though he appreciated the Canal Office's concern, he saw no reason to delay foreclosure. A few days later, Dern wrote Roper a testy letter, demanding that legal procedures against Amtankers be halted at once: "It is the opinion of the Panama Canal authorities, in which I concur, that so long as American Tankers Corporation is able and willing to keep up the insurance . . . and to maintain the vessel in a fairly satisfactory condition, every opportunity should be afforded that Corporation to retain the vessel."

Once again, Ludwig and Malone had managed to reach into their bag of tricks and come up with a maneuver to save the *Ulysses.* Now they were pitting the secretary of war against the secretary of commerce. They were also able to bring in some heavy pressure from Capitol Hill. Several congressmen, including John McCormack of Massachusetts and William Sirivich of New York, wired Roper, asking for a delay in foreclosure. Sirivich's telegram put things on a personal basis: SOME DEAR FRIENDS OF MINE ARE OWNERS OF TANKER SS ULYSSES UPON WHICH SHIPPING BOARD THREATENS IMMEDIATE FORECLOSURE OF MORTGAGE.

D.K. and Malone had sized up the situation correctly. The Commerce chief was a man honest Interior Secretary Harold Ickes would later describe as "a consummate politician"; he never raised his voice and would go out of his way to keep from offending anyone. Roper obviously did not like being caught in the middle of this foreclosure mess. As long as there was no real pressure, he had been willing to go along with the Shipping Board's decision. Now that he was getting heat from high places, he passed the buck to Peacock, with a strong hint that discretion should be used in dealing with the situation.

On December 7, Peacock caved in. To save some face, he wrote

Ludwig a harshly worded letter, saying that Amtankers would have to do some immediate repair work on the *Ulysses* (a task D.K. had already consented to do); then, almost as an afterthought, he added that the Shipping Board was giving a six-month extension on the foreclosure.

During the first two months of 1935, Ludwig was supposedly making the required repairs on the *Ulysses*. Actually he was doing nothing to the ship, which sat quietly in dry dock. Contrary to his previous statements, he had not found a new charter for the tanker, and he saw no point in spending money to fix her up before she was ready to earn an income. In March he reported to the board that heavy snows had held up the repairs, and asked for additional time to complete the work. Peacock, still smarting from the previous foreclosure attempt, was not inclined to stir up new trouble for himself, so he quietly agreed to the extension.

In October, D.K. notified the board that he finally had a charter for the *Ulysses* and was sending her immediately to another shipyard for the necessary repairs. But he was vague about the specifics of the charter, saying only that it was with the David C. Reid Company and involved carrying a cargo of fuel oil to the west coast of Italy. What he neglected to inform the board of was that the David C. Reid Company, with which he was closely connected, sharing the same 21 West Street address in Manhattan, had made a contract with the fascist government of Benito Mussolini to haul oil for Italy's war of conquest against Ethiopia.

With this one maneuver, Ludwig had once again thrown himself squarely into the middle of a complex international crisis. President Roosevelt, since his 1932 election, had been handling Mussolini with kid gloves, playing up to Il Duce's ego while exerting quiet diplomacy to foil his expansionist ambitions. Earlier, while governor of New York, Roosevelt had accepted the conventional wisdom that perhaps Mussolini was just what Italy needed — a strong leader who could unite the country's work force, put down communism, make the trains run on time, and, above all, create a safe, stable climate for U.S. business investments.

The three Republican administrations of the 1920s had all worked behind the scenes to engineer Mussolini's rise to power. President Harding, after being elected as a machine candidate from Ohio, had appointed an old crony and fund raiser, Richard Washburn Child, as ambassador to Italy, and Child had become a personal booster and patron of Mussolini. After the fascist leader had seized power, Child urged him to write an autobiography so that the world could see what a great man he was. Mussolini had complied, and Child edited and wrote a glowing introduction to the English-language version, helping it get wide distribution in the United States.

Both the Coolidge and Hoover administrations had continued to support the dictator, but by the time FDR became president, he had begun to have second thoughts about Il Duce and to wonder whether fascism did not present as great a threat to world peace as communism. When Mussolini's intentions of taking over Ethiopia became manifest, Roosevelt began to exert quiet diplomatic pressure on the Italians not to start hostilities. In 1933 he made a direct, though secret, appeal to Mussolini to keep the peace in the Mediterranean and was silently furious when the Italian ignored the plea and sent troops and warships to Ethiopia. Outwardly, FDR had maintained a dignified calm and a strictly neutral position, saying only that the United States, as a nonaligned nation, would not ship weapons to either of the belligerent countries.

Now, late in 1935, Ludwig's little oil deal with Italy forced Roosevelt's hand. If the shipment was allowed, it would look as though the United States was softening its neutral stance by supplying Mussolini with a vital commodity for waging war. If the shipment was prohibited, the fascists could claim America was reneging on long-standing trade agreements with Italy.

The man caught on the horns of this dilemma was J. C. Peacock. Aware of the president's true feelings about Mussolini's recent invasion of Ethiopia, the Shipping Board director immediately recognized the seriousness of Ludwig's proposed oil-hauling charter to Italy. Unwilling to ruffle Roper's feathers again, and afraid to act on his own, he sought the advice of Colonel J. M. Johnson, assistant secretary of commerce. After filling him in on the background of the *Ulysses* case, Peacock told Johnson that, so far, the Shipping Board had not interfered with normal trade between the United States and Italy. But this was different. The board did not want to write insurance on this charter voyage of the *Ulysses,* which was obviously war-connected and provocative. On the other hand, the only way to stop Ludwig from shipping oil to Mussolini would be to foreclose on the *Ulysses,* and this, after the Shipping Board's recent promise of forbearance, would look arbitrary and suspicious.

Couldn't Amtankers be reasoned with? asked Johnson. Not a chance, said Peacock: "Our past dealings with this Corporation indicate that it would not in any way be amenable to suggestions or hints, and that we would probably have to threaten or resort to immediate foreclosure in order to make effective any suggestion."

Amtankers, he added, was not even dealing directly with the Italians; it was working through the David C. Reid Company, a ship brokerage firm. (Peacock and the other Shipping Board and Commerce Department officials seem to have known nothing about the Reid Company or D.K.'s close ties to it.) The problem was, Peacock continued, that Ludwig had to be given a decision soon. But a few days remained to kick the problem around. The *Ulysses* was still in New York; it had not left for Philadelphia to start loading the oil.

Johnson knew a crisis when he saw one. He immediately tossed it to Secretary of State Cordell Hull, and Hull wasted no time taking it to Roosevelt. The president didn't equivocate. He picked up the phone and called Peacock. A note in Commerce Department files tells the result. Dated November 13, 1935, and written in Peacock's hand, it reads: "*Ulysses:* President very clear that the vessel should not be allowed to sail with oil for Italy. If they proceed, we will foreclose. If not, we will give them more time."

Two days later, Cordell Hull went on nationwide radio to proclaim a new national policy: the United States intended to restrict trade with "the belligerents" not only by banning shipments of weapons and ammunition but also by embargoing cargoes of oil, scrap metal, trucks, tractors, and other commodities and products that might be essential to the waging of war.

As expected, both the Italian government and American Tankers took umbrage at Hull's announcement. The Italian embassy in Washington sent a strongly worded protest to the State Department, calling the new policy a violation of trade agreements between the United States and Italy dating back to 1871. Malone, on Ludwig's orders, fired off an angry letter to Peacock, arguing (1) that the Italians were likely to sue the Reid Company for failing to honor the oil-hauling contract and (2) that Amtankers had just gone into debt for more than $25,000 to make repairs on the *Ulysses* in order to ready her to sail for Italy. Perhaps, Malone suggested archly, the government should pay this repair bill, since it was responsible for stopping the voyage after giving tacit approval.

Malone's letter was also a carefully worded ultimatum: either reimburse us for the repair bill, it said, or let us go to Italy. Unless you do one or the other, we'll sell the ship to pay for the repairs and leave the Shipping Board with nothing. After posing this double-barreled threat, Malone, feeling he had the board on the defensive, concluded, "It occurs to us that you may wish to determine whether our Company may not, with the sanction of the Government, proceed to execute its contract."

Peacock was gunshy now, and not thinking very straight. He could appreciate Malone's point and was more than half inclined to go along with the reasoning. After all, the government *had* ordered the voyage stopped after the contract had been drawn. So he may have felt guilty at causing Amtankers to run up the big repair bill it now seemed unable to pay. But he was no lawyer, and his close involvement with the case had caused him to lose perspective.

Fortunately he still had the presence of mind to ask a Commerce Department solicitor for a legal opinion, and this attorney, after reviewing the facts, pointed out, quite correctly, that the government was under no legal obligation whatsoever to pay the repair bill. Under the original loan agreement, the purchaser — Amtankers — was solely responsible for keeping the *Ulysses* in good enough condition to protect the Shipping Board's investment. Since Amtankers had been negligent in letting the ship deteriorate to the point where expensive repairs had to be made, it was entirely up to the company to pay for the work. As for Malone's threat to sell the vessel to pay the repair yard, that was a bluff. The board held a preferred mortgage as a condition of making the construction loan, meaning that its claim for payment took precedence over claims of other creditors. Amtankers could *not* sell the *Ulysses* without the board's permission.

Peacock was relieved to hear this, because it got him and the board off the hook. But over at the State Department things were not going so well. Here the matter was more diplomatic than legal, and the hornet's nest FDR and Hull had stirred up with the new embargo policy had U.S. diplomats sweating through numerous meetings, trying to calm the excited Italians and come to an understanding. From another direction came the angry objections of certain U.S. corporations that felt the shipping ban would deprive them of substantial profits.

After a few weeks of this, Roosevelt finally threw up his hands.

Retreating to the haven of Warm Springs, Georgia, he sent back word that he was leaving the matter entirely up to the State and Commerce departments and wanted nothing more to do with it. With no backing from the White House or his own staff, most of whom were too busy apologizing to the Italians, Hull was not prepared to stand alone on the issue. Within a week, State sent word to Commerce that Ludwig should be allowed to proceed to Italy with a cargo of oil if he chose. The government would do nothing more to interfere with the shipment or with trade in any of the other commodities Hull had mentioned in his embargo speech.

But by the time this news reached Ludwig, he had lost interest. Having finally gotten the *Ulysses* repaired, he had found a better-paying long-term charter for her and had no wish to resume negotiations with the Italians.

A number of other American companies, though, were pleased with the reversal of policy and Roosevelt's defeat. Trade between the United States and Italy resumed, and war profits filled many corporate coffers. The Italian Army, its supplies replenished, shook off its initial defeats and went on to crush the underequipped Ethiopians, forcing their leader, Emperor Haile Selassie, to flee into exile.

Nearly three decades later, in an ironic twist, Daniel Keith Ludwig would play host to the emperor, who had been restored to his throne after World War II, when he came to the United States on an official visit. After spending a public day in New York City, Selassie, accompanied by his entourage and security guards, stayed overnight at Ludwig's home in Darien, Connecticut. The visit was not strictly social. Ludwig, with help from the State Department, was negotiating to establish a potash-mining operation in Ethiopia, and the emperor, after discussing the matter over dinner, readily consented. It's a safe bet that he was not aware of the role his host had played many years earlier in helping the Italians conquer his nation. And it's even more sure that D.K. did not see fit to enlighten him.

Early in January 1936, Secretary of War George Dern wrote Secretary of Commerce Daniel Roper to ask what was happening these days with the *Ulysses*. Roper replied that, after declining the government's invitation to carry through with her Italian voyage, the ship had gotten a long-term charter hauling oil from the Gulf of Mexico to a refinery in a northeastern state and was now on her second trip. Her initial profits were being used to pay off the shipyard that had repaired her, and the Shipping Board was biding its time and taking no steps to foreclose.

Several months later, though, when the debt was nearly paid off, the board started showing signs of impatience. At a conference called by J. C. Peacock, Ludwig promised to begin repaying the board $5000 per voyage as soon as the repair debt was retired. The new payments he wanted to deposit in an intermediate Grace National account, where they would be available for sixty days. Ludwig also promised that the *Jay* would be sold soon — something that did not come to pass. Grace National, a few weeks after the Ludwig-Peacock meeting, moved to foreclose, and Ludwig quietly turned over the title to the bank.

The *Ulysses,* at least, was safe for the time being. Peacock was pleased with its income-producing current charter but unhappy over the proposal for an intermediate bank account. As a compromise, Ludwig was permitted a lower figure for loan repayments and got a promise from the board that there would be no move to foreclose on the *Ulysses* for at least a year. Marshall B. Hall was a co-signer to the agreement.

What the government apparently did not know was that it was dealing with the wrong company. Amtankers of Massachusetts was now only a shell, because the Ludwigs had bought out the Hall and Leahy interests in its two ships. Its only reason for continued existence was that it remained the legal owner of the ships and was the entity responsible for paying off the debt.

There was another, unspoken, reason. The Shipping Board considered Marshall Hall to be the only one of the borrowers financially responsible enough to see that the loan was paid back. It would have frowned on any move to transfer the *Ulysses* to another company. In this, too, it was ill informed. Hall was on his way down financially, and Daniel Keith Ludwig, backed by his father's money, was in the ascendant. Amtankers of Massachusetts was moribund, and Amtankers of Delaware (though listed in Delaware corporate records as "inactive") was very much alive and part of a small but growing empire.

One sign of the new prosperity was a new address for D.K.'s office — 650 Fifth Avenue in Manhattan, far more prestigious than 21

West Street. An amusing note on the identity game D.K. was playing relates to his impressive new letterhead: American Tankers Corporation of Delaware. Whenever he wrote to a federal agency on this stationery, he was always careful to cross out the last two words.

During the 1930s, the Ludwigs bought several more ships and set up Delaware-registered corporations to operate them. They were the Transford Corporation, to operate the *Transford II;* the Tankers Oceanic Corporation, to operate the *Chiloil;* the National Petroleum Transport Corporation, to operate the *Transoil;* and the American Petroleum Transport Company, to operate the *Caliche.* The two Ludwigs and Robert Schober usually were the officers and directors of these firms. Daniel F., nevertheless, stayed firmly in the background, and his son was the chief executive officer of each company. From available evidence, the ships were all owned outright, were not bought through the Shipping Board, had no visible mortgages and — what was most important — were all earning money.

By the spring of 1936, D.K. was ready for another expansion. This one had both a bit of a problem and the beauty of a new idea. The problem was to get the Shipping Board to sell him more surplus ships though he was still encumbered by the *Ulysses* loan. The new idea was a way of renovating those freighters into a new type of cargo hauler: the bulk carrier.

The advantage of bulk carriers was versatility; these ships were to be designed in such a way that they could haul either dry cargo (coal or metal ores) or liquids (petroleum or gasoline) without expensive, time-consuming structural conversion. If the oil market fell off, a bulk carrier could haul ore for a while. Or it could haul oil in one direction and coal or ore on the voyage home.

The bulk carrier was a major improvement over the less versatile tankers, colliers, and ore haulers then in merchant service. From the records available, though, it is difficult to say whether this was purely Ludwig's idea or whether he was responding to a suggestion being pushed by the new Maritime Commission, which had just been created within the Commerce Department to replace the old U.S. Shipping Board.

The evidence suggests that Ludwig was reacting to the Maritime Commission's call for fast merchant ships to replace the old, slow tankers and colliers currently plying the trade routes, and that, with his eye for economy, he figured he could make more money by converting old freighters into bulk carriers rather than ordinary tankers.

Whether the bulk carrier was his idea or not, D.K. was quick to see its advantages and cash in on it. He set up another Delaware company, National Bulk Carriers, Inc., on June 1, 1936; this later became the flagship corporation for his fleet of companies.

It is worth remarking that Daniel F. Ludwig, president or vice-president of all the other Ludwig-owned Delaware corporations set up thus far, was nowhere visibly connected with National Bulk. A possible reason is that this new company was to do business with the federal government, and the earlier ones had not been. Delaware officials showed a conspicuous lack of curiosity about the officers of corporations registered in the state, but federal personnel tended to be somewhat nosier. It would not do if someone at the Maritime Commission chanced to recognize the name of an indicted former operator of rumrunning vessels.

With the advent of National Bulk, a new figure appeared on the scene. William W. Wagner was about the same age as D.K., but in managing money he seemed much older and wiser. A former Shipping Board auditor, he would, over the next thirty-four years, provide the financial expertise the Ludwig enterprises had previously lacked.

Wagner's first miracle was to sell off the old *Ulysses* for enough money to pay off the Shipping Board mortgage and have several hundred thousand dollars left over. It so happened he lived in Syosset, Long Island, where among his rich neighbors was the prominent attorney George de Forest Lord, senior partner in the New York firm of Lord, Day & Lord.

Lord represented wealthy interests willing to buy the huge *Ulysses* and convert it into a mother ship for a whaling operation. To this end, he helped form a company, Western Operating Corporation, with himself as a director and Hans Isbrandtsen, head of the Isbrandtsen Steamship Company, as president.

When Ludwig announced that the *Ulysses* was being sold for a high price, the sigh of relief from the Commerce Department could be heard for miles along the Potomac. The government, after eight years of wrangling and excuses, had almost resigned itself to taking a big loss on the ship loan. Now D.K. was saying he would soon pay the debt in full.

But the bureaucrats should have learned by now that no Ludwig deal was ever without a catch. D.K., under circumstances that are still unclear, had recently bought from the Maritime Commission two surplus freighters — each with a market value of around $200,000 — for the incredibly low price of $25,000 apiece. Now, as a reward for finally paying off the *Ulysses* loan, he wanted to buy other similar vessels at the same price.

Maritime attorneys balked at this, reasoning that allowing Ludwig to buy ships without going through a competitive bidding process was in violation of government policy. The commission offered an alternative. First sell the *Ulysses,* it told him, and pay off your loan. Then maybe we'll consider putting the ships you want out for bids.

Ludwig didn't push the point. He proceeded to complete his $800,000 deal with Western Operating Corporation, getting about four times what the *Ulysses* was worth on the tanker market, and paid off the construction loan. There is no evidence that he ever repaid the Panama Canal Office its $118,000 purchase loan.

Twenty years later, Dero Saunders recounted it all this way: "In the middle Thirties, everything began to happen at once to Ludwig, and all of it right. . . . In 1937, he sold the *Ulysses* to a whaling syndicate for over $800,000, which was at least four times her value as a tanker, and thereby got out of debt."

# Five

# The Rockefeller Connection

For most of the world, 1936 was an ominous year. Europe and North Africa were teetering on the brink of all-out war. Mussolini had already invaded Ethiopia; in Morocco, General Francisco Franco was fomenting a revolt that, with Nazi backing, would erupt into the Spanish Civil War and end in a fascist government for Spain. In Germany, Adolf Hitler was building a juggernaut that would enable Third Reich armies to roll over much of Eastern and Western Europe and the northern Sahara. In the Far East, Japanese expansion into Manchuria and the Pacific island community was threatening U.S. trade and hegemony.

All this news was sweet music to the ears of Daniel Ludwig and other shippers. Wars and rumors of wars presaged an upturn in international commerce, which, for cargo haulers, meant greater demand and higher revenues. A tanker or other merchant vessel that had been sitting idly at the docks since the start of the Depression or begging for occasional, low-paying charters could now be spruced up and hired out on a long-term basis at high rates or, should the right offer come along, sold for a handsome price.

Ludwig was in good position to take advantage of the shipping boom, thanks to his sale of the *Ulysses* to the Western Operating Corporation. But there was one small drawback. Selling the ship would leave him short of tonnage at a time when the tanker market was ready to climb. Ludwig and his father, to be sure, had four other, newer tankers chartered and earning money, and Amtankers of Delaware was still operating the old *Phoenix*. But if he was going to make any real money hauling oil, he needed to expand now, while the market was rising and he had the means to do so.

Once the *Ulysses* sale was concluded, he would transfer the *Phoenix* to a new Delaware-registered company, Phoenix Steamship Corporation, and let Amtankers of Delaware become inactive. But it was through National Bulk Carriers that he planned to carry out most of his expansion. If Britain and the other European allies were to keep pace with the war machine Hitler was building in Germany, they needed all the coal, oil, and iron ore they could get. The United States could supply these; it was a question of how to get them across the Atlantic safely and speedily. Maritime wanted U.S. shippers to start building fast bulk carriers in lieu of the traditional tankers and freighters.

Ludwig's initial contribution to this innovative design was to advocate converting existing ships into bulk carriers rather than building new ones from scratch. His first moves in this direction had been to arrange to buy from the Maritime Commission two surplus freighters — the *Daniel Webster* and the *John Adams* — for a mere $25,000 apiece plus a pledge to spend at least $225,000 for converting each ship to a speedy bulk carrier. How he managed to get the ships for such a low price is something of a mystery, since there are no contemporary records describing the purchases in Maritime files. The National Bulk Carriers file does not begin until the spring of 1937, nearly a year after Ludwig started the company and purchased the *Webster* and *Adams*.

There *may* be a simple explanation to account for the lack of documentation of the sale. Perhaps the transaction was carried out in haste during the transitional period when the Shipping Board was giving way to the Maritime Commission. The lack of records would not be worth remarking, except that Ludwig got the *Webster* and *Adams* at such bargain prices. Since each of these ships was a 13,000-tonner in good condition, D.K. bought them for less than $2.00 a ton. Comparable ships were then being sold by Maritime for around $200,000 apiece.

It should not be overlooked that D.K. now had two former Shipping Board employees on his payroll: Malone, who was adept at using his influence with former associates to get favorable treatment for his boss, and Wagner, who, having just left the Shipping Board's auditing department, was privy to inside knowledge that could work to Ludwig's advantage.

Although he bought the *Adams* and *Webster* at giveaway prices, D.K. was obligated to spend a minimum of $225,000 on each, renovating the cargo areas and putting in new engines that would enable the ships to attain a cruising speed of sixteen knots or better. For the present, he was short of ready cash; though the *Ulysses* deal had been signed, he still had not delivered the ship or received the $800,000 for it.

Ludwig needed a way to obtain ready money without either taking partners or assuming heavy mortgages. His early experiences with partnerships had been costly, and borrowing to finance ship renovation was no better. He had lost the *Jay* to foreclosure and had managed to hang on to the *Ulysses* only by the skin of his teeth. Surely there was a better method.

It was at this time that D.K. came up with the "two-name paper" arrangement he later told Dero Saunders was the chief reason for his wealth. It all sounded so simple: go to an oil company; get it to sign a long-term charter to ship so much oil on a regular basis; take the charter to a bank and, using it as collateral, obtain a loan to build or renovate a ship to haul the oil to fulfill the charter.

This may sound like "the house that Jack built," but it was advantageous to all parties involved. And Ludwig would have a steady income as long as he fulfilled his charter obligations. He would also be free of most of the bookkeeping. The oil company, instead of paying him directly, would send the charter fees to the bank, which would take out the loan payment due and deposit the rest in Ludwig's account. The plan was legal, logical, and ingenious.

But there was much more to the two-name paper than D.K. explained to Saunders. One fact he did not mention in the *Fortune* interview was that in 1936 he was able to start his climb toward being the world's biggest shipper mainly because he had finally managed to hook into the big time. He was now hauling oil for the Rockefeller empire.

Up to now, Ludwig had been chartering his ships to smaller refineries — the little operation in Fall River, Atlantic, Sinclair. His new charterer — the company for which he was buying and converting the *Webster* and *Adams* — was Pan American Petroleum &

Transport Corporation, a major subsidiary, since 1925, of Standard Oil of Indiana.

To appreciate the significance of this, it is helpful to digress for a moment and recapitulate briefly the history of the American oil industry, and of Standard Oil in particular.

The saga started in 1859, when Colonel E. L. Drake drilled the world's first oil well near Titusville, Pennsylvania. Five years later a young accountant named John D. Rockefeller ventured into the oil fields of western Pennsylvania to make his fortune. America was in the last throes of the Civil War, and many of Rockefeller's contemporaries were fighting and dying to preserve the Union, but the young man's mind was on other matters. Not far removed from an insecure, tumultuous childhood, he had already developed an obsession for mathematical order.

What he saw in the oil fields both fascinated and revolted him. The infant oil industry was a classic example of free enterprise at its rowdiest. The search to find and drill new fields was already creating a boom-or-bust instability in the marketplace. No sooner would someone think of a new use for "black gold," raising demand and prices, than a fresh horde of eager prospectors would rush to the area, buying up options, sinking holes, and bringing in gushers, all of which saturated the market and drove prices back down.

It was a textbook case of supply and demand, and to young Rockefeller it was a horror story. How could he hope to make any money if the bottom kept falling out of the oil market? He had to find a way to impose order — stabilize prices in such a way that a shrewd investor like himself could reap the maximum benefits of his cleverness.

Rockefeller soon abandoned the idea of trying to get a monopoly in the oil fields themselves. This was much worse than the California gold rush. A virtually unlimited supply of petroleum lay beneath the ground, just waiting to be tapped. The prospect of buying or taking options on all the potentially oil-rich land in the region was beyond possibility. Nobody had *that* much money.

But the same effect could be achieved in another way. Crude oil wasn't good for much of anything except relieving coughs (early settlers had learned to drink the viscous liquid straight as a cough syrup) and starting fires. Only after it had been refined could it be used for lighting and heating homes and serving as raw material for hundreds of manufactured products.

The trick, then, was to control the refining and transporting of petroleum and its products. Let the wildcatters in the fields cut each other's throats as they would. John D. Rockefeller, aided by a few carefully selected friends, would monopolize the supply of oil on a different level and then set prices to suit himself.

Fortunately for Rockefeller, only a few refineries then existed. Those he could buy, he did. Those he couldn't, he hired gangs of thugs to blow up. Soon there was little competition left. To critics who screamed that such practices were immoral, criminal, and un-businesslike, John D. would only smile and reply, "The American Beauty rose can be produced in all its splendor only by sacrificing the early buds that grow up around it."

While his competitors' "early buds" were being sacrificed to Alfred Nobel's recently invented dynamite, Rockefeller's American Beauty — the Standard Oil Company — flowered into magnificence. Although he couldn't gain the same sort of control over oil transportation that he had over refining, he soon found it possible to make secret deals with railroad tycoons, who gave him rebates and allowed him to undercut the competition in the marketplace. If it cost him less to haul oil, he could sell it more cheaply than his rivals and squeeze them out.

By the end of the nineteenth century, Standard Oil and the railroads had managed to get a stranglehold on a large segment of the American economy. Over the next several decades, the emerging auto industry broke the back of the railroads (just as it supplanted water transportation as a way for people to travel). But automobiles required refined oil and gasoline in order to run, and this, plus his investments in auto-manufacturing companies, only made Rockefeller richer.

He was fully aware that he had almost single-handedly ushered in a new era of capitalism — one characterized not by competition and free enterprise but by secret deals, combination, and control. By this time he had learned that the winning formula was not to destroy your competitors but to join and absorb them. Working together, a few companies could soon gain control of an entire industry and stabilize the market to their mutual advantage. Later, Rockefeller boasted of his method: "This movement was the origin of the whole system of modern economic administration. It has revolutionized the way of doing business all over the world. The time was ripe for it. It had to come. . . . The day of combination is here to stay. Individualism is gone, never to return."

And, as recent history has amply proved, he was right, largely because his prophecy was a self-fulfilling one. A monopoly as powerful and as necessary to modern industrial society as he had created is nearly impossible to crack. Theodore Roosevelt tried by bringing a suit that, in 1911, culminated in the U.S. Supreme Court's famous "breakup" of Standard Oil.

But the Court-ordered breakup had no more effect than cutting off the arms of a starfish. Each severed limb just regenerates a new body. The Court's decision required only that Standard dissolve by turning its assets back into the hands of its stockholders. The immediate result was that the one company broke into four — Standard of New Jersey (now known as Exxon), Standard of New York (Mobil), Standard of Indiana (Amoco), and Standard of California (Chevron) — which remained firmly in the hands and under the control of John D. Rockefeller, his heirs, and associates. A glance at the top of the *Fortune* 500 list of largest American corporations will confirm that, far from being broken, the Standard Oil empire is alive and healthier, richer and more powerful than ever.

By 1922 it was already apparent that the Standard Oil trust had not really been hurt by the Supreme Court's order. After a long, arduous investigation, the Federal Trade Commission that year concluded, "There is . . . an interlocking stock ownership in the different organizations [of the four Standard companies] which has perpetuated the very monopolistic control which the courts sought to terminate."

But by this time, it was too late to do much about the situation. The Standard owners had reached deeply into the government itself and were using their influence to try to control policy in Washington, from the White House on down. The chief spokesman at that time for the Rockefeller interests — the New Jersey Standard chairman, Walter Teagle — was a close friend and adviser of President Harding (as he would later be of Presidents Coolidge and Hoover). None of these three administrations of the 1920s, it might be noted, made the regulation of business in general — or of the oil industry in particular — a high-priority item.

They should have. But not even the widely publicized Teapot Dome scandal would curb the growing power and influence of the

Rockefeller oil interests. In 1928, Walter Teagle — using John D.'s success formula of *conspire, combine, control* — met secretly with the heads of the two largest European oil companies, British Petroleum and Royal Dutch Shell, at Scotland's Achnacarry Castle to draw up an agreement that would control the world's oil supplies in a way similar to what the Standard companies were already doing in the United States.

This pact — later known as the Achnacarry or Red Line Agreement — in effect froze each existing major oil company's fractional share of the petroleum market at 1928 levels, creating a cartel and eliminating competition. Thereafter, each oil major would be assigned "drawing rights"; it could draw a certain amount of petroleum out of the ground each year. If it wished to draw more, it would have to pay the cartel a premium on the extra quantity, thereby making the cost of production noncompetitive.

The Achnacarry Agreement accomplished on a global level what John D. Rockefeller and his Standard Oil Trust had done earlier for the American oil market. By dividing the market fractionally among collaborating companies in such a way as to limit supplies and control prices, the oil majors imposed a stability that virtually guaranteed profits. The operating principle was that there was enough money in oil production for everyone to make a good living, as long as "everyone" was defined as including only those companies willing to curb their competitive impulses and desire for quick profit in favor of long-term control and assured revenues.

Once Teagle and his British Petroleum and Royal Dutch Shell counterparts had hammered out the basic agreement to create a petroleum trust, it was sent to other oil companies of appreciable size for their signatures. The cartel would work only if every significant player in the game abided by the rules. Any company not willing to cooperate could easily be driven out of business by the cartel members. It was get on board or get out of the industry.

Although the Achnacarry Agreement was a well-kept secret (the U.S. government did not find out about it until nearly a quarter of a century later, and even now it has received very little public attention), its effects were enormous and far-reaching. Oil was and is, after all, the lifeblood of all industrial societies, supplying the most basic form of energy to run factories, produce electricity, fuel automobiles and trucks, trains and planes, heat homes and offices, and provide the raw material for thousands of manufactured products, including plastics, drugs, synthetic fibers — the list is almost endless.

Consequently, it is no overstatement to say that whoever controls oil controls the world. Naturally, this applies in a political sense as well. It is important to realize, for example, that one of the major "oil companies" that formulated the Achnacarry Agreement, or at least the majority owner of same, was none other than the British government. In 1914, Winston Churchill, while serving as first lord of the admiralty, had been instrumental in having Britain purchase — for £2 million — controlling interest in the Anglo-Persian Oil Company, which became Anglo-Iranian Oil and then British Petroleum. So Great Britain, both as a nation and as an industrial power heavily dependent on large supplies of Mideast oil, had a vested interest in seeing the international oil cartel succeed and remain successful.

One immediate effect of the Achnacarry pact was to make long-term chartering a viable proposition for petroleum haulers. Only in a market where supplies and prices were controlled and relatively predictable could an oil company afford to commit itself five or ten years into the future by contracting to ship a specified amount of oil at a fixed rate.

And only in that kind of stable market was it possible for a young tanker operator like Daniel Keith Ludwig to go to a major oil company and ask it to sign a charter to collateralize a loan to build (or renovate) a ship to haul the company's oil for five years or more. By signing a charter agreement with the Rockefeller-controlled Pan American Petroleum & Transport, D.K. was getting into the international cartel at a very basic and vital level. As long as the cartel prospered, he too would prosper.

Why, one might wonder, would an oil company in such an advantageous position charter ships from an outside operator rather than building (or buying) and operating ships of its own? Partly for the same reason there continues to be a number of oil companies instead of a single one: the illusion of competition and decentralization has to be maintained. The U.S. government still had laws on the books dating from the muckraking days at the turn of the century when public outcry led to trustbusting. What was in fact a tightly controlled situation must not look like one from the outside.

Another question is how D.K., after struggling in the bush leagues of oil transport for a decade, was suddenly able to get in with the big-time operators. He probably had his father to thank for that. If Daniel F. knew people who could pull strings to get a British ambassador and an American secretary of state to work on his behalf in freeing a bootleg ship, he may have also had enough influence to get his son an entry into the Rockefeller establishment. The fight to keep the *Ulysses* had revealed that when the situation became desperate, D.K. and Malone were able to call for help from the secretary of war, a number of congressmen, and a Republican Party official from New York. How had they managed to get such powerful friends?

As much as D.K. has been portrayed as a "lone wolf," the fact remains that he could never have attained billionaire status by operating in a vacuum. By allying himself with the biggest game in town, he served as a useful cog in a gigantic machine that kept oil and money circulating all over the globe.

One thing the Rockefellers had already learned (and that Ludwig would learn later) is that simply making money is not enough. It is necessary to hang on to it — and keep recycling it — if one is to remain rich. In fact, it is not even essential to *own* a lot of money to have economic power. What's important is to *control* wealth — to determine where it goes and how it's used.

The heirs of old John D. Rockefeller had come to realize that mere control over the world's supply of oil was not enough. It would make them money, but it was only a beginning. Money attracts money in much the same way that matter attracts matter. The larger the pile, the stronger it pulls smaller piles toward it. This, of course, can be self-defeating. What happens when all the smaller piles have been sucked into the large central pile is either total stagnation or a big bang.

The way to avoid either effect is to keep a lot of the smaller piles in orbit, much like planets around a sun, or electrons around the nucleus of an atom, thereby creating a self-balancing system. In economic terms, this requires having a sizable portion of money always in circulation, doing the world's work, building, making jobs, moving commodities from one place to another. The trick is to move money around without losing control over it.

And this is why a Rockefeller-controlled oil company and a Rockefeller-controlled bank were willing to go along with Ludwig's scheme and let him use oil-company credit to acquire ships for himself. It was almost like transferring money from one pocket to another. The oil company — Pan American P & T — paid the bank — Chemical (controlled by a Rockefeller–Du Pont group of stockholders) — directly, so Ludwig didn't even get to touch most of the money after borrowing it.

But money was not the main thing he was after. For now D.K. wanted ships. Once he had accumulated enough tankers to gain a sizable fraction of the oil-hauling business, the money would come rolling in. And the two-name paper was a way of getting those ships without having to raise investment capital or mortgage his own holdings to the limit.

When talking to Dero Saunders in 1957, Ludwig gave himself credit for introducing this method of financing into the shipping industry. It may be so. Other writers have credited Aristotle Onassis with the innovation, but since Onassis did not start investing heavily in tankers until a few years after 1936, such claims have little foundation. A more debatable point is whether D.K. thought of the idea himself. Until 1936, though he served as treasurer for all the corporations he had a share in, he had revealed a decided ineptitude for handling money.

The two-name paper made its appearance at just about the same time D.K. hired William W. Wagner, so it is very likely that the idea was Wagner's. But it may have been the brainchild of a Chemical Bank vice-president named J. A. W. Richardson, with whom Ludwig worked closely in putting together the financing package to purchase and renovate the *Webster* and *Adams*. The relationship was evidently a friendly one, for D.K. soon named the bank official as a director of several of his corporations — an honor usually reserved for Ludwig himself, members of his family, close friends, and a few of his most trusted lieutenants. As with the insurance man Stuart Betts, D.K. seems to have found Richardson a man whose judgment, discretion, and loyalty he could rely on. But the presence of Richardson on the boards of several Ludwig-owned corporations also gave Chemical Bank a line into D.K.'s business activities.

While D.K., with the help of Wagner and Richardson, was getting his financial arrangements in better order, he was also straightening out his personal affairs. In 1937, shortly after the birth of his daughter, Patricia Margaret, and the divorce from Gladys, Ludwig took a new wife. G. Virginia Ludwig — usually called Ginger — was to prove an enduring and reliable companion to her husband. Very little is known about her, however. She had a son (and perhaps another child as well) by a previous marriage, but there are no pictures of her in media files, and the only personal reference to her in the press is in an article about D.K. in which it is reported that during a party she asked a servant to bring her husband a glass of buttermilk.

Other articles have stated that neither she nor her son takes any interest in Ludwig's business affairs. This is probably so, but starting in the late 1940s, she was listed as a director of several of D.K.'s corporations. This, of course, indicates no active participation by Ginger in the running of her husband's companies, but it does suggest that, after a decade of marriage, Ludwig felt secure enough to start making financial provisions for her in the event of his death. The creation of two cancer research foundations later provided mechanisms for him to pass his wealth on to her more or less intact.

Sometime during 1938, another family tie was severed. Daniel F. Ludwig dropped out of his son's business activities as quietly and mysteriously as he had reappeared in 1933. This time, judging from available evidence, it was for good.

When D.K.'s father had stepped in during the depths of the Depression to lend a hand, the younger Ludwig was mired deep in debt, saddled with do-nothing partners, desperately pressed to keep the Shipping Board and the banks from foreclosing on his few ships, and burdened with an unhappy marriage. Now, five years later, D.K. was in good financial shape, the owner of a growing fleet of ships and corporations, out of debt, and enjoying a profitable relationship with the government, the banks, and the oil companies. Moreover, he was building a reliable staff and he had a happier marriage.

Just how responsible was Daniel F. Ludwig for his son's remarkable turnaround? All that can be said for certain is that his name appears as an officer and director of five new Delaware corporations set up between 1933 and 1936, and that this coincides with the change in D.K.'s fortunes from abysmal to good. He almost certainly brought several new ships and an infusion of money into his son's moribund oil-hauling operation.

It is clear that by 1938 D.K. had put most of his earlier troubles behind him and was now on the way up. And sometime between April of that year and January 1939, corporate records reveal, Daniel

F. dropped off the list of officers and directors of the five companies he had helped start, leaving his son in full charge as sole owner. Where he went, and why, is not known. In 1938 he was still shown as living on State Street in Stamford, Connecticut, and the state's papers contain no record of his death. But he never showed up again in the corporate files of D.K.'s companies, so it may be assumed that the younger Ludwig, now just past forty, was no longer dependent on him. But D.K. had found a substitute parent to take Daniel F.'s place. He had been adopted by the Rockefeller empire.

*Six*

# D.K. Welshes on a Deal

President Franklin D. Roosevelt, up for re-election in 1936, saw shipping as a weak link in his administration. Though most of his first-term Cabinet members had proved themselves to be honest, effective, and loyal to the principles of the New Deal, Secretary of Commerce Daniel Roper, FDR saw, had caved in to business lobbyists and was allowing unscrupulous shippers to feed greedily at the federal trough.

Having served as assistant secretary of the Navy under Wilson, Roosevelt knew a few things about the shipping industry and the rampant corruption that often pervades the relationship between ship owners and the government officials who are supposed to regulate shipping. The president did not want to tackle Roper directly. The man still had powerful allies, and it didn't pay politically to call attention to the shortcomings of one's own appointees.

But it wasn't necessary to point an accusing finger. Reform could be accomplished through agency reorganization, and Roper could be eased out later, at a time when such a move would not be politically damaging.

To accomplish the reorganization, FDR sent Congress a bill that became the Merchant Marine Act of 1936. Among other things, the act abolished the scandal-tainted Shipping Board and replaced it, in 1937, with the Maritime Commission. One of the commission's chief purposes was to phase out the old, renovated war-surplus vessels that made up most of America's Merchant Marine and replace them with newer, faster ships able to outrun or elude German submarines. One way of doing this was to cut off the sale of World War I ships and encourage shippers to build new ones instead.

The move took Ludwig by surprise. It was hardly capricious, since every one of the war-surplus hulls was now nearly twenty years old and not, from the government's point of view, worth remodeling. But D.K. had just set up National Bulk Carriers with the idea of buying many of these old ships cheaply and turning them into moneymaking tankers or bulk-cargo haulers.

He was even now engaged in renovating the *Webster* into a bulk carrier. To be sure, it would take $250,000 to buy and fix the ships, but the money was all Pan American P & T's, lent to Ludwig by Chemical Bank on the oil company's credit. After conversion, each vessel could be expected to yield a profit of more than $100,000 a year. At this rate, Ludwig could pay off the loans for each ship in about two and a half years and, over the remaining life of the ten-year charter, net $1.5 million. It was not a bad return on the original $50,000 investment.

Dismayed by Maritime's intent, D.K. had Robert Malone write immediately to Telfair Knight, secretary of the commission, asking that the policy be suspended until National Bulk Carriers could buy several more vessels. There weren't enough American building ways to meet the demand for new vessels, Malone argued, and it made sense to continue converting the old ones for a while. Ludwig offered $25,000 apiece for two ships, the *Andrew Jackson* and the *William Penn* — sister vessels to the *Webster* and *Adams* — and four smaller ships of 11,000 tons each — the *Invincible, Courageous, Triumph,* and *Defiance.*

The commission, thereupon, seemed curiously willing to abandon its new policy and invited bids — but not at the $25,000 fire-sale price. This concession was the opening of a three-year contest in which Ludwig used every trick against a nearsighted and ponderous bureaucracy. From his early matches against the Shipping Board, he had learned the strategy; now he was a pro, and his displays of gamesmanship are worth noting.

It was an annoyance to have to pay more for the ships, but it was still cheaper to renovate an old ship than to build a new one, and he was not yet set up to build new ships. In April 1937, Malone submitted a Ludwig request to buy six more tankers, in addition to the ones requested earlier. He added that National Bulk, recognizing Maritime's interest in new ships, planned to build at least two and perhaps as many as six that would meet the commission's national defense standard of a sixteen-knot cruising speed.

Malone also included some sales figures for National Bulk Carriers. In 1936, he boasted, the company's six ships had carried almost five million barrels of cargo, earning a net profit of $323,723. (The irony of this particular disclosure is reflected in an aspect of Ludwig's personal life. At the time Malone was bragging about National Bulk's earnings, D.K. was falling behind in the $200-a-month alimony and child-support payments to his ex-wife, Gladys, with the excuse that he couldn't afford them because of business reverses.)

Maritime was enough impressed with Ludwig's recent successes to put the six ships he had requested up for bid, but by now he had decided he only wanted four of them. He therefore entered two sets of bids: one of $745,000 for the *Jackson, Invincible, Triumph* and *Defiance,* and one of $800,000 for all six ($36,000 for the *Penn,* $19,000 for the *Courageous*).

The commission had set a value of $175,000 to $250,000 on each of the six vessels, so his four-ship bid, while a little low, was not unreasonable. The frivolously low bids on the *Penn* and *Courageous,* however, were presumably a signal that Ludwig was no longer interested in them.

Maritime, after considering both bids (there were no competing bids from other companies), decided to accept the four-ship offer. Ludwig put down the required 25 percent good-faith deposit and soon took delivery of the *Andrew Jackson* to begin converting it to a bulk carrier at his small Hampton Roads shipyard.

Shortly after, he began what was to be a long delaying game. In October 1937, he asked for and was granted a delay on taking delivery of the next ship in line, the *Invincible.* In November, he informed the commission he wanted to put off the final purchase of this vessel for another six months. Just before Christmas, he made a plea for more time on the grounds that he was being held up by red tape at his bank.

What he did not tell Maritime was that he had applied to the Rockefeller-controlled Bank of the Manhattan Company (later

Chase Manhattan Bank, after its merger with Chase National) for funds to complete the *Triumph* sale, and was having some difficulty getting this loan through. But, as he had already made up his mind to get out of the *Invincible* contract, his bank problems could be turned into an excuse for buying time.

The loan problem stemmed from Ludwig's wanting to use his newly signed charter on the *Phoenix* as collateral for the *Triumph* purchase. Since the *Phoenix* was old and in poor condition, the bank's officers were understandably cautious about accepting her as security.

One Bank of the Manhattan official recalled this deal with amusement:

> He wanted to borrow only about $200,000, but it took a year to talk the bank into it. Finally, the bank's officers said to me, "Okay, go ahead if you want to, but we think it's a lemon." The ink wasn't dry on the contract when the 1938 hurricane came along. I couldn't sleep that night because the ship [the *Phoenix*] was in northeastern waters. The next day, I called up and asked, "How's my collateral?" Ludwig answered, "When we find the goddamned thing, I'll let you know," and slammed down the phone. What had happened was that she was tied up at a Fall River dock, and when the hurricane came, the dock crew had cut her loose. She ended up on a street in Fall River, and Merritt-Chapman [a contractor specializing in large projects] had to dig a channel to get her back to the ocean. But she had insurance coverage of every kind and we never lost a penny. I carried pictures of her around the bank, and I was a laughingstock. But the loan was paid on schedule and we had no trouble.

In February 1938, Ludwig was still stalling on the *Defiance* and *Invincible* contracts. In March he finished the *Andrew Jackson* conversion but had Malone notify Maritime that National Bulk did not want to buy the *Invincible,* but also did not want to forfeit its $50,000 good-faith deposit on the ship. With customary vagueness, Malone gave no reason for Ludwig's change of mind, saying only that "the purchase and conversion of the *Invincible* at this time would be uneconomic and non-self-supporting." He asked that the contract be put on indefinite suspension until National Bulk could come up with a proposal to build new tankers as a trade-off.

Maritime's special expert Huntington Morse was an obliging fellow, but he couldn't think of a single excuse for letting Ludwig off the hook on the *Invincible* contract. Why not let me give you another six-month extension? he asked in reply.

Seeing this was all he could get, Malone accepted, but soon sent Morse a progress report saying that Ludwig had decided to put much faster engines in the *Triumph* and *Defiance,* which would so increase the speed and efficiency of his present fleet that the *Invincible* wouldn't be needed. Malone also repeated Ludwig's offer to build new tankers as a trade-off.

How is it, Morse wondered in reply, that National Bulk, having signed a contract and made a good-faith deposit, can't afford to buy and renovate the *Invincible* but can afford to build new tankers?

It was a pertinent question, but Malone hedged in his answer. The banks, he said, preferred lending money on new construction rather than on renovating old ships. Morse couldn't buy this, and still couldn't find a reasonable way to let Ludwig out of the contract without forfeiting the deposit. Instead of saying no, however, he temporized by granting another extension for nine months.

During this period, Ludwig offered a concrete proposal to build a new eighteen-knot tanker if Maritime would pay for the national defense feature of extra speed. Under the National Defense Act of 1936, Maritime was empowered to subsidize merchant shipping by paying for more powerful engines that would allow a cargo vessel to outrun or elude enemy submarines. This was what Ludwig was asking for, his rationale being that the new tanker would be more useful to the government should it be requisitioned for war use. He did not dwell on the point that a faster engine would also make *him* more money, since it meant that the tanker could make more trips in a given period of time.

Morse could not rule on this request, so he passed it along to Navy's Commander Howard L. Vickery, second-in-command to Maritime's Chairman Admiral Emory Land. Vickery, wanting to know more about National Bulk's financial situation before making a decision, sent an auditor to Ludwig's Manhattan offices.

The audit showed some interesting facts but also uncovered some mysteries. National Bulk had a current net worth of $555,000 and would, with a pending $100,000 investment by Phoenix Steamship, have a capitalization of $624,000. Ludwig owned about half the stock in his own name, the other half being held by two of his other companies, Phoenix and American Tankers Corporation. When the auditor tried to learn more about these companies, he ran into a stone wall. Ludwig, he reported to Vickery, declined to furnish "any specific information concerning the ownership . . . financial status . . . and general operating activities" of any company besides National Bulk.

Why the secrecy? Possibly D.K. was trying to shield his father from government scrutiny. While Daniel F. had no visible connection with National Bulk, he was still president of American Tankers and several other Ludwig-owned corporations.

Another revelation — although it seems to have caused no reaction at Maritime — was that the *Ulysses* had been sold by Amtankers of Massachusetts to Amtankers of Delaware before its sale to Western Operating Corporation. This bit of information should have provoked a furor, for such a sale would not have been legal in the eyes of the government, since Maritime had held a preferred mortgage on that ship with Amtankers of Massachusetts that would have to be satisfied before any sale could take place. But the Ludwigs had pulled a fast one without anyone at Maritime being the wiser, and, since the mortgage had been paid, nothing was said about it now.

Based on what the Maritime auditor could find out, National Bulk's financial position didn't make it appear a very good risk. It had only $17,000 in cash on hand and current assets of only $50,000 against debts of $400,000 — an unhealthy one-to-eight ratio. While its ships were employed and earning money, their projected income would not be enough to service the debt load for the near future. "Assuming these figures are correct," the auditor's report concluded, "it will be 1942 before any money can be taken out of the company's treasury for new construction."

Maritime, looking over this gloomy analysis, was reluctant to consent to the national defense subsidy Ludwig was seeking for a new tanker. It decided to wait until National Bulk could offer a more substantial proposal. With war on the horizon, the commission didn't want to scuttle completely a project it might need later.

In June 1938, Ludwig got an extension on completing the *Triumph* and *Defiance,* and requested permission to change their names. Each would be named after a state, with the prefix *Pan* designating an affiliation with Pan American Petroleum & Transport. The applications reveal an interesting fact: the ships carried heavy mortgages that were not reported by Vickery's auditor. In all, Ludwig had borrowed more than $2.75 million to buy and convert the ships, so his debt load was much heavier than previously realized. Maritime seems to have taken this news without a blink.

In December 1938, for reasons still not clear, Ludwig's persistence in pushing the new-tanker-for-old trade finally paid off. Huntington Morse, acknowledging that it was not very logical for National Bulk to claim it couldn't afford to buy the *Invincible* while offering to build a new vessel, nevertheless recommended just such a plan to his boss, Admiral Land, who then got the commission's grudging approval to allow Ludwig to put the new tanker out for bids.

In accepting the trade-off in principle and allowing D.K. to use new tanker construction as a bargaining chip, Maritime was choosing to ignore the fact that Ludwig had announced two years earlier that he was planning to build at least two new tankships in addition to renovating old ones. Thus he wasn't really giving the commission anything except the option of paying for a faster engine.

With Maritime's approval, he now asked for bids on the proposed tanker and got only one, for $2.8 million. Too much to pay, D.K. told the commission, and announced he was returning to his original plan of building a slower tanker *without* national defense features. You're lucky, he told Maritime; now the government won't have to pay a nickel toward the new tanker.

Instead of being happy, Land's assistant, Commander Vickery, was livid. He felt Ludwig had been playing games all along to deceive the commission and had probably never intended to build a fast tanker. He also called Ludwig a liar for asserting that Maritime had ever agreed to finance a faster ship. "This statement is not accurate," he wrote. "The Commission at no time definitely accepted the proposition of National Bulk Carriers. The Commission *did* agree to allow the company to take bids and stated that it would *then* reach a decision."

To keep Ludwig's little subterfuge from succeeding, Vickery recommended that the commission either force the shipper to build the fast tanker he'd proposed or forfeit the $50,000 *Invincible* deposit.

D.K. realized he'd overstepped the mark. He quickly countered with a new and different offer. What if we build *two* new tankers, he asked Maritime, one of them slower than you'd like but faster than we'd planned, say, about fifteen knots, and this won't cost the government anything. We'll also build a smaller 40,000-barrel tanker you can use as a tender in case of war.

Again, Ludwig seems to have been operating on the assumption that Maritime had forgotten his earlier announcement that he was planning to build these ships anyway. But he was not one to offer even a specious deal without asking something in return. This time he wanted two concessions: permission to transfer his old 20,000-barrel tanker *Transford II* to foreign registry; and Maritime's agreement to take the $50,000 *Invincible* deposit, plus his earlier $36,000 bid on the *William Penn,* as a new $86,000 offer for the *Penn.*

This was a classic example of Ludwig horsetrading: offer something that appears reasonable on the surface and maybe they'll buy it without looking closely enough to see what they're really getting.

At first glance, the government seemed to be getting a fair deal. Three ships — the *Penn* and two new tankers — would be added to the U.S. merchant fleet without a subsidy from Maritime. Ludwig would also be forfeiting, in a way, his good-faith deposit on the *Invincible* for backing out of the contract to purchase it.

What would he be getting in return? This takes some analysis. Let's look first at the initial concession he wanted — his request to transfer the *Transford II* to foreign registry. Here he was trying to take advantage of policies growing out of the recently passed Neutrality Acts.

When President Roosevelt had retreated to Warm Springs, Georgia, in 1935 in the wake of his unsuccessful attempt to place an embargo on the shipment of oil and other vital materials to Italy, he had returned to Washington determined to do through legislation what he had failed to do by executive order: keep crucial supplies from being exported to aggressor nations. The result was the Neutrality Acts.

But as well intentioned as the acts had been in 1936–1937, Roosevelt in 1939 suddenly found his own hands tied by these same laws. Now, with Britain and France almost at war with Nazi Germany, FDR could not order strategic goods to be sent from America to French and British ports.

The administration's solution was not to repeal the laws (which would have allowed American companies to trade with Germany as well) but to go around them. Certain private shippers were to be given Maritime's consent to transfer some of their vessels to foreign registry, where they would not be subject to U.S. law. These ships would then be free to haul any sort of cargo to any port in the world.

This procedure was a throwback to Prohibition, when American rumrunning vessels flew foreign flags — usually British — to avoid search and capture. Now the same ruse was being employed so that American oil could aid the British war preparations.

Initially, Panama, which had been virtually a U.S. colony since its separation from Colombia early in this century, was chosen as the country to host foreign-registered U.S. vessels. In order to persuade shippers to participate, however, FDR had to hand them a blank check: few restrictions, token taxes, and low maintenance standards would be imposed by Panama on ships flying the Panamanian flag of convenience. There would be no inspections to speak of, and owners could hire foreign crews as cheaply as possible — no worrying about the higher wages paid to unionized U.S. merchant seamen. In short, foreign registry was tantamount to a license to steal. It seemed very attractive to Daniel Ludwig, but he was not in good position to take advantage of it.

For one thing, all his ships were already on charter to a U.S. company. For another, they were mostly larger ships, which Maritime wanted to keep in the U.S. merchant marine, and under an American flag, in case of war or other emergency. FDR's flag-of-convenience program was being carried out quietly and couldn't be officially acknowledged, so D.K. couldn't seek help from a congressman or Cabinet member. His only ploy, then, was to argue that the *Transford II* was so old and slow that it was no longer useful to the U.S. merchant navy.

Ludwig's second request — that Maritime accept an $86,000 bid on the *William Penn* — was a shrewd piece of hocus-pocus. At the time he had made a bid of $36,000 for her, D.K. knew that Maritime had set a value of around $200,000 on the ship, and he was obliged to make an offer since the *Penn* was one of the ships he'd asked to be put up for auction. And he knew the commission would not accept a $36,000 bid. Now that he had changed his mind and decided he wanted the *Penn* more than the *Invincible,* he was still hoping to get the former for the same low figure with the addition of a deposit he'd probably have to forfeit anyway.

At Maritime, the matter provoked an argument between Huntington Morse, who was willing to accept Ludwig's proposal, and the commission's general counsel, Carl Farbach, who wasn't. Farbach held that an unacceptably low bid plus a deposit that should be forfeited didn't add up to a fair price for the *Penn*. His main objection, though, was that if Maritime accepted the deal, it would in effect be subsidizing new tanker construction in a way not authorized by law.

Farbach's arguments finally prevailed, and on November 20, 1939, Admiral Land wrote Malone to notify National Bulk that the commission had turned down the trade-off. Malone, acting for Ludwig, replied at some length, saying that National Bulk was having a brief prepared which would show that everything proposed was strictly legal and aboveboard.

One of Malone's chief points was that Ludwig couldn't afford to offer much for the *Penn* because he was going to have to spend considerable money converting her to meet Maritime standards. If the commission wanted to realize as much as $200,000 from the sale of the ship, it would have to sell to a foreign buyer, and that, of course, would be contrary to Maritime's goal of building a strong U.S. merchant navy.

Malone's argument was both sophistic and shrewd. The sophistic element was the lobbyist's omitting to mention that Ludwig had only recently agreed to pay nearly $200,000 apiece for four similar ships and spend an equal amount converting them. The shrewdness was his realization that Maritime would be hard put to explain why it would sell an American ship to a foreign buyer if an American shipper wanted it. This was the sort of agency move certain congressmen liked to pounce on.

Then, in a completely uncharacteristic burst of candor, Malone suddenly admitted in his letter to Morse why Ludwig had taken such pains to avoid buying the *Invincible*. One of the main reasons he had been buying old ships was to salvage and sell the parts removed during renovation. When he purchased a surplus ship — unless it was forbidden by the contract — he could recoup much of his investment by selling off the old engine and other machinery. Marine salvage was as familiar to D.K. as his own face in the mirror. (Years later, *Fortune*'s Dero Saunders would quote the Baltimore scrap dealer Morris Schapiro's admiring statement about Ludwig: "He knows where every piece of equipment being sold as scrap or surplus is. . . . He is a brilliant man; it gets you all upset sometimes, the way his mind runs.")

But even geniuses make mistakes, and Ludwig had made a monumental one on the *Invincible*. The marine engineer who inspected the ship for him had pronounced its engines sound and salable. After signing the contract, however, D.K. had found the engines to be experimental turbo-electric units made only briefly during World War I. The problem was that they tended to give off sparks that might ignite a petroleum cargo and blow a ship to kingdom come. No shipper in his right mind would touch one of them for love or money. If Ludwig couldn't resell the *Invincible*'s engines, he didn't want the ship. It was that simple, and had been all along. All the delays and excuses over a period of two years had been so much smoke to conceal that fact that Ludwig had signed a contract to purchase a ship he couldn't immediately recover his money from through salvage profits.

Huntington Morse, ever the friend of the shipping industry, was sympathetic. He urged Malone to submit Ludwig's rejected proposal again. But Carl Farbach stood as firmly opposed to the deal as ever.

Ludwig, however, was now ready to back the resubmission with heavy bombardment of the Maritime legal department. This time he came armed with a supporting brief from the Washington law firm of Cummings & Stanley. Just the fact that Ludwig had hired this firm showed how serious he was about winning; it was a heavyweight among legal offices in the nation's capital. The head of the firm, Homer S. Cummings, had been Roosevelt's attorney general from 1933 to 1939. Before that, he had served as National Democratic Party chairman.

Cummings did not write the brief, though; that task was given to another senior partner, Carl McFarland, who produced a thirty-two-page discussion of the options available to Maritime.

McFarland's brief was based not so much on law, where Ludwig didn't have a leg to stand on, as on practicality and expediency. What would happen, the lawyer asked, if Maritime drove National Bulk to default on the *Invincible* sale? The government, he wrote, answering his own question, might get to keep the $50,000, but the default would cost a lot of jobs at a time when the country was still trying to pull itself out of the Depression. And Maritime might *not* get the default money for years, or ever, for National Bulk could keep the case tied up in court for a long, long time. Forget the law and the contract, McFarland was telling Maritime; you don't want to do something that both you and my client would probably be sorry for later.

The argument might have been weak on points of law, but it seems to have convinced everyone at the commission except Farbach. Even his own assistant wrote him a memo urging him to give in. In January 1940, he did. He had learned, as a number of honest government officials had before him, that when Daniel Ludwig made up his mind to do something, it was prudent not to stand in his way.

Shortly after Farbach had thrown in the towel, the commission met and agreed to a solution. It would keep the *Invincible* deposit as a forfeit, but would sell National Bulk the *Penn* for $36,000. The company would agree to build a new tanker capable of sixteen knots.

This was all fine with Ludwig. He'd won — game, set, and match — avoided a potentially costly mistake, bought a cheap ship he could use instead of an expensive one he didn't want, and suckered the bureaucracy in the process. By February, the *Invincible* flap was history and his Norfolk yard was busy converting the *Penn* to a bulk carrier.

# Seven

# The War Years

The war clouds that had been building over Europe for more than a decade finally reached their saturation point. On September 1, 1939, Hitler's armies moved into Poland.

A new kind of conflict had broken out, one in which machines would play a larger role than men. During the First World War, tanks and airplanes — for all the publicity they received — had been little more than novelties. Now, perfected into weapons of deadly efficiency by Nazi arms makers during the early-to-mid-thirties and battle-tested in the Spanish Civil War, they formed the spearhead of the German attack, smashing their victims simultaneously from the ground and air, hitting with no warning, allowing no orderly regrouping or retreat.

This mechanized form of swift attack was *Blitzkrieg,* "lightning war." Having watched their crack infantry divisions get bogged down in the trenches of France and picked to pieces during the first war, the Germans were not going to make that mistake again. This time they depended on fast, death-dealing machines, instruments of destruction whose lifeblood was petroleum.

Until the attack on Poland, Britain and France had pursued a policy of appeasement, watching passively but with growing anxiety as Hitler gobbled up large chunks of Eastern Europe without a struggle, trying to believe that each new conquest would be his last.

But in both France and Britain, and in the United States as well, there were a powerful few who, following the Nazi expansion into

Eastern Europe with quiet interest, were smiling to themselves that all was going according to plan. These people — industrialists and bankers for the most part — regarded Hitler as an ally rather than an enemy. *Their* enemy was Soviet Russia. Ever since the Bolshevik revolution at the end of World War I, they had lived in a nightmare that someday communism was going to sweep out of the East like the Mongol hordes of old and bring the capitalist empire crashing to the ground. If that happened, this elite class would find themselves killed, imprisoned, or forced to live like common laborers. While they still had their money and power, the men were determined to see that nothing of the sort happened. Their remedy was to encourage, secretly but efficiently, the buildup of strong, military-oriented regimes in Central Europe — forces capable of halting the Russians before they reached Western Europe, forces that might themselves expand eastward and crush the communists in their own Russian homeland.

To these Americans and Western Europeans, then, Hitler in Germany and Mussolini in Italy were not enemies but protectors. Call them National Socialists, Fascists, or what you would, they were leaders of corporate states dedicated to putting down communism and making Europe safe for corporate investment. Some industrialists in the United States and Europe had helped Hitler and Mussolini rise to power. Henry Ford and Adolf Hitler had a mutual admiration society: Hitler had copied Ford's mass production techniques in building the Third Reich's military strength, and he kept a picture of Ford on his office wall. Ford sent Hitler a present of fifty thousand Reichsmarks every year on his birthday.

Many other heads of corporations admired the German leader's style and sent their representatives to make deals with large German corporations. Several of the Standard Oil companies and Rockefeller-controlled banks, along with the Du Pont Company, International Telephone and Telegraph (ITT), and others had close business ties to the Nazi regime.

Some political leaders in the United States and Britain, on the other hand, were much concerned about the rise of Nazism and fascism. President Roosevelt viewed Mussolini and Hitler as threats to world peace, and Winston Churchill feared Axis expansion southward into the Mideast and North Africa, which could cut off Britain's oil supplies.

During the late thirties, arguments for and against Hitler and

Mussolini had grown ever more heated in the Western countries, with the political left decrying the Axis chiefs as dangerous dictators and the right defending them as the wave of the future and valuable allies in the struggle against communism.

Then, in August of 1939, Hitler confounded his defenders by signing a nonaggression pact with the Russians and by invading Poland on September 1. Britain and France now had no choice; they had signed a treaty to defend Poland if that country was attacked. Two days after Hitler's invasion, they declared war on Germany.

Hitler had hoped this wouldn't happen. He admired Britain and had made frequent overtures to the British to join him in an alliance against Russia. Many British conservatives, along with many Americans of the same political leanings, considered this a possibility. They had visions of a world controlled by five major powers: Britain would keep its empire; the United States would control the Western Hemisphere; Japan would govern the Far East, including China; Germany and Italy would rule Europe (including Russia), Africa, and the Near East.

But the current political leaders of the United States and Britain did not subscribe to this thinking. Churchill, though he did not like the Russians, felt Nazi Germany to be an even greater threat. Roosevelt was of a similar mind. Hitler, he knew, had designs on Latin America and constituted a definite threat to U.S. supplies of raw materials from that area. Nor could the Japanese be trusted to stay on their side of the Pacific. Britain and the United States had to form their own alliance against Germany and Japan, even if it meant siding with the Russians.

British and American conservatives were now caught in a dilemma. Having helped create the monster that was Hitler, they could either band together and destroy him, or they could try to persuade their fellow countrymen to reject Churchill's and Roosevelt's position and join with the Axis to defeat Russia. President Roosevelt had no doubt where *his* loyalties lay. He had pledged Churchill "all aid short of war," and had every intention of fulfilling his promise.

Much of the need was for ships. During the first four months of the war, the Allies lost half a million tons of shipping, mostly to German submarines and surface raiders. Britain, in order to maintain her lifeline to the Mideast oil fields, needed tankers, and needed them fast. British shipyards were running around the clock but couldn't build ships nearly as fast as the Germans could destroy them. American yards had to pick up the slack.

Government-run shipyards in the United States were already working at full capacity. In order to get more building ways, the Navy started taking over privately owned yards for the duration of the war. One of the yards requisitioned was at Little Branch, Virginia, just outside Norfolk; Daniel K. Ludwig had recently leased it from the Pennsylvania Railroad as a site for converting the war-surplus freighters he'd bought from Maritime into bulk carriers. He had completed all but one, and was just putting the finishing touches on the *William Penn,* when the Navy notified him that it needed his yard and he would have to move.

By luck, he had not yet started work on the new tanker he had promised to build for Maritime in return for being released from the *Invincible* contract. Moving out of Little Branch, then, was mainly a matter of transferring some heavy equipment and sailing the *Penn* to another yard where she could be completed. The question was where to go.

By now, Ludwig had enough contacts in Washington that he could always find a string to pull. Using his influence with the War Department, he was soon able to locate space on a section of the Norfolk Army Base where the James River flows into Chesapeake Bay. By July 1, 1940, he had transferred his entire operation to this new site and was ready to resume work on the *Penn.*

All, however, was not going smoothly. Although he always seemed to get along well with the War Department, he was having another of his spats with Maritime. As usual, the issue was money. The commission, under pressure from seafarers' unions, was insisting that D.K. make improvements in the *Penn*'s officer and crew quarters so that they would be fit for human habitation. Ludwig was balking.

It was necessary to spend money to keep his ships running. This was an investment which would produce additional income, but making the officers and crews of those ships more comfortable would not earn Ludwig an extra dime. Wagner wrote to Huntington Morse that National Bulk Carriers was sorry, but it was not going to make the changes.

Several days later, D.K. was called to Washington to confer with the commission's Crew's Quarters Committee, which had initiated the suggested changes. A memo in the commission's files, dated July 5, 1940, recounts a stormy meeting. Ludwig and Malone sat on one side of a conference table. On the other side were three committee members, J. A. McKeown, F. F. King, and L. E. Weaver. They shoved across the table a paper containing a list of improvements Ludwig would have to make on the *Penn* if he was to get her through Maritime inspection. D.K. reported that, according to his contract, he did not have to meet the standards until twelve months after taking delivery of the ship, and he was damned if he was going to make the changes until after the *Penn* had had her sea trials.

Next day, one of the committee members, King, sent Ludwig a shortened list of things that had to be done before the commission would certify the *Penn* as an approved American flag vessel. The committee was aware, King said, that the vessel in question was old and small. Nevertheless, her officers and crew were entitled to reasonable space and comfort. D.K. was to install decent metal bunks or berths and adequate drawer space in the officers' and crew's quarters. Also, he was to equip each mess with a refrigerator, a drinking fountain, and a sink large enough to accommodate the appropriate number of dishes.

Even with these improvements, King added, the *Penn*'s living area would not be up to Maritime's usual standards, but they would suffice to get the ship through inspection. To reinforce the Crew's Quarters Committee's recommendations, Commander Howard Vickery, who had never gotten along well with Ludwig, wrote a strongly worded letter emphasizing that D.K. had to comply if he wanted the *Penn* approved. Ludwig grudgingly agreed to make the improvements, but at a later date.

Ludwig's stinginess would become legendary in the shipping industry. Even Dero Saunders, who held Ludwig in awe, felt compelled to comment on it: "The captain of a Ludwig ship sleeps in a bunk, not a bed; he has but two easy chairs in his cabin, which has plain, durable linoleum on the deck. Luxuries like the white carpeting in the owner's suite on Niarchos' *World Glory* are not to be found on a Ludwig ship — which would never have an owner's suite anyway."

Nor did D.K. mellow as he grew richer and older. A 1970 *Time* article remarked: "Few, if any, of the [Ludwig] ships have air conditioning, and none has the swimming pool for the crew that is common on ships owned by less parsimonious men."

A little later the author Kenneth Lamott wrote: "When I asked a friend of mine who used to sail on tankers what he thought of Ludwig, he almost dropped his drink in the violence of his reaction. Respectable tankermen, I gathered, looked on Ludwig's ships as hardly more humane than the ships of the African slave trade. In fact, except for the officers, American seamen are never tempted to sign on any of Ludwig's ships."

Over the years, Ludwig earned the reputation of being the Scrooge of the shipping industry. One of his employees, a story goes, on being asked to suggest a design for a fleet flag symbolizing the Ludwig enterprises, submitted a drawing of two hands stretching a rubber dollar bill.

Some years later, the captain of a Ludwig ship made the extravagant mistake of mailing in a report of several pages held together by a paper clip. He received a sharp rebuke for his prodigality: "We do not pay to send ironmongery by air mail!"

Ludwig was not the only shipper noted for stinginess. Back during the Depression, it is said, Stavros Livanos answered one crewman who complained about his meager wage: "Look, maybe it's only one pound a month. But in a thousand months that would be a thousand pounds. If you saved your money, think what you could do with a thousand pounds!"

D.K.'s tightfistedness, however, persisted after the Depression, putting him in sharp contrast to such free spenders as Onassis and Niarchos. It also was largely responsible for many of his innovations in the shipbuilding industry.

One technique he did not originate but did pioneer and help make standard in the industry was welding ship seams together rather than riveting them. All-welded ships were being produced in British yards during the mid-1930s, and Ludwig relied on a similar technique in his renovation work. His experience in 1926 on the *Phoenix* had convinced him of the wisdom of this method. And his naming the shipbuilding operation Welding Shipyard shows that he intended to set himself apart from other American yards, which were still riveting.

Another motivation, in addition to safety, was certainly cost; it was cheaper to weld seams than to rivet them. Other yards eventually learned the lessons Ludwig had, and during the course of World War II nearly all American shipyards laid off Rosie the Riveter and replaced her with Wanda the Welder.

One more Ludwig innovation was the launching of ships sideways off a dock rather than stern-first out of a building way. Necessity played a large role in this invention. When D.K. was forced to move out of his Little Branch shipyard to the Norfolk Army Base, he was hampered by the lack of a building way on the new site. Installing one would be time-consuming and expensive, and since he was only leasing the property, he was not eager to add a permanent facility he would have to leave behind on his next move.

His solution was simply to lay the keel of his new tanker atop the existing dock and, when the ship was finished, remove the props and let her drop over into the water. The method was effective if somewhat undignified. Certainly it did not lend itself to the sort of ceremony frequently shown in contemporary newsreels, in which an expensively dressed woman broke a bottle of champagne over the prow just before the new vessel started to slide out of the way and into the water. Had any woman tried such a christening at one of Ludwig's tanker launchings at the Norfolk Army Base yard, she would have been guaranteed a good soaking. But D.K. was not one for ceremony anyway; his launchings were always private affairs.

Most of Ludwig's shipbuilding innovations were aimed toward a single goal: increasing payload without increasing cost. He was ever on the lookout for ways to reduce tanker design to the bare-bones minimum. His ships, for example, had much thinner decks than the industry standard — a modification that meant less weight and a smaller fuel bill.

Another cost cutter and weight saver was D.K.'s elimination of all but a single stack on his vessels. Most ships at the time were equipped with two or three rakish stacks, which gave a pleasing symmetry but had little function once modern propulsion systems replaced the old steam engines. Ludwig was among the first builders to realize that a ship did not need more than one stack.

One of his ideas that did *not* work led to another that *did*. After realizing that the mast on a modern ship was only a long, hollow cylinder of heavy steel, Ludwig asked his marine architect, George Drake, to design a mast capable of being filled with oil. There was no sense in hauling a mast full of nothing but air all the way across thousands of miles of ocean. When Drake reported that such a design was neither practical nor cost-effective, Ludwig decided to eliminate masts from his future ships and install small, thin pipes just strong enough to carry the required running lights.

D.K.'s ridding his ships of any feature that did not contribute to profits pleased his own obsessive sense of economy and kept him a step ahead of the competition. When someone asked why he didn't put a grand piano aboard his ships, as Stavros Niarchos did, Ludwig snapped, "You can't carry oil in a grand piano."

The Ludwig presence was not immediately visible in D.K.'s first shipbuilding (as opposed to ship-renovating) company. Welding Shipyard, Inc., was incorporated in Delaware in November 1938, with headquarters in New York. Its first officers were H. R. Ryan, B. E. Slocum, and I. M. Halfpenny. After a few months, the address was shifted to 4655 Stenton Avenue in northwest Philadelphia. This was just above Fairmount Park and not near a river or dock area, so it must have been only an office.

The company also got a new set of officers, but Ludwig still wasn't visible. John B. Hendrickson was now president, Charles L. McCormick was vice-president and treasurer, and Clarence W. Smith was secretary. This organization was maintained for a few years while the real Welding Shipyard was being established near Norfolk.

After getting in place at the Army base and putting the final touches on the *Penn,* Welding finally got around to the work for which it had been started — building new tankers. The first ship on line in 1940 was the tanker D.K. had promised Maritime he would build as a trade-off on the *Invincible* contract. She was to be large — 10,731 gross tons and better than 17,000 deadweight tons — and fast — powered by 9430-horsepower engines capable of pushing her to a cruising speed of over sixteen knots.

No major problems were encountered during construction, and in the spring of 1941, the first ship Ludwig ever built from scratch was ready for launch. Named the *Virginia,* in honor of the state where she was built, she was put through trials, approved by Maritime, and immediately put into service hauling oil for Pan American Petroleum & Transport.

Soon after the *Virginia* was launched, Ludwig started another ship — the little tanker he had offered to build to sweeten the pot in the *Invincible* trade-off. Ultimately this offer had not been part of the final deal, and his building the vessel anyway demonstrates that he had intended to, regardless of how the *Invincible* affair turned out.

This small ship — 8000 gross tons, 12,000 deadweight — was called the *Bulkoil,* a name D.K. briefly had used for the converted

*Daniel Webster* before rechristening that ship the *Pan Carolina.* The little tanker was nearly finished when, on December 7, 1941, the Japanese bombed Pearl Harbor and wiped out much of the U.S. Pacific fleet. America, after having maintained at least an official neutrality for more than two years, was now at war, not only with Japan but also with Germany and Italy, both of which had signed a secret pact with the Japanese to act in concert should hostilities break out in the Pacific.

The rules of the shipping game were now abruptly changed. For Ludwig, it meant that his charters with Pan American P & T were null and void for the duration of the war, with less than half their terms completed. The government requisitioned all the oceangoing vessels D.K. owned, as it did most merchant ships flying the American flag. The War Department, with the cooperation of the Department of Commerce, set up the War Shipping Administration as part of the Maritime Commission to oversee and coordinate wartime merchant-shipping activities. To handle oil transport, a three-way partnership evolved among the WSA, the major oil companies, and the tanker operators. To haul the petroleum being supplied to the government by the oil majors — at a healthy price, of course — the War Shipping Administration requisitioned tankers from private owners but allowed the shippers, as newly appointed agents of the government, to continue operating their own vessels under an arrangement called the General Agency Agreement.

In some ways, then, things had not changed much. The shippers were still plying their trade, just as they had under charter to oil companies. The main difference was that the WSA now determined the destination of the cargo. The government was also paying the bills — setting up joint accounts with ship owners and depositing, every two months or so, whatever money the shippers needed to meet expenses and make a profit.

Another difference, of course, was that the Atlantic now bristled with the periscopes of Nazi U-boats, whose main purpose was to disrupt Allied supply lines. On February 19, 1942, D.K. lost his first ship of the war. The bulk carrier *Pan Massachusetts,* which he had converted from the World War I freighter *Triumph,* was torpedoed and sunk on her way to Europe. Three months later the *Virginia* met the same fate, just weeks after being requisitioned by the WSA. Ludwig lost one more ship during the war: the *Pan Pennsylvania* hit an enemy mine on April 16, 1944, just a year after Welding Shipyard had built her.

By April 20, 1942, the WSA had taken over all of Ludwig's fleet except the little Great Lakes vessel *Transoil.* (What happened to the tanker *Transford II* is not clear. D.K. had tried to get it transferred to alien registry as part of the *Invincible* deal. Perhaps he succeeded. Or maybe he sold it.) On the list of appropriated tankers and bulk carriers were the *Caliche, Chiloil, Pan Carolina, Pan Delaware, Pan Georgia, Pan Virginia, Petrofuel, Phoenix, Virginia, William C. McTarnahan,* and *William Penn.* Two of these, the *Petrofuel* and *McTarnahan,* were recent acquisitions. The rest, except for the newly built *Virginia,* were renovated ships Ludwig had had before the war started.

Chartering his ships to the government instead of to privately owned oil companies was to prove exceedingly profitable for Ludwig. In prewar days, with its ships under charter to Pan American P & T, National Bulk Carriers had been projecting profits of about $850,000 a year for the period 1939 to 1946. Now, with the war going on, the company was looking at profits of well over $1 million a year. The government paid D.K. as much as $84,600 *per month* for each of his ships, even at the beginning of the conflict.

One disadvantage of working for the government, though, was the large amount of paperwork involved. The bureaucrats wanted everything documented in multiple copies, and Ludwig, with his small staff, was having trouble staying abreast of the record keeping. Part of the problem was that he was trying to run too many companies. Earlier, and especially with the firms his father had helped start, he had usually set up a new corporation to run each new ship acquired. When he was a small operator, this was a useful way to hide assets. Now that he was larger, and a government contractor, it was too cumbersome. If he was going to get the job done, he would have to consolidate and streamline.

In May 1942 he had three of his companies transfer ownership of their tankers to National Bulk as a way of cutting down the bookkeeping. Tankers Oceanic, American Petroleum Transport, and Phoenix Steamship gave up title to the *Chiloil, Caliche,* and *Phoenix* respectively and became inactive corporations.

Before the *Phoenix* transfer became effective, though, D.K. decided to sell the ship. He and the old tanker had been together a long time. He had owned at least a share of her since 1925, when he became a partner in American Tankers of Massachusetts. She was the first large ship he had been associated with, and she had almost killed him in 1926 when her tanks had blown. Despite occasional periods of idleness, she had performed well since then, and had paid back her original purchase price of $57,000 several times over.

But she was showing her age now and was no match, either in size or speed, for the other vessels in his growing fleet. In a few years at best, he would have to scrap her. Now, while there was a shortage of tankships and he had a good offer, was the right time to sell.

The records say that the *Phoenix*'s buyer was an Argentine company called Sud Americano de Vapores, S.A. (*Vapores* means "steamship" as well as "steam.") In reality, the purchasers were a consortium that included two of the investors who had just bought the *Ulysses* from Western Operating — Aristotle Onassis and Stavros Niarchos. The two young Greeks each owned 40 percent of Sud Americano de Vapores, with the remaining 20 percent divided among Catherine Negroponte (11 percent), wife of another wealthy Greek shipper and a relative of Niarchos; a Captain Scoufopoulos, Niarchos's commander in the Greek Navy (6 percent); and a Captain Georgeacopoulos, another Greek naval officer with close ties to Niarchos (3 percent).

Tankers were scarce in the early days of the war, and the Greeks were buying anything they could get their hands on, even if it was old and worn. They were willing to pay Ludwig $465,000 cash for the ancient *Phoenix,* and he had no objection to selling, even to an Argentine company that might use the tanker to supply oil to the nation's enemies.

By late 1942, D.K. had pared down his corporate structure. National Bulk Carriers was his lead company, in charge of operating the tankers the WSA requisitioned from him and contracting for new ones.

Four years after its founding, Welding was finally looking like a Ludwig company. Hendrickson was still nominally president, but D.K. was now listed as a director and vice-president, J. A. W. Richardson (of Chemical Bank) was a director, Stuart Betts and Robert Malone were vice-presidents, and William W. Wagner was assistant treasurer and comptroller. Most of D.K.'s other corporations were currently inactive. National Petroleum Transport was still operating the *Transoil* in the Great Lakes, but American Petroleum Transport, the Transford Corporation, Tankers Oceanic, and Phoenix Steamship, with no vessels to run, existed mainly on paper.

In December 1942, though, Ludwig decided to reactivate American Petroleum Transport. The reason was that the War Shipping Administration, wanting to increase oil shipments to Europe and elsewhere, asked whether National Bulk, in addition to the ships it was presently operating under the General Agency Agreement, could run a number of government-owned tankers — perhaps twenty or thirty — under the Tanker Service Agreement.

Ludwig was eager to get the additional business, because it would substantially increase his revenues, but he had Wagner ask whether APTC could do the work instead, since National Bulk was "engaged in a heavy construction project at the present time." The switch would make little difference to the government, Wagner pointed out: APTC operated from the same office as National Bulk, had the same staff, and would be able to handle the operation of a large number of tankers.

Thus Ludwig, using APTC, came to operate many government-owned tankers — more than thirty by 1945 — in addition to his own ships, which were being run through National Bulk. Like his other government contracts, this one would be lucrative. The accounts National Bulk was jointly maintaining with the WSA at Chemical Bank and the Bank of the Manhattan were bulging with money. At one point late in 1942, Wagner had notified a government auditor that it was fine if the government withdrew $300,000 from each account; National Bulk was "presently carrying large cash balances at both of our depositories, so it won't hamper our operations at all."

Under the Tanker Service Agreement, APTC would set up similar joint accounts with the government, and the WSA would make regular deposits, based on Ludwig's estimates of what it cost to run the ships. Initially there was a balance of $100,000, but as a result of Wagner's persistent requests, this soon grew to more than $1 million, from which D.K. was free to draw and run the ships as cheaply as he could, pocketing the rest.

But though it paid well, working for the government did entail occasional inconveniences. Late in 1942, just after he had completed his third ship and second large tanker at the Norfolk yard (he named this one the *Virginia* to commemorate the one sunk a few months earlier), Ludwig was notified that he would have to move his ship-building operation again. The Navy wanted the Army base site for building warships.

There was nothing to do but comply. After a few hassles with the Navy, during which he was admonished to "clean up unsightly debris" and restore the site to its former condition of neatness, D.K. found a small strip of land at nearby Sewalls Point, midway between Virginian Railway's coal-loading docks and the Norfolk Naval Base, and started to move Welding Shipyard there. He had less room than before, and only a single building way, but the smallness was actually an advantage. The new location was too cramped to be of interest to the Navy, so Ludwig would be able to build ships here for the rest of the war and several years beyond.

By the spring of 1943, D.K. had completed the move to Sewalls Point and was building tankers of the *Virginia* type. These 18,500-tonners were more than 2000 tons larger than conventional T-2 and T-3 tankers most other American yards were building, and were classified as T-3s of a special sort. Ludwig was holding to his conviction that bigger is better — that larger ships were more economical to operate than smaller ones.

In 1943 Welding Shipyard built three more of these ships, all nearly identical: *Pan Massachusetts* (named for a previously lost bulk carrier), *Pan Pennsylvania* (his older ship of this name had been rechristened *Petrofuel*), and *Bulklube*. All were contracted by National Bulk, using the Maritime Commission as middleman, and all were requisitioned by the WSA when built, which then assigned them to National Bulk to operate.

The financial arrangements involved in this roundabout scheme are worth examining. National Bulk, in effect, was buying ships from itself, and laying in profit at both ends, all with the consent and cooperation of the Maritime Commission and the War Shipping Administration.

At National Bulk's end, the mechanism was the construction reserve funds the company had opened jointly with the government at Chemical Bank and the Bank of Manhattan. Any money Ludwig made from his wartime activities he could deposit in these funds and avoid paying taxes on it. He could then use it to pay Welding Ship-yard — himself — to build new tankers and could write up the bill at that end any way he pleased, as long as it was not absurdly out of line.

Like the Rockefeller organization, D.K. had mastered the practice of keeping his money by transferring it from one pocket — one company — to another while appearing to spend it. And as the tax-exempt cash flowed out of the National Bulk–WSA accounts to Welding Shipyard, the government agencies were providing Ludwig with exceedingly profitable ways of replacing it. The WSA agreed to buy some of his older ships at inflated prices, and Maritime allowed him to trade in others on new construction at similarly high rates — eight to ten times what the vessels were actually worth.

The Maritime Commission, which had been created to replace the corrupt U.S. Shipping Board, was now itself rank with corruption. Under the guise of procurer of merchant shipping for wartime, it had become a cornucopia of profits for wily ship owners — Ludwig included — eager to dip into the U.S. Treasury.

Vermont's Senator George Aiken, a fiscal conservative, after probing into Maritime's financial records during 1943, charged that the agency had misspent $6 billion of taxpayers' money in overpayments to ship owners and shipbuilders. With the war going on and most elected officials either preoccupied with other matters or compromised themselves, Aiken could get little support among his fellow senators for a full-scale investigation. But he did produce enough hard evidence to persuade Auditor General Lindsay Warren, chief of the General Accounting Office, to initiate an audit of the Maritime Commission's books.

A GAO team of auditors confirmed Aiken's charges, wrote a scathing report on the glaring shortcomings in Maritime's bookkeeping practices, and sent it to Admiral Land, chief executive officer of both the commission and the WSA. Land promptly deep-sixed it, and no significant corrective action was taken.

Meanwhile, Ludwig was selling — at obscenely high prices — four of his old tankers to the WSA (the *Transoil,* the *William C. McTarnahan* — now renamed the *St. James* — the *Caliche,* and the *Bulkoil*), and trading in — at bloated rates — five other old ships (the *Chiloil, Pan Carolina, Pan Georgia, Pan Virginia,* and *William Penn*) to Maritime for allowances on new construction. These were precisely the kinds of deals Aiken had raised an alarm about, but almost no one was paying heed.

When trading in its old tankers to Maritime, National Bulk was required to fill out a form indicating how its stock was distributed. Ludwig's answers show how he had divided the shares of his chief company. As of May 21, 1943, National Bulk had 3810 shares of common (voting) stock outstanding and 3555 shares of preferred. D.K. owned 3808 shares of the common in his own name, allowing Wagner and Schober to hold one share each for tax purposes. Of the preferred, Wagner owned 200 shares, and American Petroleum Transport held the other 3355. This company had issued 200 shares of stock, of which Ludwig held 198 and Wagner and Schober a single share apiece. Since Tankers Oceanic was still owner of record of the *Chiloil,* one of the ships being traded in, its stock distribution was listed as well. True to form, the company had 250 shares outstanding, with D.K. owning 248 and Wagner and Schober one each.

Although Ludwig's exact worth at this time is difficult to assess, it is safe to say he was now a millionaire several times over. He was sole owner of several prospering companies and was operating a growing fleet of tankers, each one earning $1 million or more a year. In less than a decade, thanks to his father, his Rockefeller connections, and a world war, he had climbed out of a deep hole of debt and was now sitting well up the mountain.

At about this time, Ludwig decided to move to a new home. Since 1939, he had given his address on corporate forms as Darien. The community, less than forty miles from his Manhattan offices, was, and is, a small, wealthy commuter town between Stamford (where D.K. and his father had lived earlier) and Norwalk.

As of 1943, Ludwig changed his address to Noroton, an even smaller, wealthier town adjoining Darien. He was listed as living on Swifts Lane, a short street that ended at a branch of Long Island Sound in the most exclusive part of the posh community. (In 1960, he again listed his address as Darien, but this probably represented no change of domicile. At that time the Noroton business district was demolished to make way for the Connecticut Turnpike, and the town's residential areas were annexed to Darien.)

In Darien and later in Noroton, Daniel and Ginger Ludwig seem to have taken no active part in the life of their community. They kept aloof, refraining from socializing even casually with their neighbors. One local resident described seeing D.K. walking around his yard once, scowling at the crabgrass. But a next-door neighbor of seventeen years, Mrs. Edward P. Moore, confessed to a reporter that she would not have recognized the Ludwigs on sight: "They hardly ever came out of the house. They just kept to themselves."

Another neighbor confirmed this: "We almost never saw them. They never came to cocktail parties around town or anything like that. Nobody knew exactly who they were. I always thought he was some kind of bank executive — you know, a salary guy, maybe forty grand, nobody very important."

So successful was D.K. at maintaining his anonymity that he could ride the New Haven Railroad commuter train to and from Manhattan every working day, unnoticed and inconspicuous even in later years, when he was one of the richest men in the world. This invisibility suited him fine. He hated nothing more than public attention. But it must have been a very lonely life for Ginger.

The Ludwigs' house in Noroton has been described as comfortable without being ostentatious — not the sort of dwelling an exceedingly wealthy man might be expected to live in. But D.K. was concerned with the wealth itself, not its trappings. Making money, not spending it, was his passion, and he could do that much better if most people didn't give him a passing glance.

By 1944 the tide of war was beginning to turn. The Allies had chased Field Marshal Erwin Rommel out of North Africa and were taking the offensive, with invasions of Sicily, Italy, and — on June 6 — the coast of Normandy. In the Pacific, U.S. warships had destroyed much of the Japanese fleet, and assault forces were recapturing, in one bloody battle after another, the islands Japan had taken earlier.

During this year, Ludwig, through National Bulk Carriers and American Petroleum Transport, was busy operating more than forty tankers for the government, and Welding Shipyard was building three more *Virginia*-type tankers — the *Bulkfuel, Bulkcrude,* and *Bulkero* — and starting construction on the first of a new design with much greater capacity than its predecessors. This new tanker was 23,600 deadweight tons — a third larger than conventional T-2s and 5000 tons bigger than the *Virginia*-type vessels. It was also faster. Its 13,200-horsepower engines could attain speeds of more than eighteen knots.

In building this bigger ship, Ludwig may well have been looking ahead, past the end of the war, to a time when Europe and Asia, needing to rebuild their shattered industries, would require vast quantities of petroleum products hauled from abroad. If he had bigger ships than his competitors, he would be in excellent shape to win a significant portion of this business and reap the rewards of his foresight.

He named his new tanker the *Phoenix,* in memory of the old ship, and soon followed up with three more of the same size: the *Nashbulk, Amtank,* and *Hampton Roads.* Before he finished the last one, the war was over.

Steady Allied bombing of German factories, cities, and transportation lines had taken a heavy toll. On the eastern front, the Russians had finally stopped the Nazi advance at Stalingrad and pushed westward. Hitler committed suicide in his Berlin bunker on April 30, 1945, just eighteen days after President Franklin D. Roosevelt died of a stroke in Warm Springs. On May 8, the German government ratified an unconditional surrender to the Allies, bringing the war in Europe to an end.

The United States then turned its full attention to the Pacific. In August, President Harry S Truman ordered atomic bombs dropped on the cities of Hiroshima and Nagasaki, and shortly afterward Japan surrendered unconditionally. On September 2, 1945, six years plus one day after Germany's invasion of Poland, World War II was formally terminated with the signing of surrender documents aboard the battleship *Missouri* off the Japanese coast.

In America there was dancing in the streets. The war was over, the boys were coming home, the women could leave their factory jobs and become housewives again, and the enormous wartime bureaucracy could begin unwinding.

Where shipping was concerned, this would be a very gradual process. Traffic was still heavy across the Atlantic and Pacific, what with returning servicemen and vast amounts of vital supplies still needed in war-torn areas. Under the Tanker Service Agreement, Ludwig's American Petroleum Transport would continue for several more years to operate government-owned tankers carrying oil abroad.

For Ludwig's other companies — chiefly National Bulk and Welding Shipyard — the end of the war signaled a time for settling accounts. Welding had to be decommissioned as a government-contract shipyard, and the federally owned surplus materials there had to be disposed of in an approved manner.

At most yards this was routine, but in D.K.'s case it proved to be something of a problem. The reason was that, as usual, he had demanded and received special treatment. During the course of the war, at his insistence, he had been allowed to operate without government inspectors on site. How he managed to arrange this is not in Maritime records, but a November 28, 1945, wire from a Maritime inspector to the commission's general counsel discussed the problem. After remarking that, in most yards, qualified inspectors must approve disposal of surplus materials, the telegram continued:

> HOWEVER, THE SITUATION IN WELDING SHIPYARD, INC., NORFOLK, VIRGINIA, IS DIFFERENT IN THAT NO REPRESENTATIVES OF THE CONSTRUCTION OFFICE ARE OR HAVE BEEN STATIONED IN THAT YARD. . . . PLEASE ADVISE HOW YOU WISH WELDING SHIPYARD SITUATION HANDLED, AND WHETHER YOU DESIRE ANY CHANGE IN THE PROCEDURE WITH OTHER SHIPYARDS.

Maritime, having granted Ludwig the special privilege of running his yard without government inspectors to oversee operations, was not going to cause him any problems now. The general counsel advised the inquiring inspector to work things out with Welding Shipyard's management in the simplest way possible.

Other records in Maritime files show that the commission bent over backward during this period to give Ludwig every break possible. For instance, when National Bulk tried to close the joint account at Chemical Bank it had maintained with the government — an account that had been inactive since mid-1943 and showed a balance of only $295.55 — a Maritime official pointed out to Wagner that further tax advantages might be gained by keeping the account open, and the National Bulk vice-president gratefully — and hastily — withdrew the request.

This particular account had been used only briefly. Early in the war, Ludwig made two large deposits — a $1 million insurance settlement he had received for loss of the *Pan Massachusetts* and $2.25 million he had been paid for selling the little tanker *Bulkoil* to the WSA. Soon after, he withdrew $3,332,000 to pay Welding Shipyard for new tanker construction and just about cleaned out the account. There were other accounts to settle, including several claims by companies National Bulk had employed as agents overseas. When Maritime asked for a list of Ludwig's foreign affiliates, Wagner responded with a roster showing that D.K. had been closely tied to Standard of New Jersey and several of its overseas subsidiaries and agents: Asiatic Petroleum, Panama Agencies, Anglo-American Oil, Furness Withy, Ltd., and others. National Bulk's tankers had been hauling oil mainly from refineries in Aruba and Curaçao to Europe, Canada, South America, the Canal Zone, the Middle East, and the Far East.

If Maritime needed things from Ludwig, Ludwig needed things from Maritime as well — namely, war-surplus ships. What was to become of all the tankers idled by the war's end? He had started in the tanker business by taking World War I surplus vessels and renovating them. Now there would be more surplus ships available, and he was in a far better position to exploit the situation.

The end of World War II saw Ludwig with an impressive tanker fleet. In numbers alone, his gains were not impressive. At the start of the war, he had nine ships, had added fifteen, lost, sold, or traded thirteen, and ended with eleven. But these figures did not tell the real story. In 1939 his ships were mostly twenty-year-old hulls he had remodeled into tankers or bulk carriers after most of their useful life was behind them. In 1946 his eleven-vessel fleet — with the lone exception of the *Pan Delaware* — was composed of large, fast ships built in his own yard from his own designs, and none was over five years old. And though he had only two more ships in 1946 than in 1939, his cargo capacity had more than doubled. The 1939 fleet had totaled 94,000 deadweight tons; his current fleet was over 207,000. So, having gone into the war with a handful of old remodeled vessels, D.K. had come out with the fifth largest private independent tanker fleet in the United States, and all of his ships were fully employed for the foreseeable future.

He wanted more. His first priorities were to get back the other two ships he had built during the war. The little *Bulkoil* he sold the WSA in 1942 for $2.25 million might soon be available, and the *Hampton Roads* was still sitting unfinished at his Sewalls Point yard near Norfolk. (Although the WSA had requisitioned his other ships, he retained title to them under the General Agency Agreement.) Once he had all his own ships back, he wanted as many surplus tankers as he could manage and find charters for. Oil transportation was booming in the postwar years, and the more ships he had, the richer he could become.

At the time, bills had just been introduced into both houses of Congress setting standards for disposing of war-surplus vessels. Included in the legislation was a pricing system based on a percentage of the prewar market value of each class of ship to be offered for sale. For example, if a T-2 tanker had been selling in 1939 for $1.9 million, a surplus tanker of the same type would be offered in 1946 for a specified fraction of that amount. This was its statutory price. Below that, a floor price could be pegged to leave some room for bargaining.

In the cases of the *Bulkoil* and *Hampton Roads,* prices could not be set in this manner, since neither tanker was of a standard type that had existed before the war. But Ludwig was nevertheless intensely interested in the surplus ship sales legislation, since it would set prices for other tankers he might be buying from Maritime.

After the two similar but slightly different bills passed the House and Senate, D.K. wrote a lengthy letter to Lieutenant William A. Weber, Maritime's point man on the legislation, stating what he wanted the commission to push for in the compromise version. One of his concerns was that Liberty ships, which had been mass-produced cheaply and in great numbers toward the end of the war, would be sold at surplus at such low prices that they would tempt many small entrepreneurs into a market presently controlled by a few large shippers, including himself. He wrote, in part:

> As the Bill is now set up I feel these vessels will be so cheaply priced that they will be sold, which will result in retarding the sale of the T-2s, and also depress the tanker chartering market which, naturally, we are most interested in. I am certain that it is not the intent of Congress that a vessel, put together merely as a makeshift, should be priced at a figure so far out of line that it will prohibit the main purpose of the Bill, namely, the disposal of the T-2 fleet. . . .
>
> I am enclosing our thoughts on the subject, which I think will correct this condition.
>
> I would like to discuss this matter with you in further detail on my next visit to Washington. . . .

The suggestions D.K. wrote to Weber, most of which found their way into the final version of the bill — the Merchant Ship Sales Act of 1946 — were aimed, first, at distinguishing between Liberty dry-cargo vessels and Liberty tankers; second, at making sure that the Liberty tankers were sold at a high enough price to obviate serious competition with his own tankers; and third, at forbidding buyers of cheap Liberty dry-cargo vessels from converting them into tankers. In insisting on this last point, Ludwig was closing off to other shippers the very path he had followed after World War I.

Even before the legislation passed, Ludwig asked Maritime for an application form to submit toward purchase of the *Hampton Roads.* He assured the commission that he did not intend to file until the bill was law, but he wanted to have everything ready to move as quickly as possible. Soon after, he asked for similar forms to submit for the *Bulkoil* and for immediate notification when Maritime put any T-2s or T-3s up for sale.

There were two reasons for D.K.'s haste. If he delayed, some other shipper might get the ships first. Second, the boom market would last only a few years, and he wanted to put as many tankers in service as he could while charter rates were still high. He currently had five of his ships out on charter to major oil companies and the remaining six running single-voyage "spot" charters (so called because they were based on the spot price of oil on the commodities market) at high rates. Normally Ludwig did not trust the spot market, preferring the security of long-term charters, but he wasn't going to pass up sure money.

While he was trying to buy more tankers, D.K. was also reactivating Welding Shipyard to build more. Plans for the "world's biggest tanker" were already on National Bulk's drawing board — a 28,000-tonner he was going to name the *Ulysses,* in memory of his earlier ship. He expected to submit plans for four even larger vessels — 30,000-tonners nearly twice the size of the T-2s and T-3s he was trying to buy. Except in the case of the little *Bulkoil,* "bigger is better" remained Ludwig's rule of thumb in tanker construction. Now that the war was over and he had plenty of money, he planned to show other shipbuilders exactly what this could mean. He intended having the largest tanker fleet in the world, both in number and size of ships.

These ambitious expansion plans were causing some concern at Maritime. In May of 1946, C. G. Cornwell, acting director of the Division of Vessel Disposal and Government Aids, sent a memo to

J. M. Quinn, director of Finance for Operations, asking, in a round-about way, whether Ludwig could afford all these ships. Some of the assets National Bulk was carrying on its books, Cornwell pointed out, were unadjusted insurance claims and unexpired premiums. Besides wanting to buy T-2s and T-3s, Ludwig was now asking to build four new tankers at $1,740,000 each, with a 12.5 percent down payment. He was also buying the *Bulkoil* for $1,200,000, with 25 percent up front. Add in the *Hampton Roads,* whose price hadn't yet been determined, said Cornwell, and we're looking at mortgages approaching $10 million. Can National Bulk carry this kind of debt load?

Don't worry, Quinn replied. The company was in fine shape and could meet the payments easily. To give Cornwell a better picture, he enclosed copies of National Bulk's audits from 1939 through the first quarter of 1946. During this period, Quinn explained, the company had purchased and was purchasing a total of twelve ships through Maritime — the seven built during the war by Welding Shipyard, the *Bulkoil,* and the four newly proposed tankers.*

The first seven cost $20.8 million, of which National Bulk had already paid nearly $11 million and still owed nearly $10 million. On the four projected tankers, the total cost would be $7.2 million, with $900,000 down and $6.3 million in mortgages.† The *Bulkoil* would cost another $1.2 million, with $300,000 down and $900,000 on time.

Taking the twelve ships together, Quinn wrote Cornwell, National Bulk would have $29 million invested overall. Counting the down payments, the company would already have paid more than $12 million; the previous month, just after the audit of the first quarter of 1946, it had paid $3 million on its existing mortgages. So when the *Bulkoil* and the four new tankers were taken into the picture, National Bulk would have paid off about half its mortgages on the twelve tankers and would have $14 million left to pay over the next fifteen years. This was less than $1 million a

---

*It should be remembered that, with National Bulk buying ships from Welding Shipyard through the Maritime Commission, Ludwig was actually purchasing the ships from himself.
†This gives a good picture of the cost padding that went on at Welding during the war. National Bulk, drawing out of its construction reserve funds, paid an average of nearly $3 million per ship for its seven wartime vessels. After the war, Welding built much larger ships for $1.8 million, or 60 percent of what the wartime ships cost. On a cost-per-ton basis, Welding charged $144 per ton for its wartime ships and only $61 per ton for its postwar ones.

year, a debt the company should have no trouble handling if all its ships were employed.

Included in the package Quinn sent Cornwell was a balance sheet showing National Bulk's current assets of $30.5 million against liabilities of $25.5 million — a healthy ratio of 1.2:1. (Eight years earlier, according to a government audit, the company's balance sheet had shown assets of only $50,000 against liabilities of $400,000, a dismal ratio of 1:8. In that same year, 1938, National Bulk's total assets were just over $500,000. Now, in 1946, the total assets were nearly $43 million, with $10.5 million in capital and surplus.)

A summary of profit-and-loss statements from 1939 through the first quarter of 1946 was equally promising. In the two years before America entered the war, National Bulk had shown before-depreciation profits of around $800,000 per annum and had forecast about the same level for 1939 through 1945, based on income from chartering its vessels to Pan American P & T. But as a result of the war and the government requisitions, profits had soared. Operating as a government agent, National Bulk showed before-depreciation profits averaging more than $1.5 million a year during 1941 through 1943. In 1944 this had more than doubled, to over $3 million; in 1945 it was over $4 million. In the first quarter of 1946, the company already had more than $1 million in profits.

What Quinn showed Cornwell was that National Bulk Carriers had risen from a small struggling company in 1938 to a giant of the oil-hauling industry — a thriving, multimillion-dollar corporation — during the war years. For Quinn, this was ample reason to extend further credit and let National Bulk buy and build as many ships as it wished.

But Quinn's assessment, bright as it was, left out a most important factor. Most of National Bulk's liabilities were owed to Welding Shipyard. Thus, the figures on the debit side of National Bulk's ledger were really assets for Daniel Ludwig, who paid himself to build the tankers he operated. And since American Petroleum Transport brought in a good steady income by operating a fleet of government-owned tankers, he got additional revenue from U.S. taxpayers. Exactly how much money he made from Welding Shipyard will probably never be known; with no government inspectors at Sewalls Point to oversee construction, D.K. may have indulged in one of his chief moneymaking talents — scrounging up cheap secondhand parts from his contacts in the marine salvage business and using them in place of new machinery.

All in all, and largely as a result of his wartime activities, Daniel Ludwig was on his way toward becoming a very rich man. He was not yet in a class with J. Paul Getty or Howard Hughes, but he was headed upward and gaining steadily.

# Eight

# The Maritime Scandals

If the war years had been a period of padding and profiteering for shippers and other government contractors, the postwar years were a time of scrambling and scavenging. Ludwig and other ship owners were maneuvering to get their hands on as many surplus ships as they could grab, and the Maritime Commission was being as helpful as possible.

D.K., having submitted applications at the earliest possible moment, first wanted the *Bulkoil* and the *Hampton Roads*. As the builder, he had an inside track on both vessels. It was just a matter of filing the necessary forms and making sure he got the best deal possible.

He did not really want to keep the *Bulkoil* now; she was too small. He intended to operate bigger tankers than his competitors so as to undercut their rates. But he had a prospective buyer and could turn her over for a profit as soon as he could take possession. And the 1946 Merchant Ship Sales Act (which he himself had helped write) enabled him to buy her back for around $1 million, of which he had to put down only 25 percent.

For around $250,000 up front, he purchased the *Bulkoil* from Maritime in 1946 and immediately resold her to Sabine Transportation Company — a Pure Oil affiliate — of Port Arthur, Texas. Port Arthur was now a major oil depot from which Ludwig himself was hauling millions of barrels of petroleum in the Gulf-to-Northeast trade. It was also the town where, three decades earlier, he had had his first shipping job, as a chandler's assistant.

The second of his government-owned ships was one D.K. *did* plan to use. The *Hampton Roads,* last and largest of the tankers the WSA had contracted with Ludwig to build at Sewalls Point, was sitting in the yard's only building way when the war ended, a few months from being completed. Legally, she was still the property of Welding Shipyard, but Ludwig, utilizing a provision of his contract dealing with unfinished vessels, was able to sell her to the government in September 1946 for $3 million and buy her back a few months later under the Ship Sales Act for $1.3 million, turning a quick $1.7 million profit at the expense of U.S. taxpayers.

While he was buying back his own ships, Ludwig was also maneuvering to get as many other surplus tankers as he could. He did not want shoddily built ships, like the Liberty tankers he was trying to keep out of the hands of competitors. He was after better vessels — T-1s, T-2s, T-3s, and even dry-cargo ships and small aircraft carriers that might be converted to oil haulers. In shopping for surplus ships, he gravitated toward those built by Alabama Dry Dock and Shipbuilding and a few other yards where he maintained close contacts. He had operated many of these tankers during the war through American Petroleum Transport and was thoroughly familiar with them.

By early 1947, the Sewalls Point yard was again humming with activity. In the single building way, from which the *Hampton Roads* had recently been launched, the keel had just been laid for the "world's biggest tanker" — the 28,000-ton *Ulysses.* But the rest of the yard was being used to renovate or repair an assortment of other ships D.K. had bought as surplus. He was performing a shipbuilder's version of turning swords into ploughshares by converting vessels of war into commercial oil haulers for peacetime use. But his motive may have been less pacific than pecuniary.

Many of the surplus ships needed repair work before they could be put into service, and Maritime usually contributed generously to cover the cost of repairing war damage. But there was also a clause in the purchase contracts stipulating that any materials removed from these ships during renovation had to be scrapped. This condition was now standard in Maritime ship sales contracts, but D.K. did not want to abide by it. If he could make some money by finding a buyer willing to pay more for removed parts than a scrap dealer would, why shouldn't he be allowed to do so? It was a shame to waste anything that could be turned into profit.

So when he got a particularly tempting offer, Ludwig wrote the Maritime Commission with a proposition. International Paper Company was offering to pay $100,000 for a turbine he had just removed from a damaged T-2. Let me sell the engine, D.K. said to the commission, and I'll split the proceeds with you fifty-fifty.

On its face, the offer was in violation of the contract. But the commissioners accepted Ludwig's proposition with a single modification: Maritime wanted $55,000, not $50,000. However, to make sure this extra bite did not cost D.K. anything, the commissioners suggested that he raise his price and charge International Paper $105,000.

Done and done. On these terms the deal was made. The paper company got its turbine, the commission got a nice piece of change, and Ludwig got a lot more out of the engine than he would have by selling it for scrap.

He also got something else — Maritime's permission to violate contract terms and sell excess equipment and materials for whatever he could get, as long as he was willing to cut in the agency for a share of the money. With this understanding, he was free to turn Welding's repair and renovation work into an even more profitable undertaking. To handle the sales of what he was removing from his surplus ships, D.K. set up another company, Atlas Metals Corporation, registered in Delaware but operating in New York. Until its merger intò the parent corporation, National Petroleum Transport, Atlas Metals gave Ludwig a profitable little sideline.

If he occasionally had to give something to Maritime to get what he wanted, D.K. had ways of getting it back in spades. One of the ships he bought from the commission was a damaged T-2, the *Silverpeak.* The government not only gave him a good price on the tanker but allowed him a subsidy of $207,000 to repair it — $111,000 to fix the hull and $96,000 to install a new engine and generator, to be supplied from Maritime stockpiles.

After purchasing the *Silverpeak,* Ludwig notified the commissioners that he had decided to install a different type of propulsion system from the one originally agreed upon. He had taken the liberty of pricing the kind of unit he wanted, and General Electric had quoted him a figure of $187,000. Therefore, he was asking that the commission increase his repair subsidy to $298,000 — $111,000 for the hull work and $187,000 for the GE propulsion unit.

The commissioners went along with the request without a murmur. Not until three years later did a Maritime inspector discover that the engine D.K. had installed in the *Silverpeak* was not the new GE model at all, but a secondhand turbine he had bought from a salvage dealer, with a new gear system and condenser thrown in, for $66,000. With this one move, he had gotten $121,000 from the agency and put in an inferior engine. But even after receiving the inspector's report, Maritime took no action to chastise Ludwig or recover the money.

D.K.'s long experience with government officials had taught him how to get nearly anything he wanted from Maritime. In the spring of 1947, for example, the commission put out for bid three unfinished cargo vessels in a sale open to foreign as well as U.S. shippers. A Swedish firm offered $125,000 each for two of the ships, but the commission awarded Ludwig — who had bid $81,000, $78,000, and $71,000 — all three.

In a memo attempting to justify acceptance of these lower bids, a Maritime official explained lamely that, though D.K.'s offers might admittedly "appear to be somewhat inadequate," he was planning to finish the vessels in an American shipyard (his own), which was a sufficient reason for rejecting the Swedes' higher bids. Nothing in the invitation to bid, though, had hinted that doing the repair work in an American yard would be a factor in the commission's decision.

On the rare occasions when Ludwig did not get "most favored" treatment at Maritime, he was quick to cry foul. Late in 1947 the commission put up for sale a group of eight T-2s, five of them operational and three damaged. D.K. entered bids, informing the agency that he wanted at least four of the tankers. When the awards were announced, he was furious to learn that he had been granted only one operational ship and the three damaged ones. What made him particularly angry was that the other four operational ships had been awarded to a syndicate headed by Aristotle Onassis and Stavros Niarchos.

Onassis and Niarchos were becoming thorns in Ludwig's side. He regarded them as upstarts who had come up from nowhere during the war — partly by buying and making money from old, worn-out ships, such as his own *Phoenix* and *Ulysses.* Suddenly they were powers to be reckoned with in the tanker trade. Most galling was that in an area where he was supposed to have a tremendous edge — the purchasing of surplus ships from a U.S. government agency — he was getting the worst of the bargain. How could Maritime give an American citizen and long-time customer like himself three damaged ships and only one usable one while awarding these Johnny-come-lately foreigners four tankers ready for immediate service?

> It is difficult for us to believe [he complained to the agency] that the Maritime Commission would do anything to handicap and place at a severe disadvantage the largest independent tanker owner and operator of American tanker tonnage afloat in the world today, by placing aliens and "newcomers" in a more favorable position than an American citizen who has built and converted more tanker tonnage during the past twenty years than any other independently owned steamship company.

What Ludwig either did not understand or was powerless to change was that Niarchos and Onassis had also developed powerful contacts in the government. It was true that he was now "the largest independent tanker owner and operator of American tanker tonnage afloat in the world today." By building large tankers and buying up surplus ships as fast as he could, he had risen from fifth to first in the two years since the war's end. But there was little consolation in being the biggest independent *American* tankerman if competitors were kicking his behind in the international market. And this is exactly what Onassis and Niarchos were doing to him.

How were they managing to do this if oil and oil transportation were controlled by an international cartel of large companies? Obviously they had influence with the cartel. And how had they gotten this influence? The evidence suggests that they had acted as instruments for carrying American-owned oil to Nazi Germany.

It is now known that Standard Oil of New Jersey and other U.S. companies had been supplying Hitler's forces with petroleum and petroleum-based fuels throughout much of the war, and Onassis, headquartered in Buenos Aires and operating a fleet of Panamanian-flag tankers, probably carried oil from Standard's refinery on Aruba, in the Caribbean, to various ports where the Germans could obtain it. Such valuable services evidently earned Onassis (and Niarchos, too, since the two brothers-in-law were still close at this time and operated as a partnership) the gratitude of the powerful Standard empire. If Ludwig had his Rockefeller connections, so did the Greeks, and they were using them to great advantage. They had virtually cornered the Mideast-to-Europe oil-hauling trade, taking business away from Ludwig and other American shippers by cutting their charter rates. Flag-of-convenience ships, with no taxes and regulations and with inexpensive foreign crews, could still make money at rates that would bankrupt an American shipper who paid U.S. taxes and wages and had to maintain his ships in an adequate state of repair.

Now Onassis and Niarchos were buying up U.S. war-surplus tankers in competition with Ludwig and other American oil haulers, and not only in sales open to foreign bidders. If a Maritime sale was restricted to Americans, the Greeks simply set up a U.S. company with a few American citizens as front men to bid on the tankers. And when they got the better of Ludwig, as they did in this eight-tanker sale, they were not above rubbing his nose in the dirt. In his complaint to Maritime, D.K., without mentioning them by name, groused that the Greeks were already approaching several of his regular customers and offering their newly awarded ships at spot-charter rates, telling them it would be a while before Ludwig could get his damaged ships in service.

While Ludwig had been concentrating on becoming America's largest shipper, Onassis and Niarchos had been using Panamanian registry and cheap rates to beat him where it counted — getting charters to haul oil.

Not that Ludwig had ever had much of a chance to get into the game. In 1939, when flag-of-convenience shipping was initiated to give FDR a chance to ship oil to England without violating U.S. neutrality, nearly all of Ludwig's tankers had been under ten-year charters to Pan American P & T.

Logically, flag-of-convenience shipping should have ended as soon as the United States entered the war. As a belligerent nation, America no longer needed a subterfuge to ship oil to the Allies. It could do so directly, and in its own tankers.

But having started the mechanism, Roosevelt found it impossible to shut off. Allowing shippers to run under the Panamanian flag was equivalent to giving them a license to steal, and now that they had it, they were not about to give it up. The oil companies loved it too, because it lowered transportation rates and removed several layers of regulation. Also, they could hide profits earned abroad; as long as they did not bring their foreign earnings into the United States, they paid no taxes on them.

By 1947, Ludwig, who had a bigger, better, faster fleet than any of the Greeks, had figured out that if he was to compete in shipping, he would have to go Panamanian. If he couldn't lick 'em, he'd join 'em. And *then* he'd lick 'em. But it wasn't going to be easy. All his ships were American-flag vessels operating in the U.S. Merchant Marine. And if there was one thing that was tough, it was prying a fast new ship out of the Merchant Marine and transferring it to foreign registry.

During the war, as before it, he had been unable to go foreign, because his fleet was requisitioned by the government straight out of charter and remained in WSA service. But now there was an opportunity — if he was quick and stealthy about it.

During the first few months of 1947, D.K. was out of New York and probably out of the country. A letter from a National Bulk subordinate to Maritime, dated February 21, 1947, and concerning a possible ship purchase, revealed this absence: "Please be informed that this matter has been under the personal direction of Mr. D. K. Ludwig, President of this company. Mr. Ludwig has been away for some time under circumstances which make it impossible to reach him, but is expected to return on or about March 20, 1947."

The letter gave no clue as to his whereabouts, but the date suggests that he may have been in Panama, setting up a pair of corporations into which he could transfer much of his fleet. Soon after returning to New York, D.K. wrote to Maritime, asking to transfer three unfinished tankers he had just bought (the same three the commission had awarded him despite the Swedish firm's higher bid on two of them) to a Panamanian company, International Tankers, S.A.

The commissioners had no records or knowledge of this company, but Ludwig hastened to assure them it was not really foreign. Its officers, he wrote, were himself as president, William Wagner as vice-president and treasurer, and Samuel D. Antopol, a National Bulk attorney, as secretary. Its only stockholders were his wife, G. Virginia Ludwig, and Wagner.

International Tankers was to be D.K.'s small-tanker company for several years. Into it he would put a number of surplus ships, along with the old *Transoil,* to run Standard of New Jersey's shuttle service between the company's oil fields in Venezuela and its refinery on nearby Aruba.

Later in 1947 D.K. bought through Maritime seven unfinished tankers he had found sitting in a Florida shipyard, and he transferred them all to Panama. He got an exceptionally good deal. In a sale open only to U.S. bidders, he was able to buy two of them for $125,000 each in the name of National Petroleum Transport. When the remaining five were offered in a sale open to foreign bidders, he bought them all in the name of International Tankers for $50,000 apiece. In both sales he was the only bidder.

Ludwig could be fairly open with Maritime where International Tankers was concerned, since he was transferring to foreign registry only ships that were old, small, unfinished, or in some other way unsuited to the needs of the U.S. Merchant Marine. This wasn't a big operation, as such things went, but it was a highly profitable one, and it enabled him to start learning the ropes of flag-of-convenience shipping.

One problem he had was finding crews. Onassis, Niarchos, and the major oil companies had already hired nearly every able-bodied seaman in the Panama area, and D.K. was too stingy to offer high enough wages to tempt them away. But he soon found another solution. Some 650 miles due north of Panama lay the Cayman Islands, inhabited chiefly by the descendants of slaves brought over during colonial times. Gentle, friendly, naïve, the islanders lived a happy, relaxed existence not dissimilar to that of the Polynesians before the war. Heavily dependent on the bounties of the sea for survival, they were also superb sailors.

In short, the Cayman Islanders were just what Ludwig was looking for. Nonmaterialistic and docile, they asked little except food and shelter, and could be hired for next to nothing. D.K. soon recruited nearly all the healthy males of working age on the islands and shipped them off as crewmen aboard his Panamanian tankers.

So far everything was going right. But to give the Greeks some real competition, he needed big ships under flags of convenience as well as smaller ones — tankers that could haul oil from the Middle East to Europe more cheaply than Onassis and Niarchos could, cheaply enough to help Ludwig regain a sizable share of this lucrative market.

For this purpose Ludwig created another Panamanian corporation, Oceanic Tankships, S.A., to be his large-tanker company and own and operate the supertankers he was starting to build at Norfolk. The *Ulysses,* at 28,000 tons, was the first of these, and its launching in 1947 set off a three-way race between himself, Onassis, and Niarchos to see who would own the world's largest tanker. The contest would go on for decades and produce gigantic vessels three, five, ten, a dozen times the size of D.K.'s 1947 supertanker.

As soon as the Greeks started building tankers as large as the *Ulysses,* Ludwig started building one even larger — a 30,000-tonner. But the problem now was to get these enormous vessels transferred to Panamanian registry so that he could compete head to head with Niarchos and Onassis. It was easy to shift the *Ulysses* to Oceanic Tankships in Panama, because D.K. had built her with private financing and without government funds. Maritime had no say over what flag she would fly. But with the others — the 30,000-tonners — it would be tougher. He wanted some government financing for these, and if he got it, Maritime would be hard pressed to find an excuse that would let him transfer the ships' registration. It was a tricky situation requiring an equally tricky solution. And, as usual, Ludwig found one. He made a detour around Maritime.

During the war years, as one of America's key defense contractors, he had built up considerable influence at the Pentagon. Now it was time to turn some of this to advantage. He approached the Navy with a proposal. Let me build you five new supertankers at Norfolk, he told naval procurement officials, larger, at 30,000 tons, than anything afloat, and the Navy can charter them at a rate several percentage points below what it is paying the Voluntary Tanker Pool (which had been set up collectively by private shippers at war's end to meet the continuing fuel needs of the military). In return, the Navy will supply much of the steel and mechanical equipment to build the ships and contribute to the cost of construction.

On paper it looked balanced enough to pass the scrutiny of most budget-conscious administrators. Over the length of the charters the Navy stood to recoup through lower rates what it laid out initially in construction expenditures. But there was a catch — a factor not apparent in the cost-accounting sheets or the contracts Ludwig would sign with the Navy. It did not exist, in fact, except as an understanding between D.K. and a few top-echelon naval officers that when the new supertankers were completed and ready for service, the Navy would quietly decline to exercise its option to charter them. Having formally made the offer, and having been formally turned down, Ludwig could then put on a glum face and transfer the new vessels to Panama.

The maneuver was so clever, and executed so smoothly, that nobody — not Maritime, not congressional investigators, not seafarers' union officials bemoaning the loss of American jobs — ever seems to have twigged on to what was happening. As each ship was finished — *Bulkpetrol* in 1948, *Bulkoceanic, Bulkoil,* and *Bulkstar* in 1949, and *Bulktrader* in 1950 — D.K. would tender its services for charter to the Navy. Each time, the answer would be a polite "No, thank you." If anyone asked why the Navy, after furnishing all that money and material to build the ships, now decided it did not want them, all Pentagon officials had to do was say that they had changed their minds or found there was no present need for the tankers. But no one asked, and D.K. was able to go against clearly stated U.S. rules and policies, and transfer 150,000 tons of new tanker tonnage to a flag of convenience without causing anyone to raise an eyebrow.

By the autumn of 1949, with all his supertankers under Navy contract finished, registered in Panama, and chartered for Mideast-to-Europe operations, Ludwig had made up the distance between himself and the Greek shippers. His Panamanian fleet tonnage now rivaled what Onassis and Niarchos had accumulated, and the larger size of his vessels gave him a competitive edge. Now it was the rivals who would have to play catch-up.

But D.K. was not slackening his pace. In November 1949, seeking to increase his foreign tonnage even more, he requested permission to transfer five other American-flag tankers to Panamanian registry. These vessels, he said, were surplus T-2s that, with the oil market starting into a postwar slump, were sitting idle. They had been laid up, in fact, for the past four or five months, and it made little sense, D.K. said, for him to keep building supertankers if his smaller ships were out of work.

He would like to sell the idle T-2s, Ludwig said, in the foreign market, which he could probably do if Maritime would let him transfer the ships. And he needed the money from the sales so that he could keep building supertankers in his American yard. Otherwise, the one he was currently building — *Bulktrader* — would be his last, and he would have to close Welding Shipyard permanently.

The transfer of the five T-2s in question, he continued, would not affect U.S. jobs, since the ships were already idle. On the contrary, it would provide money to help Welding remain open and keep its fifteen hundred workers employed.

He was aware, Ludwig concluded, that Maritime had recently turned down other companies' efforts to transfer ships (this was a reference to an attempt by Standard of New Jersey to move ten of its tankers to Panamanian registry) but, because tankers were his only means of livelihood, he needed to transfer the aforementioned T-2s and sell them if he was to stay in business.

D.K.'s letter was a carefully worded mixture of fact and fiction. That Ludwig was presently considering closing Welding Shipyard and idling fifteen hundred workers was true. Much of the rest was not.

But the letter served its purpose; at Maritime's next meeting the commissioners approved letting Ludwig transfer the five T-2s to Panama. It was a decision they soon regretted. Hardly had the news been published when Maritime started getting angry letters from officials of seafarers' unions "strongly protesting" the move as "an attempt to scuttle the American merchant marine."

This favor to Ludwig, said the union officials, was the first approval given by the Maritime Commission for transfer of new ships to foreign registry. Heretofore only old ships with no value to the Merchant Marine had been allowed to change. By letting National Bulk put new tonnage under a foreign flag, Maritime was encouraging other shippers to transfer, which would result in a loss of jobs for American merchant seamen.

The T-2s in question, said the protesters, were neither old nor obsolete, but they would indeed be run down after operating under lax flag-of-convenience regulations for a few years. In short, the unions said, the commission's approval of Ludwig's transfer application was "an ill-advised and untimely action."

The reaction was not surprising. The commission had expected, when it granted D.K.'s request, to take some flak from representatives of labor organizations. What it had not expected was a disturbing piece of news sent in by a Los Angeles union: all five of the tankers just approved for transfer to Panama — the T-2s Ludwig claimed had been laid up for months — were actually busy as bees carrying oil between San Diego and South America.

This was a serious charge and could not be ignored. Checking through shipping schedules, Maritime inspectors found that, sure enough, National Bulk's "idle" tankers were presently taking on cargo in California.

On contacting National Bulk, commission officials were told that, well, yes, as a matter of fact the ships in question *were* temporarily employed. It seems that Ludwig had found some short-term charters for them and neglected to inform Maritime. Merely an oversight, though; the ships would soon be idle again, so the transfer permission should be allowed to stand.

After a month's wait, Maritime checked back. Yes, admitted a National Bulk official, the tankers *were* still employed. After another wait, the commission checked again. The T-2s were still busy. By now Maritime was beginning to lose patience. It insisted that Ludwig file an affidavit saying the ships would be through with their charters and idle again by the middle of April. But when that time came, Ludwig stated blandly that the lay-off date had had to be postponed for another two or three months. On May 1, he put it off still further.

It was becoming apparent even to the long-suffering commission that D.K. had been lying all along about the vessels' laid-up status and that he was merely stalling for time so that his ships could make as much money as possible before being transferred to Panama. On May 2, the day after his latest postponement, the commissioners met and rescinded their earlier approval of the transfer. This would be one of their last official acts. In June 1950, President Truman issued an executive order abolishing the Maritime Commission entirely and replacing it with an agency organized along different lines.

For years — indeed, almost since its creation — the commission had been a target of reformers. Charges were often heard that the agency, rather than policing the shipping industry, had become its servant. The hard truth was that the shippers — not only collectively but individually — were not going to tolerate effective regulation if they could find a way to undermine it. No matter how good the intent — and FDR had certainly had reform in mind when he set up the commission — ship owners and operators found ways to co-opt the regulating agency and get what they wanted from it. And during the war years, they had wanted quite a lot.

Senator Aiken's 1943 charges leading to the GAO probe and the critical report on its accounting practices had produced no effect at Maritime, chiefly because the men in charge of the commission — Admirals Emory S. Land and Howard L. Vickery and Finance Director Robert Anderson — had simply buried the report and forgotten about it.

But in 1946 Aiken was back with another probe. Now that the war was over, he and a few other congressmen were investigating wartime profiteering by U.S. military contractors. During a series of hearings, case after case of unmitigated greed and corruption was uncovered, and it soon became apparent that abuses in the shipping industry were among the most blatant and expensive of all. After months of sifting through stacks of evidence, the Joint Maritime Strike Commission charged publicly, "U.S. ship owners have plundered $21 billion from the U.S. Treasury."

The figure was substantial. America had spent an estimated $350 billion waging World War II, and these illicit war profits by shippers represented 6 percent of that total. In launching the investigation, Aiken had said, "An examination of Maritime Commission affairs . . . will be the most shocking story of collusion, corruption, and disregard of public interest ever presented against an agency of the U.S. government."

GAO investigators sent to Maritime to obtain accounting records and other documents, however, immediately ran into an insurmountable obstacle: many of the records pertaining to ship sales and other wartime transactions between the government and private shippers had been destroyed. Top Maritime officials blamed the loss on "disgruntled employees who feared they'd lose their jobs," but the probers suspected a gigantic coverup initiated by Land and major ship owners.

Suspecting it was one thing; proving it was another. Without the incriminating documents, congressional investigators had little to base a case on. After wading through the remaining records for several weeks, the GAO team of auditors gave up in disgust. They couldn't make heads or tails of what they were looking at. It would take a team of two hundred expert accountants six months, said a GAO spokesman, to put Maritime's records in shape, and even then the missing documents would preclude a proper audit.

Working with the little they had, the auditors reported that ship owners had gotten at least $8 billion of the misspent money by grossly inflating estimates of their vessels' actual worth. These were some of the practices:

1. During the war the Maritime Commission and its War Shipping Administration had bought sixty-nine ships twenty years old or more for seven to eight times their book value.
2. Owners of 758 ships at least twenty years old and with a total book value of less than $38 million had been paid nearly $200 million in charter fees. Had the government taken over these ships and paid their owners fair market value, it could have saved more than $160 million.
3. Old vessels being traded in had been assigned exorbitant values — ten times book price in numerous cases.
4. Owners of 690 ships at least twenty years old had insured them for a total of $477 million — many times their market value. One owner collected a claim for sixty-four times what his lost ship was worth. Settlements of ten, fifteen, or twenty times book price were common. (One senator reviewing these figures remarked dryly during a hearing, "Many of the vessels were of much greater value to their owners after they hit the bottom of the ocean than they were while operating.")
5. Maritime never cashed many of the insurance premiums shippers were required by law to pay. Instead, the agency simply held quarterly premium checks for three months, then returned them to the ship owners in exchange for new checks. If a loss did occur, the commission would cash the appropriate check and backdate the necessary forms accordingly. Shippers, in effect, were getting government insurance free of charge.
6. Maritime allowed shippers to deposit their earnings in tax-exempt "construction reserve" accounts held jointly with the government. This practice, as one congressman noted during a hearing, was not only illegal but also contrary to the advice given Maritime officials by the commission's own general counsel. According to GAO reports, these "construction reserve funds cost the U.S. Treasury at least $80 million in lost revenues at a time when the monies were needed for the war effort."

As one of a relatively small number of shippers under contract to Maritime and the WSA, Daniel Ludwig unquestionably was a beneficiary of government largess stemming from these corrupt practices.

Exactly how much he benefited will probably never be known because of the destruction of Maritime records. It can be assumed that many of those missing documents concerned transactions between the government and Ludwig-owned companies, for the records of activities up until the war years are fairly extensive, telling a good deal about relations between Maritime and National Bulk and other of Ludwig's firms. Then suddenly, during the war years, the documentation drops off to a trickle. There are great gaps and holes, and the records contain almost nothing about ship sales, leasing agreements, trade-ins, insurance, or other areas where it was possible for Ludwig to garner inflated war profits.

From the few documents available, though, certain facts are clear:

1. He did sell old ships to the WSA. Of the sixty-nine such vessels purchased for seven to eight times their value, four of these were probably D.K.'s.
2. Even during the early stages of the war, he was chartering as many as a dozen tankers (and more later) to the government at rates of more than $1 million a year each, which was several times the market value of the ships.
3. D.K. traded in five of his old tankers to Maritime for sums far in excess of their market price.
4. He collected several million dollars in claims for three lost tankers whose value was much less than what they were insured for.
5. He kept his wartime earnings in construction reserve funds to avoid paying taxes on them.

If one adds the money he made through these activities to what Welding Shipyard made by building government-contracted ships at inflated prices, one can see how Ludwig, after struggling through most of the Depression years in debt, became, by the end of the war, the multimillionaire owner of one of America's largest privately owned tanker fleets. He was by no means the only shipper to get rich from wartime profiteering; he was certainly one of a handful who did. As one GAO investigator remarked in the course of a hearing on Maritime Commission corruption, "At no time in the history of American business have so few men made so much money with so little risk — and all at the expense of the taxpayers, not only of this generation, but of generations to come."

Yet, almost to a man, the ship owners got off scot-free, with not a charge brought against them. Few shippers, yards, or companies were even mentioned by name in any of the hearings. Shipping magnates Henry J. Kaiser (later famed as an auto, steel, and aluminum tycoon) and Michael Todd (later famed as one of Elizabeth Taylor's husbands) were both called to testify but, guided by sharp lawyers, were able to muddy the waters enough to escape prosecution. Frank Costello was also called before an investigating committee that discovered he had found the pickings at Maritime so tempting, he had set up a dummy corporation and gotten a government contract to use as a tax dodge. Justice Department officials drew up an indictment against the former bootlegger, charging him with nonpayment of taxes, but after a secret meeting with his lawyers decided not to pursue the case.

Other well-known names cropped up during the Maritime corruption hearings; they were those of people who had used their positions to profit illegally or unethically as a result of agency favors to shippers. Many of those who had become rich through Maritime's generosity, though, weren't shippers; they were fast-buck artists who had seen the chance to cash in on a one-time good deal. As one GAO prober testified, the only know-how needed to make a fortune in wartime shipping was "knowing how to secure a contract from the Maritime Commission."

As the hearings continued and scandal after scandal came to light, it became disturbingly apparent that Maritime had indeed been guilty of participating in the largest, most flagrantly illegal giveaway of public money in the history of the American government.

But something else emerged from the hearings, helped considerably by an intense, carefully planned public relations campaign mounted by the shippers and their friends in Congress. This was a double standard, according to which the ship owners were not really to be blamed. They had been doing what businessmen do — trying to make a profit. Hey, if they'd made a few dollars — or a few billion — more than normal, well, didn't they deserve a bonus for helping America win the war? The Maritime officials, however, were either dishonest scoundrels or bumbling incompetents whose laxity in office encouraged the profiteering. It was all a big bureaucratic bungle; and if anybody was going to be hanged, let it be the bureaucrats.

And so it was. The shippers, including Ludwig (whose name was never mentioned at the hearings), were allowed to go on with business as usual. Admirals Land and Vickery resigned in disgrace, their reputations permanently tarnished by the disclosures. Finance Director Robert Anderson and several other staff members were fired a few days later by the remaining members of the commission, who had kept their mouths shut and played dumb throughout the investigations.

After Rear Admiral Earl W. Mills served a short stint as acting Maritime chairman, Vice-Admiral William W. Smith was brought on as the commission's new chief executive. But he was too friendly with the shipping industry to make more than cosmetic changes. Furthermore, during his two years' tenure, he worsened an already precarious situation by allowing nearly all merchant vessels being built in the United States (including Ludwig's new supertankers) to transfer to Panamanian registry in violation of the stated Maritime policy of maintaining a strong U.S. Merchant Marine. This and other transgressions brought another wave of investigations, and the new chief didn't last long after a commission employee told a Senate committee that Admiral Land, just before his resignation, had told panicky staffers, "Don't worry, boys. Everything will be all right once Smith gets over here."

In a desperate effort to clean up Maritime's badly soiled image, Truman reached outside the Navy and brought in Major General Philip Fleming to replace Smith. But Fleming didn't know enough about the shipping industry to get a handle on regulating it, and fresh stories of scandal and abuses prompted Truman a year later to scrap the whole commission, retire Fleming, and set up the Maritime Administration and the Federal Maritime Board to have a try at policing the shipping industry.

But the effort was too little and too late. The sad fact was that the U.S. Merchant Marine by now was in a shambles. American shippers who, like Ludwig, could manage to do so were transferring their foreign fleets to stay in competition with the Greeks. The rest were either scaling down to run small, local operations or getting out of the business entirely.

Shipbuilding was in a similar state. Foreign yards were building ships at much lower cost than American yards could afford to. For some years U.S. shipbuilders had stayed in the game only by getting subsidies through the Maritime Commission. Now that this practice had been exposed through congressional investigations and the well had gone dry, the builders had to face the hard realities of the free-market system. They, too, had to go foreign or find another line of work.

For Ludwig the choice was obvious. He had already — mostly through Maritime's dereliction — taken much of his ship-chartering operations abroad. Now he would go foreign to build, too.

*Nine*

# Going Japanese

In 1949, Senator Owen Brewster of Maine, on a tour of the world's shipyards, reported back to congressional colleagues that most of Europe's maritime nations, including several who had been our allies during World War II, were more than a little angry about American moves to subsidize and stimulate shipbuilding in West Germany and Japan.

German workers, said Brewster, were eager to get jobs paying forty to fifty cents an hour, and would work overtime or second or third shift at the same rate. As a result, German shipyards were doing repair work for half the cost and in a third the time required by the European yards that paid their workers a decent wage. Japanese yards were even cheaper than German ones. "The British and Swedes," Brewster continued, "resent the German and Japanese competition, and blame America for permitting it."

And indeed it was very easy to get the impression in the postwar years that the United States was turning its back on its former allies in its zeal to restore the industries of its defeated enemies. Nor was this impression far from the truth. Under the auspices of the European Recovery Program and other aspects of the so-called Truman Doctrine, Japan and West Germany were being rapidly built back to their former industrial strength, and, with massive infusions of American aid, were already outstripping their neighbors and becoming the dominant economic forces in Asia and Western Europe.

The outcome of the Second World War had also left the United States and American business interests in a unique position. The country was now dominant in the world — the only major industrial nation whose resources and manufacturing capability had not been destroyed or severely crippled by the war. The question was how to use this power. It could be used humanely, to work for a peaceful world in which all people had enough food to eat and supplies of energy to make their lives easier. Or it could be used for exploitation, to give certain corporate interests a long-term lock on global resources and cheap labor supplies.

During the late 1940s, old antagonisms between capitalists and communists that had lain dormant during the recent conflict were reemerging to push a world tired of war toward new violence. In Europe and Asia, armies representing the Eastern and Western superpowers faced off against one another across demarcation lines bristling with weaponry.

On June 25, 1950, the uneasy peace in Asia was broken by the sudden onset of war between North and South Korea. By the end of June, American troops were on their way to support the South Koreans, and by the middle of October, Chinese troops were coming to the aid of the north.

While the war was savaging that mountainous peninsula, it was doing wonders for the economy of Japan, which now found itself attracting many sorts of industry from the United States as support for the war effort. Among the new industries was a major shipbuilding operation being set up in the city of Kure by an American-based firm named National Bulk Carriers.

It had become apparent to Daniel Ludwig that if he intended to build larger supertankers, he would have to move out of the Sewalls Point yard at Norfolk. The limited facilities could not accommodate a vessel larger than around 30,000 tons, and he was already building ships of that size. The question was where to go. There seemed little point in continuing the operation in the United States. The Maritime scandals had given the American shipbuilding industry a black eye and severely diminished opportunities for builders to get fat government subsidies. And postwar inflation and heightened union activity were driving up U.S. labor costs.

Early in 1950, Ludwig sent Elmer Hann, his top man at Welding

Shipyard, on a trip around the world to locate a site for a new yard. D.K. had hired Hann away from Henry J. Kaiser's yards after the war, and the tough, heavyset, cigar-chomping executive had proved himself an effective producer; he built Ludwig's postwar supertankers on schedule.

Hann went to West Germany, which was D.K.'s first choice. Ludwig was familiar with that country's North Sea ports, since his tankers had been carrying oil there since the end of the war. But the Berlin blockade and continued tense relations between East and West Germany made the political situation too unstable, and Ludwig decided the time wasn't right for tying himself to the area (though he would establish a shipping operation — Emden Tankschiffahrt-GmbH — and invest in 15 percent of a 30,000-barrel-a-day oil refinery — Erdölwerke Frisia, A.G. — in West Germany).

So Hann was soon on his way to Japan, where he found a situation much to D.K.'s liking. The former Imperial Navy Shipyard at Kure (only a few miles from Hiroshima) was sitting empty and idle, and there was a ready supply of skilled labor in the city, workers who had been employed in the yard during the war. The very size of the yard — it was many times bigger than the narrow facility at Sewalls Point — was also an inducement. The largest vessels in the Japanese Navy, including the giant battleship *Yamoto,* had been constructed there, so there was plenty of room for building as huge a supertanker as Ludwig might dream up. As an additional bonus, the shipyard could be leased for almost nothing.

Kure it would be. Ludwig sent word to Hann to make arrangements with Japanese officials to get an option on the yard; final details could be worked out later. Then the Welding Shipyard chief could come back home and start closing down the Sewalls Point operation.

Two projects needed finishing first. The *Bulktrader* — the last of D.K.'s Navy-contracted 30,000-tonners — was almost ready for launching. As for the other, Ludwig had decided to indulge himself in a little uncharacteristic luxury: he was building a yacht for his own use.

Gleaming white, 191 feet long and displacing 381 tons, this luxury vessel was an exceptional craft. Designed by the marine architect John W. Well, she was intended — as Ludwig bragged in a letter to Maritime — to be "the last word" in privately owned pleasure boats.

Going against his usual custom, he had spared no expense in building the *Danginn* (named for *Dan*iel and *Ginger* Ludwig, with an extra *n* so that no one would think he was advertising liquor), fitting her up with every expensive frill he could think of and spending $25,000 just carpeting the staterooms. The total cost of the ship — more than $2 million — was about what he spent to build a supertanker nearly a hundred times larger.

The contrasts between the *Danginn* and a Ludwig-built tanker were, of course, enormous. It was as if the ghosts of Christmas past, present, and future had visited the Scroogelike D.K., making him put aside his customary stinginess and construct a pleasure craft that was the stuff of dreams.

Assuming there had been no such ghostly visitations, what would prompt such a radical departure from his habitual penny pinching? Perhaps there were two reasons: Aristotle Onassis and Stavros Niarchos. By now the two brothers-in-law had dissolved their wartime partnership and were busy competing for their father-in-law's — and the world's — attention. The chief weapon in this duel was money; each was trying to outspend the other, making a display of his own wealth in order to put his rival in the shade. And each made a point of hobnobbing with wealth and royalty — kings and queens and Middle Eastern potentates and titled nobility and heads of state and old, established money. But while they were lavishly entertaining the leaders of European and Arab aristocracy, they were also winning contracts to haul oil to make enough money to keep the spending spree going.

And Ludwig, watching these glamorous men steal contract after contract from him by dazzling those who had the power to grant such concessions, had begun to realize that if he was going to compete with them successfully, he would have to do more than build bigger and more economical tankers. He had to do a little dazzling of his own.

He had gotten by up to now without such nonsense. In America, people had a great tolerance where the rich were concerned. They expected millionaires to be eccentric, and didn't care whether they wore old, baggy clothes or spat tobacco juice or picked their noses. Money was money, and if you had enough of it, you could get respect no matter how you dressed or looked or acted.

In Europe it was different. The aristocratic tradition required that if you had money, you had to spread it around a little to prove you were worthy of keeping company with the nobs. Onassis and Niarchos were succeeding wildly by outswelling the swells.

Ludwig would never have the bonhomie of Onassis or the polish of Niarchos. He lacked the ability to be witty or make clever small talk. He wasn't a member of the horsey set, and he had no taste for art. But he was going to have to compete with the Greeks on their turf.

He would have to attend white-tie parties, and he would need a yacht as opulent as the Greeks' on which to entertain Arab sheiks and European oil barons. Maybe he couldn't make them chuckle the way Onassis and Niarchos could, but at least he wouldn't look like some hick tankerman from western Michigan. And as long as he got the chance to talk with them face to face, he felt, he could convince them it was worth their while to charter his tankers instead of his rivals'.

Over the next decade, D.K. would use the *Danginn* frequently in this way, cruising the Mediterranean or the Atlantic with a boatload of wealthy guests, usually ones from whom he needed a business favor. For him, the yacht was as much a business craft as any of his tankers, and probably earned him more money than any of them. For example, he hosted Saudi Arabia's King Ibn Saud in the Persian Gulf as a way of procuring a charter to haul Saudi oil.

But not all of D.K.'s yacht trips were connected with business. In 1956 he took Clark Gable and his new wife, Kay, on a South American cruise — a voyage during which the Ludwigs' pet monkey and poodle were reportedly seasick most of the time. Gable was enamored of the excellent food served aboard the *Danginn* and put on some weight. Ludwig was a great admirer of the virile actor. "He was all man," D.K. told a *Business Week* interviewer three years after the actor's death. "He stood head and shoulders above all those two-bit phonies in Hollywood today. I still watch his movies on TV."

Ludwig's personal relationship with Gable, though, may have sprung from his and Ginger's friendship with Kay, an association that perhaps dated back to the years of her marriage to the sugar heir Adolph Spreckels. The friendship was an enduring one. In 1976, some two decades after the voyage to Venezuela, *Newsweek* reported, "Ludwig with his second wife Ginger gets together with a small circle that includes Gable's widow Kay and former California Governor Ronald Reagan."

But during the 1950s, at least, D.K. was generally too busy to spend much time socializing on his yacht. According to one account, the *Danginn* logged an average of forty thousand miles a year, carrying business acquaintances and friends on tropical cruises and jaunts to exotic pleasure spots, but it usually sailed without Ludwig, who was in his Manhattan office, scheming up new ways to make money. Still, he probably got more than his investment out of the boat, which he kept for ten years before selling it to a midwestern multimillionaire contractor, Ralph M. Parsons (who renamed it the *Argo*), in 1960 in order to build an even larger, more expensive yacht that would rival a new one J. Paul Getty had just bought.

Once Welding Shipyard had completed the *Danginn* and the *Bulktrader* in 1950, D.K. closed down operations at Sewalls Point and put the yard on a standby basis. He laid off all the line workers, keeping only a few key executives and technical people on the payroll in case he wangled another government-subsidized contract to build ships.

In fact, he almost did. Shortly after the new Maritime Administration took over supervision of the Merchant Marine, its chairman, Admiral E. L. Cochrane, announced a government program for subsidizing efforts to revive the moribund American shipbuilding industry. Ludwig pricked up his ears and immediately wrote Cochrane a fawning letter, asking to build either tankers or dry-cargo vessels under the new program. There was a problem, though: he wanted government funding for building ships he intended to register immediately under flags of convenience.

Cochrane was willing to go partway. He would recommend the subsidies, but he was leery of letting the ships go foreign immediately. If they could be kept in U.S. service for a while, transfer would be less of a problem. But D.K. was impatient. He considered trying the Navy-contract route again, as he had with the last several tankers he had built at Norfolk, but changed his mind and, after keeping things in the air for years, finally abandoned the project without reactivating the Sewalls Point yard.

This facility, though small, had made possible D.K.'s current status as a shipbuilder as well as an owner and operator of tankers. During the 1940s he had built nineteen ships there — twenty, counting the *Danginn* — and repaired or renovated a number of others. In terms of capacity, Welding Shipyard had constructed 438,000 deadweight tons of shipping at the site, more than a quarter-million tons of it during the war, when peak employment was twelve hundred workers. Ludwig would later boast that Sewalls Point had built more tonnage for its size and labor force than any yard in the United States.

But the time had come for him to move on. First, however, he had to work out a deal that would allow him to transfer his shipbuilding operation — and $1.5 million worth of heavy equipment — to Japan.

Negotiating with the Japanese was not difficult. Japan was, after all, a conquered country ruled by a puppet government whose strings were pulled by forces in the United States. And though there was still a Democratic administration in Washington, Ludwig had a powerful ally in John Foster Dulles, who in 1950 was a "bipartisan consultant" at the State Department and with his friend General MacArthur was running things in the Far East. President Harry Truman was no longer the tough fighter he'd been in the 1948 election; he had won that battle only to lose the war. Hounded by forces from the right led by Wisconsin Senator Joseph McCarthy, he was accused of harboring Reds in office and of being sympathetic to communism.

In the late 1940s, at the same time the Maritime Commission investigations were going on, other congressional committees and federal agencies were probing related areas of war profiteering. They found, among other things, that ARAMCO, the Arabian-American Oil Company, a consortium made up of Standard of California and Texaco, had been overcharging the U.S. Navy outrageously for petroleum during World War II. Through evidence brought forth by these probes, President Truman also learned of the existence of the oil cartel that had existed since the 1928 Achnacarry Agreement.

He was furious, and he gave the green light to the Justice Department to proceed with an antitrust action against twenty-one large oil companies, which, if successful, might succeed in breaking the cartel once and for all. But he didn't know how powerful an enemy he was tackling.

He was about to find out that, even if he was president of the United States, he was up against forces much bigger than he. The Justice Department's suit, stalled repeatedly by the maneuvers of the oil company lawyers, dragged on, untried and unresolved, through the remaining years of Truman's term. As soon as Eisenhower took office in 1953, the antitrust suit, in a legally unprecedented move, was somehow transferred from the Justice Department to the Department of State, where, under newly appointed Secretary John Foster Dulles, it died a quiet death.

But in 1950 Dulles was shuttling back and forth across the Pacific between Washington and Tokyo, not only negotiating the Japanese peace treaty but also overseeing efforts to turn Japan into a corporate capitalist society modeled after the United States, with a few important differences. No established labor movement existed in the country, and there were no antitrust laws. Japan and all of Southeast Asia outside the communist countries were a potential source of cheap labor ready to be exploited by U.S. investors.

It would not look good, though, if Japan were suddenly swarming with American companies seeking to exploit the conquered nation. Better to set up a local infrastructure in the form of a series of companies headed by Japanese officers and directors to manufacture products that could be shipped to the United States and Europe.

Certainly this would cost thousands of American jobs, but many U.S. companies were tired of paying union wages and listening to union gripes. They wanted workers willing to accept small wages and poor working conditions without complaint. For many American investors, it made little difference whether a product was labeled "Made in Japan," "Made in West Germany," or "Made in U.S.A." as long as the money invested in its manufacture returned a healthy profit. The only real competition was for jobs.

Turning Japan into a Western-style industrial nation would be complex and difficult, but not impossible. Despite the wartime propaganda, which had pictured them as sadistic savages, the Japanese people were by and large industrious, obedient, and elaborately polite. Moreover, they were quick learners and good imitators, and were somewhat compulsive about work.

John Foster Dulles knew this better than most. His grandfather had been an expert on the Far East, and Dulles had absorbed much from the old man. He also knew that postwar Japan presented financial opportunities that might not come again.

Development of Japanese industry must be done in a rapid but orderly manner, and American technology grafted onto an Eastern culture. But Japan had started becoming an industrial nation well before World War II. If the Japanese had been able to get the raw materials they needed, it might have been a much harder war for the United States.

Now they could get those raw materials. As an independent nation whose needs and interests threatened those of the United States, Japan had had to be fought and defeated. As a captive nation of the United States, it would be able to succeed economically in a way hitherto undreamed of. All that Japanese businessmen had to do to become rich was to follow the gospel according to John Foster Dulles and cooperate while the old Rockefeller formula — *conspire, combine, control* — was applied to the Far East.

Many corporations were to be set up in Japan and run by Japanese, but nearly all would be owned and controlled by a half-dozen huge holding companies called *zaibatsu*. These, in turn, would be owned and controlled by both Japanese and U.S. investors. Many of the latter were cooperating groups of American corporations.

The government of Japan was headed by Prime Minister Shigeru Yoshida. During the war he had been one of Emperor Hirohito's advisers; more recently he had become a Dulles protégé. Incarcerated as a suspected war criminal after the surrender, Yoshida had proved so tractable in the hands of his American captors that by early 1946 he was serving as foreign minister in the occupation government Cabinet of Prime Minister Kijuro Shidehara.

In May of that year, General MacArthur, as chief of U.S. occupation forces in Japan, ordered Shidehara ousted. Hirohito then, on MacArthur's orders, appointed Yoshida as the new head of state.

The appointment was instantly unpopular. Over 125,000 protestors gathered in front of the Imperial Palace in Tokyo, chanting, begging for food, and waving banners that read DOWN WITH YOSHIDA. MacArthur ordered in U.S. troops to disperse the demonstrators.

Despite the response of his countrymen, Yoshida was viewed very favorably by Dulles. Obsequious to those above him, the new prime minister was ruthless and highhanded with inferiors and enemies. He had no scruples about crushing dissent. On the other hand, he could bend when it came to negotiating with American businessmen. When Daniel Ludwig's emissary Elmer Hann came to Tokyo to discuss leasing the Kure yard, Yoshida went along with the proposal.

Evidently there was arm-twisting from some U.S. source, either military or civilian. A later State Department dispatch notes: "Although the Japanese Government was at first loath to sell or lease its former naval construction facilities to a foreign company, it was persuaded to do so in the belief that such lease or sale would remove the facilities from reparations designation."

At this time, some five years after Japan's surrender, the Allies were just getting around to negotiating a peace treaty that would end the occupation. Several of the Allies were demanding heavy reparations as part of the treaty, but the U.S. State Department, as represented by the bipartisan consultant John Foster Dulles (this was his title because the Truman administration, still smarting from remarks Dulles had made against it during a recent election campaign, was unwilling to call him an ambassador) was taking a flexible view of the reparations question.

The Japanese were in a tight spot. They could either negotiate with Ludwig and agree to let him have the Kure yard at a low price or they could hold out and run the risk of losing the yard entirely as part of the reparations settlement. They chose the less costly alternative.

Serious negotiations began in late summer or early fall of 1950, shortly after Dulles held a series of meetings with Yoshida, and dragged on for nearly seven months. Neither the State Department nor the American occupation government (hereafter referred to as SCAP — General Headquarters, Supreme Commander for the Allied Powers) seems to have been aware, at least officially, that such discussions were taking place until they were well under way.

But somehow the word leaked out, and Representative Franck R. Havenner wrote to the State Department on April 9, 1951, requesting information about the alleged leasing of certain Japanese shipbuilding facilities to an American company for tanker construction. How Havenner happened on the information is unclear, but the secret was out and State was obliged to respond to the query. A department spokesman replied that indeed negotiations had been going on for some months between the Japanese government and National Bulk Carriers and that reports had been appearing in Tokyo newspapers. In late 1950, State acknowledged, officials of Japan's Finance Ministry had informally approached SCAP's Industry Division, Economic and Scientific Section (ID, ESS), and asked about the possibilities of leasing Kure to Ludwig. The Industry Division, also informally, had advised the Japanese not to submit an application for such a move, saying it would recommend disapproval.

As a result, no formal application had been submitted, but negotiations between Ludwig and the Japanese had continued anyway. On April 20, 1951, a news agency in Japan announced that, except for minor details, an agreement had been worked out between National Bulk and the Finance Ministry whereby Ludwig would lease the Kure yard for ten years, with an option to renew for another five, at the rate of $8700 a year. He would also pay $850,000 for facilities on the property, with the understanding that he could sell these back to the Japanese government when his lease expired. (This purchase clause, according to a State Department document, was put into the package at the informal suggestion of a SCAP official. Ludwig had initially proposed leasing everything.)

In final form, the agreement between Ludwig and the Japanese government contained these provisions:

1. Starting in 1951, as soon as U.S. approval could be obtained, D.K. would lease the Kure shipyard for $725 a month for as long as fifteen years, if he chose to stay that long.
2. He would pay $85,000 a year to buy certain on-site buildings and equipment, which he would sell back to Japan when he left.
3. He could sublease a small section of the yard to Harima, a Japanese shipbuilding company that was already using it.
4. He would use at least seven thousand tons of Japanese steel each month.
5. He would use Japanese labor, except for a handful of supervisory personnel.
6. He would build ships for his own companies only.
7. He could import engines, mechanical equipment, foreign steel, and other shipbuilding materials, duty free.

Taken item by item, the agreement certainly seems slanted in Ludwig's favor. Rent for the mammoth yard was incredibly low; D.K. was getting a fifteen-year lease on one of the world's largest shipyards for $130,500. With the Japanese government committed to buy back the facilities he was purchasing, he was, in effect, getting these free.

Subleasing part of the yard to Harima would not only bring in extra income but also provide an on-site subcontractor to handle some phases of the shipbuilding operation. Using Japanese steel was a condition that would presumably benefit the Japanese economy, but, as will soon be seen, this was not a section of the agreement Ludwig felt obligated to follow. Employing Japanese labor could hardly be considered a concession by D.K., since a primary reason for his wanting to come to Japan was to take advantage of the cheap, experienced workers at Kure, thousands of whom were currently unemployed and eager to find jobs even at subsistence wages.

Building ships for his own companies only was no hardship; this was what Ludwig had been doing all along, although he customarily chartered his vessels to other corporations. What one writer has called "an attractive assortment of tax and tariff deals" built into the agreement would save Ludwig millions while costing the Japanese treasury the same amount at a time when the country was trying to rebuild its shattered economy. Yet D.K. had insisted on the right to import certain materials and equipment instead of using Japanese-made products. Ship engines were one example. Engines then being manufactured in Japan had a reputation for breaking down, and Ludwig wanted to continue buying from U.S. firms with which he had long-standing relationships. And it was nice to be able to import American-made engines, boilers, and other equipment without having to pay duty on them.

Once Ludwig and his negotiating team had worked out details of the agreement with representatives of Japan's Finance Ministry, they had to get SCAP and Washington to approve the package. The middle-echelon managers at SCAP's Industry Division had been anything but encouraging. Their job was to build up Japanese industries, not to encourage American companies to siphon off available opportunities. But Ludwig, as always, had contacts in high places who could override the objections of middle management. Even when his demands were unreasonable, he could usually get what he wanted with a little help from his friends.

For instance, while his application to lease Kure was being considered anew by SCAP, D.K. made an additional request. Instead of using seven thousand tons of Japanese steel per month, as he had already agreed to do, he wanted to import American steel. He had found, he said, that Japanese steel was not well suited to welding. Its sulfur content was too high. Besides that, it was more expensive. Because he did not have to pay duties, he could bring American ship-plate steel of welding quality to Kure for two thirds of what it would cost him to buy the Japanese product.

It appears from State Department records that Ludwig had never intended to honor the stipulation relating to the use of Japanese steel. He had already taken an option with a West German manufacturer to supply ship plate, but the option had expired while his negotiations with the Japanese government dragged on. Now he wanted steel from the United States for reasons of quality and price.

SCAP had serious problems with this request. High-quality steel was scarce worldwide. The amount of steel Ludwig was asking for to build his tankers was almost the entire government-approved allotment of U.S. steel to all of Japan. Also, steel of the type Ludwig wanted was scarce even in the United States. There was no understanding, in the Kure agreement SCAP was about to approve, that American steel would be required. One reason the occupation government was even considering approval was that it would boost the Japanese steelmaking industry. Japanese shipbuilders, because of regulations that forced them to buy the local product, were not being allowed to purchase the same steel Ludwig was asking for and would be put in a noncompetitive position. And, since D.K. had already (to quote one State Department document) "been given a great advantage through permission to use low-cost Japanese labor and facilities," it was hardly fair to other shipbuilders either in the United States or Japan to give him the additional benefit of high-quality American steel at cheaper prices. He would be getting the best of it both ways: American shipbuilders were having to pay higher United States wages; Japanese shipbuilders were having to use inferior, high-priced steel.

With all these objections, it seems that SCAP would have turned down Ludwig's steel request as a matter of course. But D.K. once more got what he wanted. In a document dated August 11, 1952, a State Department analyst, R. A. Ericson, revealed that factions had developed over National Bulk Carriers' application:

One group of officials within the Economic and Scientific Section (ESS) of GHQ, SCAP, said to have been composed of higher ranking officers, were sympathetic to the NBC request. . . . Officers on the operating level within ESS, however, were bitterly opposed to the allocation of . . . materials to NBC. . . . They believed that . . . would give that company undue advantage over both American and Japanese shipbuilders, greatly reduce benefits to the Japanese economy, and remove the incentive for Japanese production of higher quality materials.

As officials at the operating level assessed the situation, giving National Bulk the steel it wanted would benefit nobody but the company. The American embassy in Japan agreed:

> The Embassy is . . . of the opinion that permitting NBC to obtain such materials outside the Japanese economy would defeat SCAP's purpose in approving the acquisition by NBC of the Kure facilities and that NBC should be required to use critical materials of Japanese origin where they are satisfactory to the certifying agency and where their export from the United States would reduce the supply available to American shipyards building for American flag operation. In addition, NBC has either failed adequately to investigate availabilities of Japanese supplies or has been blinded by its desire to economize in the construction of its ships, since several of the items which it categorically stated were not available in Japan . . . can be made by Japanese firms to any specifications, although admittedly at prices which exceed those charged by American manufacturers.

But it was apparent from the outcome that Ludwig's friends in SCAP outranked the officials opposed to his request. "The weight of their opinion," a State Department analysis reads, "was such that official SCAP justification for all desired quantities was dispatched," and D.K. got his American steel, along with approval of the Kure lease.

Final approval of the lease by the U.S. government, however, had to be delayed for reasons of diplomacy. John Foster Dulles, who had almost certainly been instrumental in helping Ludwig bring his shipbuilding operation to Japan, was at this time in London, leading discussions that would result in a mutually acceptable Japanese peace treaty.

Britain and Australia, in particular, were taking a hard line. Both countries were claiming reparations for war damages. Dulles was trying to make them back off. In his mind, World War II was a dead issue. He was much more concerned about what he perceived as the

Soviet threat and felt it important to build West Germany and Japan up to industrial strength as quickly as possible so that they could be bulwarks against the advance of communism.

One point of disagreement between Dulles and his Allied counterparts was Japanese shipbuilding. The British-Australian argument was twofold: Japan should not be allowed to build a large Navy or Merchant Marine that might pose a military or economic threat. Also, Britain in particular did not want the Japanese to re-emerge as a major shipbuilding power. The British looked on shipbuilding as one of the major industries in which they could excel, and they feared the competition from West German and Japanese yards.

Dulles had never been sympathetic toward British aims, and he wasn't now. The faster West German and Japanese shipbuilding grew, the better. But he had to be very careful about how he handled the issue. One thing he didn't want known was that Daniel K. Ludwig was starting a move that would soon turn Japan into the world's largest producer of commercial shipping.

Presumably he had kept a close eye on the Kure project when he was shuttling back and forth between Tokyo and Washington during 1950 and early 1951. Now that he was in London, the U.S. State Department dutifully kept him informed about the progress of the Ludwig agreement with the Japanese. On June 4, 1951, Secretary of State Dean Acheson cabled Dulles in London to get in touch with Tokyo about the matter. Three days later, Acheson wired Tokyo: IN ORDER GIVE PROPER OPPORTUNITY ASSESS LIKELY EFFECT OF PROJECT ON PEACE TREATY NEGOTIATIONS, REQUEST YOU STRONGLY URGE DECISION BE DEFERRED UNTIL NEXT WEEK WHEN DULLES CONVERSATIONS IN LONDON WILL BE COMPLETED.

On the same day, Dulles cabled Acheson to report progress in the London talks:

AUSTRALIAN AND OTHER COMMONWEALTH COUNTRIES ORIGINALLY PROPOSED PEACE TREATY CONTAIN DEFINITE PROVISION DISMANTLING "EXCESS" SHIPBUILDING CAPACITY OF JAP. HOWEVER IN RESPONSE TO AMERICA REPRESENTATIONS HAVE AGREED LEAVE SUCH CLAUSE OUT OF TREATY, BUT HAVE EXPRESSED HOPE THAT JAP WLD VOLUNTARILY MAKE SURVEY OF ITS PRESENT SHIPBUILDING CAPACITY WITH A VIEW TO DISMANTLING OR DIVERTING TO OTHER USES THAT WHICH NOW IS SURPLUS AND THAT BECAUSE OF DIFFICULTIES IN OBTAINING RAW MATERIALS UNPREDICTABLE

FUTURE WILL PROBABLY REMAIN SURPLUS FOR SOME TIME TO
COME. WE HAVE TOLD BOTH AUSTRALIAN AND UK REPS THAT WE
WLD DISCUSS MATTER WITH JAPS TO DETERMINE WHETHER OR NOT
THERE WERE ANY PRACTICAL STEPS ALONG THESE LINES WHICH
CLD BE TAKEN. IT IS SUGGESTED YOU INFORMALLY CALL THIS
POINT TO JAP ATTENTION AND INFORM IGUCHI THAT I SHALL WISH
TO DISCUSS THE MATTER WITH HIM AND QUALIFIED JAP WHILE IN
TOKYO WHERE I NOW EXPECT TO ARRIVE IN ABOUT TWO WEEKS.

On June 12, a State Department employee named Johnson sent a
lengthy message to Dulles through the Far Eastern office presided
over by Dean Rusk. The message noted that National Bulk was
"very anxious to proceed with the agreements" and that these had
the backing of Admiral Callahan, head of the Military Sea Transport
Service. Dulles was also asked whether he thought a public announcement of the project might have an adverse effect on the peace
treaty negotiations.

Dulles cabled back:

I STRONGLY URGE THAT NATIONAL BULK CARRIERS, INC., NOT RE-
CEIVE SCAP APPROVAL PURCHASE OR LEASE OF KURE SHIPYARD FOR
AT LEAST FEW WEEKS. BELIEVE IF ANY PUBLICITY GIVEN AT THIS
TIME TO PLANS OF NATIONAL BULK CARRIERS IT WOULD HAVE
SERIOUS DELETERIOUS EFFECT, PARTICULARLY IN UK WHERE
THERE IS STILL CONSIDERABLE APPREHENSION OVER JAP SHIP-
BUILDING CAPACITY AND POTENTIAL. DELAY OF SEVERAL WEEKS
SHOULD NOT PREJUDICE EVENTUAL CONSUMMATION OF ARRANGE-
MENT.

In deference to Dulles's wishes, SCAP held off approving the
agreement until the delicate negotiations could be concluded and the
peace treaty signed. The British, deceived into thinking that Dulles
would talk seriously to the Japanese about reducing their shipbuilding capacity, put their signatures to the document. Little did they
realize that their shipbuilding supremacy was already doomed
— that Dulles had deliberately withheld information. Thus Dulles
got his treaty, and Ludwig got his shipyard.

Having finally gotten SCAP's approval for the Kure deal, Ludwig
set Elmer Hann to work hiring laborers and producing ships. Before
the end of 1952, the first tanker, the 38,000-ton *Petrokure,* was
completed and launched, and Ludwig already had plans for three

more of the same size to be built the following year. These ships were larger by nearly 10,000 deadweight tons than any tankers previously built. But he had an even bigger one on the drawing board — the 44,500-ton *Phoenix* (the third Ludwig-owned ship to carry that name) — and due to come off the ways in 1954.

Such gigantic vessels took a lot of steel. About two thirds of Ludwig's shipbuilding costs were for materials, and over half of this was for steel to build the hulls. He was building ships that were probably cheaper per ton than those built by anyone else, but he still wanted to cut costs, and the best way to do so was to obtain a cheap, abundant supply of steel.

It was not easy. World War II had taken a tremendous toll on known reserves of iron ore, and even the United States was beginning to run short. The vast iron fields of Wisconsin's Mesabi range and other smaller reserves had been almost depleted. American steelmakers had begun to explore elsewhere for new sources of ore.

United States Steel, for example, had secured a large concession in the Cerro Bolívar region of Venezuela's Bolívar province south of the Orinoco River. Early tests had indicated that iron ore reserves in the area, near Standard Oil of New Jersey's petroleum fields, might be as large as the Mesabi's had been, and of far higher quality. By late 1949 U.S. Steel had completed more extensive geological and technical tests confirming the value of the find, and plans were being made to set up extensive mining operations.

The plans were running into considerable political opposition. Venezuela was being run by a military junta basically sympathetic to foreign investment, but there were those in the country who felt Venezuela should develop its own steel industry rather than allow foreigners to carry off the ore and smelt it elsewhere. Nevertheless, U.S. Steel and other North American steelmakers were going ahead with plans to exploit Venezuela's rich ore fields.

Daniel Ludwig was familiar with these efforts and had great interest in them. Furthermore, he saw a way of benefiting the Japanese steel industry by supplying it with higher-grade ore than it was presently using. No altruistic motives need be assumed. If D.K. could provide Japan with a steady supply of top-grade iron ore, he could negotiate for less expensive, better quality steel than he was then bargaining to import from the United States. He could also expand his shipping enterprise to handle dry cargo.

Ludwig began negotiations with U.S. Steel to get a concession to haul iron ore out of Venezuela once the mines started producing. Not far into these talks, new opportunities opened up that caused D.K. to think about diversifying his operation far beyond shipping and shipbuilding.

U.S. Steel was looking for a variety of things besides ships to haul its ore. Specifically, the company was searching desperately for farmers and cattle ranchers who would raise beef and agricultural produce to provide food for the construction crews and miners who would be working at Cerro Bolívar.

Ludwig had not tried this sort of thing before. He was a shipper, not a farmer or cattleman. But it was a golden chance. If there was enough money in it, he could hire the experts he needed. All he would have to do was to make sure they were doing *their* jobs.

The steel company wanted somebody it could trust in this job of supplying food. An American businessman like D.K. would be loyal to his corporate customers. So a deal was worked out. U.S. Steel would give Ludwig a concession to haul 20 percent of the iron ore mined at Cerro Bolívar. It would also use its influence with the junta to help him get a huge tract of land near the mines and oil fields — half a million acres or more — which he would clear in order to grow beef and other edibles, and could also exploit for whatever oil or minerals were there. For his part, D.K. would supply the iron mine workers with food. He would also help U.S. Steel get contracts to supply Japanese steel mills with iron ore, then haul the ore, or a sizable fraction of it, to Japan, taking other cargoes to U.S. Steel's smelting operations in Philadelphia.

Ludwig and the steel company had substantially come to an agreement by the middle of 1951, for a State Department document dated June 12 of that year notes, referring to National Bulk, that "the Company has tentative plans for building a 60,000 ton ore carrier which could be utilized to carry Venezuelan iron ore to Japan at a substantial savings over other iron ore now available to Japan."

Ludwig's plans for his Venezuelan land are reflected in an amendment to National Bulk's corporate charter. Dated September 11, 1952, the new section expands the company's allowable activities to include "exploration and development of petroleum, gas, asphalt, hydrocarbons, metals, ores, coal, other minerals . . . operation of oil wells, mines, drilling equipment, all kinds of oil, gas and mineral development, also farms, ranches, livestock."

From this time forward, National Bulk would list itself not as an oil transportation firm but as a holding company, and D.K. was no longer just a simple shipper and shipbuilder. He was now a highly diversified one-man multinational corporation.

Exactly what Ludwig did on much of his Venezuelan land is not generally known; those connected with it have not talked about it. Indications are that it was never even surveyed, and estimates of its size vary considerably.

It *is* a matter of record, though, that D.K. had several thousand acres cleared for a cattle ranch, called Hato Vergareña, and that this enterprise was having some problems. Ludwig sent his administrative assistant, William B. St. John, down to try to straighten things out, and an agricultural attaché at the site, James H. Kempton, wrote an amusing report of the visit for the Venezuelan ambassador. It reads:

> Bulk Carriers' Bolívar ranch, Hato Vergareña, is developing the troubles to be expected in a venture of this sort. . . .
>
> Mr. Wm. St. John, who is representing Bulk Carriers on the ground, has spent the last month on the property while the cattle round-up for inventory purposes was in progress. The cowboys managed to bring in 1,200 animals which is a few short of the 2,000 claimed as being on the property. In the course of this operation they succeeded in breaking the legs of two half breed Cebu bulls and two cows. Shortly after the 1,200 animals were secured behind the fence, the fence was cut and the animals dispersed. This operation is laid to the ex-owner.
>
> Mr. St. John is convinced he is dealing with an accomplished group of cut throats which include the ex-owner and Bulk Carriers' Venezuelan advisor, together with a choice lot of local characters who are all set to pluck the stranger from New York.
>
> At the moment he is in Caracas hoping to find, evidently at the local bars, a two-gun Spanish speaking Texan out of employment who knows cattle and who will be willing to live on the Hato Vergareña for a modest salary and protect the interests of Bulk Carriers.
>
> Mr. St. John is not discouraged, though he is anxious to get back to his New York desk where the banditry, though just as effective, is conducted with better form and more style than it is in the wilds of Bolívar.
>
> It is Mr. St. John's comforting opinion today that there is only one route over which cattle thieves can make off with Bulk Carriers' four-footed assets. This opinion is not shared by your reporter.

More will be heard of Hato Vergareña before it electrifies investors
by declaring a dividend.

For the ambassador:
James H. Kempton,
Agricultural Attaché

Despite these early difficulties, D.K. remained committed to the
Venezuelan ranching venture and to the ore-hauling project as well.

Meanwhile, at Kure, D.K. had Elmer Hann start building ore carriers. The shipyard was by now a considerable operation. On the
payroll were less than a dozen foreigners and some twenty-five hundred Japanese workers, plus another fifteen hundred on subcontractors' rosters. In 1954 they produced the *Ore Chief* and *Ore Transport,*
to be followed by the *Ore Titan* in 1955. Each of these ships, at
60,000 deadweight tons, exemplified Ludwig's "bigger is better" thesis. But as soon as the *Ore Chief* went into service, it became apparent that D.K. had made a costly miscalculation. He had failed to
realize that Venezuela's Orinoco River, down which U.S. Steel's ore
had to be hauled from the mines to the Caribbean, tended to silt up
badly during rainy seasons, creating shoals at its mouth. Though
Ludwig's new ore carriers had no trouble going upriver empty, they
usually ran aground coming back down fully loaded. The only way
they could get safely back to sea was with half a load.

Ludwig did not like admitting a mistake. Years afterward he
insisted to an interviewer that his 60,000-ton ore haulers, operating
even with half loads, were economical enough to make money. But
the ore ships he built later were around 45,000 tons: the *Ore Prince*
(1955), *Ore Monarch,* and *Ore Convey* (both 1956). He also built an
even smaller ship — the *Sinclair Petrolore* — which, as its name
implies, was a bulk carrier able to haul either petroleum or ore, and
was built for charter to a long-time customer, the Sinclair Refining
Company. The mixture of cargoes, however, presented a hazard.
Fumes from a previous oil cargo tended to accumulate in the hold,
where a spark could ignite them. In December 1960, the *Sinclair
Petrolore* exploded and sank off the coast of Brazil.

Meanwhile, Ludwig had to solve his problem on the Orinoco. He
brought one of National Bulk Carriers' old T-2s, the *Pan Georgia,*
over to Kure and converted her into a dredge, renamed the *Sealane.*

On completion, she was to be taken to Venezuela and put to work cutting a channel in the Orinoco deep enough to allow his ore carriers to sail downriver, fully loaded, without scraping bottom.

At the same time, he brought another T-2, the *Pan Massachusetts,* to Japan for renovation into a 30,000-ton ore hauler, rechristened *Commonwealth.* Both of these remodeling jobs were part of a large-scale restructuring of Ludwig's shipping empire. He was gradually phasing out most of National Bulk Carriers' oil-hauling operations. The major part of his U.S.-flag fleet was still under charter, but as contracts expired, he either sold his old ships or converted them to other uses.

His new ships were being registered foreign. Around 1950, the congressional criticism of Panamanian operations, plus his desire to have a headquarters nearer the Persian Gulf–Europe oil trade he was then courting, prompted D.K. to move much of his foreign operation from Panama to Liberia. This mainly involved setting up an office and a tanker-servicing facility in Liberia's capital, Monrovia. Like Panama, Liberia had long been a kind of unacknowledged U.S. colony; it was established in the early 1800s as a country for freed slaves.

It was there that Ludwig started two new companies, Universe Tankships and Seatankers, Inc., as his latest big-tanker and little-tanker corporations. Universe was to operate the big ships, which were transferred from Oceanic Tankships in Panama. Oceanic, however, would remain in place as a holding company and official owner of Universe Tankships, providing a buffer in Ludwig's increasingly complex corporate empire. Seatankers was to take over most of the little boats of Panama's International Tankships.

These moves represented Ludwig's entry into an international oil trade that was shifting its center from North and South America to the Middle East after the end of World War II. It was the market that the Greeks had almost managed to get a lock on.

Onassis nearly pulled off a coup in 1954 that would have given him clear domination of what had become a three-man race for the title of "world's tanker king." Working quietly and insidiously, he had managed to talk King Saud, ruler of Saudi Arabia, into signing an agreement that would make him the only non-Arab involved in hauling the forty million tons of Saudi oil exported each year.

Onassis's clever manipulation of the Saudi monarch made a lot of people angry, including Stavros Niarchos. It also disturbed the major oil companies, whose tight control over the international petroleum cartel was predicated on a carefully maintained balance between all of the working parts. By going behind the scenes and making his own deal with Saud, Onassis had violated the rules of the game and threatened the system's equilibrium. This upstart would have to be taught a lesson and the balance restored.

In the early days of the Eisenhower administration, there were means of doing both. Besides the regular network of intelligence professionals, there was also what Jim Hougan, in an article in *Playboy,* called "an archipelago of private-detective agencies and so-called public-relations firms — ostensibly private businesses that operated with the secret sanction of the Federal intelligence community and that did its bidding on the home front."

One such detective agency was being run by a former FBI agent, Robert A. Maheu, who was building a reputation for taking on sensitive jobs that the CIA did not want to dirty its hands with. Shortly after the Onassis deal with Saud leaked out to interested parties, Maheu and a secret operative named John Gerrity went to Washington for a meeting with Vice-President Richard Nixon. Their purpose was to work out a way of bringing Onassis to his knees and canceling his deal with the king of Saudi Arabia.

What was Nixon's interest in the matter? After making a national reputation for his prosecution of the Alger Hiss spy case in the Senate, he had become allied with oil and banking money and been viewed by prominent Republicans as a man on the rise.

In 1952, the Republicans wanted the presidency badly, and it looked like their year. Truman was stepping down; the Democrats did not yet have a strong leading contender. But the Republican front-runner for the nomination was Ohio Senator Robert Taft. Son of a former president, Taft was a strong conservative, but also a man of great intelligence and integrity. He would not be easily controlled. The Rockefeller interests were looking for a man who could be. Dewey would have suited their purposes very well; he was a smart lawyer who knew how to walk the edges of the legal precipice, and was also part of the inner circle of political power. And Nixon was a good possibility. He met all the criteria except one: he probably was not electable. He was well known, but not *that* well known. The Rockefeller Republicans wanted a sure winner this time around.

They found him in General Dwight David Eisenhower, a popular war hero who had presided over the victory in Europe. Nixon, meanwhile, was being groomed for the vice-presidency. He was also part of the inner circle, privy to secrets of power that only a few people shared. His nomination to the nation's second highest office had been carefully engineered by a handful of men representing the Rockefeller interests: Thomas E. Dewey, the unsuccessful candidate in the 1944 and 1948 elections; the Dulles brothers; and Herbert Brownell, who would become Eisenhower's attorney general.

It was Nixon, the Dulleses, and Brownell, then, who had real political power in the Eisenhower administration. They pulled the levers and kept the wheels turning the way the corporate powers wished. Just now these men were concerned with bringing Onassis down a few pegs. They did not want to destroy him completely, for that might expose the oil cartel. The situation had to be handled with delicacy and finesse. This was why Maheu was brought in and why Nixon was overseeing the operation.

The plot would involve phone taps and the planting of stories — some true, some half true, some false — in cooperative foreign and domestic newspapers, all with the purpose of changing Onassis's image from that of a glamorous celebrity to a cunning villain. After he had been sufficiently smeared, the U.S. Department of Justice would start suits against him that, it was hoped, would force him to relinquish his exclusive rights to haul Saudi oil. A government attorney, Warren Burger, would be instrumental in bringing such legal actions.

The money for funding the operation was to be passed through an emissary of Stavros Niarchos's. Niarchos had a vested interest in seeing the Saudi contract — the Jidda Agreement — scrapped. So, of course, did Daniel Ludwig, and the question arises as to whether Ludwig was also involved in the plot. There is no hard evidence to tie him in. Given D.K.'s secrecy, though, this does not necessarily rule him out. His later ties with Nixon included hiring the former vice-president (and future president) as National Bulk Carriers' attorney in the sixties and entertaining him in his Connecticut home. It is also known that Ludwig was a close friend of Herbert Brownell, whose supervision of the Justice Department would include authorizing the suits against Onassis.*

---

*Brownell, before being appointed attorney general, was a member of the New York law firm of Lord, Day & Lord, one of whose partners, George de Forest Lord, had once been instrumental in buying the *Ulysses* from Ludwig. The firm had also advised Onassis earlier that his ship purchases were legal.

Maheu flew to Arabia to hold secret talks with Saudi officials, who subsequently ordered Onassis to sit down with ARAMCO representatives and work out their differences. He had no choice but to comply, and the Jidda Agreement was broken. Like magic, the suits and attacks against him ceased, and his chief troubles were over. When the Suez Canal was closed in 1956, the unprecedented demand for tankers made him richer than ever — as it did Niarchos and Ludwig.

But in 1954, with the tanker market still in a slump, D.K. was busy shifting from petroleum to iron ore as a way of guaranteeing himself a steady income. Having gained a concession to haul U.S. Steel's ore from South America to Japan, he was now breaking into the North American market. When he learned that a small corporation, Ore Transport Company, had begun hauling ore from Quebec and Labrador to U.S. Steel's Philadelphia smelters and expected to increase its annual loadings from a current two million tons to eight or ten million over the next few years, D.K. started thinking about a takeover.

Ore Transport was jointly owned. Half the company's stock was held by a consortium of six steel companies. The other half was in the hands of an established but floundering shipping firm, American-Hawaiian Steamship Company. AHSS had prospered for half a century, but it was encountering hard times in the postwar years. Though its Ore Transport affiliate was starting to show a profit, the parent company was burdened with a fleet of outdated ships that racked up yearly losses in the intercoastal trade. Clearly it was vulnerable.

The takeover would not be friendly. Although American-Hawaiian was a public company, most of its stock was held by a few well-heeled investors, some of whom would not take kindly to D.K.'s close-fisted style of management. Unquestionably they would also be squeezed out; Ludwig did not like sharing control with anyone. Once he acquired enough stock, he would probably convert American-Hawaiian to a privately held company.

But if D.K. had enemies among the firm's stockholders, he also had powerful friends. He had made it a point to establish close relations with several key officers and directors, among whom were:

Samuel H. Moerman, an attorney who would become chief executive officer after the takeover.

H. J. Coyle, who would be another top executive.

J. A. Kennedy, another important functionary.

Hal A. Kroeger, a stockholder-director who would become involved in several of Ludwig's other ventures over the years.

William Keith, a director also on the boards of Lockheed Aircraft and Hilton Hotels.

Lawrence C. Marshall, a director who was also one of the top officers of Chase Manhattan Bank.

George E. Allen, a director and one of the most powerful men in America. Allen was a wheeler-dealer who, using his ability to make people laugh, gravitated unerringly toward centers of power. He had become the intimate of several U.S. presidents, and he wrote a book called *Presidents Who Have Known Me* — including FDR, Truman, and Eisenhower. In the Truman years he had not only been one of the Missourian's inner circle of advisers but had been appointed head of the Reconstruction Finance Corporation. When Truman left office, Allen promptly abandoned him and ingratiated himself with Ike as a favorite golfing partner. Hurt, Truman publicly called Allen a "fixer." Drew Pearson had earlier called him "a dangerous influence in government." The charges were merited. Behind Allen's clownlike demeanor lurked a shrewd, conniving mind. He knew everyone who was anyone in Washington and corporate America, and sat on many boards of directors. Besides being president of Allen Oil Company, he was a director of Chemical Bank, New York Trust, Atlas Corporation, AVCO (Aviation Corporation of America, on whose board Daniel Ludwig, probably through Allen's influence, would also sit, beginning in 1960), Occidental Life, Republic Steel, and many others.

Working with and through these men, Ludwig managed to buy up 69,500 shares — over 27 percent of the stock outstanding — before Wall Street caught on to what was happening. This was enough to give him working control of the company, and a tender early in 1955 got him another 35,000 shares. But it also stirred protest from a number of stockholders who resented the takeover. Several directors of AHSS resigned in a huff, including James S. Rockefeller, president of New York's National City Bank; Arthur A. Ballantyne, former under secretary of the treasury; and Ellsworth Bunker, chairman of National Sugar Refining Company (and later U.S. ambassador to South Vietnam).

Just as Ludwig was making his move to take over his first public company, he was besieged by trouble from another direction. It almost cost him his shipyard at Kure. In August 1954, a committee of the Japanese Diet charged Prime Minister Shigeru Yoshida and about half his Cabinet with accepting bribes from certain government-subsidized shipbuilders in exchange for favors. No specific builders were named in the charges, but Ludwig — the largest shipbuilder in postwar Japan and the recipient of numerous benefits granted by the Japanese government — may have been involved.

There were demonstrations at the Kure yard, and rumblings of discontent with the deal the Yoshida government had made earlier with D.K. were heard all the way to the Maritime Administration in Washington. But for the most part the pressure was on Yoshida and his cronies.

The Diet committee pressed for a full investigation and called on the prime minister to come before it and answer questions. But the cagy Yoshida kept stalling for time. As the heat intensified, he took off on a worldwide junket, first to Europe, then to the United States, where he stopped off in New York to see his old boss, General Douglas MacArthur. Then it was on to Washington, where Yoshida had closed-door meetings with Secretary of State John Foster Dulles.

Apparently it was agreed that the only way to salvage the situation was for Yoshida to bail out. Following the conference with Dulles, the Japanese prime minister flew home and resigned rather than answer the Diet committee's charges. The matter was largely hushed up, and the ruling Liberal Democratic Party managed to keep control of the government and install Ichiro Hatoyama as Yoshida's successor.

Japanese politics for a long time remained under the control of men closely tied to U.S. corporate interests, chief among whom was a shadowy figure named Yoshio Kodama, long known to U.S. drug enforcement officials as "the Al Capone of Japan" because of his international trafficking in narcotics. Kodama nevertheless, after being "retrained" by American occupation forces, had proved useful to his captors for his ability to organize gangs of Japanese hoodlums to beat up left-wing demonstrators. Rising in power, Kodama had become a paid agent of American military contractors as well as a kingmaker. Later he was a key figure in the Lockheed bribe scandals, which brought down the Tanaka administration in the early 1970s.

But it is a political truism that covering up one scandal only leads to a worse one later, and had the Yoshida bribe charges received better coverage, the Lockheed episode might not have happened. The world press, however, and the American press in particular, were strangely silent on the fall of Shigeru Yoshida, head of state of a major country. The charges and his resignation were mentioned only briefly in U.S. newspapers, which made no attempt to go below the surface or uncover the names of shipbuilders who had allegedly paid the bribes. As with the Maritime scandals in the United States, government officials took the punches, and private interests sustained nary a scratch.

*Ten*

# Grand Bahama Island

During the autumn of 1954, as charges flew and tensions mounted in the Japanese shipbuilding bribery scandal, Prime Minister Shigeru Yoshida and his Cabinet members were not the only ones who worried. Unless the issue could be defused, Daniel Ludwig might have to move his ship-construction operation elsewhere.

He looked around for a place where he could start afresh in case he suddenly had to leave Kure. There were several possibilities. He could still go to West Germany, which he had considered doing in 1950, or to one of several other European sites. But no area seemed more likely than the Caribbean.

Ludwig did not want to come back to the United States to build ships. There was too much wrangling with the Maritime Administration and other government agencies over regulations, and too many taxes to pay. In Japan he had — for the time being — virtual autonomy. He was free to do things his way without government interference, at least while Yoshida and his cohorts could hang on to power.

But if they couldn't and he had to move, he wanted the same kind of arrangement elsewhere. It wouldn't be that hard to find. Rulers of small or underdeveloped countries were usually eager to please if they smelled money. There were other factors to be considered, though. Geography was important, which was why the Caribbean basin was an attractive prospect. Ludwig's activities in Panama and Venezuela and the Cayman Islands had given him a strong presence there. And, though he did not want to set up a shipyard *in* the United States, it would be convenient if the yard were *near* the United States.

The choice soon narrowed down to Grand Bahama Island, a narrow stretch of land in the Bahamas chain about eighty miles east of Palm Beach, Florida.

Topographically, the Bahamas seem like little pieces of paradise dropped down into the warm Caribbean. Their surrounding waters are emerald green, and so clear that a swimmer at their surface can observe schools of bright-colored fish darting among coral outcroppings several fathoms down. Their sands are clean and white under the hot tropical sun.

Their human history is something else, filled with episodes of plunder and exploitation since the coming of the white man. Columbus had first set foot in the New World on one of these islands; he found it inhabited by Lucayan aborigines, whom he erroneously called "Indians." "Gentle, peaceful people of great simplicity" was how he described them in his journal; then he added, after appraising them with a conquistador's eye, "They ought to be good servants, and of good skill."

By the end of the next century, the entire native population of the Caribbean islands — more than two million Lucayans, Arawaks, and Caribs — had been removed, many slaughtered outright, most hauled off to die slower deaths in the mines of Cuba and South America. By the time the Spaniards discovered that sugar cane could be grown on some of the larger islands, they had to import other slaves from the mainland — later from Africa — to do the sweat work.

Late in the sixteenth century English freebooters began raiding the Spanish islands, and during most of the seventeenth and eighteenth centuries the Bahamas were a base for pirates — Blackbeard, Morgan, Lafitte, and many others. Spain and England both claimed ownership of the islands in this period; the English finally established primacy in 1783 through the Treaty of Versailles.

During and after the American Revolution the Bahamas became a refuge for Tories fleeing the mainland with their slaves and whatever other possessions they could take away by boat. These new colonists perpetuated the planter economy previously practiced by the Spanish; a white minority controlled a steadily growing population of blacks. Even after slavery officially ended in the island in the mid-nineteenth century, nothing much changed, except that the blacks were afterward referred to as "natives." (As one present-day "native" expressed it, "They couldn't call us 'Indians,' so they called us 'Bahamians.' ")

During the American Civil War, the Bahamas, and especially their capital, Nassau, on New Providence Island, became a headquarters for Confederate blockade runners sneaking guns and cotton past Union warships. After that bloody struggle, the islands were more or less quiet until the advent of Prohibition in the United States, at which time they hosted a new breed of blockade runner — bootleggers seeking to move liquor into the United States in violation of the Volstead Act. The traffic in contraband booze brought money to the Bahamas, which became a center for offshore banking, tax-avoidance schemes, and fly-by-night operations run by everyone from petty swindlers to top figures of organized crime, always with the hospitality and cooperation of local officials.

Such dubious activities, continuing after the end of Prohibition, were augmented by another importation during the 1930s and 1940s. Attracted by the islands' white-elitist tradition, rich Nazis came to take up residence. One was the Swedish industrialist Axel Wenner-Gren, owner of the Electrolux Corporation. An outspoken advocate of the doctrine of Aryan supremacy, Wenner-Gren bought little Hog Island in Nassau Bay and turned it into an outpost for Nazi machinations in the Western Hemisphere during the late thirties and early forties. He also used it to play frequent host to the governor of the Bahamas — the Duke of Windsor — and his American wife, the former Wallis Warfield Simpson, after the duke and duchess were sent to the islands as a kind of exile for admiring Hitler too openly.

It was not surprising, then, that after more than four and a half centuries of use and abuse by conquistadors, freebooters, pirates, Tory slave owners, Rebel blockade runners, bootleggers, con men, corrupt officials, and Nazis, the Bahamas would roll out the red carpet for Wallace Groves.

In 1948, when Groves came over from Miami at the head of a boatload of laborers bearing saws and axes, Grand Bahama Island was forested with stands of slender, graceful Caribbean pines. It was these trees Groves had come after. South Florida, in the years following World War II, was experiencing an unprecedented building boom as hundreds of thousands of Americans, having endured the Depression and the war, were ready for retirement or at least a little fun in the sun. They had saved their money during the early 1940s and now wanted to spend it in Florida, and they flocked south as fast as houses, hotels, and apartments could be thrown up to accommodate them.

Most of the stands of timber in central and south Florida were being exhausted in the rush of new construction, and Groves was looking for new sources close by. He remembered Grand Bahama from the good old days — those freewheeling years during and after Prohibition when, as the "whiz kid of Wall Street," he had been on top of the world. He had had the Midas touch then, and would pop down to Miami or the Bahamas for a deal or a pleasure cruise, living high and loving every minute of it. Then it had all gone sour.

Groves had first made national news in 1931, when the Bank of the United States collapsed. Reasons for the failure were unclear, but evidence pointed to shady dealings by the institution's top officers. New York City's police commissioner called it "the biggest racket of the year," and Governor Franklin D. Roosevelt tried to get to the bottom of the matter.

Wallace Groves was probably not involved in the bank's collapse. A Virginian by birth and rearing, he had made a name for himself in Baltimore banking circles. Then he had headed to New York to try to pick up some of the pieces of the Bank of the United States, either for himself or the interests he represented. There was a bit of the vulture in him, and he was looking for a feast among the dying businesses on Wall Street. No one knew where his money came from, but he was soon making fortunes by buying up failing companies, turning them into moneymakers — at least on paper — and then selling out. Some old financial hands, noting that many of his deals were financed through Canadian or Bahamian banks, suspected that he might be fronting for bootlegging interests.

Whatever his connections, Groves was getting rich on Wall Street at a time when many established companies were struggling to meet their payrolls. By 1934 he had acquired a Park Avenue penthouse, his own private island, Little Whale Cay, in the Bahamas, and a beautiful new wife, Monaei, who had given up a stage and screen career to marry him and bear him a son and heir.

Things were going swimmingly for Groves until the spring of 1937, when he took Monaei on a Bahamian cruise to meet some of his Miami friends. He wanted to show her what a big man he was in Florida, but she was thoroughly disgusted. She considered his friends crude hoodlums and began looking at Groves himself in a different light. When the couple returned to Manhattan, she left to go to the bedside of her ailing father in Indiana. Soon after she arrived there, terrible news came from New York. Her young son, whom she had left with a servant, was missing and presumed kidnaped.

Beside herself with grief and fear, Monaei rushed back to New York, only to learn that she had been the victim of a cruel hoax. Groves had merely removed the child to a nearby hotel suite in the care of a nursemaid and staged the "kidnaping" to get his wife back.

The plot blew up in his face. Furious at having been tricked, Monaei, recovering her son, packed him and herself off to California to live with friends. She then made a short trip to Reno to get a quick divorce. Four days later, by coincidence, federal agents who had been tracking Groves charged him with tax avoidance, stock manipulation, and fraud. According to the indictment, he had acquired a company, the General Investment Corporation, built its assets through deceptive advertising, then looted it.

After a four-year court battle, Groves was convicted of using the mails to defraud purchasers of General Investment stock and was sentenced to two years in a federal penitentiary. Released in 1943, he headed south to Miami and was soon enmeshed in land-speculation schemes. Every kind of con game was going on in south Florida, many of the schemes being run by ex-bootleggers who had used their booze profits to buy up cheap land along Florida's east coast and were now making another killing in land sales and construction. Miami was fast becoming known as a city where organized crime called the shots.

As a financial wizard and ex-con, Wallace Groves fitted right in. He obviously couldn't go back to Wall Street, where his record and reputation would haunt him; but in south Florida his past carried no stigma, and he soon found numerous contacts and opportunities to make money.

By 1948, Groves was popping over to Grand Bahama to cut timber. The island was covered with pines just waiting to be cut. All he had to do was find a few complaisant Bahamian officials willing to grant him a logging permit for a small fee and some cash passed to them under the table.

The seat of government was in Nassau, 120 miles southeast of Grand Bahama Island. Officially the Bahamas were a colony of Great Britain; in practice they were nearly autonomous. They were ruled by a governor appointed by the Crown (currently the Earl of Ranfurly), aided by a nine-member Executive Council and a Parliament comprising representatives elected from the inhabited islands.

Bahamian politics were in fact tightly controlled by a clique of white merchants, lawyers, and doctors, most of whom had their shops and offices along Nassau's main thoroughfare, Bay Street. For this reason they were known in the islands as the Bay Street Boys, and without their approval, nothing significant could be done in the Bahamas. All the members of the Executive Council, including the premier, Sir Roland Symonette, were Bay Street Boys, but the most powerful was a massive man named Stafford Sands.

A direct descendant of one of the first English families in the islands, Sands was the Bahamas' leading corporation lawyer. He was also minister of tourism and finance. Born into wealth, he had increased his fortune several times over by a simple device. As the attorney representing a corporate client, Sands would present the client's proposal to the islands' minister of tourism and finance. Then, switching hats, he would obligingly approve the project. Sands drew no salary as a government official, but as an attorney he raked in legal fees by the armful. Questions of conflict of interest bothered him not at all. Let others moralize. He had a country to run.

In his double role Sands had become so rich and powerful that some referred to him as King Stafford the First. If he wasn't officially king of the Bahamas, he undeniably had royal tastes and powers. He dwelt in a million-dollar mansion in which he housed a world-renowned collection of antique paperweights and a closetful of expensive smoking jackets he was fond of wearing while entertaining. And entertain he did. His parties were the talk of the islands; even when he had in a few friends for an informal dinner, he would set out enough Beluga caviar for a hundred guests.

If someone had decided to make a movie of Sands's life in those days, he would certainly have picked Sydney Greenstreet for the lead. Or, scaling the plot up to higher levels of international intrigue, he could have used the three-hundred-pound lawyer as chief villain in a James Bond epic. Clever, urbane, and totally corrupt, Sands was greed personified.

Groves soon discovered it was an easy matter to make a deal with the corpulent minister. But things were not to end there. Over the next five years, while Groves, operating as Abaco Lumber Company, Ltd., was leveling pines and shipping them off to Florida, he was forming an ambitious plan.

It would be a shame, after clearing all this land, just to go off and leave it. There was room for a city here, if only he could get someone to come and build it. Groves envisioned a duty-free center for manufacture and international trade. The duty-free aspect would be the lure. Any manufacturer would be able to come in, set up a plant, and import raw materials and equipment without paying a tariff. The Bahamas were already free of most taxes, including those on income, so a businessman could keep almost everything he made.

There would be a little fee, of course. As the developer of the project, Groves would hold licensing power and get a percentage — say around 10 percent — of whatever a company earned in profits. But this would still be less than what the U.S. government would take in taxes and tariffs if the operation were in the States.

By 1953 Groves had his plan worked out clearly enough to take to Sands. He would develop a duty-free port on Grand Bahama's south shore, and ships and businesses would flock in to make him rich. He would call the place Freeport so that there could be no mistaking the advantages it offered. And it would be his to run as he pleased.

Sands, after looking over the plan, suggested a few modifications. First, as chief financial officer of the Bahamas, he did not like the idea of the port being entirely duty free. The government would receive no money that way. Industries and other commercial operations could import goods free of tariff, but people would have to pay some duty. Groves agreed to this.

Second, there had to be financial backing from a reputable source, somebody who could afford to come up with a few million in startup funds. Much of this money would have to be spent dredging a deep-water harbor if large ships were to be able to dock at Freeport.

The translation of Groves's plan into the reality that became Freeport is a puzzle from which several pieces are still missing. What is apparent is that, at some early stage of development, Groves was able to come up with two American backers for his scheme: Charles Robert Allen, Jr., of the New York investment banking firm of Allen & Company, and Daniel Keith Ludwig.

Charlie Allen was a colorful figure who later earned the reputation of being the richest man on Wall Street, and he was demonstrably one of the richest men in America. A hardheaded businessman, he was nevertheless known to take an occasional flyer on a long shot. He had made his first million in the market by 1929, only to see it go down in the Crash. Worth remarking is that he had made it all back by 1931, when the stock market was bottoming out. From that time on, he and his brother Herbert, doing business as Allen & Company, grew steadily richer.

Although much of his money and reputation were made on the Street, Charlie Allen was also a mover and shaker in other areas, including Hollywood. His first wife, Rita Friedman, had been a theatrical producer, and Allen had developed a strong interest in show business. He eventually owned controlling interest in several major Hollywood studios. And in the mid-1950s, he was willing to invest several million dollars in the development of Groves's Freeport.

Daniel Ludwig's role in the Freeport scheme is both more and less clear than Allen's. D.K. had a function to perform. It would be his job to dredge the harbor and an entrance channel through the coral-filled shoals surrounding the island so that large vessels could get close to shore. He had the equipment to do the job. His large dredge *Sealane,* which he had converted from a T-2 tanker at Kure, was just finishing the deep-water channel in the Orinoco that would allow his ore carriers to come downriver fully loaded. Once that job was completed, the *Sealane* could be brought north to begin work on the Freeport harbor and channel.

D.K. also wanted to start a shipyard on Grand Bahama, either to replace or supplement his Kure operation. At this time, the Yoshida situation had not yet been resolved, and Ludwig did not know whether he might have to pull out of Japan in a hurry. If he did, he needed a place to jump to, and Freeport looked like the place.

Initially, then, D.K. had two obvious reasons for getting involved in Freeport. A mystery, however, surrounds the depth of his involvement. A question that has lingered since Freeport started is where

Groves got the money and power to take over much of Grand Bahama and build the city in the first place. It has been speculated that Ludwig, from the very beginning, was Groves's silent partner and chief financier. Leslie Waller, in his 1972 book *The Swiss Bank Connection,* remarked, "Whether or not the Ludwig ownership was long ago transferred to Switzerland for protective reasons, the fact remains that in every move Groves made over the years he had an exceedingly silent associate who, some say, owned more of Groves than Groves."

It would help if we knew how Groves, Ludwig, and Allen got together to begin Freeport. Had they known one another earlier? Had D.K. and Allen helped Groves hatch the plan? Had Ludwig and Allen been acquainted in New York? These questions, like many others surrounding the project, remain unanswered.

Whatever the case, Groves soon returned to Sands with adequate financial backing, and Sands took the plans to the Earl of Ranfurly. It sounded like a good idea, said the earl, but it was a pity, since the Bahamas were, after all, a British possession, that Americans should reap all the profits. Why not bring in a British investor as well, he asked, and suggested an old friend, Sir Charles Hayward, head of Firth-Cleveland, Ltd., a diversified English conglomerate.

After some haggling back and forth, the matter was settled. Groves, Allen & Company, and Firth-Cleveland would cooperate in a joint venture and form a new company, Grand Bahama Port Authority, Ltd., to build Freeport. Groves would hold a 50 percent interest in the authority; the other two partners would hold 25 percent each and put up much of the financing. The Bahamian government would sell the authority fifty thousand acres (about one sixth of the island) for £1 (then $2.80) per acre.

The Port Authority would also be granted numerous other concessions, including the right to exempt any Freeport business from corporation taxes until 1990 and from customs duties on imported business goods until the year 2054. The concessions given the authority, someone later remarked, were the greatest ever granted by an established government to a private company since England's Charles II, in the late 1600s, conferred almost unlimited rights to the Hudson's Bay Company to exploit Britain's Canadian territories.

All the Port Authority had to promise in return was to build and develop a port and dredge its harbor to a depth of thirty-two feet.

The conditions and concessions were incorporated into the Port Authority charter and submitted as legislation. The Hawksbill Creek Act (so called after a stream running through the property, which in turn was named for the hawksbill turtles which laid their eggs on the island) sailed through the Bahamian Parliament early in 1955 and was quickly signed into law.

Once the plan was authorized, Ludwig brought the *Sealane* up from Venezuela to start dredging the ship channel and harbor, a job for which he later presented the Port Authority with a bill amounting to $5.6 million. Allen & Company, as part of its investment in the project, picked up the tab.

From the outset, D.K. may have been playing a dual role in the development of Freeport. On the one hand, he was having some of his companies perform various operations connected with the project, such as doing the dredging and starting a shipyard. On the other, the venture itself has the earmarks of a Ludwig deal. For example, press releases about the dredging note that the Port Authority was supplying its own equipment, even though the dredge belonged to D.K. Also, the authority soon announced that it was starting a new ship-refueling operation in the harbor, for which it would be the sole owner and operator, with Gulf Oil Company supplying the fuel.

This refueling station would in itself be a sizable project, benefiting the tanker traffic — including most of National Bulk Carriers' fleet — between the Texas Gulf Coast and the Northeast. The tankers were currently carrying not only their cargoes of petroleum but also their own supply of fuel. If they could stop en route for refueling, they could carry less fuel to start with and devote more of their tank space to cargo.

The Port Authority's ship-refueling station, then, looks like a classic Ludwig maneuver to save and make money. Almost certainly it was his idea, since none of the visible partners in the authority had any connection with oil transportation. The choice of Gulf Oil as the supplier of fuel also supports the notion that Wallace Groves had by now become the front man for interests much larger than himself — that the idea of Freeport, though it may have been his originally, was being shaped by Daniel Ludwig in cooperation with Gulf Oil.

Two of the first industrial projects for the new Freeport development were announced on November 29, 1955. The Earl of Ranfurly issued a press release stating that D. K. Ludwig was planning to build a $30 million shipyard and a 100,000-ton-per-year chemical lime plant on Grand Bahama. But the earl, it seems, had jumped the gun. Reporters calling National Bulk Carriers' offices for confirmation were told that the release of information was premature. Yes, the company was interested in starting these projects, but plans would not be completed for another six to nine months. No other details were available.

Ludwig always hated having news of his ventures leak out before he was ready to make them public. Nevertheless, he went ahead with getting the necessary Bahamian licenses for the announced projects. He set up two new corporations, Bahamian Shipyards, Ltd., and Bahamian Chemicals, Ltd., in Nassau to handle the operations.

The shipyard company, under its charter, was empowered to dredge two basins in the Grand Bahama industrial area large enough to accommodate ships of 80,000 deadweight tons (about the size of the largest vessels Ludwig was then building at Kure), with the option of adding a third basin later. Bahamian Chemicals was licensed to export lime rock, but there were indications in its charter that the company was planning to engage in related operations, too. This corporation came about because Ludwig was dredging lime rock out of the Freeport harbor and looking for profitable ways to dispose of it. A less thrifty man would probably have hauled it away and dumped it in the ocean, but D.K. was not one to waste thousands of tons of dredge spoils if there was a way to make money from them.

The rock was almost pure limestone, the calcified remains of billions of tiny marine animals forming the coral base of Grand Bahama Island. Chemical lime was useful in a number of industrial processes, including the making of steel and cement.

Rather than trying to go it alone, Ludwig brought in some professional help. He worked out a deal whereby U.S. Steel, his ore supplier in Venezuela, would buy a million-dollar parcel of land on Grand Bahama and put up a cement plant. He would supply the raw material and buy some of the finished product — an arrangement similar to the one in which he hauled iron ore to Japanese steel mills and then bought some of the finished steel to build his ships.

D.K. needed cement. He was planning to bring eight hundred of his Japanese workers and their families over from Kure to start the Grand Bahama shipyard and wanted housing for them. Groves had removed most of the timber from the island, so there wasn't much left to build with except lime rock and sand. But with cement, he could turn those materials into concrete.

Out of these simple beginnings was to come a construction innovation that made Daniel Ludwig one of the world's largest house builders. The method would be known as Con-Tech (evidently short for "concrete technology") and, like most of his innovations, would be simple, quick, and cheap, designed to eliminate waste and maximize profits.

The basic idea was to set up lightweight, portable aluminum molds on a construction site and pour the concrete into them. There was no wooden framing to bother with, no carpenters or lumber or nailing involved. And no particular skills were needed. All the workers had to do was to set the molds in place (these would be custom-made from ore Ludwig was hauling from his bauxite mines in Venezuela), bring in truckloads of concrete mix to fill them, then remove the molds when the concrete had dried.

The Con-Tech method was soon perfected to the point where half a dozen unskilled or semiskilled laborers, using a few aluminum forms each light enough for one man to carry, could erect all the exterior and interior walls of a house in half a day's time. As a brochure put it, "The entire cycle of removing the form from the previous day's work, setting up new forms, and pouring concrete can be finished in less than eight hours, completing a wall with wiring, plumbing, and window and door frames all in place."

This inexpensive method which Ludwig and his engineers developed to build houses for the Japanese workers on Grand Bahama was, ironically, never used for that purpose, for the shipyard itself never materialized. As soon as dredging started on the two basins mentioned in the charter, it was found that the coral bedrock was not strong enough to bear the weight of the supertankers D.K. was planning to build. At any rate, this was the excuse given for scrapping the project, and it may have been true. But by this time Prime Minister Yoshida's resignation and the appointment of a new head of state had taken most of the pressure off Ludwig. Finding an alternative to Kure as a place to build ships was no longer imperative. Finding an alternative building method that was cheaper, easier, and quicker than anything else around, however, was of prime importance.

To utilize and market Con-Tech, D.K. started two more companies. International Concrete Company was to handle U.S. operations, and International Housing, Ltd., was to oversee foreign operations. Within less than two decades these firms, often through joint ventures or local franchises, would have more than a hundred thousand housing units built or in progress around the world. The cost of building most of these units was next to nothing. In 1974, Ludwig put up houses in Mexico, each of which — with three bedrooms, a large kitchen, and a fully equipped bathroom — was designed to sell for $2500 and still make money for the builder. But another beauty of the system was that by using more elaborate molds, D.K. could build larger houses, offices, and commercial buildings. Con-Tech could construct for princes *and* paupers. It could even create walls that, when painted, looked like brick or stone.

While his engineers were working to perfect Con-Tech, Ludwig decided to relax a bit. When he wasn't traveling to his various enterprises, he was dividing his time between New York and Los Angeles, where he had established another residence to be nearer his Latin American and Japanese operations. It was in January 1956, when he was in California, that he took the *Danginn* on a cruise from the West to the East Coast, with a stopover in Venezuela so that Clark Gable could try some jaguar hunting.

But for Ludwig, the trip was really more than a pleasure jaunt. It gave him the chance to look at several sites where he was thinking of starting projects. One was on Mexico's Pacific coast, about halfway down the Baja peninsula. Here, at a place called Guerrero Negro (Black Warrior) Lagoon, were huge underground deposits of brine. Concentrations of salt in the water were around 30 percent, nearly ten times the salinity of sea water.

By the simple process of pumping this brine to the surface and letting it stand in pools where the hot sun could evaporate the water, one could produce millions of tons of salt, which could be gathered and exported. The economy of the procedure appealed to D.K. All he had to do was bring up the brine, and nature would do the processing.

The main problem was labor. This part of Baja California was nearly unpopulated, and he would have to import workers and build places for them to live. Not only to live, but to shop and go to church. The Baja coast was so remote that he would have to build an entire town if he was going to develop the salt deposits.

But he had learned something by now. Opportunities exist on the frontiers where most men dare not venture, and it is often the case that the farther the frontier, the greater the opportunity. The majority of men, even businessmen, are tied to cities, where the ingredients of development already exist — labor, energy supplies, building materials, transportation, and so on. Competition also exists there, and the way to escape it is either to do something no one else is doing or do it where no one else is doing it.

Much of Ludwig's success was due to his willingness to venture where more timid entrepreneurs dared not go. If he needed to bring along men and equipment to carry out a project in a remote area, he had the ships to get them there. He *could,* if there was enough money in it, move the mountain to Mohammed, and he *would.*

Late in 1956 Ludwig sent shiploads of crews and heavy equipment to Baja to build a new town at Guerrero Negro Lagoon. Streets were laid out, lots surveyed, and Con-Tech workers with their aluminum molds and truckloads of wet concrete were soon busy putting up houses, stores, and churches. The community was designed to be self-sufficient, except for the foodstuffs and other necessities that would have to be imported.

The salt operation would be known as Exportadora de Sal. Ludwig, operating through National Bulk Carriers, also owned, in joint venture with Dow Chemical, a company in Salt Lake City called Solar Salt. Whether he was supplying this company with salt from his Mexican operation or processing it locally is not clear. It may be that he was marketing Exportadora's salt in the United States until he had large enough volumes to ship abroad. Once the Baja plant's output increased to as much as four million tons a year (making it the largest producer of solar salt in the world), D.K. built special self-unloading ships at Kure to haul the salt and constructed a deepwater port facility off Cedros Island near the Baja coast to load the vessels. Most of the salt went to Japan and Canada, and one of the ships, the S.S. *Cedros,* had enough capacity to keep Japan supplied with all the salt it could use.

Ludwig kept the project going until 1973, when, in response to threats by the Mexican government to nationalize the operation, he sold it to Mitsubishi for $20 million while retaining his contracts to haul the salt. A year earlier, he had sold National Bulk's share of Solar Salt to the American Salt Company.

As he was starting Exportadora in 1956, though, he was also

embarking on an even more ambitious project in Panama: the building of a 55,000-barrel-a-day refinery and an adjoining petrochemical complex. This was to be a joint venture with Continental Oil Company (Conoco) costing an estimated $33 million, two thirds of it for the refinery, the other third for the petrochemical operation. Still another corporation, Central Industries, would be set up to manage the project.

Ludwig was to furnish at least some of the crude petroleum from his wells in Venezuela. He could refine it in Panama, then ship the finished product through the canal to Japan. He and Conoco had worked out a very favorable deal with the Panamanian government whereby they would have to pay a tax of only a penny on each barrel of crude refined.

Before starting construction, however, D.K. had a little chore to perform, one that he intended to do personally. Twice he had trusted the word of specialists, and twice he had been burned. He had believed them when they told him he could bring fully loaded 60,000-ton ore carriers down the Orinoco without running them aground. And his geologists had failed to discover, until after considerable work was done, that the coral rock underlying Grand Bahama Island was too fragile to support giant supertankers.

These episodes had cost D.K. considerable time and expense, so before building a refinery in Panama, he decided to check out the site himself. Dressed in baggy work clothes, he caught a night flight out of New York to Panama City and arrived at Tocumen Airport just about dawn. A car was waiting to drive him the fifty miles to Las Minas Bay on the Caribbean side near Colón. The refinery site was out in the bay, on Pavardi Island.

He sauntered into a little village store at the bay's edge just as it was opening, casual as any gringo tourist down for a holiday and a bit of fishing. Pulling a quarter out of his pocket, he paid for his purchases: a heavy bolt costing a nickel and a twenty-cent ball of string. As a few loiterers watched with amused curiosity, he unwound the string, measured it out in six-foot lengths, and tied a knot at each interval. Then he made a slip knot at one end and drew it tight around the bolt. This done, he went outside, made arrangements with the dock owner to rent a motorboat, and spent the rest of the morning and afternoon puttering around the bay, checking with his weighted line the accuracy of every sounding marked on a nautical chart he had brought along. Only when he had satisfied himself that the water was as deep as the chart said did he fly back to New York and give the signal to begin construction.

The start of the Panama refinery (which became operational in 1962) marked another step in Ludwig's efforts to integrate his oil activities into a smoothly flowing whole. He was already a producer, having struck oil on his Venezuelan lands, and he had long been a transporter. But soon he would be able to haul his own oil from his own wells to his own refinery (he bought out Conoco's interest soon after the project was completed) in his own ships, then haul the refined products, again in his own ships, to Japan and other consumer countries. Hypothetically this would make him an independent oilman. Actually he was part of the complex network of producers, refiners, and transporters that constituted the international cartel.

Ludwig was getting more heavily into oil for the same reason Willie Sutton gave for robbing banks: that's where the money was. Dwight D. Eisenhower had been put into the White House primarily by oil money, and, once there, he approved while package after package of legislation favorable to the oil industry was rammed through Congress. The oil-depletion allowance, expensing of drilling costs, foreign tax credits — these breaks and others allowed oil companies to become incredibly rich and at the same time get credits on their tax returns. Ludwig, as a member of this exclusive club, was growing so rich that, despite his efforts to avoid publicity, he was drawing attention to himself. The "New Argonauts" article in *Time* mentioning him as one of the world's largest shippers was soon followed by *Business Week*'s "Tanker King" piece, revealing the diversity of his activities.

It was now more imperative than ever for him to move secretly if he was to conduct his business in private. And just now he was plotting a deal that had to be done quietly. He was aiming to become the major oil supplier for the southeastern United States.

*Eleven*

# Seadade

The article in the June 8, 1959, *Miami Herald* attracted little attention. It said basically that a land syndicate headed by D. K. Ludwig, one of the richest men in America, was bidding on a 1280-acre parcel of land in south Dade County, Florida.

But the reporter who had learned about the bid thought it important enough to do some digging. Land deals in Dade County had a way of growing pretty big. In north Dade, where Miami was located, real estate values were rocketing higher than anything being shot from Cape Canaveral, a couple of hundred miles up the coast.

Land along Florida's Atlantic seaboard had been attracting investors and speculators ever since Henry Flagler, a friend of John D. Rockefeller's, had come down from Pennsylvania with pockets full of Standard Oil money and, in the 1880s and 1890s, opened up the southeast coast to rail transportation. Since World War II, though, things had really gone crazy. Fortunes were being made overnight on land schemes, particularly in the Miami area, and those in the know were saying that the mob was involved in many of the deals. Land bought for little could be sold and resold through dummy corporations until it was appraised at many times its real worth; then it was dumped, for huge profits, on unwary homesite buyers looking for their place in the sun.

The growth of the military in response to the cold war was also bringing many new residents to Florida. South Dade, for example, was now the site of Homestead Air Force Base, a giant Strategic Air Command facility. Except for that, and the town of Homestead, there wasn't much in the lower county except the Everglades in the west and coastal mangrove swamps in the east.

The inflated land prices in north Dade, then, had not yet affected the southern part of the county. The state of Florida, which owned the 1280-acre parcel, had considered cutting it up into small lots that could be sold for more than the $175-per-acre appraisal value. State officials had decided against subdividing, though, when they learned that the land was subject to periodic flooding and that small landowners, if they wanted to drain their lots, would have no place to divert the water. If the land was to be drained, this could be done more easily as a large project.

But when the state got an offer for the entire property at its appraised value of $224,000, the price seemed awfully low. Perhaps a new appraisal was needed. Perhaps the company making the offer should be questioned about its plans.

Seadade Realty, Inc., had been chartered as a Florida corporation only a short time before, on April 29, 1959. Its officers were D. K. Ludwig, president; W. W. Wagner, vice-president and treasurer; and I. M. Halfpenny, secretary. Its business address was 380 Madison Avenue, New York. Its local business agent was Preston Bird, a prominent real estate agent and a former mayor of Homestead and Dade County commissioner. Its reason for wanting the land was to build a housing development on it.

Not until nearly two and a half years later would the people of Dade County get an inkling of what Daniel Ludwig was really up to. The light dawned when a Seadade employee filed an application to have two thousand acres of land between Homestead AFB and the ocean rezoned for heavy industrial use. When queried, a spokesman for the realty company divulged that a $40 million, 50,000-barrel-a-day refinery was being planned for the site, to be followed by a $300 million petrochemical complex.

The refinery would take a twelve-hundred-man construction force two years to build and would then employ seven hundred workers. The petrochemical plants using the refinery's byproducts would eventually employ twenty thousand more.

By now, Seadade had acquired at least eighteen thousand acres of cheap real estate — land that would have been priced far higher had

Ludwig's intent been known. On the land still zoned for residential use, D.K. planned to build housing and necessary commercial buildings to accommodate upwards of a hundred thousand people — the more than twenty thousand employees of the refinery and petrochemical plants and their families.

The refinery would be the first in the entire Southeast. Not another one existed on the entire length of the coast between Louisiana and Delaware. It would presumably supply not only Florida but Georgia, Alabama, the Carolinas, and Virginia with gasoline and other refined petroleum products.

The reason there had been no refinery in the region earlier was that no oil was produced there. But Ludwig would make up for that lack by bringing in crude petroleum from Venezuela and the Middle East. South Florida would soon become a major refining and petrochemical center, resembling Philadelphia and the Gulf Coast of Texas and Louisiana.

Some Dade officials and residents were excited about the prospect, particularly real estate agents and other businessmen, who saw an influx of population that spelled money, money, money. Local environmentalists, on the other hand, were horrified. They foresaw forests of smokestacks spewing black billows and poisonous chemicals into the atmosphere. They pointed out that the county had no regulations to deal with the probable pollution problems. County officials conceded the point and agreed to hold off on the rezoning decision until new pollution regulations could be drawn up and put in place — a process estimated to take nine months.

In the interim, more of the details of Ludwig's project emerged. Along with building a refinery and petrochemical complex and a city for the workers to live in, he was planning to dredge a deep-water harbor and channel through some of the upper keys to establish a port where his supertankers could come in close to the refinery to load and unload.

Some county officials began having reservations about the size and scope of the project. They were not entirely satisfied with the assurance of Seadade spokesmen that the refinery and chemical plants would be almost free of pollution. They asked for federal help in evaluating the impact of the proposed refinery on south Dade's ecology, and got back some surprising replies.

There had been a changing of the guard in Washington. President

Eisenhower had delivered a memorable farewell address, warning of the dangers inherent in what he called "the military-industrial complex." John F. Kennedy and his band of New Frontiersmen had stepped in. Among Kennedy's appointments was a devout environmentalist. Secretary of the Interior Stewart Udall advised Dade County officials not to give Seadade permits to build a refinery until Seadade could provide meaningful assurances that the operation would not damage air and water quality in the Everglades and other nearby national parks. "It's the long-standing interest and function of this department," said Udall, "to protect wildlife."

The U.S. Public Health Service came forward with some disturbing figures. The refinery, it said, could be expected to emit an estimated thousand pounds of sulfur dioxide per hour — nearly as much as was then being produced by all four electric generating plants in Dade County. In addition, its emissions would measurably increase hydrocarbon and carbon monoxide pollution, and give off twice as much nitrogen oxide as all the automobiles in the county combined. This pollution, said the agency, would damage or kill vegetation in the area over a prolonged period of time.

After reading these federal reports, Dade County environmentalists redoubled their efforts. They turned Seadade into a public issue, sparking debate in the local media among businessmen and citizens. The refinery became a hot topic of conversation, and county residents chose sides; the split was mostly along geographical lines. The town of Homestead was strongly in favor of the project because of the business it would bring in. Miami was about evenly divided. Many business leaders welcomed the idea, but thousands of new residents who had moved down from northern industrial cities to escape pollution were opposed to it. Miami Beach began to fear for its tourist industry. If the air and water and beaches became fouled by oil spills and the pollution from the refinery and petrochemical plants, hotel owners and other businessmen dependent on those seeking recreation could kiss their investments goodbye. Owners of expensive beach houses started picturing what would happen if a tanker ran aground in Biscayne Bay and broke apart. About the only point everyone agreed on was that if the refinery did come, south Dade County would be radically changed. Many saw it as a change for the better. Many did not.

County officials were in a quandary. How strict should they make the regulations? If they were too harsh, D.K. would not build. If they were too lenient, the environmentalists would raise Cain. Then there was the dredging to worry about. Would a 300-foot-wide, 32-foot-deep ship channel through the keys and the bay disrupt water flow and cause beach erosion? It was rumored that Ludwig was going to pile his dredge spoils alongside the channel, creating a long artificial island that would run crossways to the keys. How would that affect boat traffic?

Some people sprang to Ludwig's defense. Mitchell Wolfson, a member of the Committee of 21, a local businessmen's association, said in a newspaper interview: "It [Seadade] could well become one of the great ports of the world because of the strategic geographic location. . . . I believe Seadade is destined to bring tremendous benefits to south Dade as well as to the rest of the state if given encouragement."

The author Philip Wylie responded with a heated article giving reasons that Seadade should not be allowed to come in. Preston Bird (who had bought most of the land — now amounting to more than twenty-five thousand acres, or nearly forty square miles — cheaply for Ludwig before the nature of the project became known) gave a newspaper interview pleading Seadade's case, but he weakened his credibility as an objective observer when he admitted making a lot of money as D.K.'s land agent.

By now the matter had dragged on for more than two years as Dade County officials kept putting off a decision. (Surprisingly, the national media, except for *Business Week,* which carried a couple of paragraphs, ignored the Seadade struggle entirely.) The *Miami Herald,* after sitting on the fence throughout the debate, finally came out with a lukewarm endorsement.

Nevertheless, county officials, when they finally made a decision, voted unanimously to kill the project. More accurately, they voted to accept Ludwig's withdrawal of the refinery application. Some ambiguity still lingers about the decision. Did the commissioners go along because D.K. had changed his mind and decided not to build? Or did he withdraw the application because he knew it was going to be denied?

Ludwig then sold off much of the land to Florida Power and Light. He kept some land, though, on which to build housing developments as a way of recouping his initial investment. He tried to get a few tracts rezoned for various commercial purposes, and, as late as 1982, was still trying — and failing — to obtain permits to dig lakes in the middle of mangrove swamps in order to erect condominiums around them. But the Seadade project had raised environmental awareness in south Dade County to the extent that local ordinances were passed to discourage development and protect the area's natural attractions.

Ludwig finally had had an encounter with aroused public opinion, and, rich as he was, he had lost. But the most probable cause of his defeat — the group that gave the Seadade project its kiss of death — was not the environmentalists or the citizens or the county commission but the Miami Beach hotel owners. During the public debate, Morris Lansburgh, owner of five hotels and a close friend of Meyer Lansky's, had said, "Why take a chance? Who needs it?"

Ludwig got the message. He turned to other projects. If he couldn't lick the hotel owners, he'd join them. There was more than one way to make money.

# Twelve

# American-Hawaiian

While Daniel Ludwig was taking a flyer in Florida real estate, he was also investing in California land. Having observed the exodus of people from the North and Midwest to these two warm states after World War II, and the resulting growth of the tourist and recreation industries along the ocean, he saw the shift as a profit-making opportunity.

D.K. liked getting in at the beginning of a trend and riding the wave as far as it would carry him. He felt that U.S. census figures were bound to keep rising, and that all these people would need places to live and play. Beach property in warm climates would be especially valuable. There was only so much of it, and its value was bound to rise.

Ludwig had created Seadade Realty to handle his Florida land acquisitions. In California he used the American-Hawaiian Steamship Company, the intercoastal cargo-hauling firm he had bought control of in 1954.

AHSS had begun the postwar period by doing much the same thing Ludwig's National Bulk Carriers had done — buying up surplus T-2 and T-3 tankers in order to continue serving oil-company customers on the East and West coasts. Unlike D.K., though, the company failed to anticipate that its American-flag carriers would be unable to compete successfully against the flag-of-convenience fleets of the Greeks and Ludwig himself. By 1948 AHSS was starting to hemorrhage red ink, and by 1954 the mounting losses appeared fatal, at least to some of the officers, directors, and large stockholders of the company. These were the men who helped D.K. wrest control of American-Hawaiian from other stockholders.

The prospect was tempting. While it was true AHSS was losing money, it was also true the company still had considerable assets, including its fleet of ships and a sizable portfolio of stocks accumulated over the years as investments. It also had several million dollars' worth of claims against the U.S. government for war losses, which had dragged on for nearly a decade without settlement.

Ludwig had not taken over a public corporation before, preferring to create private companies entirely owned and controlled by himself and unregulated by the government. But, by investing a few million dollars to buy control of AHSS, he could recoup his outlay almost immediately by selling off the company's ships, acquiring the portfolio of stocks, and pressing the government for settlement of the war claims.

He had several plans for reviving the moribund company, only a few of which had anything to do with shipping. But one that did was a method that would revolutionize dry-cargo hauling and cost thousands of dockworkers their jobs. The idea was not Ludwig's; it's not clear who first thought of it. But it emerged about the time Harry Bridges and his longshoremen's union were striking to win higher pay and other benefits for the men who loaded the ships at dockside. The strikes were interrupting shipping schedules, and the shippers were looking for ways around this problem.

The answer was a technique called roll-on-roll-off loading, or RORO. Traditionally, many dry-cargo commodities — canned food, for example — were trucked from factory to dockside, unloaded by dockworkers, and reloaded aboard a waiting freighter. This process was both labor-intensive and time-consuming.

The RORO approach would allow truckers, driving tractor-trailer rigs, to haul the same cargoes directly on board a ship, unhook the cab from the trailer, and drive away. At the ship's destination, another truck tractor could drive on board, hook up to the trailer, and drive off. The trailer would function as a packing crate on wheels, containing the cargo from the time it left the factory until it reached a distribution point in some far city.

RORO may not have been Ludwig's idea, but it was his *kind* of idea, and he immediately saw its advantages. He never liked using manpower for any job a machine could do less expensively, more quickly, or more efficiently. If he had to employ human labor, he preferred it to be foreign and cheap, except for a few top managerial and technical positions. His aim was to eliminate the human factor whenever possible in getting his projects accomplished.

There was, however, another problem. With RORO, the shippers not only could roll on and roll off their cargoes; they could roll over the dockworkers' unions. But they had to have the cooperation of the truckers, who were also unionized. If the Teamsters decided to strike in sympathy with the longshoremen, RORO would never work. It was necessary, then, to break the Teamsters away from the body of the U.S. labor movement, a move soon accomplished through bribery and infiltration by elements of organized crime working secretly with and for the shippers. Once deals had been made with Teamster head Dave Beck and his men, roll-on-roll-off shipping could become a reality, and the pesky, persistent Bridges and his dockworkers could be sacrificed to the gods of economic progress.

Ludwig's part in the RORO scheme lay in his plans to build specially designed container ships, equipped with ramps allowing trucks to drive on and off the vessels at dockside. By building these ships, he hoped to get an early jump on the competition and gain control over RORO shipping contracts. The business was to be handled through American-Hawaiian.

First, though, he wanted to gain better control over the company, but the continued hostility of some embittered stockholders who refused to sell gave him trouble. He had put attorney Samuel H. Moerman in as chief executive officer, and, as a way of driving the company's stock prices down so that other stockholders would become discouraged and sell out to him, D.K. instructed Moerman to draw up a pessimistic annual report, saying, in effect, that AHSS's prospects for the immediate future looked grim indeed.

As required by law, American-Hawaiian, a public company, had to submit the report to the Securities and Exchange Commission for review before issuing it to stockholders. The SEC criticized the document for giving an unbalanced picture and advised against mailing it. But Moerman sent it out anyway, drawing a complaint from the SEC that American-Hawaiian's officers were trying to manipulate stock prices downward.

To take the heat off, Moerman resigned and went to Washington, where he set up a law office and acted as Ludwig's lobbyist in the nation's capital. In 1958, when things had cooled off somewhat, he reassumed the chairmanship of American-Hawaiian. By this time, D.K. had sold off all the company's ships for around $7 million and had settled (with Moerman's help) the war claims against the government for $4 million. The $11 million would be put into a construction reserve fund at Maritime, where it could be held — tax free — until such time as Ludwig decided to start building RORO container ships.

Financing the project was a problem. D.K. did not want to risk so much of his own money, and private lenders were skittish about lending such a large amount on what was still a highly speculative venture. Ludwig's approach was to apply to the Maritime Administration for permission to build ten new container ships and ask the government to underwrite 87.5 percent of the mortgage insurance necessary to obtain funds for construction.

Maritime was not eager to get involved. First, like the banks, it felt the proposal to be highly risky. Next, the agency itself was a branch of the Department of Commerce, and just now Commerce was in the midst of a bitter dispute between shippers and railroad owners over whether water or rail was the cheapest, speediest, most efficient form of intercoastal transportation. (When the Department of Transportation was set up, it arbitrated such matters.) Maritime's endorsement of Ludwig's container-ship proposal would force Commerce to commit to the shippers' side at a time when the department was trying desperately to maintain a neutral posture.

Third, three companies were currently trying to get into the intercoastal container-ship business: American-Hawaiian; Luckenbach Steamship Company, a family operation that had been in the shipping business for 112 years but was now having difficulty staying afloat; and Sea-Land Services, an affiliate of McLean Industries, whose owner, a Winston-Salem entrepreneur, had expanded a fleet of trucks into a nationwide operation he was now trying to combine with RORO shipping.

All three of these companies were applying for government aid from Maritime. But it was generally understood that there was enough intercoastal business to sustain only one operator profitably. This meant the agency could not approve one application without drawing charges from the other two companies that it was playing favorites.

From the outset, the container-ship race shaped up as a two-man battle; Luckenbach did not have the money or political clout to wage a sustained struggle. Ludwig, of course, as the world's largest independent shipper — or in the top three, at least, depending on what Onassis and Niarchos were doing at the moment — was a powerful force to be reckoned with. He had influential friends in the Defense Department and was able to call on support in Congress if he needed it. But Malcolm McLean was not without friends. He was being backed by the huge conglomerate Litton Industries, owner of a substantial chunk of McLean stock and actively interested in seeing Sea-Land get the franchise. Another McLean friend was North Carolina's former "businessman governor," Luther Hodges, whom President Kennedy had picked to be U.S. Secretary of Commerce.

With Litton and Hodges in his corner, McLean was a formidable opponent. Moreover, Ludwig had made an enemy who just might undermine American-Hawaiian's chances, a man who could hit him where it hurt.

Loring Revere Hoover had been intensely angered in the mid-1950s by what he considered D.K.'s highhanded takeover of AHSS. Hoover had been associated with the company since 1929, as a stockholder and as a member of the board of directors (he had stepped down as a director in 1950), and he had a strong sentimental attachment to it. Ludwig was used to riding roughshod over people, but Hoover, a New York lawyer and investment banker, was not a man to be trampled underfoot. He had been around a long time, and he knew how to make himself felt.

Throughout the container-ship struggle, Hoover, as a minority stockholder, wrote long, carefully worded letters to Maritime full of embarrassing questions designed to hurt Ludwig's chances of getting the mortgage insurance money. For example, he wrote — after D.K. had finished selling off the last of American-Hawaiian's old vessels — "May I ask how a steamship company in name only *without* any ships or tankers or containers of its own to be put up as collateral and guarantees is able to get a hundred-million-dollar mortgage loan?"

It was a good question, but one Maritime chose to ignore, as it would most of Hoover's other queries and comments. Finally, in

1959, seeing that he could get no satisfaction from the agency, Hoover enlisted the aid of several other dissident stockholders and filed suit in federal court, charging that Ludwig, Moerman, George Allen, and several other officers, directors, and stockholders of American-Hawaiian were conspiring to maintain the firm nominally as a shipping company when in reality it was operating as a real estate investment firm. As a result, Hoover and his fellow plaintiffs claimed, they could not get tax credits due them because of the company's concealed purposes.

It was not really the higher taxes that bothered Hoover and his friends; that was merely an issue to give them legal standing in the courts as injured parties. The stocks they were refusing to sell to Ludwig were earning greater dividends than they could have expected under the previous management. Rather, their loyalty was to the company itself, which they felt had been taken over by a corporate raider who was looting it and deceitfully insisting that it was still a shipping company, even though it had no ships and was being used for purposes far removed from shipping.

If American-Hawaiian was still a shipping company, Hoover asserted, let it act like one. If it was to be operated as a real estate investment firm, let the change be made honestly. If it was not going to do either in an ethical manner, let it be liquidated. Better the company die a quiet death than be prostituted by the likes of Daniel Ludwig and George Allen.

In the stockholders' suit, Hoover and his associates charged specifically that AHSS, though continuing to masquerade as a shipping company, was investing its available monies in real estate ventures in New York, the Washington, D.C., area, and California.

A reading of American-Hawaiian's 1961 annual report confirms the truth of these charges. In it, Moerman mentioned that the company had just sold off the last of its old ships and was still seeking Maritime-backed mortgage money in order to proceed with the container-ship project. It was also trying to rescue a small subsidiary, the Journapak Corporation (a manufacturer of lubricators for railroad car axle housings) from near bankruptcy. Then Moerman got to the meat of the report — the real estate ventures.

American-Hawaiian, he said, had just formed a wholly owned subsidiary, Hawaiian Realty, Inc., which entered into a fifty-fifty partnership with Fisher Brothers Construction Company to build a forty-four-story office tower, the Burroughs Building, on Third Avenue in Manhattan between Thirty-ninth and Fortieth streets. The structure, Moerman added, would have eight hundred thousand square feet of office space to lease.

In a connected project, AHSS was investing $4.5 million in a joint venture with Fisher Brothers to build a co-op apartment building at Fifth Avenue and Sixtieth Street, overlooking the southeast corner of Central Park. (This structure, seventeen stories high, would contain fifty-eight apartments, each with four to ten rooms, to be rented to wealthy occupants. Ludwig himself would reserve the penthouse for his own residence.)

American-Hawaiian, through another wholly owned subsidiary, Hawaiian Washington, Inc., had formed a partnership with a Washington realty company to buy and rehabilitate an office building on Pennsylvania Avenue, not far from the White House, to lease to a federal agency for five years. American-Hawaiian was investing a million dollars for a 50 percent interest.

Through yet another wholly owned subsidiary, Hawaiian Freestone, Inc., the company was investing $250,000 to buy five hundred acres of land at Freestone Point in Prince William County, Virginia, to resell or develop.

American-Hawaiian had sold off some company-owned land in San Diego at a profit and still had a lot of acreage left in that city.

On August 15, 1961 (Moerman continued), AHSS, through the wholly owned subsidiary Cargo Despatch, Inc., went in with a New York realty group in a joint venture to sublease and operate the Empire State Building. Cargo Despatch put in $2.25 million for a 37.5 percent share, but was selling out its interest in the project four months later for a profit.

Moerman ended the report by noting that, on December 26, 1961, the company's directors had approved the filing of a registration statement with the SEC that would allow American-Hawaiian to devote up to 70 percent of its total assets to real estate development, and, at the same meeting, had approved the purchase of a parcel of land — 11,500 acres — located in Los Angeles and Ventura counties, California, for $32 million.

It is obvious from this report by Moerman that the charges in Hoover's court suit were essentially correct, and that Ludwig, after buying a majority interest in American-Hawaiian, had turned the company from shipping to real estate while keeping up a charade. It is also apparent that he was using the firm's assets to plough perhaps ten times what he'd paid for it (probably between $5 and $10 million) into development schemes. The acquisition of American-Hawaiian was evidently making D.K. considerably richer than he had been previously.

Acquiring the tract in California was itself a coup that would bring in hundreds of millions of dollars and create a new city. The property was the Albertson Ranch, a large spread used primarily for cattle raising for almost a century. Now, with Los Angeles mushrooming, the land was a prime candidate for development. It was only forty miles northwest of downtown L.A. and a short distance from Topanga Canyon (soon to be made famous by the Manson gang). The L.A.–to–Ventura freeway had already been built through the tract. The Rocketdyne Division of North American Aviation was only twenty minutes away; the rapidly growing Conejo Industrial Park only ten. Over the next decade, big defense industry payrolls in the area would draw a large population, according to Ludwig's sources of information, and he figured on attracting between fifty and a hundred thousand people to live on the Albertson Ranch property — which would soon be known as Westlake Village.

First he had a fight on his hands to buy the land. By the time he learned it was for sale, in the fall of 1961, a Beverly Hills Realtor, John O. Gottlieb, had already put in a bid of $30 million for it. Ludwig upped the ante to $32 million ($2782 per acre), and the battle began. Gottlieb went to court, and lawyers kept the deal tied up for the next two years. Then the Beverly Hills entrepreneur settled, taking a $500,000 payment from AHSS for giving up his claim to the property.

By this time, according to *Business Week,* which was following the suit with interest, the value of the land had risen to an estimated $45 million. "Ludwig's plans for the development still are vague. It is likely he will build for low, middle, and high income housing, together with shopping and recreation centers, schools, churches, roads and hospitals. When the 20-year project is completed, the price tag will be well over $1 billion."

Unspecific as the details were, *Business Week* was getting them directly from the horse's mouth. For the better part of a decade, the magazine had been almost the only member of the American media (assuming Dero Saunders's *Fortune* article to be a puff piece deliberately arranged by D.K.) to regard Ludwig as an item of news interest and show curiosity about his financial activities. *Business Week* had provided the first significant — and unauthorized, since its reporter couldn't get past the National Bulk Carriers reception room — look at this secretive man who was on his way to becoming the world's wealthiest private individual. Its March 16, 1957, article was entitled "Tanker King Who Shuns Crown."

Now, six years later, D.K. had finally allowed the magazine to send one of its writers over to National Bulk's offices — and past the reception room — for a personal interview. The observations of the reporter — perhaps the only reasonably objective newsman ever to get this close a view of Ludwig — are worth repeating at some length.

The headquarters staff for his entire empire numbers less than 260 persons — including secretaries. . . .

The inner sanctum from which Ludwig controls his network of operations has but a single black telephone. And Ludwig's working desk is so small and cluttered with papers that even this single phone is exiled to a little table close to Ludwig's left hand.

D.K.'s taste in décor, while still Spartan, was mainly nautical.

The office itself is modestly furnished with a leather sofa and five brass-studded leather chairs. The pastel-blue walls of the L-shaped room are bare except for two pictures, one depicting a Japanese pagoda. Two barometers, a barograph, and a double-chiming ship's clock are set at strategic points about the room.

Other hints of the sea are provided by four ship models, including one of the sailing frigate *Essex,* made for Ludwig by one of his retired captains. The floor is covered with a light gray wall-to-wall carpet. Through a window, at a distance of several blocks, can be seen the sheer black walls of the new Burroughs building, one of Ludwig's many real estate projects.

The interviewer offered a rare word-portrait of the tycoon himself.

Ludwig likes to work in his shirtsleeves, and when he takes off his jacket he usually reveals a pair of gaudy suspenders. Often his concentration is so intense that his usually neatly combed hair falls over one eye. His speech offers little hint of his South Haven, Mich., origin. He meets visitors with a mixture of confidence and shyness, head down, eyes peering warily from under shaggy brows. It is this shyness — or modesty — which has kept him resolutely turned away from publicity for himself or his companies. He has allowed himself to be interviewed only twice during his entire business career.

D.K. was obviously not quite what the writer had expected.

Many of Ludwig's more bitter critics have charged him with being a kind of remote, ogre-like automaton. The fact is that he has a sense of humor that ranges from the fey to the downright folksy. But he is reputed to have something of a blind spot in matters involving evaluation of human emotion. "He'll outguess all comers on a set of impersonal probabilities," says one former acquaintance. "But I doubt if he'd do well in a game such as poker, where judgment of human reactions is essential."

The *Business Week* writer also gave an updated overview of Ludwig's varied business ventures; he mentioned Seadade (which was still pending) and D.K.'s recent purchase of more than 1.3 million shares — about 15 percent of the total outstanding — of Union Oil Company stock, which he had acquired by plunking down a cool $100 million.

Ludwig's move to buy a substantial piece of a major California-based oil company was puzzling to the *BW* reporter, who also fretted about the ethics of the situation:

The reason for Ludwig's recent purchase of 15% of Union Oil Co. stock is still something of a mystery to industry observers. The company owns some much-sought-after crude reserves in Canada, Louisiana, Australia and elsewhere. It also owns 33% of Maruzen Oil Co., Ltd., a Japanese refiner and marketer, and has plans to sell Alaskan natural gas to Japan.

Even a cursory glance reveals some ambiguities for Ludwig. By buying a piece of an oil company, he may risk alienating many of the producers who employ his tankers. Also, the possibility of conflict-of-interest charges from smaller stockholders could make it very difficult for him to carry much of Union's cargoes in his own vessels. For the same reason, it is unlikely that Union will have a hand in the operation of the projected Miami refinery.

The writer, who was unaware of the incestuous habits of the oil industry or was naïve, tried to raise moral issues in an amoral business, and Wagner reassured him that Ludwig "is primarily interested in the appreciation of the value of the stock," not looking for tanker cargo in his purchase of Union shares. And indeed D.K., nineteen months after buying the stock — which had split three-for-one while he held it — would sell it for $146 million ($35.50 a share for 4,117,510 shares), reaping a handsome $46 million profit on his short-term investment.

The Union Oil deal seems to have evolved this way. In 1960, Phillips Petroleum, planning to take over Union, bought up 1,340,517 shares of the target company's stock. The purchases, however, came to the attention of the Justice Department's Antitrust Division, and the department started a suit to block Phillips's takeover of Union. It opened the battle with a restraining order banning Phillips from buying any more Union stock.

Headed off at the pass, Phillips decided not to fight, and saw no point in keeping the Union shares it had already acquired. But the dumping of such a big block of stock on the market would cause Union shares to plummet disastrously. A rescue operation was called for. What was needed was a big buyer who could afford to purchase the stock as a package for a reasonable price. With Union's plans for expansion, its stock was due to rise soon (which is why Phillips had tried to grab the company), but only if no obstacles got in the way.

Ludwig, for reasons still unknown, was in the right place at the right time, and with enough cash (or credit) to be of assistance. By putting up $100 million (about $75 per share) for the stock, he could get both Phillips and Union shareholders off the hook. The following month, Union made D.K. a director, and a year and a half later bought up his stock for a price that gave him the $46 million profit. *Fortune* believes that Ludwig sold out because he objected to Union's proposed takeover of Pure Oil, but Wagner's statement to the *Business Week* writer suggests that D.K. had bought in only as a short-term investment and planned to get out after the split, which he may have known was coming.

As a longer-term investment, D.K. was expanding his Latin American activities, said *Business Week,* by becoming an orange grower.

A few years ago, some friends sent him a sack of oranges grown in Panama. Ludwig decided they were the most succulent he ever had tasted. Three weeks later two U.S. soil experts arrived in Panama unannounced to make a study of soil conditions. On the basis of their report, Ludwig decided Panama's climate was ideal for orange growing: there are no hurricanes to spoil the crops, and it takes only 3½ years, against the usual seven, for the trees to bear fruit.

Citricos de Chiriqui, S.A., a $25 million Ludwig project, was soon under way. In 1960, Ludwig bought 10,000 acres of land at Dolega, in the interior of Panama. The land was cleared, roads and bridges were built into the region, and the planting of 800,000 Valencia orange trees began. When full production is reached in 1967, the plantation probably will be the largest privately owned venture of its kind in the world.

Ludwig took special pride in being the biggest in the world at whatever he undertook. He wanted the biggest ships, the biggest fleets, the biggest fortune . . . and he was now well on his way to another title — the biggest private landowner in the world. He also aspired to be the biggest builder by using his patented Con-Tech method to erect more houses more quickly than anyone else could, and even to build entire cities when the situation called for them.

Westlake Village was to be his biggest building project so far. It would take him some time after acquiring the land, though, to get plans drawn up and crews organized. In the meantime, he did not intend to let the 11,500-acre tract of land sit idle, without earning money.

In 1963, just after signing the papers that gave him possession of the huge Albertson Ranch, Ludwig set up a company to manage the property. Glenmoor Cattle Ranch Corporation's charter describes its role as "managing agent for a joint venture engaged in cattle raising and location for film and television productions." The project indeed was a joint venture, with the Prudential Insurance Company putting up much of the money for development. Also, a Hilton Hotels executive from Beverly Hills, Benno Bechhold, was in on the deal and would serve as director of several Westlake-connected companies.

Probably the largest ranch remaining in the Los Angeles area, the Albertson spread had become familiar to TV viewers as the Ponderosa in the long-running "Bonanza" series. It was also the locale for many episodes of another popular Western show, "Gunsmoke."

Ludwig saw no reason that the studios shouldn't continue using the property until he got ready to build on it, particularly if they were willing to pay. He had friends in the movie and TV industry, notably Clark and Kay Gable and Charlie Allen, the Wall Street investment banker who, as a part-time Hollywood mogul, would take control of such studios as Warner Brothers and Columbia and become known to many as the "godfather of Hollywood."

Soon after D.K. bought the Albertson Ranch, he received an offer from a famous actor-producer who wanted to use the spread for the locale of his latest movie. Old Blue Eyes himself, Frank Sinatra, was looking for a place to film parts of a musical gangster movie. Ludwig was happy to cooperate. A National Bulk Carriers publication a decade later boasted that "*Robin Hood* was filmed in a wood [on the Albertson Ranch] that became known as 'Sherwood Forest,' now the site of a riding school." Actually, the title of the film was *Robin and the 7 Hoods,* fourth in a series of Sinatra-produced movies with numbers in the title, slyly suggesting dice points (the others were *Oceans 11, Soldiers 3,* and *4 for Texas*) to reflect their maker's fondness for casino gambling.

Not much more filming would be done at the Albertson Ranch. By 1966, Ludwig was ready to start building. The Glenmoor Cattle Ranch Corporation was renamed Westlake Communications, and D.K., using American-Hawaiian as a holding company, began creating subsidiary corporations under its ownership to handle various aspects of Westlake Village business. One of the first moves was to establish a local cemetery, Valley Oaks Memorial Park. Then came Westlake Properties Company, Arboles Development Company (which in its first year of existence was Conejo Patrol Services, providing security for the ranch), Buena Tierra Development Company, Westlake Realty, Westlake Escrow, Westlake Inn, Westlake Water Company — and more.

These companies were the instruments through which Ludwig developed his eighteen-square-mile tract of property between Woodland Hills and Thousand Oaks, California, by building streets, shopping centers, restaurants, utilities, and of course thousands of housing units, all with the Con-Tech system.

By controlling the stores and services as well as the housing in the area, D.K. was taking steps to ensure that much of the money the new residents of Westlake Village would be spending would quickly find its way into his own pockets. Although he was not employing most of these people, he was building what amounted to a company town. When they bought homes, they were buying *his* homes. When they shopped, they were shopping at stores *he* had built and either leased or sold to small businesses. When they paid their utility bills, they wrote their checks to Ludwig's utilities.

Buying the homes in the first place, of course, brought them in contact with Ludwig's realty companies, which got commissions on every Ludwig-built house or commercial property sold. To borrow mortgage money, they often went to savings and loan institutions in nearby Thousand Oaks, Woodland Hills, or other towns. Here, too, although they didn't know it, they usually dealt with Ludwig. Starting in the early sixties, while he was negotiating for the Albertson Ranch, he had started buying up the area's savings and loan companies, beginning with Woodland Savings and gobbling up others as fast as he could make satisfactory deals. He soon had so many that he was exercising almost monopolistic control over S & L mortgage money in the region, raking in, as the loans were repaid, both the principal and interest, and managing to get himself some major tax write-offs at the same time.

If anybody in California state government regulatory agencies had been looking closely at D.K.'s near-total control of the financial aspects of Westlake Village in the late sixties and early seventies, he probably could have found good legal basis for breaking up this little empire. But Ludwig had a friend in Sacramento, the state capital. Former actor Ronald Reagan, two years after making a moving speech in the losing Goldwater campaign of 1964, had been picked up by a clique of Los Angeles millionaire power brokers and elected governor of California as a first step in a run for the White House. Reagan perfectly represented Ludwig's whole-hog-anything-goes philosophy of relations between business and government, and the two men were soon close friends. Exactly when, how, or through what mutual acquaintance D.K. and Reagan first met is not clear, but it is certain that, once introduced, they formed a lasting friendship.

To consolidate the savings and loan institutions he was buying up, Ludwig grouped them into two holding companies: Colonial Savings of the North (with assets of $105 million) and Colonial Savings of the South (with assets of $80 million). D.K. constantly reshuffled their holdings. His method, initially, was to buy up small S & Ls, build them up with Westlake mortgage loans, then sell them off for quick profits. In 1971–1972 Ludwig merged Colonial of the North into H. F. Ahmanson & Company, owner of Los Angeles–based

Home Savings & Loan, the largest savings institution in the United States. Through this merger, D.K.'s National Bulk Carriers became a substantial shareholder in Ahmanson.

At about the same time, Colonial of the South was merged into Imperial Savings & Loan, another major S & L holding company with branches in four states. Through this merger, Ludwig became the largest single stockholder in Imperial.

Finding his S & L acquisitions profitable, D.K. kept buying new ones as he sold others. In the early seventies he bought a substantial interest in American Savings & Loan of Utah, which had twenty-one branches in Utah and Hawaii. He also pushed into Australia, where he invested in several projects — coal mining, iron-ore mining, ranching, real estate development, and insurance. In 1970 he started up Western Pacific Permanent Building Society, an S & L with three offices in Melbourne and a dozen agencies throughout the country. This was in connection with the erection of Ocean Shores, a resort community he was building on three thousand acres of Australia's "Gold Coast," some two hundred miles north of Sydney. Though not quite on the scale of Westlake Village, Ocean Shores was expected by D.K. to have an eventual population of fifty thousand, about half of them year-round residents. To attract buyers he built a marina, a championship golf course, swimming and therapeutic pools, and facilities for riding, tennis, and of course water sports. He also constructed streets and utilities to serve the community. (Similar developments were going up simultaneously in Florida and in Acapulco, Mexico.)

Along with his other interests in Australia, D.K. bought up insurance companies. In 1970 he purchased the Greater Pacific Life Assurance Company (more than $200 million insurance in force). Shortly after, he bought another insurance firm, Skandia of Australia, and merged it into Greater Pacific, which soon became a whole chain of companies, including Greater Pacific General (fire and casualty insurance), Greater Pacific Fund Management (investment counseling), and Greater Pacific Finance (consumer credit). To house these allied companies, he built "the most prestigious office building in North Sydney," the twenty-five-story Greater Pacific Building, containing 140,000 square feet of office space. (He also erected a similar but smaller office tower, the Kapiolani Building, in Honolulu to house his Hawaiian ventures.) Continuing his westward expansion, Ludwig, operating as Greater Pacific General, went into a joint venture with the Bank of Canton to start the Hong Kong and Shanghai Insurance Company, Ltd., with branches eventually in Singapore, Malaysia, Indonesia, and Taiwan.

Ludwig's ventures in the Pacific resulted in such a proliferation of companies that he was obliged to create a new holding company, Berkshire Industries, Inc., to cover most of them. Under this umbrella, American-Hawaiian was able to operate as Ludwig's chief West Coast company without spreading itself too thin. It also endeavored to re-establish its claim to being a shipping company, a status it needed to rebut Loring R. Hoover's charge that Ludwig had turned it into a real estate investment firm.

Thus, while D.K. was using American-Hawaiian to buy the Albertson Ranch and transform it into Westlake Village, he also had the company continue to press for Maritime mortgage insurance guarantees for the building of ten giant container ships. Throughout the same period, Hoover was writing bitter letters to Maritime accusing Ludwig of looting American-Hawaiian and saying that, far from being an asset to United States shipping, the tycoon was helping drive the industry down by building and operating ships under foreign flags and by using cheap labor from the Caymans and other backward areas instead of American seamen to crew his vessels. Thousands of U.S. merchant sailors were being deprived of jobs, Hoover wrote, because of Ludwig's stinginess, and this could only lead to conflicts with organized labor groups in the United States.

An example of what Hoover meant had already happened. On October 21, 1960, when Ludwig's *Ore Monarch* arrived at a Philadelphia pier with a load of Venezuelan iron ore for U.S. Steel's Fairless Works, local dockworkers had refused to unload it and formed a picket line alongside. The longshoremen, said a spokesman for the International Maritime Workers Union, were protesting on behalf of the *Ore Monarch*'s crew and the crews of other Ludwig vessels. These seamen, claimed the union, were helpless victims of unfair labor practices and substandard living conditions, mainly because D.K. was not allowing them adequate union representation.

A Universe Tankships official called the charges untrue. Its ships' crews, he said, were sufficiently represented by the Global Seamen's Union. Poppycock, replied IMWU leaders. Global, they said, was a sham organization formed by Ludwig stooges in the Caymans in 1959 to make it *appear* that the islanders he had recruited to man his ships had union representation. Why, IMWU asked, if the Global

Seamen's Union was representing them satisfactorily, had most of the *Ore Monarch*'s crew signed pledges to support the American union's efforts on their behalf?

A battle royal was shaping up. D.K.'s *Ore Prince,* fully loaded, soon arrived at Philadelphia to keep her sister ship company, but the *Ore Mercury,* also loaded, was diverted to Baltimore. The gambit failed. Baltimore dockworkers, supporting their Philadelphia counterparts, formed their own picket line and refused to allow unloading.

The matter was soon in the courts, and, as usual, Ludwig was able to put a heavyweight into the arena to carry the day for him. Under Secretary of State Douglas Dillon (a Wall Street fixture as head of the giant Dillon, Read brokerage firm, and a staunch Rockefeller Republican, who, despite his party affiliation, was later appointed secretary of the treasury by President Kennedy) pressured the Justice Department on D.K.'s behalf to have the National Labor Relations Board ban picketing of foreign-flag vessels. A Supreme Court ruling several years later would overturn this ban and restore the unions' right to picket flag-of-convenience ships. But in the meantime Ludwig's ore haulers had unloaded their cargoes and sailed back to Venezuela for many another load.

While Dillon was using his clout to aid D.K.'s ore carriers Ludwig was leaning on a number of California congressmen, including Representative James Roosevelt, eldest son of the late president, to write letters to the new Maritime administrator, Donald Alexander, in support of American-Hawaiian's container-ship application.

Some Pentagon friends were helping out as well. A NASA representative dropped by Maritime to say that if American-Hawaiian got the go-ahead, the U.S. space program would use the company's container ships for intercoastal service, carrying the Apollo rockets and boosters from Los Angeles to Cape Canaveral. Just in case Maritime officials weren't getting the point, the NASA man stressed that no other shipper would do: only American-Hawaiian would be a satisfactory carrier for the nation's moon rockets.

The reason for the hard push was that Malcolm McLean of Sea-Land Services had decided to steal a march on Ludwig. In April of 1961 he had announced that, whether it got government mortgage insurance money or not, Sea-Land was going to start intercoastal container-ship service by June 1962. An American-Hawaiian official was doubtful that McLean could carry that off without government aid: "If we get the mortgage insurance, he's dead. If he gets the insurance, we're dead."

But McLean's move was a bold stroke. By not waiting for Maritime's decision, he was out of the gate first, and Ludwig would have to run like the devil. He rounded up all the political help he could, Democrat as well as Republican. Deputy Secretary of Defense Roswell Gilpatric, a powerful voice in the Kennedy administration, wrote a letter to Maritime urging acceptance of American-Hawaiian's application. So did Senator Clair Engle of the Senate Armed Services Committee. Under Secretary of Commerce Franklin D. Roosevelt, Jr. (probably at his brother James's request), notified Deputy Maritime Administrator James W. Gulick that he "would like to have advance notice" before any decision unfavorable to American-Hawaiian was made. Other messages poured in to Maritime pleading Ludwig's cause — from Pennsylvania's Senator Joseph Clark, New York's Senator Jacob Javits, Massachusetts's Senator Edward Kennedy, and from Representatives Emanuel Celler, James Delaney, William Miller, Leo O'Brien, and Steven Derounian, to name a few.

Obviously, Donald Alexander was under pressure to settle the container-ship matter in American-Hawaiian's favor. Less obviously, he was also under pressure not to. Despite his brave leap in front of the field, Malcolm McLean was still quietly fighting Ludwig's application from behind the scenes. There were even persistent rumors that he was asking his old friend Luther Hodges, who, as commerce secretary, was Alexander's boss, to get the Maritime chief to turn down AHSS's bid.

These rumors, in fact, were becoming so widespread that Alexander felt obliged to write a letter — to be placed in Hodges's files and his own — denying them. This done, the following week he came to the long-postponed decision and, with Hodges's backing, formally rejected Ludwig's application. A reason for the turndown, Alexander said, was Ludwig's asking the government to assume 87.5 percent of the container-ship project's risk. That was too much. If the project was such a good idea, D.K. should not mind taking more of the gamble himself. The Maritime chief, however, did leave the door open by stating that Maritime would be willing to consider a new application asking for 50 percent mortgage insurance. This was tantamount to saying that Maritime would be willing to underwrite half the money if Ludwig was willing to risk the other half.

This suggestion was fine with D.K., who probably had not expected to get all he'd asked for. He had Samuel Moerman write back immediately, asking Maritime to consider the application amended to 50 percent. Shortly afterward, James Roosevelt wrote to FDR Jr. at the Department of Commerce, bringing his brother up to date on the container-ship situation and adding, "I hope very much that the matter can go forward expeditiously now."

It would, but not in a way the Roosevelts anticipated. Shortly after giving American-Hawaiian his decision, Donald Alexander left Maritime, to be replaced by a new administrator, Nicholas Johnson. Johnson approved the American-Hawaiian amended application with little ado. By this time, however, Ludwig himself had scaled down the project considerably. Instead of planning to build ten container ships, he now proposed only three, at a cost of roughly $20 million each. He wanted the government to underwrite half of the total amount.

After pushing so hard for so long, Ludwig was now the one to delay things. Moerman wrote to Johnson, saying that an assistant secretary of the Navy wanted to discuss with American-Hawaiian a modification: Would the company consider powering the new ships with nuclear fuel, thus making them capable of attaining a cruising speed of thirty knots rather than the twenty-four possible with conventional engines?

It would be another first for Ludwig. No commercial vessels had ever used atomic power, and none was capable of thirty knots. Of course, wrote Moerman to Johnson, such a change would take more time. Discussions were still in the preliminary stages, and the container ships would have to be redesigned. He ended by asking Maritime for a postponement on starting work until the atomic power issue could be worked out.

Maritime, understandably assuming that Ludwig was eager to get started, had already put the construction of the three ships out for bid, and General Dynamics (one of the nation's largest shipbuilders and defense contractors) had gotten the contract. Even if D.K. was in no hurry, the shipyard was; it was keeping people on its payroll to build the container ships.

American-Hawaiian, though, continued to delay and refused to be pinned down to a likely starting date. As the months dragged on with no action, both General Dynamics and Maritime became increasingly impatient.

What they did not realize was that Ludwig was busy working out another deal. He had apparently decided that if he was going to get only half a loaf instead of 87.5 percent of one, he would prefer taking it another way. He had not really liked the idea of putting up half the risk capital to build container ships that would then have to compete with McLean's Sea-Land for the limited amount of inter-coastal business. So, while Maritime was processing the revised application, he had opened talks with McLean and his chief backer, Litton Industries.

McLean already had the routes and some business, but he had stuck his neck out by getting into the intercoastal RORO trade without government backing — something D.K. had not been willing to do. Sea-Land was dangerously short of operating capital and was running its ships on a shoestring. Litton had already come to the rescue once, buying 800,000 shares of McLean stock, but now, in 1964, another transfusion of cash was needed badly.

Ludwig had plenty of money. The $11 million he'd gotten from selling American-Hawaiian's old ships and settling its war claims against the government was still sitting in a construction reserve joint account with Maritime. He had tried to pry some of it loose in 1961 for real estate investments by offering to deposit in its place several million dollars' worth of American-Hawaiian-held stock (large blocks of shares in such companies as A T & T, Bethlehem Steel, Chrysler, Dow Chemical, Johns Manville, Montgomery Ward, Philadelphia Electric, Standard Oil of New Jersey, Union-Camp, and Union Pacific), but Maritime had nixed the proposal as "a violation of generally accepted accounting principles."

So the cash was still there, and Ludwig could free it simply by closing the account in the name of American-Hawaiian. But he would have to pay taxes on the money, and probably a penalty for reneging on the container-ship contract. He might also get slapped with a breach-of-contract suit by General Dynamics. Unless, of course, he could fox Maritime into canceling the contract unilaterally.

This was probably why Moerman had started stalling — asking for extensions, telling Maritime he was meeting with Assistant Secretary of Defense Kenneth BeLieu to discuss atomic power and design changes, and preparing for an eventual meeting with Secretary of Defense Robert McNamara.

But while Maritime was getting this busy-busy-busy talk from Moerman, it was hearing nothing from the Defense Department to confirm the excuses. Logically, somebody from the Pentagon should be interceding on American-Hawaiian's behalf and asking for more time. But from that direction there was only silence.

Finally, in January 1965, after nearly a year of delays and excuses by Moerman, Maritime Administrator Nicholas Johnson began to suspect something. In a memo to his deputy, James Gulick, he wrote:

> With every passing month I become more and more convinced that American-Hawaiian is never going to build boats, and I don't see why we should be a party to whatever it is they are trying to achieve.
>
> We gave them their time and they did not meet it. The yard [General Dynamics] is willing to extend them until January 30, and I do not see why we should go beyond that.
>
> So far as this nuclear business goes, I think it is highly questionable. Based on the decisions now being made by the Secretary of Defense's Office and the Navy Department, it is almost inconceivable to me that they would recommend government expenditure to make these ships in domestic service nuclear-powered. Someone (who I cannot recall) told me that this was simply a delaying tactic on their part with some very low-level friend of American-Hawaiian's in the Navy Department and that this had no high-level support at all. It would seem to me that we would be fully within our rights to stick to our original decision and hold them to their time. If they want to make another application, that's up to them.

A short while later, a Maritime section chief wrote Johnson, "Mr. Gulick advised me this date that Mr. Martin [another Maritime official] had been advised by Assistant Secretary of the Navy BeLieu that he had never heard of American-Hawaiian and was not interested in nuclear commercial ships."

Later — perhaps to cover for Ludwig and his friend in the Navy Department — BeLieu backtracked and told Maritime he had not meant to say he'd never heard of American-Hawaiian, but that it was a jurisdictional matter and Defense was not going to get involved until Maritime took a position regarding the use of nuclear power in commercial vessels.

Had Moerman been lying about the meetings with BeLieu and McNamara and the discussions about atomic-powered container ships? Probably, though BeLieu's belated retraction and hedging make it hard to prove. What *was* clear, though, was that the Defense Department was not about to make any commitments to put nuclear-powered propulsion systems in American-Hawaiian's ships.

All of which suited D.K. perfectly. By exhausting Maritime's patience and pushing Johnson into letting the contract expire, Ludwig seems to have accomplished exactly what he had set out to do. He was now off the hook with both Maritime and General Dynamics, and without penalty. After a respectable interval of a few months, American-Hawaiian could, and did, ask to withdraw the $11 million from the construction reserve fund and close the joint account with Maritime.

Ludwig could then take most of this money and buy a million shares of McLean Industries stock (then trading at $13.75 per share) for $8.50 each. This $8.5 million would provide some desperately needed operating capital to Sea-Land, which, by default, was now the only company operating in the intercoastal roll-on-roll-off trade. But in return D.K. got a substantial share of the profits not only from the container ships but also from Malcolm McLean's lucrative trucking operation.

Two years later, in 1967, Ludwig and Litton put more money into the venture, each buying an additional 250,000 shares of McLean Industries for $4.5 million — $18 per share, because the stock had gone up considerably since D.K.'s initial purchase. He now owned 11 percent of McLean, and Litton owned 10 percent. He was also getting some of his own money back, since Malcolm McLean had agreed to use the fresh cash to lease from Litton and National Bulk Carriers seven tankers converted into container ships. Ludwig would do the conversions, which Sea-Land would pay for over the ten-year life of the lease.

In 1969, however, the giant tobacco conglomerate R. J. Reynolds, looking to diversify its holdings, bought out McLean Industries. For his 11 percent share, which he had bought for $13 million, Daniel Ludwig received $60 million — a profit of almost 500 percent.

## Thirteen

# Freeport

Meyer Lansky had enjoyed a nice setup in Havana for quite a few years. Shortly after the end of Prohibition, the diminutive junior partner of the Bugs and Meyer gang had gone to Cuba, looking for a place to set up shop. Lansky had learned something during the years of the Volstead Act that had escaped other bootleggers: a lot of Americans loved to gamble even more than they loved to drink. With the repeal of Prohibition, it was now legal to drink, but gambling was still against the law.

That an activity was illegal had never deterred Lansky if he thought he could make money out of it. He and Bugsy Siegel had gotten rich by running an efficient escort service for bootleggers and had later expanded their business to include murder-for-hire.

But gambling had become Lansky's first love, and he had set up craps and blackjack tables, roulette wheels and slot machines, in some of New York's most fashionable speakeasies during the Jazz Age and found them so profitable that he had no intention of stopping. But it was harder after Repeal. He could not put the same tables and machines in legal, duly licensed bars and restaurants.

By means of payoffs, he was able to keep a few private gambling clubs open in the United States — in New York, Kentucky, and Florida — but this was a risky business. Some crusading cop or reformer was always butting in to stage a raid or make headlines.

What Lansky wanted — and found — was a place close to the

United States where he could operate in complete freedom while pulling in American tourists to spend their money on games of chance. In Cuba he made friends with a tough, stocky army sergeant named Fulgencio Batista, who, with Lansky's help, was soon the chief power on the island.

With Batista running the country, Lansky had casinos and hotels operating in Havana, which became a playground for rich Americans. Things started getting a bit too hot in 1944, when several U.S. politicians called attention to organized crime flourishing openly just two hundred miles south of Miami. It was deemed advisable for Batista to step down for a while and for Lansky to make gambling less visible in Cuba.

In 1952, Batista, with the help of friends in the Miami mob, stormed back into power in Cuba. Soon there were two new casino-hotels in Havana: the $14 million Riviera and the Hotel Nacional. These were owned by the Lansky brothers, Meyer and Jake, and run by Lansky lieutenants — George Sadlo, Dino and Eddie Cellini, Mike McLaney, Frank Ritter (also known as Red Reed), Max Courtney (born Moishe Schmerzler), and Charles Brudner, known to familiars as Charlie Brud. Nearly all these worthies had received their gambling training in Lansky's illegal casinos in New York, Kentucky, and Florida before moving on to "legal" operations in Vegas and Havana.

During most of the Eisenhower years, Cuba was a haven not only for gambling but also for a host of other mob-connected activities: prostitution, drugs, con games. It was also a center for the foreign activities of many U.S. corporations. But many Americans had reservations about the Batista regime and its blatant corruption. It was tolerated officially only because of its leader's strong anticommunist stance.

Then came the revolution, and Castro ousted Batista and from 1959 on ran the country. He did not close the gambling casinos right away, and there were even rumors that he might leave them open if the mob cut the Cuban government in on some of the profits.

But Lansky was furious. He wanted Castro dead. When his attempts to get Castro assassinated came to nothing, he decided to set up his gambling operations elsewhere in the Caribbean near Florida — and he chose Freeport, on Grand Bahama Island.

Sir Stafford Sands, the Bahamas' roly-poly minister of tourism and finance (he had been knighted by Queen Elizabeth), would later testify that Lansky came to see him late in 1960 and offered him a $2 million bribe (Sands first said $1 million but later changed his story) to allow casinos in Freeport. Sands tried to make a board of judges believe that he had indignantly shown Lansky the door after the offer, but the fact remains that, almost immediately, plans for Grand Bahama's first casino-hotel were in the works.

These plans revolved around one Lou Chesler, a Canadian-born wheeler-dealer almost as fat as Sands himself. Chesler was a man of many parts. He had made a fortune in Florida real estate schemes as chief executive officer of Miami's General Development Company, whose directors included people like Trigger Mike Coppola, former bodyguard of mob boss Albert Anastasia and now a big man himself in the numbers racket, and Max Orovitz, a partner in the mob-controlled Bank of World Commerce and a director of Florida Power and Light (which, it will be remembered, would soon help bail Daniel Ludwig out of the aborted Seadade project by buying from him much of the land he had acquired to build a refinery and petrochemical complex on).

Chesler also had close connections with one of the Grand Bahama Port Authority partners, Charlie Allen of Allen & Company. Their mutual interest was movie-making. After getting rich in Miami land deals, Chesler had decided to become a film mogul and had founded his own studio, Seven Arts Productions, which, among other ventures, had brought Ray Stark's popular Broadway hit *Funny Girl,* starring Barbra Streisand, to the big screen. (Chesler's Seven Arts would later be merged into Allen's Warner Brothers.)

During the latter months of 1960, Chesler, Allen, Wallace Groves, and Sir Charles Hayward of the Port Authority (and perhaps Ludwig, standing in the shadows) worked out a deal. Chesler would be brought by the authority to Grand Bahama to do two things: (1) develop much of the land the authority had acquired for $2.80 an acre into luxury building sites selling for as much as $40,000 to $50,000 an acre, and (2) put together a consortium to invest $12 million in the building of a casino-hotel.

The timing was perfect for attracting American investors to the Caribbean, but there was a lot of competition. The Eisenhower administration wanted badly to check the spread of Castro's influence. If similar revolutions occurred in other countries, U.S. corporate influence and investments in Latin America might well become a thing of the past. To prevent this, the Republicans were pouring billions of dollars of aid into the Caribbean through the Inter-American Development Bank, the Export-Import Bank, and the Development Loan Fund.

The idea was to pull as many U.S. companies into the Caribbean as possible — and as soon as possible. The corporate sector was largely willing to cooperate. The tax situation under Eisenhower had been excellent, but if Kennedy was elected, it was certain that he would want revenues to spend on social programs. The more money that could be gotten out of the country, the better. Also, many of the companies were in good position to get some of the U.S. aid funds by increasing their Caribbean presence.

On January 11, 1961, just nine days before JFK was to be inaugurated, the *New York Times* printed a special section made up entirely of enticing stories and large ads about investment opportunities in the Caribbean. Small countries, such as Haiti, Suriname, Trinidad and Tobago, the Netherlands Antilles, and the Bahamas, vied with one another as shamelessly as whores in a red-light district to lure corporate johns into their clutches. A typical package of inducements looked like this:

Five-to-ten-year exemption from taxes.
Generous depreciation allowances on plant equipment.
Duty-free importation of plant equipment and raw materials.
Abundant supplies of adaptable low-cost labor.
Full repatriation of capital and dividends to any country.
A friendly, highly cooperative, stable, democratic government.
Excellent labor relations and productivity.
Low electric rates.

Some of the countries advertised bounteous supplies of natural resources as well. President François (Papa Doc) Duvalier of Haiti, whose "friendly, highly cooperative, stable, democratic government" was kept in power by the brutal Tonton Macoutes, beckoned alluringly to U.S. industry with such blandishments as "our resources of manganese, bauxite, petroleum, iron and copper are practically untouched" and "new protective laws grant up to ten years of tax and duty exemptions to all investors."

This coordinated effort to attract U.S. investment to the Caribbean was obviously not a spontaneous act on the part of several local business groups. Large forces were at work — forces that, with the tacit blessing of the Eisenhower administration, would cost the U.S. Treasury many billions of dollars in lost revenues and U.S. workers many thousands of lost jobs as American companies packed their bags and headed south.

In many ways, this Caribbean basin initiative was an expansion of what Wallace Groves and the Port Authority had tried to start on Grand Bahama without much success some six years earlier. Except for Ludwig's lime plant, U.S. Steel's cement factory, Charlie Allen's Syntex, the Gulf Oil–supplied ship-refueling operation, and a handful of other ventures, the Hawksbill Creek Act had not succeeded in attracting much industry to the island.

Now the local pitch would be tourism and recreation; Lou Chesler would erect a casino-hotel as the chief draw. The casino part would have to be kept quiet for a while, because gambling was illegal on the islands, and a special exemption would have to be secured. This could be done by greasing the palms of the right people, but in the meantime the hotel could be built.

For Chesler, this meant coming up with $12 million for construction costs. Most of his own money — what he had made in Miami real estate deals — was tied up in Seven Arts and in two Canadian mineral companies, Lorado Uranium Mining and Canadian Dyno Mines. He figured on putting together a consortium of investors, to be called Grand Bahama Development Corporation, Ltd. (or DEVCO for short), to which he could divert funds from the other companies he owned an interest in.

He could also get some of his friends to buy shares, and Port Authority partners would come in as well. DEVCO was chartered in Nassau on March 17, 1961. Its directors included Eliot Hyman of Seven Arts, Sir Charles Hayward of the Port Authority, Max Orovitz of the Lansky interests, and a mysterious New Yorker named C. Gerald Goldsmith. Chesler and his friends and companies held 52 percent interest in the company; Groves and his Port Authority partners held the other 48 percent. The Chesler interests were supplying most of the money for the hotel; the Port Authority was furnishing the land.

Once these details were worked out, construction began on the hotel, to be called the Lucayan Beach. On various sets of blueprints, the large room that would house the casino (since the gambling exemption had not yet been approved) was variously labeled as a convention hall or handball courts.

But to those in the know, there was no mistaking the room's intended purpose. In November of 1962, Chesler flew to Florida for a meeting with the "experts." In a suite at Miami Beach's Fontainebleau Hotel he sat down with Meyer and Jake Lansky, Trigger Mike Coppola, Charlie (the Blade) Turine, Dino Cellini, Frank Ritter, Max Courtney, and Charlie Brud to map out the casino's floor plan in minute detail.

Sir Stafford Sands, meanwhile, was moving in mysterious ways to obtain the gambling exemption for the casino. He couldn't ramrod this through the Bahamian Parliament as he had the Hawksbill Creek Act, because the activity in question was clearly against Bahamian law and was bound to raise protest even among the usually pliable representatives. Besides, if word leaked out to the world press that Sands was trying to get an illegal casino in the Bahamas, all hell could break loose. The exemption had to be made legal before news of it got out.

There was one way to do this: through the Bahamas Executive Council. Here, Sands would have to deal with only nine votes — eight besides his own — and the proceedings could go on behind closed doors. He knew he could count on the premier, Sir Roland Symonette, so only three other votes were needed for a majority. He did not foresee trouble. The Executive Council was made up of men like himself — businessmen who drew no salary for their public service but were not above compensating themselves by rendering official decisions that would bring them in a little money on the side.

By April 1963, Sands had pulled off his little miracle. The Lucayan Beach Hotel, still under construction, had its exemption from the Bahamas' antigambling statutes, courtesy of the Executive Council. To quiet local protest, the council had included a proviso that Bahamian citizens were banned from gambling in the casino. Groves also helped silence religious objections on Grand Bahama by spreading some money around for the building of churches for several denominations.

In the summer of 1964, the Lucayan Beach Hotel and its Monte Carlo Casino had their grand opening. It should have been a gala event, and outwardly it was, but some of the main characters in the drama were wearing forced smiles.

For months, Chesler and Groves had been feuding. Partly it was a clash of personalities. Groves, with his soft Virginia drawl, seemed very quiet and low-key. "When you talk to him," one local resident would say later, "you get the impression he's a nice old man who knows nothing. But it could be very uncomfortable for somebody to cross him." Chesler, on the other hand, was big, loud, and brash. His pushy manner had grated on Groves's nerves since the start of the project.

But mostly it was a matter of money. A terrific salesman, Chesler was a poor manager, with little patience for administrative details. He had finished the hotel and casino, but his costs had overrun original estimates by $8 million. Groves had been planning to have the Lucayan Beach built cheaply enough to keep room rates low — say, $30 to $40 a night for double occupancy. At those prices, tourists could be expected to flock down to Grand Bahama in great numbers to spend their money in the shops, restaurants, and casino. As it was, in order to finish paying for the hotel, they would have to charge $70 to $80 a night, which would scare away many potential customers.

When Groves confronted Chesler with these figures, the burly developer responded by offering to buy out the Port Authority's share of DEVCO (48 percent) for $17 million. Groves refused and made a counteroffer. The Port Authority, he said, would buy enough of Chesler's shares to gain a majority interest.

Chesler refused, and the contest was a standoff. But not for long. Chesler had a lot of mob contacts, but Groves could also play sneaky and dirty when the occasion called for it. All of a sudden, Chesler was attacked from the rear — by a band of dissident Seven Arts stockholders claiming he had had no right to invest their money — film company money — in the building of a casino-hotel on Grand Bahama.

The protest may well have been orchestrated by Charlie Allen. Chesler, outflanked and outvoted, had to get out of the film company he himself had started. Not only that; he had to eat five hundred thousand shares of DEVCO he had bought with Seven Arts money. Soon after Chesler and the film studio parted ways, Allen, who had recently gained control of Warner Brothers, stepped in and merged Seven Arts into his larger company.

Chesler was a beaten man. He now owned more shares of DEVCO stock than he could afford to hold on to. But he could not just dump them. DEVCO wasn't listed on any American stock exchange, and he could not sell to the other investors. His own companies and friends were carrying as much as they could handle already, and the Port Authority partners were willing to buy only enough to gain majority control.

Chesler had no choice. He caved in and sold Groves and his allies enough shares to bring the Port Authority holdings up to just over 51 percent.

Throughout the battle for control of DEVCO and the Grand Bahama casino-hotel (which *Newsweek* had labeled an attempted buyout by Chesler and the Miami mob), Daniel K. Ludwig was nowhere to be seen. Now he stepped forward and, operating as Seatankers, Inc. (the small-tanker company he had created in Liberia and later transferred to Hamilton, Bermuda), purchased two hundred thousand shares of Chesler's stock.

In July 1966, a major reorganization allowed Chesler to sell many of his shares to British and Canadian investors. The change was made possible by a resolution to alter DEVCO's Bahamian charter by adding the sentence "The Company may exercise any power conferred by law to dispense with distinguishing or denoting numbers on shares."

What this amounted to was a four-for-one stock split, which opened DEVCO to wider ownership. Much of the new stock issue was sold in blocks of a few hundred or a few thousand shares, but there were some large buyers as well, notably companies representing financier Bernard Cornfeld and his Investors Overseas Services; the Marquess of Hamilton; and the Canadian millionaire E. P. Taylor, to whom Ludwig in 1981 would sell his overseas Con-Tech building company, International Housing, Ltd.

At about the same time he was buying into DEVCO, Daniel Ludwig was expanding his visible activities on Grand Bahama by going into the casino-hotel and luxury housing business himself. It was as if he was picking up where Chesler had left off. During the early sixties, Chesler had developed what is known as the Lucayan section of Freeport — not only the hotel and casino but also most of the local houses and shops. (Whether Ludwig Con-Tech companies contracted for some or most of this work is not clear, but it's a strong probability.) Another corporation, the Florida-based Mary Carter

Paint Company, had bought up a failing local firm, Bahama Developers, Ltd., and used it to construct a luxury housing project called Queen's Cove.

Now, in 1964, with the blessing of the Port Authority, Ludwig started developing a section of Freeport to be known as Bahamia. It would dwarf what Chesler and DEVCO and any other builders on the island had done. He would erect not one but three new hotels and a separate, Moorish-style casino nearby to serve them all. There would also be the International Bazaar, where tourists could buy — without paying duty fees — merchandise imported from all over the world. Other features of Bahamia would be two championship golf courses, tennis courts, a marina, fine restaurants, and several luxury housing developments.

The first phase of the multimillion-dollar development was the King's Inn, a three-hundred-room hotel located on a thousand-acre site, with an adjoining golf course designed by the famed U.S. golf architect Dick Wilson. To build the hotel, Ludwig started a company, Sunrise Properties, Ltd. (so called because the new hostelry would be located on Freeport's Sunrise Highway). The design looked more like a motel than a hotel, consisting of several long, low buildings grouped in a semicircle around a large office complex that also featured a three-thousand-seat auditorium and a swimming pool with grottolike rocks.

To bring people in, D.K. was planning to supplement the junket tours offered by a local airline with a thousand-passenger express liner running regularly between Freeport and Miami. He was also offering rock-bottom room rates: $16, $20, and $24 per night for double occupancy on the European plan — far below what the Lucayan Beach had to charge. He had either built his hotel cheaply enough to permit low room rates or was prepared to take a loss until more tourists could be lured to Grand Bahama. The *Freeport News,* announcing the opening of the King's Inn in January 1965, remarked that Ludwig's investment in Freeport was already $35 million, with much more to come.

The King's Inn was not Ludwig's first hotel. In 1960, according to *Business Week,* he had gone to officials in Bermuda and asked whether they would like their main island enlarged. What he had in mind, apparently, was dredging a deep-water harbor at Hamilton and piling the spoils alongside to increase the land surface. He may have had a more ambitious project in mind, or he may simply have been looking for a way to employ his dredge, which had finished the Freeport harbor and was being held up from working on Seadade. Whatever the case, Bermuda was not interested. But Ludwig had been impressed by Hamilton's grand old hotel, the Princess. He had taken such a liking to it, in fact, that he decided to buy it. A relic of prosperous Victorian times, it was starting to decay but was still salvageable. With renovation and enlargement, it could be better than ever. On taking it over, D.K. installed a new water-purification system, doubled the number of rooms to five hundred, and reopened it in 1964.

After finishing the King's Inn in 1965, he was now owner of two hotels. Soon he started constructing a third and fourth. One, the Xanadu, was a small, exclusive, nine-story building that fronted on its own private beach. It was off Freeport's main tourist drag and definitely not for ordinary folk. John Q. Sightseer and Ken Conventiongoer were welcome at the King's Inn, but the Xanadu was being built to cater to the very rich.

Ludwig's fourth hotel, though, was for tourists. The International, ten stories and block-shaped, was rising across the street from the King's Inn. Adjoining, and in the same Moorish-Mediterranean architecture, with white, onion-shaped domes, minarets, and Arabic arches, was the casino, to be named — without much inspiration — El Casino. But what it lacked in imaginative nomenclature it made up for in size; it was larger than any gambling house in Las Vegas and far bigger than the Lucayan Beach's Monte Carlo Casino.

Again there is the question, as there was with his yacht (he was now on his second *Danginn*): What would make Ludwig, the proponent of no-frills marine design, step so far out of character as to build pleasure palaces Kublai Khan might envy? And again the answer is probably the same: He was trying to keep up with his old archrival, Aristotle Onassis.

In 1952 — three years before Ludwig went to Grand Bahama — Onassis had surprised the world by quietly buying up, on the Paris Bourse, the controlling shares of the Société des Bains de Mer. What made this significant was the fact that the Société owned most of the tiny principality of Monaco — its hotels, its golf course, its only theater, and, most important, its famed Monte Carlo Casino.

There were undoubtedly social and personal reasons for Onassis's purchase. Monaco, despite its tiny size — under four hundred acres — was the playground of Europe's wealth and nobility. The old money and the titled aristocracy gathered there to take the baths during the day and go gaming in the evenings.

Being accepted in Monaco was the *ne plus ultra* of social climbing. You couldn't go any higher. And if you *owned* the place, they would have to accept you. Onassis, a Greek born in Turkey, had always felt socially inferior, and having to compete with a brother-in-law like the polished, handsome Stavros Niarchos, who chummed around with Queen Elizabeth and Prince Philip at Ascot, didn't make things any easier.

So Onassis had bought Monaco, where he could rub elbows with the royalty of the rest of Europe. But he had gotten a lot more in the bargain. Monaco, however small, was its own country, with its own laws. No other nation's laws applied. If you owned Monaco, you could do what you pleased there, and nobody could object. Well, almost nobody. There was Prince Rainier, of course, the country's titular ruler. But he and his beautiful wife, the former American movie star Grace Kelly, could be won over easily enough. Once that was done, Onassis was master of all he surveyed — within Monaco's borders. He had acquired what Howard Hughes would later refer to as "empire status" — a lofty pinnacle above the laws of men. He didn't even have to pay personal or corporate income taxes; Monaco levied none. Not a bad bargain for just over a million dollars invested in Société des Bains de Mer stock!

From a distance, in 1952, Daniel K. Ludwig could only watch and envy. There was, after all, only one Monaco in the world. But in D.K.'s head the wheels were turning. If he couldn't buy a Monaco of his own, maybe he could build one.

But just as D.K. was getting his new hotels and casino finished, disaster struck. Not a hurricane or tidal wave, but something far worse: bad publicity. On October 5, 1966, on the front page of the *Wall Street Journal* was a glaring headline:

*LAS VEGAS EAST*

U.S. GAMBLERS PROSPER
IN BAHAMAS WITH HELP
FROM ISLAND OFFICIALS

236

TOP LOCAL POLITICAL LEADERS
GRANT CASINO LICENSE, ALSO
RECEIVE CONSULTANTS' FEES

IS THERE LINK TO U.S. CRIME?

The accompanying story, by the investigative writers Monroe Karmin and Stanley Penn, contained numerous charges against Wallace Groves, the Bay Street Boys, and several employees of the Lucayan Beach's Monte Carlo Casino. Some of the charges (paraphrased) were:

That Groves had acted unethically in obtaining an exemption from Bahamian law to open the casino.

That he had paid Minister of Finance and Tourism Sir Stafford Sands "legal fees" in excess of $1 million to get the exemption.

That several members of the Executive Council, including Premier Sir Roland Symonette, had been hired as "consultants" for the casino-hotel project following their favorable votes on the exemption.

That a book manuscript, The Ugly Bahamians, telling of these scandals, had been purchased by Hill & Knowlton, a prominent New York public relations company doing publicity for the Bahamas, and subsequently suppressed.

That at least three of the men running the casino at the Lucayan Beach were known associates and long-time employees of Meyer Lansky and currently fugitives from justice wanted by U.S. authorities for gambling violations. These men — Frank Ritter, Max Courtney, and Charlie Brud — were, the article implied, probably still working for Lansky.

The charges were not mere speculation. Karmin and Penn had copies of documents straight out of DEVCO corporate records showing how much money had been paid Sands and other Executive Council members. They even knew about Groves's prison record.

Groves and Sands and the Bay Streeters were now on the hot seat, not to mention Ritter, Brud, and Courtney. Instead of getting flustered or counterattacking directly, Groves invited Karmin and Penn down to Freeport as his guests to take a look for themselves.

The writers were not completely fooled by Groves's mild appearance and soft-spoken manner, though he was disarmingly convincing. Why, he was no underworld figure, he told the reporters; only an ambitious American businessman hoping to attract tourists to this island he was trying to develop. Yes, he'd had the casino built for that purpose, but that was only a small part of a much larger development plan. And yes, he was aware there were men with shady pasts running the gambling. But after all, you had to get experts to operate a business like that, and who knew it better than men who'd been in it for a long time? It was sort of like hiring the fastest gun in town to be sheriff. Besides, Mr. Chesler, not he, had hired the men in question. (Groves had made sure, when DEVCO was set up, not to involve himself directly in administrative matters.)

He also told the writers that Freeport was by no means a one-man operation. The respected investment banker Charles Allen and a British peer, Sir Charles Hayward, together owned a 50 percent interest in the Grand Bahama Port Authority. Daniel Ludwig had been granted two thousand acres of land in Freeport, part of which he had sold to U.S. Steel for its cement plant. Ludwig had also built the island's largest hotel, the King's Inn, using a $600,000-a-year subsidy from the profits of the Lucayan Beach casino, and was building other projects, too.

Before the *Wall Street Journal* writers left Freeport, Groves had succeeded in convincing them that most of the hanky-panky in their story was Chesler's doing, not his, and that he — Wallace Groves — was the unfortunate victim of a serious misunderstanding.

On October 19, 1966, two weeks to the day after their first story, Karmin and Penn published a follow-up piece in the *Journal.* If not exactly a retraction, the second article largely exculpated Groves and portrayed him as an ingenious if somewhat dictatorial entrepreneur who had performed a miracle of economic development on a nearly deserted island — even if he had inadvertently let in a few shady characters.

The two stories, taken together, won Penn and Karmin a Pulitzer Prize for investigative reporting.

An article — "Lax Laws and a Powerful Clique Invite the High-Rollers to Swarm In," by Richard Oulahan and William Lambert — in the February 3, 1967, issue of *Life* repeated some of the *Wall Street Journal* allegations and contained a good bit of new material. Casino proceeds, it indicated, were being skimmed by the Lansky organization, representing several Mafia families headed by Frank Costello of New York, Angelo Bruno of Philadelphia, Joe Adonis of New York and Italy, Steve Maggadino of Buffalo, and Santos Trafficante of Tampa.

Nor was casino skimming the only racket being run in the Bahamas. There were insurance frauds by phony "suitcase" companies based in Nassau (with Sir Stafford Sands serving as agent and attorney for many of them) that were cheating thousands of U.S. citizens out of money. There were secret accounts in a score or more of Nassau and Freeport banks, where not only mob figures but other tax evaders could hide their profits. There were companies — often no more than post office box addresses — specializing in the sale of worthless securities to unwary investors. The Bahamas, in other words, were an offshore haven for crooks running illegal scams and seeking to avoid U.S. legal authorities.

The *Life* writers also mentioned Ludwig's activities in Freeport. They characterized him as "the enormously wealthy American shipbuilder and international industrialist who came to Grand Bahama in 1955 to finance and dredge the deep-water harbor, and stayed on to build the King's Inn."

Oulahan and Lambert took note of Ludwig's Bahamia development, but seem to have misinterpreted a switch in plans:

It was Ludwig's understanding that he could also build an adjacent casino and the International Bazaar. But after Ludwig had invested millions of dollars in the resort, Groves sadly informed him he would have to take over the proposed casino project himself because his Bahamas Amusements, Ltd., holds the casino monopoly. And while the International Bazaar — an unholy mixture of Chinese streets giving on to an English mews, a Copenhagen square and a soupçon of Montmartre — was under construction, Ludwig was informed that he had lost the franchise to do business there, because he was insisting on bringing in his own shopkeepers and importing his own merchandise. The Bay Street Boys, who are, after all, primarily shopkeepers and merchants, had other ideas. As a sop for losing the casino and the bazaar, Ludwig got a barren tract of land which may (or may not) some day become a housing development. Nine of the International Bazaar's shops have already been turned over to Bay Street's Solomon Brothers.

Anyone who could accept this version of events obviously did not know Ludwig. The idea of D.K., who was used to tackling the U.S. government and winning, caving in to a pipsqueak like Wallace Groves is beyond belief. What probably happened was that Ludwig, after the *Wall Street Journal* stories appeared, decided to assume a lower profile. He could not completely hide his presence on Grand

Bahama; his dredging of the Freeport harbor and his building of the King's Inn were already matters of record. What he could do, though, was pretend that Groves and the Bay Street Boys had squeezed him out of the casino and bazaar. If there was to be bad publicity, let it fall elsewhere, not on him. Groves and the Nassau crowd were being paid well to take the heat. D.K., if he could not be completely invisible, could at least look like a victim. And the *Life* writers apparently swallowed this version.

*Fourteen*

# Whiteford

During the late 1950s and early 1960s, while Ludwig was expanding his operations in the Bahamas and elsewhere, he was also continuing to build ships in Japan. The controversy surrounding the alleged bribe taking by Prime Minister Yoshida and members of his Cabinet having died down after Yoshida's resignation, Ludwig's Kure yards were able to stay in place and keep producing.

In the early fifties, D.K. had built only five supertankers at Kure — four 38,000-tonners plus the 44,500-ton *Phoenix* — before switching over to ore carriers.

Then, responding to the demands of the Suez oil crisis, he had returned to building tankers, scaling up dramatically by constructing a ship nearly twice the size of the current *Phoenix:* the 85,515-ton *Universe Leader.* This Ludwig-built vessel, like several of its predecessors, became the world's largest tanker and was soon carrying oil from the Middle East to consumer countries. Like the other ships he had built after the war, this giant was operated under a foreign flag, that of Liberia, site of Universe Tankships, his big-tanker company. National Bulk, meanwhile, was continuing to shrink its shipping activities as it expanded its other ventures.

With tanker charter rates still high, D.K., during 1957 and 1958, quickly built seven more 85,000-tonners to capitalize on the oil boom: the *Universe Admiral, Universe Challenger, Universe Commander, Frisia, George Champion, Harold H. Helm,* and *Universe*

*Defiance.* Then he scaled upward again by more than 20,000 tons, completing the *Universe Apollo* in 1959 and the *Universe Daphne* in 1960. At 106,000 and 107,000 tons respectively, each of these ships, on launch, inherited the title of the "largest tanker ever built." Ludwig was now setting the pace again, having wrested the lead away from the Greeks, but both Onassis and Niarchos were also building tankers of more than a hundred thousand tons.

As if to take a breather and give his rivals a chance to catch up, Ludwig stopped building tankers and returned to constructing ore haulers. (Actually he and the Greeks had overbuilt, and now that demand had returned to normal, there was a glut of tankers in the world market.)

From 1959 to 1961, the Kure yard built seven more ore carriers and in addition produced a number of smaller specialty vessels: dredges, self-unloading bulk carriers, small tankers for Standard-Vacuum (Mobil) Oil, and quite a few tugs and barges. During the early sixties, activity at Kure slowed down. But Ludwig, who was then building his first hotel on Grand Bahama, was making big plans.

During the 1950s he had established what might be called "the Pittsburgh Connection." First he had gotten together with U.S. Steel's Benjamin Fairless to work out the ore-hauling deal to Japan (which led to his extensive South American ventures). Then he had cultivated a close friendship with William H. Whiteford, chairman of Gulf Oil, which led to Gulf's chartering some of D.K.'s big tankers. Since Ludwig was the only investor in Freeport to have shipping interests, he probably had a hand in Freeport Bunkering, the ship-refueling operation at Freeport owned by the Grand Bahama Port Authority and supplied by Gulf.

Ludwig and Whiteford had much in common. They were both secretive men, schemers on a grand scale, who didn't let scruples stand in the way of making money. Whiteford had come to Gulf in 1951 as executive vice-president and assumed the presidency the following year. In 1957 he was elevated to chief executive officer and became chairman of Gulf's board in 1960. But it was in 1959, while he was chief executive, that the gruff oilman earned himself a niche in American political history.

John Foster Dulles had just died, and Whiteford probably felt that Christian Herter, who had succeeded Dulles as secretary of state, was not doing enough to promote Gulf's interests abroad. Herter was

242

not the master plotter Dulles had been. He balked at things like bribery and coercion in foreign business relations, and Whiteford had no use for him.

Testimony during congressional hearings would reveal, fourteen years after the fact, that in 1959 Whiteford took matters into his own hands by setting up a secret slush fund, the purpose of which would be to influence U.S. and foreign officials to make decisions beneficial to Gulf.

According to the testimony of Joseph E. Bounds, who had been an executive officer directly under Whiteford at this period, no one except Whiteford and a few assistants reporting to him were to know about this fund. At the time he testified, Bounds was near death, suffering from the effects of a rattlesnake bite and from other ailments. The hearings were obviously an ordeal for him, but he told his story with the air of a man who had something he wanted off his conscience.

Whiteford, he told a Senate committee headed by North Carolina's Sam Ervin, had originally planned to have Sir Stafford Sands handle the fund, which was to be set up in the Nassau branch of the Bank of Nova Scotia (of which Whiteford was a director). Money was to be supplied to the fund from Gulf's Freeport Bunkering and other Bahamian operations. An initial deposit of $250,000 was made, and a courier, operating in the name of Bahamas Exploration, a small Gulf Oil subsidiary, was empowered to draw out as much as $25,000 a month. This money would never show up on Gulf's books in any form.

Sands agreed to handle the slush fund, said Bounds, but soon got greedy; in addition to his usual high legal fees, he wanted a percentage of all the money coming through the account. Whiteford decided at that point to cut him out and oversee the fund personally. The courier would bring the money to Pittsburgh, and Whiteford would put it in a safe in Bounds's office, to which only he, Whiteford, had the combination. Then (Bounds continued) the Gulf chief would draw it out as needed and send it to New York or London. Bounds testified that he did not know who received the money in those cities, and no other testimony provided any clues, but it is worth remarking that both Ludwig and Charlie Allen were in New York and that Sir Charles Hayward, another partner in the Grand Bahama venture, was in London. So, of course, were a lot of other people, but who else would Whiteford have taken into his confidence?

Whiteford, said Bounds, had told him in 1961 that other oil companies had set up similar slush funds to make political payoffs around the globe and were keeping them off their books, but Bounds told Whiteford he didn't like "the Bahamian setup"; it was too vulnerable. Whiteford replied that Bounds was being paid to like it, and Bounds had responded by asking for early retirement. Whiteford had become furious, and the two men had fought, with Bounds "decking" his boss. Whiteford could not fire Bounds without risking exposure, so he exiled him to California. After that, Bounds lost track of the slush fund and could not account for any of it.

But another witness, the Gulf lobbyist Claude Wild, told the Senate Judiciary Committee what had happened to $10.5 million of it. About $5.4 million, Wild said, went into the campaigns of Richard Nixon and some other candidates. Another $4 million was given to South Korean officials, since Gulf had major dealings in South Korea. Another million was used to buy presents for Latin American heads of state. The president of Venezuela, for example, had received a helicopter.

Despite these revelations, the Senate Judiciary Committee was surprisingly understanding. Senator Ervin treated Wild with deferential kindness. At one point he asked the Gulf lobbyist whether it wasn't a shame that government regulations made it necessary for companies like Gulf to have to resort to bribery to get favorable treatment from foreign officials.

Wild, beaming, replied, "I couldn't have put it better myself, Senator."

Ultimately a blue ribbon panel was appointed to look into charges that oil companies were routinely bribing foreign officials. The chairman, John J. McCloy, was a New York lawyer. It had already come out that Standard of New Jersey had used at least $130 million to influence elections in Italy during one brief period, but no punitive action would be taken against Gulf, Exxon, or any of the other accused companies.

Whiteford's role in Gulf's bribe scandal was not revealed until several years after his death. During the mid-sixties he continued to operate without detection. His only real problem at Gulf was that he had to step down in 1966 as chairman because of a company rule requiring retirement at sixty-five. Whiteford was just about there, but he wasn't ready to get out, and resented the fact he was being forced to. So he cooked up a little deal with Daniel Ludwig that would make Gulf pay through the nose for dumping him.

Under Whiteford's leadership, Gulf was expanding its European operations, and the plan was to set up a huge terminal on Whiddy Island in the shelter of Ireland's Bantry Bay. There, huge supertankers would bring their cargo of oil from the Persian Gulf, where it would be transferred to smaller tankers of 85,000 tons or so for hauling to the European mainland.

And how big were the supertankers that would bring the oil around South Africa? *Very* big; 326,000 deadweight tons big. Over three times larger than the biggest tankers Daniel Ludwig had ever built. And who would build these monsters? Daniel Ludwig, of course.

No other oil company was willing even to consider chartering or contracting for tankers of this size. Why, then, was Gulf? Apparently because Ludwig had promised Whiteford a cushy job after his mandatory retirement.

Whiteford had never cared much for the Mellons, Gulf's largest shareholders, and he regarded E. D. Brockett (who was to replace him as chairman) and other young Gulf executives as "Boy Scouts." Whatever his methods, he had made money for the company, and now it was shoving him out. But he and Dan Ludwig would show them.

Just before leaving Gulf, Whiteford set all the wheels in motion, and then walked out whistling. It was left to the new chairman, Brockett, to make the announcement.

On April 27, 1966, the *New York Times* ran the story: GULF OIL ORDERS SIX NEW TANKERS. Each of the six, said the article, would be longer (at 1100 feet) than the liner *France* and four times heavier than the *Queen Elizabeth*. Each would have the capacity to carry 2.2 million barrels of oil, stored in fifteen compartments that, individually, could hold as much oil as a fully loaded T-2 tanker of World War II vintage.

At the same time, Gulf announced plans to construct the Bantry Bay facility. Water depth in the bay was eighty feet, and the new supertankers would draft seventy-four when fully loaded. The port, Brockett said, would cost $28 million to build. He declined to say what it would cost to build the ships (other oilmen estimated $21 million per vessel) or who the builder was. Only later would the news leak out that Ludwig was ordering the ships. Officially, he was no longer the builder, since his lease at the Kure yard had run out and the facility had been taken over by Ishikawajima-Harima Heavy Industries. Unofficially, D.K. had very close ties with IHI and probably a substantial share of ownership.

The Bantry tanker job — the largest ship order ever given — was too big, though, even for the Kure yard to finish in a reasonable time, so three of the monstrous vessels were given to IHI to build, the other three to Mitsubishi. Ludwig, however, would be overseeing the construction of all six.

And what of Whiteford? Ludwig was seeing to him, too; he set up his friend in a new Manhattan brokerage. As for getting personnel, they were in luck. During 1965, a scandal had hit one of New York's major brokerage houses, Shearson, Hammill & Company. The SEC had come down hard on the firm for unscrupulous dealings and had taken the unusual step of suspending each of Shearson, Hammill's top five executives for sixty days each, a stiff penalty. The charge was "failure to prevent grave and extensive illegal activities."

In the wake of this debacle, Ludwig and Whiteford hired away three of Shearson, Hammill's key people to run their own brokerage. Neil Sellin, who had been getting $800,000 a year in gross commissions, was picked as chief executive officer. Raymond Forbes, Shearson, Hammill's floor partner on the American Stock Exchange, was hired to serve as floor partner of the new company. F. Randall Smith, a senior securities analyst, would head up the research department. Both Ludwig and Whiteford would lie low. Ludwig would put up most of the money, and Whiteford would maintain an office on the premises, but the new brokerage would be called Sellin, Forbes & Smith. It would, said Sellin in announcing its formation, "aim its services at wealthy individuals. . . . There are lots of brokers, who go after the big institutional investors. We'd like some of this business too, but our main pitch is going to be to individuals." He added that among his present clients were "movie stars, a big-league baseball player whose name [is] a household word in New York, heads of major companies, and so forth."

In short, what Ludwig and Whiteford were planning was an investment service for rich people like themselves, people looking for tax shelters and discreet investments. Ever ingenious at finding ways of using other people's money, D.K. was getting ready to tap into some new and fertile sources.

Yet Sellin, Forbes & Smith does not seem to have started business. At least no later record of the company has been found. The reason may be that, on September 11, 1968, some two years after his retirement from Gulf, W. H. Whiteford, while driving back to his Ligonier, Pennsylvania, home, ran head-on into another vehicle and was instantly killed. He was never able to take advantage of his part of the sweetheart deal with Ludwig. On the other hand, he was spared the embarrassment of having to testify before a congressional committee investigating bribery and corruption and slush funds.

As for the Bantry Bay project, it didn't fare so well either. During 1969 and 1970 — somewhat behind schedule — D.K.'s six Bantry tankers came off the ways in Japan. The *Universe Iran, Universe Korea, Universe Portugal, Universe Ireland, Universe Kuwait,* and *Universe Japan* were run by a specially created corporation, Bantry Transportation Company, under ten-year charters to Gulf Oil.

But on January 8, 1979 — just before the charters were due to expire — a French-owned tanker, the *Betelgeuse,* exploded at the Bantry Bay terminal, killing fifty-four people and causing a massive oil spill in the bay and on nearby beaches.

Gulf compounded the disaster by falsifying records. It attempted to cover up the fact that one of its employees, who might have prevented the tragedy, was absent from his post at the time. The officials and residents of County Cork were enraged by both the accident and the deception, and Gulf decided to end the entire project and put the terminal up for sale. There were no takers.

Soon after, in 1980, Ludwig, unable to find other employment for his oil-hauling elephants, got rid of them. He sold three for scrap and the others to Avin Oil (apparently a Niarchos company) for an undetermined sum.

The Bantry episode had ended badly for nearly all concerned, but, as usual, Ludwig had remained almost invisible throughout and emerged unscathed and a good deal richer.

*Fifteen*

# The Royal Commission of Inquiry

Bahamian Premier Lynden O. Pindling had a very short honeymoon with the American media. A lot of eyes, including those of U.S. District Attorney Robert Morgenthau, were glued on him from the moment he took office, waiting to see whether the new chief was going to do anything to clean up the gambling and corruption rampant in Nassau and Freeport. As son of a former U.S. secretary of the treasury, Morgenthau had a good notion of what such activities were costing the United States government. And as a hardheaded D.A. battling organized crime almost single-handedly, he knew how easy it was for the mob to gain control of small countries like the Bahamas.

It was soon clear to Morgenthau that Pindling himself had been compromised and was going to make only cosmetic changes in the lucrative offshore scams that had brought so much money to the islands. The righteous indignation in the Progressive Liberal Party leader's United Nations speech had been considerably tempered by the time he was elected premier. No, Pindling was not going to close the casinos and chase out the Lansky bunch. He was only going to make sure he and his constituents got a bigger slice of the pie.

So Morgenthau, frustrated because the mob was continuing to operate just outside U.S. jurisdiction a few miles off the Florida coast, resorted to the best weapon he had available: publicity. He wasn't out to get revenge; he was a lawman doing a lawman's job. And he was aware of how much politics could get in the way of that. Public disclosure was the only answer.

The *Life* magazine article in early February 1967 had reignited the issue. A *Saturday Evening Post* exposé shortly afterward fanned the flames, detailing how, even after all the previous publicity, a mob courier named Dusty Peters was still, two days a week, collecting stacks of checks and IOUs from the Lucayan Beach's Monte Carlo Casino and El Casino and flying with them to Miami Beach, where, after depositing them in a bank, he would go to the Fontainebleau and report the take to his bosses, Meyer and Jake Lansky.

It galled Morgenthau that the Lanskys could thumb their noses at American law enforcement officials while the Bahamian government was staring off into the distance and pretending nothing untoward was happening. Pressure must be brought to bear on the Pindling regime to clean up its act. Either that, or Morgenthau would see to it that American tourists were constantly reminded, through their newspapers and magazines, that the money they were dropping at gaming tables in the Bahamas was going straight into the pockets of the Mafia.

Pindling got the message. On February 28, 1967, he flew to New York to hold a press conference at the Regency Hotel, where he announced that "an authoritative investigation by outside experts" would be made into casino gambling in the Bahamas. Pressure was being exerted in Britain as well. One day earlier, the British government kicked Dino Cellini, a Lansky lieutenant, out of the country. He had been running a school to train young croupiers who would replace the American hard cases — most of them with criminal records — currently employed by the Freeport and Nassau casinos.

Pindling said he intended to "re-establish the government as the ultimate authority" on Grand Bahama, which would entail stripping Wallace Groves of his sovereign powers on the island.

Two weeks later, on March 14, a royal commission of inquiry sent over from Britain convened to hear testimony about the charges made in the *Wall Street Journal, Life,* and *Saturday Evening Post* articles. Its members were Sir Ranulph Bacon, former deputy commissioner of Scotland Yard (chairman); Detective Superintendent John O'Connell, also of Scotland Yard; a British lawyer, Robin Auld; and a Jamaican lawyer, Joseph Wharton. The hearings dragged on for more than a month without the appearance of the two most important witnesses, Wallace Groves and Sir Stafford Sands. Groves was in Switzerland, and Sands had been taking an extended holiday, first in Madrid, then in Miami, carefully keeping out of the commission's jurisdiction. Sir Ranulph decided to adjourn the inquiry until late summer, saying that Sands would testify then. He remained noncommittal as to whether Groves would also appear.

During the recess, there were several important developments. In mid-June, the Bahamian Parliament passed a revenue measure levying a $1 million tax on each of the islands' casinos. In response to this, the Lucayan Beach's Monte Carlo Casino decided to close. This, of course, meant that the hotel would close as well, since its main tourist attraction would be lost. Freeport's other gambling house, El Casino, in Ludwig's Bahamia section and near his three hotels on the island, would pay the tax and remain open.

The effect of this was to transfer nearly all tourist activity on Grand Bahama from the Lucayan section of Freeport, built by DEVCO, to Bahamia. This shift had begun even before the scandal, because Ludwig's hotels and El Casino were much bigger than the Lucayan Beach and its Monte Carlo Casino. Almost as soon as Chesler left DEVCO in 1964, D.K. had given some thought to taking over the Lucayan Beach and operating it as part of his growing hotel chain. He even went so far as to send a team of engineers to look the building over and evaluate it structurally. The casino, after all, had been a gold mine, without one losing night since its opening, in January 1964. It had made its first million in the first five months of operation and by the end of the year was able to pay back the $600,000 Lansky and his friends had lent to equip it.

But the rest of the hotel was a financial disaster. The debts Chesler had piled up in building it were too heavy a burden, and, after reading his engineers' reports and considering the whole financial picture, Ludwig decided to bow out. The Lucayan Beach was then sold by DEVCO (which Groves now controlled) to a Canadian investor, Allen Manus, for $7.6 million, $1 million less than Chesler had spent to build it.

To raise the money for purchase, renovation, and maintenance, Manus borrowed heavily from a Canadian lending institution, Atlantic Acceptance Corporation, which soon had $11 million of its capital tied up in the project. When the Lucayan Beach (most of its business drained away by Ludwig's hotels and the new Holiday Inn, which, like D.K.'s King's Inn, had been constructed with subsidies from the Lucayan Beach casino) failed to produce a profit after a few months, Atlantic Acceptance declared bankruptcy. In June 1965 it defaulted on $104 million in debts to creditors (mostly Americans) and created a serious tremor on the seismograph of international finance.

The closing of the casino at the Lucayan Beach in June of 1967 was merely the coup de grâce for an operation already mortally wounded by financial mismanagement and public scandal. But, whatever the other effects, and whatever relationship Daniel Ludwig had had with Wallace Groves before this, the demise of the Lucayan Beach Hotel and its Monte Carlo Casino left D.K. the undisputed king of Grand Bahama Island.

Meanwhile, Groves, still in Switzerland, was negotiating the final touches on a deal whereby he would relinquish ownership of another Bahamian property — Paradise Island in Nassau Bay. Groves (thanks to Sands) still owned 44 percent of Paradise Enterprises, Ltd.

On August 16, Sir Ranulph Bacon gaveled the hearings to order again in Nassau, and Groves was on the stand. His demeanor was far different from that of the mild-mannered man pictured in earlier articles. Under questioning he was arrogant and combative, as if trying to intimidate his interrogators. To the charge that he and his associates in DEVCO had bribed Bahamian officials to get the gambling exemption, he replied, "Unthinkable!" To allegations that he had conspired with notorious mobsters to bring casinos to Freeport, he growled, "Utterly ridiculous!"

Claiming to be ignorant of the day-to-day operations of DEVCO, Groves continued to stonewall through a day of questioning. By the end of the session, the commissioners had failed to dent his armor. Despite his unprepossessing appearance, he was obviously a clever man. With the *Wall Street Journal* reporters Penn and Karmin, he had been affable and charming and had turned a shocking exposé back on his enemies. Before the commission, he was closed-mouthed and hard as nails, and he emerged relatively unscathed from that encounter, too.

A week later, Sir Stafford Sands finally appeared in Nassau to testify. But if Groves had been a shark on the stand, Sands was a jellyfish. The heat didn't help. The Bahamas in August are oppressively uncomfortable for anybody, and the former minister of tourism and finance was a very fat man. He perspired profusely, continually dabbing at his brow with a sopping handkerchief, and the sweating only added to his discomfort at having to answer embarrassing questions.

For a lawyer, he was amazingly inept under fire, and he repeatedly declined to answer queries "on grounds it might tend to incriminate me." The answers he did give were often so patently contrived that the commissioners kept interrupting him with comments like "Oh, come now, Sir Stafford, are you quite sure?"

By the end of the hearing, Sands was such a beaten figure that he did not even challenge the commission's statements that he had been paid $1.8 million in "legal fees" for conspiring with DEVCO officials and other Executive Council members to push through the certificates of exemption. But if he was in disgrace, he was also wealthy enough to retire to Spain and spend the remainder of his days in ease.

The following week, Lou Chesler testified that he was positive the American mob had never had any connection with Bahamas gambling. Meyer Lansky had been consulted, he said, simply because he was the most knowledgeable person in the United States on casinos. Chesler's statements represented a kind of recanting of the earlier information leaked to the *Wall Street Journal,* and could be interpreted to mean that he had "gotten the word" from the powers that be and was now trying to make amends.

This concluded the hearings, which had gone on for over six months, with frequent recesses. In November, the commission issued its report and recommendations. Its findings were not to rock many boats presently on the water. Groves came out of the inquiry, if not smelling like a rose, at least with no taint of criticism. As for Ludwig, he had hardly been mentioned during the hearings and had escaped the scandals relatively untouched.

In 1968, Ludwig turned over the running of his King's Inn Hotel (the other two in Bahamia were still under construction) to a company called Inn Operators. The chairman of this firm was one Samuel Cohen, and its president was Morris Lansburgh. Both were big Miami Beach hotel men and both had interests in Las Vegas. They were also close to Meyer Lansky. Cohen was generally recognized by U.S. crime officials as being a Lansky front man, who, around this time, was buying out the Teamsters' interest in the Miami National

Bank. In 1969 he would be indicted along with Lansky for skimming the take from a Las Vegas casino. Lansburgh, who owned the Fontainebleau, where Lansky kept his headquarters, was, curiously, one of the hotel men who had turned thumbs down on Ludwig's Seadade project. Yet here he was, president of Inn Operators, which was going to run D.K.'s hotel.

The resort of Paradise Island, in Nassau Bay, was controlled by a man named James Crosby, who had transferred to the island the certificate of exemption he had used earlier on Nassau. Crosby had bought out Wallace Groves's interest in Paradise Island for $2.1 million. Through a front organization, the Mary Carter Paint Company (which had bought Bahama Developers, Ltd., and constructed the luxury project at Queen's Cove), he had first taken over Intertel, the security operation for Lucayan Beach's casino. Then he amalgamated his holdings, sold the paint company, and put his money into a corporation called Resorts International.

His grip on Paradise Island was as tight as that of Ludwig's on Grand Bahama. But the two men seem not to have been rivals. The question, of course, is whether Crosby worked for Ludwig, either as a partner or as a front man. Before moving to Paradise to set up a casino there, he had been on Grand Bahama, doing development work similar to that done by Ludwig in the Bahamia district of Freeport.

Soon the two men were to cooperate on a project of enormous significance: bringing the "emperor of Las Vegas," Howard Hughes, to the Bahamas.

*Sixteen*

---

# Hughes

It is a choice bit of irony that Howard Hughes, who during the last thirty years of his life was reputed to be the most secret man on the globe, has since become among the best known — the subject of several biographies, some of which quote exhaustively from piles of memos he wrote that revealed his innermost thoughts and even his bathroom habits. No laboratory frog has ever been so thoroughly studied, dissected, and picked apart as the remains of this eccentric recluse once known as the world's richest man.

And yet many mysteries remain, mostly about the last six years of his life, when he was living (if one can call it that) incommunicado outside the United States.

Most of the facts of his Nevada years are common knowledge by now: how he came to Las Vegas in 1966 to hole up on the top floor of the Desert Inn, how he bought up (or was duped into buying) many of the city's hotels and casinos, how he was kept carefully guarded in a darkened room by his "Mormon Mafia," seeing no one except his personal attendants, yet exerting a powerful influence on national policies and politicians through the use of money and an elaborate spy network.

To some, Hughes was regarded at the time as a sinister figure who used his vast wealth to exert influence over lesser mortals. To others he was a hero, one who had stepped incarnate from the pages of an Ayn Rand novel, the epitome of the rugged individualist who had attained enough money to do what he damn well pleased. Few at the time realized that he was a pathetic drug addict (the result of a near-fatal plane crash twenty years earlier which had hooked him on painkilling chemicals) who despite his fortune lived, paranoid and unkempt, in sterilized squalor.

That he bought up most of Las Vegas is a matter of record. Why he did so is another question. Some writers speculate that Robert Maheu, his right-hand man in Nevada, was conspiring with the mobster Moe Dalitz and other organized crime figures to "clean up" the casinos before the Feds closed in, and that getting Hughes to buy them was a way of taking the heat off. If this is so, and there is evidence to support the thesis, there is still a question about whose interests Maheu was really representing: Hughes's, the mob's — or the CIA's.

Maheu had been working full time for Hughes only since early 1961. But he had been employed off and on by the billionaire since 1954, and in 1957 — when Groves and Ludwig were beginning work on Freeport — he had flown down to Nassau, where Hughes was negotiating a secret real estate deal, in order to act as bagman and slip the appropriate Bay Street Boys a skids-greasing $25,000.

In 1966, it was Maheu who set things up for Hughes to come to Las Vegas, who met his boss's plane at an isolated airstrip and drove him to the Desert Inn, who acted as go-between in the deal for Hughes to buy the hotel from Moe Dalitz and friends for $13 million, who handled the negotiations for Hughes to acquire the Sands, the Castaways, the Frontier, the Silver Slipper, and, later, the Landmark, plus Harold's Club in Reno.

The bill for all this came to more than $100 million, and Dalitz and his chums could be forgiven for thinking they had hooked the biggest fish of all time in the middle of a desert. Nevada officials were also ecstatic to the point of delirium. With Hughes as resident (if not visible) owner of Las Vegas, they could now boast that the mob had been run out of town and a new day had dawned in the Sagebrush State.

So the grab continued — Hughes buying, the mob selling, and Maheu running back and forth as the billionaire's chief negotiator. But other eyes were watching with increasing disapproval. Bill Gay and Chester Davis, powerful men in the Hughes Tool Company, were seeing their boss's money, and their own influence, melting away.

At least that is the story. It is hard to say exactly why some of these things happened. The only thing clear about this part is that by 1969 certain forces in the Hughes organization, and perhaps elsewhere as well, decreed that the Hughes-Maheu relationship had to be broken off and Hughes taken away from Las Vegas. One theory is that Maheu had started drinking heavily and was becoming unreliable. Another is that Gay and Davis were simply jealous of him. In any case, Hughes was to be removed from Maheu's sphere of influence.

It would not be easy. Maheu was shrewd, a past master of stratagems and dirty tricks himself. Furthermore, he sat at the head of a thoroughly professional and efficient spy network (Hughes could afford the best, and Maheu had the contacts to acquire them) whose lines of communication reached throughout the world. Hughes might be isolated, but, thanks to Maheu, he was well informed about many things most people had no inkling of.

So the problem was to get Hughes out of Las Vegas suddenly without Maheu's finding out in advance what was happening and acting to prevent it. There was another problem that might prove even tougher: convincing Hughes himself to go along with the scheme.

In 1974, at the height of the Watergate disclosures, someone leaked a story to the columnist Jack Anderson, which he printed as an item at the bottom of a column on January 14 but failed to follow up. This is a pity, because it hints at a relationship whose significance Hughes experts have missed. This is the item in its entirety:

*Secretive Pair* — Howard Hughes' choice of the Xanadu Hotel in the Bahamas as his newest hideaway wasn't dictated by mere whim. There has been a longstanding secret link between the phantom billionaire and the international shipping magnate who owns the hotel.

The owner is D. K. Ludwig, who is reported to be both as wealthy and as secretive as the elusive Hughes. Back in 1969, Ludwig initiated a meeting with Hughes to discuss merging some of their talents and some of their millions.

According to our sources, the meeting was finally held on August 2, 1969, at the International Hotel in Las Vegas. Ludwig quickly got to the point. He wanted to manage all of Hughes' hotels and casinos. Hughes agreed to think it over. There is no available record that he ever responded.

But now that Hughes is staying at Ludwig's hotel to avoid extradition to the United States, two of the world's richest recluses may once again sit down and talk business.

What Anderson did not know, and had no way of knowing — not being aware of a connection between Ludwig and James Crosby — was that the business had already been done. Hughes had come to an agreement with Ludwig. He had consented to move out of Las Vegas and let D.K. move in to take over the hotels and gambling operations. He would go somewhere else and set up another little empire.

Late in August, after the meeting with Ludwig, Hughes, according to biographer Michael Drosnin, "let it drop to his Mormons that he was preparing a proxy that would give Gay, Davis, and Holliday [Raymond Holliday was another top executive in the Hughes Tool Company organization] authority over all his Nevada operations."

Soon after this, Bill Gay flew to Washington, D.C., for a secret meeting with Robert Peloquin, a former member of the Justice Department and now head of James Crosby's Intertel. Later, Peloquin flew to Los Angeles to talk with Chester Davis, who asked him to draw up a detailed scheme "for a change of management in Nevada."

In some ways, it seems strange that Hughes would consent to put himself in the hands of Intertel, which he must have known was mostly owned and controlled by James Crosby. Earlier (according to one of his memos) he had seemed to consider Crosby a rival and a threat to his own power, particularly in relation to Governor Paul Laxalt of Nevada. Hughes figured he owned Laxalt body and soul, but was afraid of losing absolute control over him, and had written Maheu at one point:

I am fearful that somebody or some company may be getting to Gov. Laxalt on a sub-rosa basis.

We must show enough interest to keep the Gov. solely and exclusively devoted to our interests. The first time he ties up with somebody like K [Kirk Kerkorian, a rival in Las Vegas who planned to build the biggest casino-hotel in town] or Crosby of Mary Carter Paint or any other source of financing, I think we will be forced to pull out of here lock, stock and barrell [sic]. I am ready to ride with this man to the end of the line, which I am targeting as the White House in 1972, but there is no room in our program for a second angel.

Yet in 1969 Hughes was tying up with Crosby, apparently because Daniel Ludwig had talked him into such a move.

Despite his being obsessed with secrecy, Hughes could not seem to avoid discussing his proposed departure from Vegas with Maheu. For some time he had been depressed and frightened by the nuclear tests being conducted in Nevada — blasts whose tremors he had felt in his penthouse suite — and about what he felt was the pollution of Las Vegas's water supply, nearby Lake Mead.

In September 1969, a month after his meeting with Ludwig, he wrote to Maheu:

> Bob, my future plans are in a state of complete chaos, as a result of what is happening.
>
> I have things I want you to do in both New York and Washington, and, thereafter, unless something surprising occurs, I will want you to come here to Las Vegas and supervise a massive sale of practically all of my Nevada assets.

After giving a long list of reasons that he considered Las Vegas no longer a habitable place, Hughes wrote of his plans to his long-time aide:

> I am prepared to invest almost every cent I can scrape together in the development of an entire new community and way of life in some location where some of the restraints, incumbrances [sic] and competition of this area are not present.
>
> I want to make this new development the last and, I hope, the most important project of my life.

And where did he plan this ambitious venture? He had already narrowed down his choices.

> I cannot think of any location worthy of consideration except Mexico and the Bahamas. Of course, Onassis had the really ideal setup with Monaco. However, I prefer a location close enough to the U.S. so that the U.S. would never permit any hostile intervention by outsiders. I feel both Mexico and the Bahamas qualify in this respect.
>
> So let's, for the moment, compare those two. Which government do you think would be the most reliable and lasting?
>
> It seems to me that the Bahamian situation is very unpredictable due to the recent change in the complexion of the government.
>
> I think the Mexican government is more stable, but I have less confidence in our ability to occupy a position of sufficient influence and privilege with the Mexicans.
>
> In other words, I have pretty well assumed that you felt confident of a very favorable position with the new Bahamian government,

whereas I do not somehow gain that impression in respect to Mexico.

In the light of everything we know, this is the most hopeful and very most realistic possible site for the location of the projects I have planned.

However, there are many other powerful entities located in the Florida, Bahama, Caribbean area, and they present a deeply entrenched powerful force that may not take kindly to my entry into that area. There is no way I can estimate the strength of these competitive entities since we must keep my plans the most religiously guarded secret, or everything will really be screwed up completely.

I do know that Baja has been much, much less invaded by rich American projects than the Florida-Bahamas area.

I want to consider a development in Baja that would be similar to the all-inclusive arrangement Onassis had in Monte Carlo. I don't mean that I aspire to take over the Mexican government as he did Monaco. I mean that I want to make a deal with the Mexicans which would be somewhat similar to the deal Ludwig made with the Bahamian government when Freeport was established.

Please consider the problems in obtaining "Empire Status."

This very revealing memo, besides showing Hughes rationally and lucidly weighing his options on where to relocate, also sheds light on a number of other matters.

To begin with, it shows that Hughes, like Ludwig, envied Onassis enough to emulate him. It also shows that Hughes, like Ludwig, preferred staying fairly close to home in order to take advantage of U.S. military protection. In choosing the Bahamas or Baja, Hughes would also be availing himself of another protection — Ludwig's. D.K. was already set up in both places. He had Freeport in the Bahamas and he had his salt operation and village at Black Warrior Lagoon in Baja. So the choices Hughes was sounding out Maheu on may well have been Ludwig's suggestions.

Hughes made it clear that if he decided on the Bahamas, he anticipated possible resistance from "powerful entities" already established there. He did not, however, seem to regard Ludwig as a competitor but as a role model.

For our purpose, the most important part of the memo, though, is the reference to "the deal Ludwig made with the Bahamian government when Freeport was established." Not that "*Groves* made," but that "*Ludwig* made." This indicates that Hughes thought of

D.K. as the real prime mover on Grand Bahama. And this is the sort of thing that Hughes, for all his isolation, was apt to know better than most people; he was paying his spy network to keep him informed. Besides, Hughes himself had been in the Bahamas making deals in 1957, when Freeport was just getting started, so he would have been in close touch with the situation at the time.

It had always made sense that Groves was fronting for some body. He didn't seem to have the financial or political underpinning to set himself up as czar of Grand Bahama on his own or to attract a big investor like Charlie Allen as a junior partner.

When the *Wall Street Journal* bombshell exploded, many observers jumped to the conclusion that Groves was fronting for Meyer Lansky. But that didn't make sense either. Groves had come to Grand Bahama more than a decade before the casinos opened, and his initial projects were aimed at attracting industry, not tourists. Only after the Cuban Revolution did Freeport become an attractive place for casinos, so making Freeport a gambling center couldn't have been planned in the mid-1950s.

It can be assumed, then, that Wallace Groves was no more than a Ludwig surrogate, managing one segment of D.K.'s far-flung empire. And *empire* is the proper word for what came of Ludwig's negotiations with the Bahamian government: he had no laws on Grand Bahama except his own, no taxes except his own, the freedom to dictate whatever terms he chose to anyone else coming to live on the island, and even to throw people off if he decided he didn't want them there any longer. Technically, Grand Bahama was a part of the British Empire. In actuality, it was his island, and Charlie Allen's and Sir Charles Hayward's. Leslie Waller had figured out much of this by around 1970, when he was writing *The Swiss Bank Connection*. But Howard Hughes had probably known it all along.

Hughes had been enjoying empire status in Las Vegas since 1966. But if he moved, he would have to make another deal somewhere else — either with the Mexican government or the Bahamian regime of Premier Lynden Pindling. The memo indicates that he felt he was likely to fare better with Pindling. Exactly where he was planning to build his new empire in the Bahamas is unclear. Ludwig had Grand Bahama, and Crosby was in control of Paradise, but there were plenty of other islands available. Hughes probably did not intend to move in with either of them, since, as he said later in the memo, "it just does not work out to have more than one tiger to each hill in a situation like this." But things did not go as he planned.

From around the time he talked to Ludwig, Hughes seems to have been convinced he would have to leave Las Vegas soon to escape the bomb tests and the water pollution. But in his current state of paranoia, he was not one to do anything quickly. He agonized over every possibility, and these ruminations kept him immobilized. Meanwhile, his Mormon aides, at Gay's instigation, were starting a whispering campaign designed to break him away from Maheu.

Hughes had become too dependent on his memo correspondence with Maheu to keep anything from him, and he was soon commenting on the rumors, angrily accusing the wily ex-FBI man of plotting to steal his empire away from him. Whether the charges were true, Hughes was being led to believe they were, and this was what mattered. Meanwhile, he continued to discuss in detail his escape plans with the very man he was trying to escape from, and the Mormon aides clawed the walls of the Desert Inn penthouse in frustration.

Finally, on Thanksgiving Eve of 1970, Hughes worked up the nerve to go through with the great escape. Bundled onto a stretcher, his scraggly hair and beard partly concealed by an old snap-brim fedora, he was carried down the Desert Inn fire escape and loaded into a waiting van. After being driven to the airport, he left in a private jet arranged by Intertel and was soon winging his way to the Bahamas, where he would be ensconced in another darkened ninth-floor penthouse, this one on the top floor of the Britannia Beach Hotel on Paradise Island, a plush hostelry owned by James Crosby's Resorts International.

A week passed before Maheu discovered his boss's disappearance. When he did, he immediately raised the alarm that Hughes had disappeared and probably been kidnaped, possibly even murdered, by sinister rivals seeking to take over the Las Vegas operations.

The *Las Vegas Sun,* run by a friend of Maheu's, the publisher Hank Greenspun, ran a front-page story headlined HOWARD HUGHES VANISHES! MYSTERY BAFFLES CLOSE ASSOCIATES.

Reading the story in the Bahamas, Hughes saw it as confirmation of his suspicions that Maheu had been lying to him all along. *He* knew that Maheu knew where he was, because he had been discussing the exodus with him for more than a year. In the back of his mind, he had retained a troubling uncertainty that, by believing his

Mormon aides, he was wronging Maheu. But the *Sun* story clinched it. Maheu was obviously lying in saying he didn't know what had happened to Hughes, and if he was lying about this, he had no doubt lied about other things.

His mind finally made up, Hughes sent instructions to Chester Davis to strip Maheu of his proxy. In effect, Davis was to fire Maheu. At the same time, Intertel agents moved into Las Vegas to seize control of the Hughes hotels and casinos. A desperate legal battle took place between Intertel and the Maheu forces, but was quickly resolved when Hughes called Governor Laxalt and expressed his desire that Maheu be ousted. Once it was apparent that this was what Hughes himself wanted, the matter was soon settled, and Maheu was on the outside, looking in. He wasn't about to give up easily, however. As soon as he had found out about Hughes's disappearance from Las Vegas, Maheu sent a team of his own intelligence operatives down to Paradise Island, where they took a room directly under Hughes's. They had soon been discovered, rounded up, and shipped off the island by Intertel's James Golden, a former Secret Service bodyguard for President Nixon, now in charge of security for Hughes.

This was not to be the end of it. On January 7, 1972, when Hughes set up a telephone interview from his Bahamas hideaway to talk with several newsmen as a way of convincing the world that the Clifford Irving "biography" was a fake, his answers to reporters' questions about Maheu were revealing. Asked whether the Irving book might have been done in collaboration with Maheu, he said, "My attorney thinks that it could be." And when asked why he had fired Maheu, Hughes lost his cool: "Because he's a no-good dishonest son of a bitch and he stole me blind. I don't suppose I ought to be saying that at a news conference, but I just don't know any other way to answer it."

A month later, Maheu filed a $17.5 million libel and slander suit against the Hughes Tool Company. After four months of lawyers' arguments, a jury decided that TOOLCO (which had now, against Hughes's own wishes, become the Summa Corporation, with Gay at its head) was liable for Hughes's statements to the press, and a later trial awarded Maheu $2.8 million in damages. An appellate court later overturned both rulings.

In the meantime, while the case was going on, Intertel had

launched an intensive effort to discredit Maheu, even getting the Internal Revenue Service to do a tax audit on him. Maheu fought back, and eventually revealed information before a congressional committee that threw harsh light on Hughes's own financial maneuverings.

Having made his public blast against Maheu in the telephone interview, Hughes sank back into the safe seclusion of his Britannia Beach hideout. But not for long. On February 15, 1972 (just five days after Maheu had filed his libel and slander suit), the billionaire's privacy was abruptly interrupted. Bahamian immigration officials showed up at the Britannia Beach to ask why Hughes was still on the island long after his six-month residency permit had expired.

Howard Hughes had to get out of the Bahamas, and get out in a hurry. Intertel's James Golden chartered an eighty-three-foot yacht, the *Cygnus,* belonging to a Baltimore advertising executive, and took Hughes and his aides to Sunset Island Number 2 on the Biscayne Bay side of Miami Beach, where Bill Gay maintained a rented house. Gay wanted Hughes to stop over for a few days and have some needed dental work done, but the billionaire refused to go into the house or stay in Florida any longer than he had to. A van was procured, and Hughes was driven to the Fort Lauderdale airport, where, after some delay, he was put aboard a leased executive jet and flown to Managua, Nicaragua.

Why Nicaragua? Two reasons suggest themselves. One was the presence of Ambassador Turner Shelton, who had earlier been ambassador to the Bahamas. Shelton provided a direct Bahamas-to-Nicaragua link that the Hughes people and Intertel could exploit on the spur of the moment.

Second, General Anastasio Somoza Debayle was a personal friend of Daniel K. Ludwig's. In 1971, three years after James Crosby had held a splashy grand opening for the new Resorts International Paradise Island Hotel and Casino, Ludwig had opened his own hotel in Acapulco — the Acapulco Princess, shaped like an Aztec pyramid and built at a cost of $64 million. Unlike the host of the Paradise Island bash, Ludwig had invited only a few intimate friends and associates to his grand opening. The guest list included Clark Gable's widow, Kay; California governor Ronald Reagan; the heads of Standard of New Jersey, Gulf Oil, Standard of Indiana (Amoco), Litton Industries, the Bank of America, and New York's Citibank; and General Somoza of Nicaragua.

(The opening, according to one person who attended, "seemed to go well, but, upon leaving the hotel, Ludwig summoned the new manager and said simply, 'I want you out of my hotel by five o'clock today.' No explanation and no reprieve.")

How long Ludwig and Somoza had known each other is not clear, but the relationship between the Somoza family and certain U.S. corporate interests Ludwig was tied to went back a long time, to the dictator's father, General Anastasio Somoza García, and even before.

In 1909, the United States, at the urging of several American corporations, had intervened to support a coup d'état against a reformist Nicaraguan leader, General José Santos Zelaya. A civil war broke out, and in 1912 the United States sent in Marines to support the conservatives. These troops stayed until 1925, but after they were brought home, fighting broke out again, and more U.S. Marines were sent. Their presence was vigorously opposed by a liberal leader, General Augusto César Sandino, who began a guerrilla war against the American occupation forces.

By 1933, the Marines had organized the Nicaraguan National Guard to help keep the peace against the Sandino forces. Once it was in place, the Marines were called home again by President Franklin D. Roosevelt. Left in charge of the Nicaraguan military was an English-speaking officer with close ties to U.S. corporate interests, General Anastasio Somoza García.

Not long after the Marines pulled out, Somoza persuaded Sandino and his followers to accept a cease-fire and turn in their weapons. As soon as the guns were in hand, Somoza had Sandino assassinated. Unarmed, the liberal leader's followers were unable to retaliate. In 1936, Somoza staged his own coup and deposed President Juan Sacasa. The following year, after rigged elections, he assumed the office himself.

He held the post until 1956, in the meantime working closely with the CIA to overthrow, in 1954, the government of neighboring Guatemala. After he stepped down, his older son, Luis, took office. (He later let the CIA use Nicaragua as a staging area for the Bay of Pigs invasion of Cuba.) Luis left office in 1963, and a Somoza family puppet, René Schick, held the presidency for four years, during which time, in 1965, Nicaraguan troops were sent to support a landing of U.S. Marines at Santo Domingo in the Dominican Republic. While Schick was president, Luis's younger brother, Anastasio

Somoza Debayle, headed the National Guard. In 1967, he moved up to the country's top office himself and occupied it for most of the next twenty-two years.

The Somozas were not only Nicaragua's first family in politics but in wealth as well. In fact, they were said to be the richest family in Latin America; they owned many of Nicaragua's businesses, including the national airline, a shipping firm, radio and TV stations, a newspaper, truck and automobile dealerships, a port, and concrete, cement, textile, and tobacco operations. They also controlled Nicaragua's agricultural production and owned perhaps 30 percent of the country's agricultural lands. Whether Ludwig was involved in any of these operations has not been established, but his friendship with General Somoza, and the fact that several of the family operations — the shipping company, the airline, the port, the concrete and cement plants — sound like D.K.'s cup of tea, make a business connection between Ludwig and Somoza a distinct possibility. Ludwig rarely had friends he didn't also do business with.

But it is clear that when Howard Hughes was taken to Nicaragua, Somoza wanted to do business with *him*. The general, after all, was doing Hughes a big favor. The *norteamericano* billionaire had no valid passport, so Somoza had to waive normal requirements to let him into the country.

Having landed in Managua, Hughes was taken to the Intercontinental Hotel, where he was put into a suite on the eighth floor (the ninth, where he usually stayed in hotels, was a restaurant). Once settled in, he wanted to show his host how grateful he was and also provide himself with a little insurance. He wrote in a memo to an aide:

I think that while Somoza is being so decent to me in the face of all this bad publicity, something might happen tomorrow to change all this.

The Central and South American people are very emotional and changeable. So before this happens, I think I should make a present to Somoza.

I suggest a *really* desirable automobile. We should find out whether he likes to drive himself and would prefer a sports car, or a very elaborate limousine with a bar and telephone and TV set, and the very last word in accessories.

Also, I want to be *damn sure* he (Somoza) is told *loud* and *clear* that this was *my personal idea* because I appreciate the considerate treatment he has shown me.

Somoza, however, had a better idea. His personally owned airline, LANICA, which was also Nicaragua's national air carrier, was operating in the red and in desperate need of some new equipment. Hughes took the hint. In exchange for 25 percent of the airline's stock, he ordered TOOLCO to ship down two Convair 880 jetliners. Somoza also pushed Hughes into buying some choice Managua real estate to build hotels and other resort facilities on, as well as a pharmaceuticals firm and a plywood factory.

It soon became apparent that Somoza was a bottomless pit of greed. If Hughes stayed much longer, he would become bankrupt. After twenty-five days in Managua, he and his party decided to leave. The excuse was that communications with Hughes enterprises in the United States were difficult from Nicaragua because of bad radio transmission.

Before he left, though, Hughes agreed to an unusual ceremony. He would meet personally with Somoza and Ambassador Turner Shelton just before taking off for Canada. Doing so required his taking a rare bath, getting his hair and beard cut, and having his fingernails and toenails trimmed, but the billionaire went through with the ordeal, and welcomed the dictator and the diplomat aboard his leased airplane, looking thin but with his beard a neat Vandyke.

It was important that Hughes make a public appearance of a sort. Other than his attendants, almost no one had seen him in person for fifteen years, and many suspected that he was dead. The captain of the *Cygnus* had reported, after carrying the billionaire from Paradise Island to Miami Beach, seeing a grotesque, skeletal being, naked except for a bathrobe, and possessed of long, unruly hair and beard and fingernails and toenails that looked as though they hadn't been cut for years. The meeting with Somoza and Turner, with Hughes properly groomed, would establish that he was alive and well and properly taken care of.

During the meeting, Hughes thanked Somoza for his hospitality and, in general, talked and behaved lucidly. His only gaffe was in complimenting Somoza (a West Point graduate) on "speaking English very well for a foreigner."

Following the visit of Somoza and Shelton, Hughes and his party took off for Vancouver, where he was to spend the next six months at the Bayshore Inn. Canadian officials, like Somoza, had to agree to overlook Hughes's lack of a valid passport.

In August 1972, for reasons still unclear, the entourage packed up again and headed back to Nicaragua. Some vague reference was made to Canadian taxes having to be paid by those staying longer than six months. On this visit, it is not reported whether Somoza tried to sell Hughes anything else.

But on December 23, Hughes's peace was again abruptly shattered, this time by a force of nature. Just after midnight on that date, the first tremor of a massive earthquake shook the Intercontinental, and the aides barely got their boss out of the building in time to save his life. Within hours, Managua was a shambles — more than seven thousand killed, another fifteen thousand injured, nearly three fourths of the city leveled, more than half its remaining population homeless. Hughes and his staff had been among the more fortunate. They had come through unscathed, and could fly off to London the next day.

The world, shocked by the disaster, poured more than $1 billion in aid into the devastated city. It was an opportunity for Somoza to redeem himself for his past sins of greed by rising to the occasion and becoming his country's savior. Instead, he became its biggest looter, siphoning off the aid money to benefit himself and his friends.

There were thousands of unemployed laborers in Managua, and hundreds of local contractors looking for work. Somoza usually ignored them, bypassing their bids in favor of much higher ones from contractors in Miami and the Bahamas, many with ties to organized crime.

Ludwig was one of the chief beneficiaries. As a personal friend of Somoza's, he soon formed a fifty-fifty partnership with the dictator to rebuild many of Managua's destroyed houses and public buildings, using the Con-Tech system. His International Housing, Ltd., entered a joint venture with Somoza's privately owned construction firm, CASANICA, to grab off much of the money the Agency for International Development was supplying to rebuild the city. Meanwhile, local contractors went begging for work.

In the meantime, Intertel had taken Hughes to London's luxurious Inn on the Park, owned by Rothschild banking interests and overlooking Buckingham Palace. There his good luck continued. Hardly was he settled in when news came that the U.S. Supreme Court had overturned a $180 million judgment against him in a case with TWA. The news perked the billionaire up so much that he held a meeting with Nevada's new governor, Mike O'Callaghan, and even piloted an airplane again.

Hughes spent nearly all of 1973 in London; it was the most vigorous, and seemingly the happiest, year he had had in nearly two decades. The end of the year would even see his name enshrined in the Aviation Hall of Fame in Dayton, Ohio. He did not attend the event, but he was pleased to receive the honor.

His good times, though, were just about over. On December 20, 1973, Hughes was flown out of London and back to the Bahamas. The plane carrying him and his party, a DC-9, belonged to Adnan M. Khashoggi, a Middle East arms merchant who had become incredibly rich acting as a middleman for such U.S. firms as Northrup and Lockheed in selling weapons to Arab countries. Ludwig had apparently asked for the use of the plane.

The destination this time was Freeport. Hughes was going to be a paying guest of Daniel Ludwig at the exclusive Xanadu Hotel on the beach in D.K.'s Bahamia section. The suites Hughes occupied at the Xanadu rented at $1,000 a day, but it was worth far more to him to be out of the reach of U.S. officials. In fact, it was worth at least $15 million, for that is the amount Hughes reportedly paid Ludwig to buy the entire hotel.

Whether Hughes was in what could be described as sound mind at this time is debatable. During his last days in London, he had fallen and broken his hip, and was now a complete invalid. Furthermore, he seems to have been kept more heavily drugged than before and to have been less and less in touch with the outside world. No longer the shrewd plotter who had kept Maheu hopping with contradictory memos and instructions, he was now pathetic in his paranoia. For example, when he concluded the deal to buy the Xanadu from D.K., he wrote to his aides: "Please send a personal note from me to Mr. Ludwig (just orral [sic] — not written — through Mr. Ludwig's chief representative — but with no other man present) as follows: 'It has been a pleasure to do business with you.'"

While Hughes was drifting in and out of drug-induced reveries and occasionally watching old movies, the U.S. legal system was grinding steadily along. Hughes was being charged in federal court with having manipulated stock to force shareholders of Air West (which he had worked to acquire so that he could fly people into his Las Vegas casinos) to sell out to him cheaply. A grand jury returned a true bill of indictments, and a U.S. consul in Nassau was notified to fly up to Freeport and serve Hughes with a summons to come back to the States and testify in his own defense.

The consul knew Hughes was staying at the Xanadu, but when he inquired at the hotel, he was told the management knew nothing of any Howard R. Hughes staying there. He then consulted the local postmaster and learned that a Hughes employee was regularly picking up the boss's mail. The consul tracked down the employee and handed him the summons.

A week later, the consul received a visit from Robert Peloquin, the head of Intertel, who angrily argued that the summons had been improperly served and would have to be given to Hughes in person. Fine, said the consul. Would Peloquin kindly set up a meeting? The Intertel chief replied that "any consular officer would find Mr. Hughes quite inaccessible." The summons was never served, and Hughes was never extradited.

Hughes stayed holed up in the Xanadu (now called the Xanadu Princess, having been consolidated into Ludwig's Princess International Hotels, Ltd., shortly after Hughes moved in) for more than two years, his health and mental acuity sinking rapidly during the last few months. On Christmas Eve of 1975, he observed his seventieth birthday without ceremony, but by that time he was only occasionally aware that he was in the world.

Soon after, it was decided that he should be moved to another Ludwig hotel, the Acapulco Princess in Mexico. It has been surmised that this decision was made by somebody high up in the Hughes organization, perhaps Bill Gay, but it might have been Ludwig.

The Mormon aides themselves seem not to have known who dictated the move to Mexico or why. But they had the task of explaining to Hughes that he had to move again, and made up a story that his drug supply in the Bahamas was drying up and he would have to go to Mexico to ensure a steady supply. This was a bald lie — Hughes's drugs were being flown in from New York — but it served to pacify him.

On February 10, 1976, the semicomatose Hughes was once again loaded onto a stretcher and flown away to Acapulco.

Ludwig's Acapulco Princess was perhaps the most colorful and expensive of his Princess International chain, which now numbered seven hotels: the Princess and Southampton Princess in Bermuda, the Bahama Princess (formerly the King's Inn) and the Princess Tower (formerly the International) in Freeport, the Acapulco Princess (which he had built) and the Pierre Marqués (which he had bought) in Mexico, and the Sir Francis Drake (which he had bought and operated as a Princess hotel, though it was run by a separate corporation) in San Francisco.

D.K. liked pairing his hotels, presumably so that they could share such recreational facilities as golf courses and tennis courts. He had done this in Bermuda, Freeport, and Acapulco and, in the last two locations, had surrounded the hotels and golf courses with luxury housing selling for premium prices. No expense had been spared in Acapulco to attract rich guests and potential second-home buyers. The Princess alone there had cost him $40 million to build, averaging out to better than $50,000 a room, something of a record for modern hotel-building cost.

Every luxury was available — marble baths, intricately hand-carved furniture, a huge air-conditioned, professional-quality indoor tennis court, championship golf courses, and of course a beautiful beach. For those who preferred the sedate sport of elbow bending, there was a pool where guests could swim under a man-made waterfall to their own submerged barstools and drink their rum concoctions sitting neck-deep in water.

All this, of course, was lost on Hughes, who was cooped up in his room at the top of the pyramid-shaped hotel, his windows covered over with heavy blankets. He was rarely conscious now. A staff of doctors was available, but they seem to have been little concerned with his health. He should have been in a good hospital, with round-the-clock care and modern facilities, but here he was, in one of the world's most luxurious hotels, neglected and filthy and starting to die.

On April 3, 1976, less than two months after coming to Acapulco, Hughes became delirious and repeatedly mumbled something about an insurance policy. The next day he was worse, and Jack Real, a former airline executive who had become part of the Hughes entourage so that the boss could talk to him about airplanes, called Dr. Wilbur Thain in Logan, Utah. Thain, a brother-in-law of Bill Gay, had overall charge of Hughes's medical staff.

Real, recalling the conversation later, said he told Thain that he didn't want to play doctor, but that Thain's patient was dying. Thain replied, "Well, goddamn it, you are playing doctor, and mind your own business."

Real repeated that Thain should come to Acapulco to treat Hughes. Thain responded, "I've got a party in the Bahamas and I'll come over after that."

By the wee hours of the morning of April 5, Thain still had not arrived, so a local Mexican doctor was called; he diagnosed Hughes as suffering from severe dehydration and asked two of Hughes's own doctors why the skeletal man on the bed was not in a hospital. He was told that the patient did not like hospitals.

Thain finally arrived from the Bahamas after 7:00 A.M. on the fifth, accompanied by an Intertel agent, Fenelon Richards. According to later testimony by the aides, both men went into the office adjoining Hughes's bedroom and spent approximately two hours pulling out documents and feeding them into a shredder. Only after they had completed this task did Thain go in to see his patient.

At 11:00 A.M. Hughes was finally put on a stretcher and taken to a waiting plane to be flown to a Houston hospital. By that time, it was too late. He died en route at 1:27 P.M., shortly after the plane had flown over the Rio Grande, dividing Mexico and Texas.

Once the plane set down in Houston, the body was taken to a local hospital and an autopsy performed. Cause of death was listed as kidney failure. It might well have been put down as neglect.

# Seventeen

# Mercantile Bank

The world of offshore banking is as deep and mysterious as the ocean, and harder to fathom. Things pop to the surface occasionally — fetid, putrescent things — but soon sink back into the depths whence they came, and are lost to sight and memory. To those who merely observe the surface, most of what takes place under the waters is unapparent and unreal. But it exists, and it can have profound effects on the lives of surface dwellers, even though they have no knowledge or understanding of it.

To the diver who goes below the surface, the waters are still murky but more penetrable. Strange shapes loom suddenly out of the near darkness, tangible but hard to identify. Sharp focus is impossible at these depths, and features cannot be discerned clearly. But by putting together the blurred images, the diver can sometimes form a rough idea of what these benthic monstrosities really look like.

Freeport's Mercantile Bank is a case in point. In retrospect, it is hard to get a clear fix on what happened, or know exactly who was involved, other than a few visible participants. All one can do is to put pieces together and speculate, citing evidence wherever possible. When one is researching a figure as elusive as Daniel Ludwig, this is the only course possible.

Mercantile Bank was started in Freeport at about the same time the Lucayan Beach Hotel and its casino were being built, in 1963–1964. It was put together by three companies: Cayship Investment

Company of Panama, Security (Bahamas) Company, Ltd., of Nassau, and Compañia de Navigación Mandinga, S.A., of Panama. Of these three companies, Cayship (Cayman Shipping?) was, according to an undercover IRS agent who lived and worked in Freeport for many years, generally assumed to be a Ludwig-owned firm. No connections have been suggested for Security (Bahamas), but Compañia de Navigación Mandinga may have been owned by the Goulandris family, Greek shippers.

What is known for sure is that in March of 1963 a Bahamas branch of Cayship Investments, Ltd., was started in the Nassau offices of Price Waterhouse, the international accounting firm, and soon transferred to Freeport. In November, another corporation, the Mercantile Navigation Company, was also set up in Nassau and transferred to Freeport soon after. Both companies were located in the new Mercantile Building, where Mercantile Bank would also have its headquarters. In fact, a group of related companies — the Mercantile Group — would be housed in the same building.

Officers and directors of the Mercantile Group included I. Gordon Mosvold, Frances Voetberg, John L. Schlanbusch, Serge Michaelides, Paul L. E. Helliwell, F. Eugene Poe, D. G. Stampados, Karl Glastand, and P. A. Tomkins. Mosvold, the leader, is said by knowledgeable IRS sources to be a member of a Norwegian shipping family and, in Freeport, a representative of D. K. Ludwig's interests. Helliwell was a Miami attorney in the firm of Helliwell, Melrose & Dewolf, and allegedly a close associate of Richard Nixon's. He is also said to have been the paymaster for the Bay of Pigs invasion force. Poe was an officer of the Bank of Perrine in Perrine, Florida, between Miami and Homestead, near where Ludwig had bought his Seadade land. Tomkins was a Cayman Islands banker.

Mercantile Bank, a member of the Mercantile Group, was classed as a merchant bank, the purpose of which is to represent a small number of depositors — usually wealthy ones — by channeling their deposits into lucrative income-producing ventures, such as building projects. In the Bahamas, merchant banks also offer many tax advantages. Americans need never send their money out of the States. It can simply be put in a U.S. bank but marked to a Bahamian account, where it is not subject to the kinds of regulations and taxation applicable to U.S. accounts. Offshore banking, then, as practiced in the Bahamas, the Caymans and elsewhere, was and is basically a tax dodge designed to cheat the U.S. Treasury. It is also a source of loan capital for people like Ludwig, engaged in big development projects.

The reasons for Ludwig's setting up merchant-banking operations, then, were several. He could attract investment capital. He could, by borrowing money from his own banks, pay himself the interest on the loans. He could also, by controlling the books, use the banks to launder money for a variety of purposes.

Ludwig, of course, was not the only one to benefit from offshore merchant banking. In both Freeport and Nassau, numerous banks sprang up to serve rich people eager to hide their money in offshore accounts. Some of the biggest banks in America and Europe — Chase Manhattan, Citibank, Morgan Guaranty, Barclays, Lloyd's, Crédit Suisse — built impressive structures in the Bahamas' two largest cities. In all, by 1980, there were 314 banks to serve the islands, with their population of 237,000 people. This was one bank per 755 residents — all the more remarkable when one realizes that most Bahamians are too poor to have need of banks. But then the banks weren't for ordinary people. You could stand outside one for the better part of a day and never see a customer enter or leave. Many of the banks, in fact, didn't even have cash. All they had were records of depositors. The cash was still back in the United States, but the records were removed from the scrutiny of U.S. authorities.

How were the funds of the merchant banks being used? Some of them, no doubt, were employed for Bahamas development — the hotels and casinos and luxury houses and restaurants and golf courses all required startup money. But some of the money went into land speculation in the United States as well.

For example, about the time Mercantile Bank was getting started, a major enterprise was taking shape in central Florida. The Disney interests were buying up land around Orlando for what would become the East Coast version of Disneyland, only much larger. Walt Disney World would soon draw millions of tourists from all over the eastern United States and even Europe. The announcement would not be made until 1965, because the Disney people wanted to buy up as much land as they could before word got out and prices skyrocketed. But a few other people knew. One of the chief land buyers for Disney was Paul Helliwell, the lawyer who had helped set up the Mercantile Group. Not surprisingly, while he was buying land for Disney, he was also buying acreage in Orange, Volusia, and Osceola counties in Florida — the counties most affected by Disney World's coming — for some members of the Mercantile Group. Once the amusement park got going, much of this land was sold off for big profits, but some was kept.

For a brief time in Freeport, once the first casino-hotel was completed, business boomed and the Mercantile Bank prospered. The economic signs were encouraging enough to persuade Ludwig to begin his huge Bahamia project with three hotels and a larger casino. But the Groves-Lansky-Sands scandals of 1966–1967 hit Grand Bahama hard, and business fell off. Then, when the economy and the stock market took a downswing in 1970, both Ludwig and the Mercantile Bank were in big financial trouble. And by spring of 1971, things were even worse. *Business Week* remarked, in its April 3 issue:

> Hotel and casino operators on Grand Bahama Island, already dispirited by a sluggish season, were further depressed this week by two developments. First, Pan American World Airways, facing financial troubles of its own, announced it is discontinuing service on April 25 between Freeport and Miami, chief take-off point for Grand Bahama visitors. Second, the $7.5 million International Hotel, which opened just last December, closed on Monday.
>
> The hotel, owned by multimillionaire D. K. Ludwig, is being operated under a 20-year lease by Morris (Meyer) Lansky, the Miami Beach hotelman now under federal indictment with an alleged plot to "skim" $14 million from a Las Vegas casino.

There are a couple of things worth noting here. James Crosby of Resorts International, who, as we have seen, probably had ties to Ludwig, had just been trying to take over Pan American. Was this move to forestall the airline's cut-off of service to Grand Bahama? Or was Pan Am retaliating for the attempted takeover?

Second, *Business Week* was obviously confusing Meyer Lansky and Morris Lansburgh. Lansky was indeed currently under indictment for a Las Vegas scam, but he was not connected with Ludwig's hotel. Still, considering the similarity of names and the fact that Lansky and Lansburgh were closely associated in a number of deals, the mistake was understandable. And particularly so when it is noted that Sam Cohen, Lansburgh's partner in Inn Operators, which was running Ludwig's Grand Bahama hotels, was under indictment with Lansky in the same Las Vegas case.

As for the Mercantile Bank, it too was in danger of going under. During the middle and late sixties it had lent several million dollars of depositors' funds to other companies in the Mercantile Group — companies mostly involved in construction and development and very probably connected with Ludwig's building of the Bahamia section of Freeport.

Many of the companies holding the loans had put the money to work by investing it on margin in the American stock market, with the idea of using the profits for operating capital. But when the market dived in 1970 and the debtor companies could not meet their loan payments, Mercantile was caught short. It couldn't very well foreclose; it was part of the same group of companies it had lent the money to. And in many cases there was nothing to foreclose on. The bank had made the loans without collateral.

Desperate, Mercantile chief I. Gordon Mosvold began to look for ways to plug the holes. He hurriedly set up a number of dummy corporations — "straw companies" — and used them to "buy" the assets of some of the loan holders. Through this process, nearly worthless holdings were suddenly transformed into "valuable real estate." Undeveloped acreage in the Florida boondocks — some of the land Helliwell had bought for Mercantile Group companies — was quickly subdivided, sold, resold, and sold again through the straw companies. Land that was miles from anywhere, covered with scrub pine and palmetto, and would normally be expected to bring $200 an acre, was cut up into lots and shuffled through several "owners." Some 550 acres were divided into third-of-an-acre parcels — 1650 in all — and by the time the selling dust had settled, were appraised at $17,000 apiece.

Company A had bought some of the lots from one of the loan-holding corporations for $2000 each. Company B had bought them almost immediately from Company A for $5000 apiece. Company C had paid B $10,000 per lot, and so on.

No one in his right mind would have considered paying more than a fraction of that amount for any of these lots, but that wasn't the idea. The plan was to build up assets on paper — assets Mercantile could point to and say, "Look, we've got plenty of collateral. Just see all the valuable property we're holding."

And to someone who didn't know any better, it would look just that way. Land that had been worth about $100,000 before Mosvold started his hocus-pocus with straw companies was now being valued at over $28 million — just about what Mercantile needed to hide its defaults.

The idea was not to sell the land, but to sell the *bank*. Mercantile holding over $25 million in uncollectible debts could hardly be given away, but Mercantile holding $28 million in valuable Florida real estate as collateral was a very marketable property.

Once Mosvold had built a paper raft under his sinking bank, he put out the word that Mercantile was for sale. Pretty soon he had a nibble. Late in 1972, General George Olmsted came down from Washington, D.C., to talk business.

Olmsted was now retired from the military, but after World War II, he had been one of the generals who helped set up and administer NATO. He had also taken a large responsibility in carrying out the European Recovery Program.

In performing his several duties, General Olmsted had managed to offend just about every one of America's European allies, chiefly because he continually pushed them to produce armaments they could scarcely afford. In this he was merely passing along the pressure exerted on him by the State Department, but the criticism of him became so acute that he was finally transferred to the Far East before retiring.

On leaving the Army, Olmsted joined forces with another retired general, Orval Cook, and several civilian acquaintances to form a giant bank-holding company, Financial General, Inc., umbrella for the International Bank Group. Headquartered in Washington, where it owned several banks in the nation's capital and surrounding states, Financial General spread its net to many countries around the world. One knowledgeable observer has said it virtually owned Liberia.

Olmsted, when he came down to talk about a deal with Mosvold, was a power in Republican Party politics, serving as chairman of the Republican Congressional Campaign Committee. Testimony during the Watergate hearings would reveal that he had ordered the creation, in one of Financial General's Washington banks, of forty-nine campaign committees for Republican candidates into which contributions from the dairy industry — apparently political payoffs for Nixon's having raised milk and dairy prices during his first term — could be funneled. The contributions themselves were not illegal

— D.C. had no campaign-reporting requirements — but the committees had been set up to disguise the donors so that the payoff aspect could be concealed. The chairpersons of most of these committees were E. Howard Hunt, his wife, Dorothy, and an attorney, Douglas Caddy.

Olmsted, then, was hardly a babe in the woods. But whether he was gullible in negotiating the purchase of the Mercantile Bank is a question still unanswered. It is a matter of record that he went to Freeport and spent two days in discussions with Mosvold and others before arriving at a deal. According to the agreement worked out, Olmsted agreed to buy a two-thirds interest in Mercantile Bank of Freeport and a half interest in Mercantile Bank of the Cayman Islands* in exchange for 77,574 shares of Class A stock in the International Bank of Washington, which at the time had a book value of $14 per share (totaling just over a million) and a market value of around $7.00 per share. He also agreed to pay off a million-dollar certificate of deposit to an unnamed Mercantile depositor. (Whether this was Ludwig has not been determined.) Mosvold would also be made a director of International Bank of Washington.

This deal, worked out in December 1972, was made final in March 1973. Soon after, Olmsted was revealed to be involved in an attempt to take over Chessie Systems, owner of the Chesapeake & Ohio and the Baltimore & Ohio railroads. Other members of the Olmsted group in this little Monopoly game were Gulf & Western's Charles Bluhdorn (who had sold James Crosby two million shares of Pan Am in Resorts International's attempt to take over the airline); Lawrence Tisch, head of Loews Corporation, a motion picture exhibitor that just happened to be operating Resorts International's Paradise Island Hotel and Casino; the *New York Herald Tribune*'s publisher, John Hay Whitney; Texas oil and construction millionaires Clint Murchison and his brother; and the heads of Glen Alden Corporation and the Power Corporation of Canada. The attempt failed when the target company decided to fight the takeover.

Ludwig, during the same period, was having no better success at the takeover game. In the spring of 1971 he had formed a new company, Newport Industries, as a subsidiary of National Bulk Car-

---

*Olmsted also agreed to pay, through International Bank, $122,500 in cash for fifty thousand additional shares of Mercantile Caymans — enough to give him two thirds of that bank as well.

riers, with the idea of taking control of Cinerama, Inc. Cinerama had just bought RKO–Stanley Warner Theaters, Inc. (RKO was Howard Hughes's old studio), and was short of cash. Ludwig wanted to buy three million shares of Cinerama for $3.125 per share — it was currently trading at $5.50 — and acquire an option to buy another million shares later at the same price. These would have made him Cinerama's biggest stockholder, with about 30 percent of the shares outstanding. But in June 1971, three weeks after the proposed deal was announced, negotiations were suddenly dropped, and neither Cinerama nor National Bulk would comment on the reasons for the breakoff.

In the Bahamas, things were not going well either, partly because the islands, after nearly two hundred years of British rule, were scheduled to receive their independence in the summer of 1973. To many rich white Americans who had money invested in Bahamian enterprises or deposited in Bahamian banks, this was cause for alarm. Premier Lynden O. Pindling had been reasonably pliable since taking over in 1967, but he had been at least nominally under the authority of the British Crown. What would happen when the Bahamas gained their independence? Would Pindling suddenly nationalize all foreign assets? It was a frightening thought, and American investors reacted predictably: many of them transferred their holdings elsewhere. The white flight became a green flight. Money poured out of the islands in a steady stream before Pindling could gain absolute authority and seize it.

The new Caribbean tax haven would be the Cayman Islands, the tiny Jamaican dependency where Ludwig had come many years earlier, seeking crews for his ships. There were hardly any black males left on the islands to participate in a revolt, so the Caymans were considered safer territory than other Caribbean islands with predominantly black populations.

For Mercantile Bank, this meant transferring most of its assets from Mercantile Freeport to Mercantile Caymans, a task made easy by the fact that the Mercantile Group (and now International Bank of Washington as well) had well-established branches in both places. Mosvold, when he wasn't shuttling between Freeport and Washington (where he was helping set up the American Indian National Bank as part of the Financial General bank group), was soon traveling between Freeport and Georgetown, capital of the Caymans, to transfer money from one Mercantile Bank to the other. Other Bahamian bankers were doing the same.

All this flutter in the dovecote was very interesting to U.S. Treasury officials. For years, while J. Edgar Hoover and his FBI had been looking under every bush for communists and grabbing headlines, Treasury had been the only national law enforcement agency in America actively pursuing organized crime figures like Meyer Lansky and the various Mafia dons. Although Internal Revenue agents could not go down to the Bahamas and seize all the money being stored in offshore tax havens, they could and did maintain undercover agents in Freeport and Nassau to keep an eye on what was happening. In 1973, they were trying particularly to get the goods on Lansky, but when they pulled up one net, it contained some very strange fish indeed.

The net was Castle Bank, one of the numerous merchant banks and tax havens on the islands. Castle was an offshoot of Mercantile Bank, and, according to Bahamian corporate documents, Mercantile still owned stock in Castle. Thus, if Ludwig was part of Mercantile, as IRS agents believed he was, he was part of Castle, too.

An undercover IRS agent named Norman Casper had gained access to Castle's records. In January 1973, Casper learned that one of the bank's officers, Michael Wolstencroft, was getting ready to make one of his periodic trips to Miami and would have with him a briefcase full of bank documents. Wolstencroft, knowing that Casper (who was posing as a bank employee) had friends in Miami, asked the agent to fix him up with a date. Casper, complying, furnished the bank official with an escort for the evening — actually a Miami policewoman.

When he arrived in Miami, Wolstencroft called on the lady Casper had recommended and took her out for dinner and a tour of Key Biscayne, leaving his briefcase at her apartment. Casper, who had also come over from Freeport, entered the apartment, removed the contents of the briefcase, and took them to Special Agent Richard Jaffe, an organized crime expert in charge of Operation Haven (as it was called) to be photographed. (Jaffe and another IRS agent had been waiting nearby with special photographic equipment.) Once they were copied, Casper returned the documents to the briefcase in their original order, and Wolstencroft apparently never suspected a thing. Now the IRS had a list of Castle depositors who were secretly hiding money outside the United States in order to avoid taxes.

According to sources who have seen the list (its existence was later confirmed by a secret congressional hearing on October 6, 1975), it contained the names of more than three hundred "extraordinarily prominent Americans,"* one of whom, said an IRS informant, was Richard M. Nixon. The former president, who had recently resigned in the wake of the Watergate scandals, hotly denied the charge when confronted with it. Another name, allegedly, was that of former Republican National Committee Chairman Leonard Hall. A number of Hollywood stars and a major magazine publisher were also said to be on the list, along with Moe Dalitz and other mobsters who were now in Las Vegas running the casinos.

But the list was never made public, and the investigation itself was quashed — by none other than IRS Commissioner Donald Alexander, the same Donald Alexander who, a few years earlier, as the Maritime Administration chairman, had turned down Daniel Ludwig's request for 87.5 percent mortgage loan insurance to build American-Hawaiian container ships but left the door open for 50 percent funding.

After leaving Maritime, Alexander had returned to private law practice, but had been called back to government again by President Nixon, who, after firing two other commissioners, appointed him to head the Internal Revenue Service in 1973. Nixon's own tax situation was under considerable criticism as a result of the Watergate probes, and Alexander immediately conducted an investigation and cleared the president of any wrongdoing — a finding many investigators regarded with extreme suspicion.

Alexander also set about dismantling the IRS investigative mechanisms, but he failed to stop Operation Haven, because, for most of two years, he didn't know about it. Undercover agents had discovered the name of his former law firm on a Castle Bank telephone index and, to avoid involving him in a possible conflict of interest, had not told him about the operation. Once he found out, though, he ordered Operation Haven stopped, along with several other probes involving the Central States pension fund of the Teamsters and C. Arnholt Smith, a big contributor to Nixon's campaigns. A

*Castle's clients had all been referred by two law firms, one in Chicago, the other Paul Helliwell's firm in Miami.

flap developed, but Alexander was later exonerated by the Ford administration.

The Castle Bank scandal, then, was one of those putrid messes that pop to the surface and then disappear again, most of their mysteries still unrevealed. Mercantile Bank was another. By 1977, Mercantile Freeport was virtually stripped of funds. Apparently some depositors had been warned and had taken out their money while there were still funds left. Others had not. The ones who had not then complained to the Bahamian government, which responded by voiding Mercantile's license on grounds that the bank could no longer meet its obligations to investors.

Disgruntled depositors who couldn't get their money back sued General Olmsted and two of his International Bank officers, claiming they had gained control of Mercantile in 1973 and systematically looted it of more than $25 million through fraudulent transactions. International Bank of Washington was also named as a defendant in the suit.

International Bank, in turn, sued Price Waterhouse, charging the giant accounting firm with conspiring with Mosvold to misrepresent Mercantile's assets at time of purchase by overvaluing almost worthless real estate near Orlando, Florida, and elsewhere.

In its defense, Price Waterhouse argued that Olmsted had been made aware of Mercantile's troubles by Mosvold before he bought the bank, and that International Bank had cooked up the scheme to loot Mercantile, then close it, taking a tax loss to offset sale proceeds of other properties.

Charges and countercharges flew as these two heavyweights slugged it out in court, and lawyers fired interrogatories like bullets. Some interesting names appeared in their lists: Castle Bank & Trust (which for a while had money deposited in Mercantile Freeport); Bernie Cornfeld and Investors Overseas Services, Ltd.; Robert Vesco; John M. King (once described by his friend Cornfeld as "the biggest wildcat oil driller in the world"); Paul Helliwell; the Pritzger family (owners of the Hyatt Hotel chain and reportedly holders of the largest single deposit in Castle Bank); Delafield Capital Corporation (a member of the group of companies that in buying the Mary Carter Paint Company from James Crosby, was charged with stock manipulation by the SEC); Jack Hayward (son of Sir Charles Hayward and a top executive in Grand Bahama Port Authority); Henry,

Robert, and Patrick Dowd (who will be mentioned later); and
— most interesting of all — the CIA. Lawyers on both sides demanded any materials pertinent to both the Central Intelligence
Agency and the opposing companies involved in the suit. One can
infer from this that the CIA had ties to International Bank, Mercantile, and Price Waterhouse.

The case, having dragged on for years, still sits unresolved, at this
writing, in a Washington, D.C., federal court. Until it is settled, most
of the records will be unavailable. But in the thousands of pages of
documents that *are* open to public scrutiny, there is not one mention
of Daniel Ludwig.

There are, though, some tantalizing clues that he may well have
been the gray eminence behind Mercantile Bank. All through the
records are scattered references to a mysterious, unknown person
who was an associate of Mosvold's:

Castle Bank was acting on behalf of a third party presently unknown
to International Bank.

\* \* \*

Milluna [one of the straw companies] is a Liberian company owned
by an unidentified friend or associate of I. Gordon Mosvold.

\* \* \*

Lynmar Company, Ltd. [another straw company] is, we are informed,
a Bahamian corporation owned by an unidentified American.

Many of the straw companies mentioned in the suit as having been
involved in the fradulent inflation of land values were registered in
Liberia or Panama, countries where Ludwig was strongly established. So, of course, were several other shippers, nearly all of them
Greek. What seems to clinch the argument that Ludwig himself was
the mysterious stranger is that one of the intermediate straw companies Mosvold used was named Cromarty Investments, Ltd. Shortly
before Mercantile Bank was sold to Olmsted, Ludwig had started a
company called Cromarty Petroleum at Cromarty Firth in northern
Scotland to exploit North Sea oil (another of the straw companies,
incidentally, was named North Sea Shipping), and he was in the
habit of giving the names of his shipping ventures to investment
companies using their proceeds. If, for example, Cayship Tanker
Company was a Ludwig shipping enterprise, there would also be a
Cayship Investment Company to manage the profits. Cromarty In-

vestments, Ltd., then, sounds like an offshoot of Cromarty Petroleum, which is known to have been a Ludwig-owned corporation. Besides, after one puts all the facts together — an unidentified American who owns companies in Panama, Liberia, the Bahamas, Canada, and Scotland — one is hard put to think of anyone besides Ludwig who could qualify on all counts. The evidence points to one conclusion: Daniel Ludwig was the real power behind both Mercantile and Castle banks, and Mosvold — like Groves — was only a front man.

# Eighteen

# "Welcome to Brazil, Mr. Ludwig"

There are only two seasons in the tropics of northern Brazil — wet and dry — and even the dry season is relatively wet. Farther south (Rio de Janeiro being as far below the Equator as Miami is above it), climatic changes over the course of the year become more apparent. In the Southern Hemisphere, of course, the seasons are reversed: March 21 in Rio marks the beginning of fall, not spring.

For one prominent Rio resident in 1964 — Brazilian President João Goulart — the coming of autumn would have an especially ominous meaning. It would signal the start of another kind of fall: his own.

Goulart, after taking over his nation's top office in 1961 following the resignation of Jânio Quadros, had quickly established himself as one of the most popular, albeit controversial, leaders in Brazilian history. Most of his power came from the working classes, which, despite their vast numbers, had traditionally exercised little influence in the country's government.

The new president intended to change that. His stated purpose was to make Brazil a democracy in fact as well as name. He planned to accomplish it in two ways: by giving workers and their unions the political rights and privileges hitherto enjoyed only by wealthy land-owners, merchants, and the military; and by building a solid base of prosperity in the nation.

For too many years, Goulart said in numerous speeches, multinational corporations based in the United States and Europe had been bleeding Brazil dry of its natural resources, not giving the country a chance to raise its own people's standard of living. "Brazil is for Brazilians," he proclaimed, and proceeded to act on the slogan by instituting a program of land reform and nationalizing such key industries as oil and steel.

One of the businesses most affected by these policies, the U.S.–based Hanna Mining Company, had recently moved in to claim most of the newly discovered, rich (70 percent pure) iron-ore deposits of Minas Gerais state. To Hanna, the Minas Gerais lode meant one thing — that Brazil would soon become the world's leading exporter of iron ore to the United States, Western Europe, and Japan. To Goulart it meant another — that Brazil could now start its own basic steel industry, which would put it on the road to becoming a modern industrial nation.

Goulart, by moving into the courts to expropriate the ore fields from Hanna, was well on his way to winning this clash of purposes in March of 1964. Then something happened to change the odds.

Back in the United States, Hanna officials met with business and government leaders, reminding them of what had happened just a few years earlier in Cuba. Bad enough that Castro and his partisans had taken over that little island. But if Brazil, with its vast resources, went the same route . . .

In several of Brazil's rural areas, the week after the March equinox was full of furtive movement. Shadows flitted through the tropical nights, some of them rumored to be CIA shadows. Large open-bed trucks, normally used for hauling iron ore from Hanna's mines near Belo Horizonte, now rumbled down dark country roads toward secret rendezvous spots, their cargo spaces filled with armed men in sweat-stained fatigues.

On March 31 all hell broke loose. Interior-based Army units rose in revolt against the central government, seizing control of several provincial capitals. The rebellion spread east toward the coastal cities of Rio and São Paulo like wind-blown fire through dry pampas grass.

News flashed ahead to Goulart that same afternoon. The next morning he fled Rio for Brasília, the new national capital still under construction in the interior. There he hoped to rally enough loyal forces to turn the tide. Too late. His enemies had done their work well. The rebellion was unstoppable. Realizing that the situation was hopeless, Goulart flew out of the country, his dream of a united, democratic, prosperous Brazil shattered, his administration the latest victim of those military coups which chronically overthrow civilian governments in Latin American countries.

On April 11, the victorious Army chief of staff, General Humberto Castelo Branco, proclaimed himself Brazil's new president. One of his first acts was to purge the government of Goulart's leftist supporters and suspend their political rights. Another was to sever diplomatic relations with Castro's Cuba, with which Goulart had established close ties.

Quickly — almost too quickly — the United States recognized the new regime. The U.S. ambassador to Brazil, Lincoln Gordon, immediately got busy making speeches praising Castelo Branco and the overthrow. The new president responded in kind with a move designed to please business and government leaders in New York and Washington: he named Roberto Campos as minister of planning.

Campos was already a familiar figure in corporate and official circles; colorful and outgoing, he had become so Americanized during his stint as ambassador to the United States that his American friends had translated his name to "Bob Fields." He was known to be in so tight with certain Manhattan interests that one observer remarked wryly, "It's hard to tell whether Campos was Brazil's ambassador to the United States or the Rockefellers' ambassador to Brazil."

A key figure in the Castelo Branco regime, Campos had the task of scrapping Goulart's "Brazil for Brazilians" programs and attracting as much foreign capital as possible into the country. The first priority was to encourage multinational investors to come in and open up the Amazon basin — a vast area then covered by the world's largest tropical rain forest and inhabited by a few thousand Indians, squatters, and a great variety of wildlife — for farming, mining, lumbering, and a host of other potentially profit-making activities.

Campos wanted to civilize the Amazon. Toward this end he was soon winging northward to New York in search of individuals and companies willing to invest large amounts of money turning thousands of square miles of jungle into productive land. In December 1964, he had a meeting with Daniel K. Ludwig in the latter's Manhattan offices.

Had the two men known each other previously? Probably so.

Shortly after setting up his cattle ranch and related ventures in Venezuela during the early 1950s, D.K. had become friends with a wealthy Brazilian minerals tycoon, Augusto Trajano de Azevedo Antunes. The Brazilian magnate was already involved in various enterprises with such U.S. firms as Bethlehem Steel and Scott Paper, and before long he and Ludwig were pooling money to form several joint ventures for developing natural resources. Antunes knew Campos well and may have introduced him to D.K. Or it may have been their Rockefeller connections that brought together the billionaire and the planning minister. In any case, Campos seems to have known that Ludwig was looking for a tract of several million acres of land on or near the Equator for establishing what would become the world's largest tree farm.

"I always wanted to plant trees like rows of corn," D.K. told an interviewer years later. He had conceived of the notion back in the mid-1950s, about the time he was making regular trips down to Venezuela to watch his bulldozer crews push down miles of native forest to make way for cattle pastures. Ludwig hated seeing anything go to waste that he could make money on, and we can imagine him saying, "What a shame! Too bad there's not a market somewhere that would pay me to cut these trees into usable wood and haul it out. Thirty years from now, when the population has doubled and most of the forests are down, people will pay fortunes for wood like this."

But wood was too plentiful in the fifties to be worth hauling to a distant market, so there was little alternative but to have it pushed into piles to be burned. Still, the wheels had started turning in D.K.'s mercenary mind. What if he started soon and created a mammoth forestry enterprise that, by 1980 or so, would be ready for harvesting just about the time the world was experiencing a shortage of wood? Why, he could rake in money that would make his oil-hauling profits seem like peanuts! Ludwig had already become one of the world's richest men by taking gambles no one else had the courage or foresight to risk. This seemed a choice opportunity to become even richer.

But what kind of tree to grow? D.K. knew from observation that most species native to the tropics are unsuitable for large-scale pulp and lumber use. Either they grow too slowly or their wood is too soft, and much of their bulk is waste, with no commercial value.

Most existing forestry operations were concentrating on conifers and other softwoods — pines, firs, spruce, hemlock, cedars, redwoods — because they grew more quickly and had a multiplicity of uses. If reforestation was being done primarily with softwoods, the *real* shortage of the future would be of hardwoods. It was true that a hardwood forest generally takes sixty or more years to grow back, and pines can be ready for harvest in thirty. But somewhere in the world, D.K. reasoned, there must be a hardwood tree capable of rapid growth in hot, wet, Equatorial climates and versatile enough to serve as an all-around source for paper pulp, lumber, and furniture industries. And if such a tree existed, he, Daniel K. Ludwig, would find it.

In the early 1960s, D.K. assembled a number of botanists, foresters, and other scientists knowledgeable about silviculture (some of them already working for him on projects he had started in Latin America, Africa, and Asia) and sent them out searching for the perfect tree. Soon one of the scouts, a chemical engineer named Everett Wynkoop, sent back exciting news: he believed he'd found just what his employer was looking for.

Wynkoop's candidate was a deciduous species named *Gmelina arborea* (pronounced meh-LEEN-ah — the *g* is silent and sometimes dropped from the spelling — ar-BORE-ee-ah). The engineer had located it in Nigeria, where he was doing some mining surveys for Ludwig. He had learned about it almost by accident; the Nigerians were using strong, hard Gmelina posts as props in the mines. He did some research and found that the British Colonial Office had imported the tree for mine posts from Burma and India around the turn of the century and had been growing it in Africa ever since. But besides its strength and durability, its most notable feature was its rapid growth rate. Under ideal conditions, Gmelina was capable of shooting upward at the incredible rate of a foot a month! Planted as a seedling, it could be ready to harvest for pulpwood in six years, for lumber in ten. Almost as important, there was virtually no waste; every part of the tree could be used for pulp, and most parts for other wood products.

Reading Wynkoop's report, Ludwig was impressed enough to fly the engineer back to New York immediately to confirm in person what the tree could do. Hearing this phlegmatic Dutch scientist state flatly that the tree would grow phenomenally in tropical climates anywhere near the Equator excited the tycoon in a way few things ever had. Imagine millions of acres of hardwood forest capable of being harvested and replanted every six to ten years! Think of the tonnage this would produce! If the market went as Ludwig predicted, he could make nearly half a billion dollars a year out of forestry alone. Oil had long been known as "black gold." The Gmelina tree, if he could get a head start in growing it, might become "green platinum" for D.K. in a decade or so.

Ludwig flew Wynkoop straight back to Africa to start combing Nigeria and neighboring countries for Gmelina seeds. (An attempt to locate seed-bearing specimens in the tree's native Burma and India proved unsuccessful.) Before any large-scale commitment was made, Gmelinas would first have to be test-grown. D.K. was soon sending his project managers in various Equatorial countries small bags of Wynkoop's seeds to see how Gmelinas would fare in the soils of different areas. With the bags went careful instructions on how to plant the seeds and care for the seedlings and, above all, how to keep accurate growth records. By scanning his managers' reports, Ludwig would be able to determine which locales were best suited for large-scale production.

In a few places, the Gmelinas didn't do well at all. D.K.'s manager in Mexico, for example, reported that the seedlings were unable to establish an adequate root system in the country's dry, hard-baked soils. But in Costa Rica, Panama, Honduras, and Venezuela the news was enormously encouraging: the seedlings were adapting to New World soils and growing like weeds, except that they were taller and larger.

Word of what Ludwig was doing soon leaked out, and some timber company executives, curious, came down to have a look at this miracle tree. Most, after looking, remained skeptical. In the eyes of lumbermen accustomed to the straight, soaring trunks of commercially grown conifers, Gmelina was an unimpressive prospect. It tended to grow somewhat crookedly and to branch close to the ground, both of which characteristics made it unsuitable for the production of long, straight, knot-free lumber.

After seeing this for themselves, the timber executives went away shaking their heads, convinced that D.K. had misplaced a few of his marbles in gambling on such an ugly tree. The billionaire was undeterred. He'd gotten richer than any of his doubters by flying in the face of conventional wisdom and accomplishing what lesser men deemed impossible or too risky. Confirmed in his faith by his own foresters (who naturally were telling him what they knew he wanted to hear), Ludwig went on singing the praises of Gmelina as the ultimate answer to future shortages of lumber and pulpwood.

"It's all he ever talked about," remembered one paper company president who knew him during this period. "He thought Gmelina could do anything. He was the only one in the industry who did."

Having convinced himself that he had found the tree, D.K. now set about finding a country where he could grow it in great numbers. His criteria were few but specific:

1. A large tract — several million acres — of cheap, undeveloped land on or near the Equator.
2. Access to a deep-water port (which he would dredge deeper if necessary).
3. A country dominated by a friendly authoritarian government that would give him favorable tax breaks and other financial incentives, suppress any social unrest, and keep its nose out of his business.

What he wanted politically, in other words, was what he had already acquired in several other places: empire status. Government help when he needed it, a policy of noninterference when he didn't. The autonomy of a feudal baron who was free to create his own country and make and enforce his own laws. To a degree, he had achieved this in Japan, much more so in Panama, Venezuela, Grand Bahama, Nicaragua, Mexico, Costa Rica, Honduras, the Caymans, Nigeria, and other areas into which his empire had spread. Acquiring such status was not difficult. If you had enough money, everything else was negotiable. And Ludwig had enough money.

By the spring of 1964, D.K. had considered a number of countries for his giant Gmelina plantation — Venezuela, Suriname, Brazil, Nigeria — and had almost decided on the last when two things happened to change his mind: an uprising by Biafran separatists in Nigeria's southeast, and the overthrow of Goulart in Brazil.

A few years earlier, in the late 1950s or early 1960s, Ludwig had apparently been considering buying land along the Jari River, an Amazon tributary, in northern Brazil. The tract was being offered by an American land speculator in the Amazon named Robin

McGlown. Castelo Branco, in fact, while still a colonel, had been sent into the region to investigate a rumor that a rich *norteamericano* named Ludwig was putting out feelers on a large area of jungle formerly owned by a notorious Amazon land baron, Colonel José Júlio de Andrade. Soon after, however, Goulart had come to power, and D.K., put off by Brazil's swing to the left, had abandoned the notion of going there.

Now, in 1964, with Castelo Branco's right-wing military regime in power, Brazil was once more a viable possibility, particularly because of the unsettled condition of Nigeria, and Ludwig was receptive to whatever Roberto Campos was ready to offer. Before he committed himself, though, he intended to negotiate the best deal he could get. He was in no great hurry. He still wanted to test Gmelina growth two or three more years before moving to large-scale planting.

What kind of tax advantages and other favors, D.K. asked Campos, was Brazil willing to grant if he came to the Amazon? Campos's answers were encouraging, but for any definite commitment, he said, Ludwig should talk to Castelo Branco in person. The planning minister, though, left no doubt that a satisfactory arrangement could be worked out.

The aims of the Castelo Branco government were in essence to turn one of the world's largest areas of undeveloped land into a producing region that would supply the Western industrial nations with food, metals, wood, and other raw materials. It was also understood that such production must be carried out on a large scale by multinational operators who could, supposedly, function more efficiently and profitably than small, independent farmers, ranchers, and miners.

Ludwig was an important ingredient in this plan. As owner-operator of a number of private companies, he was not answerable to stockholders and could take on risky ventures that public companies shied away from. Yet he was rich enough to run such ventures on the largest of scales, which gave him an advantage over smaller private companies. If he succeeded in the Amazon where previous entrepreneurs had failed, his achievement would demonstrate to more cautious companies that it *could* be done, and they would be less hesitant about investing in the region themselves.

Certain obstacles, however, still stood in the way of widespread development. One — the so-called Amazon Factor — was the long-held belief, substantiated by numerous failures, that money put into the region never comes out again. Another was the Amazon's indigenous human population, which, sparse as it was, still had to be dealt with. These Amazon dwellers were mostly of three types. There were European immigrants who, having failed in their own countries, had come to the wilderness to make a fresh start in farming, ranching, mining, trading, or preying on the other inhabitants. There were the poor Brazilians, usually of mixed blood, who subsisted as squatters and laborers on the fringe of the jungle. And there were the native Indians, many of whom were very primitive and had little contact with civilization but who nevertheless were recognized by the government, in theory if not always in practice, as having certain tribal land rights.

In many respects, twentieth-century Amazonia is not unlike the North American West of the late nineteenth century. Both have been characterized by disputed land claims and culture clashes between settlers and aborigines, or between one group of settlers and another. Many people, both foreign and Brazilian, who have come to the Amazon to exploit its resources regard the squatters and Indians as nuisances to be dealt with violently if necessary. Some, particularly the Europeans, have often bought acreage — very cheaply — from shady land dealers known as *grileiros* (literally, "squatters") and found their claims based more on their ability to hold the property against all comers than on any legal basis. Such a new "owner," if he found his newly purchased land already occupied by squatters or Indians, usually resorted to one of several methods to get rid of these unwanted cohabitants. He threatened to shoot them if they didn't leave, or he carried out his threat. He could always hire gangs of tough *pistoleiros* to do the dirty work for him. Or he "banana-ed" them off by flying over the huts or camps and dropping sticks of dynamite until the undesirables were dead or had fled.

Some ranchers were particularly incensed because large tracts of land were set aside as tribal preserves for the native Indians. One transplanted European grumbled: "The Paracis have 554,000 hectares [1 hectare = 2.471 acres] for 525 of them. That's 1055 acres an Indian! There's a miserable 75 Ciabis and they're locking up 47,000 hectares. And why, in the name of God, should 210 idle Bororo, who do nothing except make a few trinkets, hang on to

83,000 hectares of good grazing land? Don't get me wrong. I'm a Christian. I don't think the only good Indian is a dead Indian, as the Yanks say. But I do believe the only good Indian is a landless one."

Such an attitude is not uncommon in the Amazon today, and the ranchers who espouse it refuse to be thought of as the bad guys. "You like to eat meat?" asks one belligerently. "You like to drink coffee? Well, this is what it's all about."

In the mid-1960s, when Ludwig was considering going to the Amazon, things were even worse. At that time, not only individual ranchers but the Brazilian government felt that the only way to get rid of unwanted humans and avoid future land claims was through genocide.

In 1969, despite death threats and bribe attempts, some courageous members of a Brazilian congressional commission investigating the country's ironically named Indian Protective Service (a government agency similar to the U.S. Bureau of Indian Affairs) charged that the IPS had been systematically killing off entire tribes to open up new land for the entrance of U.S. and other foreign-based multinationals.

Among the charges, directed against 134 IPS employees, were that the Cinta Larga tribe of Mato Grosso state had been annihilated by helicopter gunships that bombed their village and machine-gunned the survivors as they ran out. The Tapaiunas, from another part of Mato Grosso, had been poisoned en masse by being fed a mixture of sugar and arsenic. Evidence indicated that the Pataxo tribe of Bahía state had been deliberately infected with smallpox, to which they had no resistance.

Grisly as these crimes were, the charges recommended by the full commission against the IPS employees were for theft and misuse of government funds, not murder. Even so, the matter was hushed up, and few, if any, were ever punished.

The hard fact was that many in the Brazilian government considered extermination of the Indians a necessary adjunct to opening the country for development. It wasn't simply a matter of moving them elsewhere. As long as members of a particular tribe were alive, some idealistic young lawyer could go to court with a land claim on their behalf.

In 1974, at an international meeting, anthropologists revealed that, of some 240 tribes listed as inhabiting the Amazon basin in a

1900 survey, more than 80 — over a third — were extinct. Individual figures were even more shocking. The Amazon Indian population at the turn of the century had been calculated at around a million. Now, seventy-four years later, it had shrunk to just over a hundred thousand — a drop of nearly 90 percent.

Indications are that no such Indian massacre was necessary to clear the Jari area of human inhabitants prior to Ludwig's moving in. One study by a Brazilian anthropologist suggests that the two tribes which had traditionally lived in the region — the Wayampi and the Apalai — had migrated northward a few years earlier. There were, however, a number of squatters — variously estimated at several hundred to a thousand — living in the territory during the mid-1960s. What had become of them by the time Ludwig's crews arrived is not in the record.

In 1966, Brazilian President Castelo Branco, at Campos's urging, invited Ludwig down for discussions about the proposed Jari project. By this time Castelo Branco had abandoned all pretense that his regime was anything but a military dictatorship. During 1965 he had abolished all political parties except his own ruling ARENA organization and had instituted repressive measures that were not only driving the left underground and into terrorist activities but also forcing middle-of-the-road anticommunist labor leaders to live in fear of their lives. Torture and political murder had become commonplace. While the European press was full of stories detailing heinous crimes against leftists and moderates by the right-wing military regime, U.S. media, for the most part, remained strangely silent about the abuses.

As vicious as Castelo Branco was toward those he considered his enemies, he was, like most military heads of state, obsequious in the presence of big money. At the Presidential Palace in Rio he greeted D.K. with effusiveness: "Welcome to Brazil, Mr. Ludwig. These days we have a safe country."

Over the next few hours of talks, the dictator seemed willing to grant his guest anything his heart desired. Yes, Mr. Ludwig could have a ten-year exemption from taxes at Jari. Yes, he could bring in whatever equipment he needed for the project without paying the customary import duties. Yes, he could run his operation in any way he saw fit without interference from the Brazilian government. Yes, in return for moving to Jari and creating new jobs and products for export, Mr. Ludwig could even write off half the taxes on profits from any *other* enterprises he might wish to undertake elsewhere in Brazil.

Finally satisfied that he had milked the government of every concession he needed, D.K. shook hands with the Brazilian ruler, left the palace, and met with his local lawyers to notify them they could go ahead with completing the land purchases, which together constituted the largest real estate deal by a private individual in modern times.

No one is sure exactly how much land Ludwig bought in Brazil. Because of varying figures and conflicting claims, the picture is hopelessly confused. At the time, it was generally accepted that he had purchased between 3.5 and 4 million acres, lying on both sides of the Jari River north of the Amazon.* By far the larger portion lay to the west in Pará state, with the smaller part in Amapá Territory (the Jari being the dividing line between Pará and Amapá in that region). The Paru River provided a natural boundary in the southwest, and the Amazon along the southern edge, although Ludwig's territory included some islands in the larger stream, including a big one, Comandari. In the north and east, boundaries were artificially drawn.

Overall, Ludwig's tract was said to be comparable in size to Connecticut. It was a lot of land for one man to own. "The project is so grandiose," remarked one U.S. diplomat in Brazil, "you would expect it only from a national government."

Some observers who were following the purchase speculated that this time even D.K. might be biting off more than he could comfortably chew. But Campos, who had been instrumental in setting up the deal, had supreme confidence in the billionaire. "Ludwig," he said, "is accustomed to investing in lunatic ventures, and just as accustomed to having them pay off. Ludwig has always been fifteen years ahead of the general run of mankind."

One probable reason for Campos's optimism is that he knew how little D.K. had paid for the land: $3 million by most accounts (although some sources give the figure of $10 million), or less than a dollar an acre.

*A study done in the late 1960s shows that the Brazilian government allowed some 50 million acres to be taken over by multinationals around this period. Ludwig's acquisition represents 7 to 8 percent of this total.

From whom had he purchased it? Again, different sources give different sellers. It is generally agreed that much of it was bought from, and with, a European-owned Brazilian company, Jari Comércio e Navigacão, Ltda., trading in rubber, cattle, Brazil nuts, and other locally produced commodities. The firm had apparently acquired the vast holdings of the ruthless Colonel Júlio around 1947, and, by buying the company, Ludwig was buying the land as well. After changing the corporation's name to Jari Florestal e Agropecuária, Ltda., D.K. set it up as his chief business entity (he would soon have at least eighteen others) in Brazil.

Evidence indicates, however, that the Jari land purchases were actually a complicated undertaking. Drs. Philip Fearnside and Judy Rankin, ecologists who have done considerable work at Jari, reported in 1980 that "the estate is covered by 170 land titles of various types, acquired from 52 different sellers."

In 1967, with all the groundwork laid, Ludwig started his giant project rolling. He shipped 18 tractors down to begin clearing land. He also set up accounts in a Belém (a large city at the mouth of the Amazon) bank, money that would provide an initial $600,000 a month in operating capital for the enterprise. He had hired an engineer-explorer-adventurer named Rodolfo Dourado to lead a work crew into the interior and begin the job of leveling the jungle to make way for the Gmelina seedlings.

Leaving Belém, Dourado and his boatload of men and machines sailed up the Amazon some 250 miles to the mouth of the Jari, turned northwest, and pushed on up that twisting river another 80 miles to a spot, near the center of the estate, that had been selected as headquarters for the forestry operation. There the tractors and workers were unloaded, to start the task of clearing an initial 250,000 acres for the planting of Gmelinas.

One of the first tasks was to saw up some of the trees to build rude houses for themselves, buildings that would be the beginning of the town of Monte Dourado, named for the expedition's leader. Then the job of leveling the primeval rain forest could start in earnest. Enormous Caterpillar "jungle crushers," each costing a quarter of a million dollars and weighing many tons, rumbled over the soft earth, uprooting trees two hundred feet tall as if they were nothing. The men had no idea what they were destroying. A few months earlier, Wynkoop and another scientist, the plant pathologist Juan Ferrer from D.K.'s Panamanian plantation, had made a quick tour of the property on foot, by mule, and canoe, taking a few soil samples and noting that a few of the trees might make good building material. But there had been no systematic survey of the life forms at Jari. Except for a few used in construction, nearly all the downed trees were pushed into piles and burned.

The Amazon rain forest Ludwig's crews were destroying was a biologists' paradise — one of the world's last great gene pools, with over a million different species of life. More than fifty thousand types of higher plants inhabited the region, besides countless kinds of mammals, birds, insects, fish, amphibians, reptiles, and numerous forms of lower plant life. The species at Jari were parts of a staggeringly complex ecosystem that had taken half a billion years to evolve, and the survival of each type was inextricably bound up with the whole. The beings that lived here were themselves creations of one another in a unique environment representing countless episodes of interaction, adaptation, specialization.

Ludwig had looked at this and seen only disorder. The idea of a jungle offended his engineer mind. It was untidy — all those trees, vines, and underbrush sprawling haphazardly over the landscape. He wanted it neat — trees standing in straight rows like soldiers, waiting to be cut and shipped to market.

He had a passion for straight lines, and he was compulsive about getting rid of every extraneous element. Pare it down. Chop off the fat. Do away with nonessentials. He had done that with ship design and with his personal life. He had a knack for locating the fine line between function and economy. This was his genius. It would also be his downfall.

What he completely failed to comprehend is that nature has its own economy — one that stresses proliferation, not reduction. If there is a niche available, nature will fill it with life. The answer to waste is to let something live on it. What Ludwig was looking at in the Jari jungle was not disorder but an incredibly complex system of interdependent life forms. Failing to appreciate that, he destroyed the very elements that might have made Jari a success. In his zeal to bring human order into what he perceived as natural chaos — to show nature how it *should* be done — he ruined his own dream and hundreds of thousands of acres of productive rain forest along with it.

It had been tried before, and not far away. In 1927, about the time

Ludwig was acquiring his first oil tankers, his fellow Michigander Henry Ford had bought four thousand square miles of Amazon jungle some five hundred miles upriver from Jari. Ford's idea was to start a huge rubber tree plantation to furnish raw material for his automobile tires. Rubber trees were native to Amazonia, but in the wild they normally grew widely scattered through the forest. Harvesting the sap from which rubber is made required considerable manpower and travel.

It made sense to Ford that leveling an area of jungle and planting it in nothing but rubber trees would save him time and money and produce a lot more rubber. But it didn't make sense to nature. What Ford did not realize was that the trees were offered a form of protection against insects and disease just because they were widely scattered. If a bug or a blight killed an occasional tree, most of the rest were far enough away to be safe. His clustering them together turned a minor annoyance into a ravaging epidemic.

Much the same thing had happened to human populations in Europe during the early Renaissance. Once large numbers of people left the farms and crowded together in cities, plagues chronically wiped out large fractions of the populace. It took hundreds of years and millions of lives for the lesson to sink in.

With Ford, it only took a decade. By the late 1930s most of his millions of trees were dying of a disease called South American leaf blight. Because of the desperate wartime need for natural rubber, he kept the project going as long as possible, but in 1945 he folded it up, leaving Fordlandia as a rusting, expensive reminder of human folly.

Ludwig was aware of the Ford debacle, but figured he had the money, expertise, and chemicals to overcome any problem of the sort that had laid the auto tycoon low. He was going in armed with every weapon human ingenuity could provide, and it would be a classic struggle between man and nature. As usual, man would win the early battles, but nature would win the war.

The troubles started early. After spending two years clearing jungle, in 1969 Ludwig's staff planted the first Gmelina seedlings. It didn't take them long to realize that the gargantuan machines D.K. had sent down to level the forest had also packed the soft, thin soil so tightly that the seedlings could not force root systems through it. And after a rain, the ground over which the jungle crushers had moved dried as hard as brick. Also, the blades the Caterpillars were using to take down the trees and push them into piles were skimming off what little topsoil there was.

Ludwig's experts had made a monstrous mistake about the soil of the Amazon. They had assumed that, because the jungle vegetation was so lush, the soil must be exceptionally rich. Not so. They hadn't understood that, over all those millions of years of evolution, the plants which had survived had done so by developing the ability to extract almost every available nutrient from the earth. Consequently, most of the minerals and organics the plants needed in order to live and grow were to be found not so much in the soil as in the other plants. As soon as a plant died, its system, in this hot, wet, tropical climate, was almost immediately broken down and its nutrients absorbed by other plants. In this way, the jungle had become adapted to living, as it were, on itself, storing in its own diversity of plant forms the ingredients to nourish new life. By leveling and destroying this complex ecosystem, Ludwig was impoverishing the land for his own trees.

One leading Brazilian agronomist, speaking only on the condition that his name not be used, remarked at the time that to try farming the Amazon "is to create a desert. The government does not allow anyone to say the soil is no good for farming, but it *is* no good. This is the most stupid project in Brazil . . . up to now."

Another factor Ludwig and his scientists had failed to anticipate was flooding. In 1970, a wet year even for Amazonia, heavy rains caused the river to rise several feet over its banks. Four million Gmelina seedlings — nearly all that had been put in so far — were washed out of the ground. The waters took so long to subside that new planting had to be postponed for several weeks.

But D.K. was not one to give up easily. Once the ground dried he ordered his foresters to redouble their efforts to get new seedlings planted. And he sent down a ship to load up the massive jungle crushers and take them elsewhere. Finally convinced the machines didn't work, he now relied on manpower. He hired dozens of *gatos* (literally, "cats") — rough Amazon adventurers who would do almost anything for money — as subcontractors, and sent them into the slums of Belém and other coastal cities, rounding up gangs of laborers to be brought to Jari, where they would be taught to practice the "slash-and-burn" method of clearing jungle that had been utilized in the Amazon, even by primitive Indian tribes, for hundreds of years. Crude as this was, it was much less damaging than the Caterpillars. In cutting down trees with axes and crosscut saws (the more mechanically adept were trained to use chain saws), the human workers did not appreciably damage or pack the soil. Moreover, when the brush was burned, the laborers could collect the ashes and spread them over the thin soil as fertilizer.

This helped, but there were other soil problems. In 1972, during one of Ludwig's monthly trips to the tree farm, Chief Forester Clayton Posey pointed one of them out. Running through the plantation in an east-west direction, he said, was a geological fault, something the soil scientists had failed to notice. South of this line, the soil was primarily arenaceous (sandy). Gmelinas needed argillaceous (clayey) soil, such as that found north of the fault line. Posey suggested pulling out the Gmelinas already planted in the southern tracts and replacing them with Caribbean pines, much better adapted to growing in sand. Ludwig took the suggestion as an insult to the Gmelina — *his* tree. "Anybody can grow pines any time," he sneered.

Posey knew D.K. too well to try arguing with him. The headstrong billionaire would fire a man for the slightest offense. Instead, after Ludwig had gone, the forester took it on himself to plant a small patch of pines in one of the southern tracts beside a stand of puny Gmelinas. The following year, when D.K. was down on another inspection tour, Posey just happened to take him out to the spot so that he could judge for himself. The evidence was too strong to be denied. The pines were healthy and putting out new growth; the Gmelinas were as scrawny as before.

Without pushing it, Posey had made his point. Ludwig gave him permission to yank out the Gmelinas in the southern tracts — about a third of the plantation — and plant pine seedlings instead. Under ideal conditions the pines would take about sixteen years to mature — two to three times as long as Gmelinas. But at least they would grow in sandy soil.

Growing trees was not the only business at Jari, although it was the largest. To the south, along the north bank of the Amazon at a place called Jarilandia, D.K. was striving toward another milestone: the world's largest rice paddy.

The land here was too wet for tree farming. Land in the Amazon is often classified into two types: *terra firme* (higher, drier ground) and *várzea* (floodplain). Ludwig's Gmelinas (and, more recently, pines) were being planted in terra firme, but the only sorts of trees that would grow in the várzea were certain native species which, like the bald cypress, are capable of putting out "knees" for support in times of flooding. However, thought D.K., the area ought to be excellent for growing rice.

Several years earlier, as part of a global effort to increase food production, the Rockefeller and Ford foundations had set up, in the Philippines, the International Rice Research Institute. The IRRI's purpose was to develop high-yield, disease-resistant strains of rice that could be grown in a variety of warm, wet environments around the world.

Ludwig's Amazon rice plantation was a direct offshoot of the IRRI experiments — an attempt to find out whether rice could be raised cheaply and abundantly in the Amazon floodplains. It was also — as the tree plantation had been in the beginning — an effort to learn whether most of the work could be handled by machines rather than human labor.

Nearly all the phases of rice growing were to be done by airplane. First, large dikes were constructed along the riverbank so that the water could be kept at a constant level of four inches. Then small planes from two nearby airfields built by Ludwig's crews would fly over, dropping seed, fertilizer, herbicides, and insecticides at the proper time during the operation. Only the harvesting was to be done by land-based combines, and the only manpower involved, except the pilots and combine operators, was the laborers, who stood in the ankle-deep water and, using flags, guided the planes on their runs over the paddy. (At first these workers — mostly uneducated *mestizos* — ignored the scientists' warnings that protective clothing should be worn when the planes were spraying pesticides. Finally one scientist hit on the idea of telling these *machismo*-conscious Amazonians that they would lose their manhood if they didn't protect themselves from the spray. The warning worked.)

As with the tree plantation, the rice project got off to a shaky start. Ludwig's overseers — most of them rice farmers from Louisiana and Georgia — were depending too heavily on chemicals. During the heaviest insect season, the planes were making as many as two hundred flights a day, spraying toxic pesticides. Though this was having a devastating effect on local bird and fish populations, the bugs were rapidly becoming immune; consequently, larger and larger doses were being applied.

This soon became too expensive. Spray levels were reduced and supplemented with light traps that attracted and incinerated the rice moths before they could lay their eggs. This worked better and was considerably cheaper, not to mention less environmentally destructive.

Another problem was more puzzling. Despite following all recommended procedures, D.K.'s rice growers were not producing anywhere near the expected yields. Unable to determine why, they called for help. Scientists from the IRRI flew over from the Philippines to conduct extensive tests. Finally they located the trouble: the Amazon soil was seriously deficient in sulfur. Once this was corrected with applications of ammonium sulfate, yields rose by 250 percent.

Encouraged by these figures, Ludwig decided that the time was right to expand the operation. After hiring Taiwan-born Dr. Chie Huang Wang, an IRRI specialist, as supervisor, he moved the rice project a few miles upstream to São Raimundo and began planting what was intended to be a 30,000-acre, 100,000-ton-per-year plantation by 1980. Some of this rice would be kept for use in Brazil; most of it was to be shipped abroad, mainly to Europe.

Another agricultural experiment going on near the rice project was the raising of cattle. For some years D.K. had been raising cattle at his ranch in Venezuela, mostly humpbacked varieties bred of stock brought from India. He found these types better suited to wet climates than other breeds. (On the drier plains of his Australian properties he was raising Herefords.) He was also experimenting with domesticated water buffalo, which he found quite adaptable to Amazon conditions. On the island of Comandari he established a herd that soon comprised over six thousand buffalo. On the mainland, near São Raimundo, he was running another herd of humpbacked cattle. Once the pine forests were established at the tree plantation, he planned to have grass planted between the rows (but not between the Gmelinas) and pasture some of the cattle there to provide manure for fertilizer and help keep down the native vegetation, which was continually trying to grow back amid his tidy forests.

Cattle raising in the Amazon was already the subject of much controversy among ecologists, who were concerned that thousands of acres of tropical rain forest were being destroyed to make pasturage where beef could be grown cheaply. Most of this meat was being exported to fill the demands of U.S. fast-food restaurants and supermarkets, and alarmed scientists and citizens were worrying that the Amazon basin could not withstand this Big Mac Attack for much longer. Land stripped of its native vegetation and turned to pasture, they said, would soon lose its ability to sustain *any* form of plant life, even with massive doses of chemical fertilizers. If the trend continued, the Amazon would look like the Sahara in another few decades.

Ludwig scoffed at such prophecies. He had no patience with those who claimed the region's ecology was fragile. "Hell's bells," he said scornfully, "I spend five million dollars a year just to whack down the wild growth that springs up among our planted trees."

Initially D.K. had started the cattle operation mainly as a means of feeding his Jari workers cheaply. He had planned to bring over a few hundred head from Venezuela, but the government there had balked, saying it needed the meat Ludwig was exporting to improve its own trade balance. That is why he had imported zebu cattle from India (where he was also involved in iron-mining operations) and the water buffalo from Southeast Asia, and had set about building herds that, by 1978, were expected to number fifty thousand animals, most of which he intended to slaughter and export to the United States and Europe.

On a smaller scale, Ludwig's agronomists were also testing a variety of other crops and livestock at Jari, both to supply food for the workers and to prepare for a potential export market. Now that he was having to feed many more laborers than originally planned, D.K. was trying to cut costs where he could. Each month he was having to provide the project with a thousand head of cattle, seventy-five thousand chickens, seventy tons of frozen fish, plus large quantities of rice, vegetables, fruits, and staples. The more he could grow on site, the less he would have to ship.

Chickens, soybeans, sugar cane, corn, squash, tomatoes, and melons were among the food crops being raised. Other crops were being tested for uses not related to food, including castor beans, cacao trees, oil palms, and manioc. Only the manioc proved successful enough to continue; it was fermented into alcohol, which could be used as fuel on the projects.

Nor was Jari strictly an agricultural venture. Ludwig was also engaged in various mining projects both on these lands and at other locations in Brazil. From the beginning, it had been said that the Jari region contained rich deposits of diamonds, gold,* tin, and bauxite. No official reports have been found of D.K.'s mining the first three minerals (though there were frequent rumors during the early years of the project that he was secretly mining gold and diamonds and smuggling them out of the country by plane from the airfield at Monte Dourado), but he is known to have operated one bauxite mine at Jari and another some three hundred miles to the west on the Trombetas River. The latter site was one of Brazil's richest deposits of the mineral, and Alcoa (Aluminum Company of America) and Alcan (Aluminium Company of Canada) also had mines there.

Ludwig had need for aluminum. The molds used in his Con-Tech construction projects were made of this light, durable metal. D.K. had decided, however, not to manufacture them himself. He had worked out a deal with Kaiser Aluminum (in which he apparently held considerable stock) according to which he would supply the bauxite and contract to have the molds built once the ore was processed into aluminum. This, however, still cost him more than he liked paying. After flying down to see the Trombetas project in 1971, he had a better idea: he would process the bauxite on site and save the cost of shipping the ore.

The problem with this idea was that the process of extracting aluminum takes enormous amounts of electricity, an energy form not readily available in the midst of a jungle. Ludwig knew how to solve that one, though. He would build a dam across a tributary of the Trombetas and another one at Jari, and generate hydroelectricity to run both projects. The dams would be expensive to build, but he could recover part of the cost by selling power to Alcan and Alcoa and to any other firms that might want to move into the region. A plentiful supply of electrical power in that part of the Amazon would undoubtedly draw other industries to the resource-rich area and hasten development. Large cities could spring up where now there was only wilderness and a few isolated mines.

In planning these dams, Ludwig expected the cooperation of the

---

*Ludwig's mines at Jari were said to be the only ones in the Amazon capable of producing 24-karat gold.

Brazilian government, which earlier had been only too eager to encourage Amazon development. But again, he had miscalculated. The present military government was no longer the tool of multinationals that the Castelo Branco regime had been. The nationalistic feeling that had characterized the Goulart days, after being suppressed for several years, was beginning to reassert itself, not merely on the left, which was still being crushed, but on the right as well. Many of the generals resented the foreign interlopers and thought they could run the country more profitably with less "help" from the United States.

Thus, when Ludwig routinely asked permission to build his hydroelectric dams, his request was politely but firmly denied. The reason, he was told, was that supplying energy in Brazil was now a national function, no longer to be handled by private enterprise. If Ludwig were allowed to build the dams, he would be in direct competition with ELECTRONORTE, the state-run utility with the task of providing power to the region.

D.K. was not used to being told no, particularly not in a foreign country, one that had so warmly welcomed him a few years earlier. He persisted with his applications, and negotiations between him and the Brazilian government over this issue dragged on for years.

On the plus side of the ledger was the unexpected discovery, in the early seventies, of one of the world's largest deposits of kaolin, the fine clay used in the manufacture of ceramics, medicines, and as a coating for certain high-grade paper to enable it to take color printing. This find on the Jari estate was a valuable one. Kaolin could be marketed for as much as $70 per ton, and the deposit was estimated at fifty million metric tons, prompting one Jari official to comment that mining might recoup Ludwig's entire investment in Brazil.

D.K. quickly set up a company, Santa Patricia Mining, Ltd. (like most of his other Brazilian companies, a subsidiary of Universe Tankships), and began strip-mining operations while constructing a $25 million factory on site, able to process 500 metric tons of kaolin per day. As soon as the plant was operating at full capacity, he expected to ship some 220,000 tons of the refined mineral — worth $15 million — each year.

The Amazon was not the only part of Brazil where Ludwig had ventures. During the early seventies he went in with his friend

A. T. A. Antunes to form a joint agricultural, farming, and mining enterprise called VERAGRO (Veredas Minas Agropecuária, Ltd.). The mining part of the operation involved exploiting the rich Aguas Claras iron reserves near the city of Belo Horizonte in Minas Gerais state. An estimated billion tons of high-grade ore (64 percent pure or better) — the same lode Hanna Mining Company had been excavating since the early sixties — was waiting to be dug up and shipped out.

Another part of the project was aimed at acquiring about 400,000 acres (an area half the size of Rhode Island) of farmland along the São Francisco River north of Belo Horizonte. Though only one-tenth the size of his Jari purchase, these tracts had already proved suitable for farming and ranching. Ludwig and Antunes planned to use them for raising six million head of hogs, thousands of head of cattle, and for growing vast plantations of oranges, pineapples, and other crops.

At first, real estate agents secretly representing the two tycoons came into the Tres Marías area of Minas Gerais and offered local farmers in this prosperous region $40 to $50 an acre for their land. Most of the farmers, knowing their property to be worth more, declined. Instead of going up, however, the offers went down by half, but this time they were accompanied by a threat: either the farmers could sell out for $20 to $25 per acre or the government might step in and condemn the land, leaving the former owners with nothing.

Many farmers, intimidated, sold out at the low prices. By midsummer of 1974, Ludwig and Antunes had acquired 160,000 of their targeted 400,000 acres very cheaply. This was part of the plan. Of the $300 million they had allotted to spend on VERAGRO, only $15 million had been budgeted for purchasing land. If they could make good their threat to have the Brazilian government exercise eminent domain and seize the farmers' land, they could get it for much less than this figure.

Some farmers, however, decided to take the matter to court, where it became mired in legal maneuvers.

Another Brazilian venture Ludwig was contemplating around 1972 never materialized. This was a $180 million tanker-repair yard to be built at the northeast coastal city of Recife. The facility was designed to service supertankers traveling between the Persian Gulf and the eastern United States. Its blueprints are revealing; there were to be four huge dry docks able to handle vessels of up to a million deadweight tons.

This gives an idea of the size of the vessels D.K. was considering building — about three times as large as any he had already built. But several factors combined to thwart these plans. The OPEC embargo and resultant oil shortages of 1973–1974, the failure of the United States to establish a deep-water oil terminal on the eastern seaboard, a worldwide tanker glut, the wreck of the giant *Amoco Cadiz* off the Normandy coast — all these contributed to reversing the trend started by Ludwig toward larger and larger tankships.

As a result, Ludwig not only had to cancel plans for his Recife ship-repair yard; he also had to back out of orders he had given Ishikawajima-Harima Heavy Industries to build four 450,000-ton ULCC (ultra-large crude carrier) supertankers. More accurately, he canceled three of the ULCCs outright and scaled back the fourth to a VLCC (very large crude carrier) of 270,000 tons.

IHI charged the billionaire no penalties for the cancelations and changes, probably because Ludwig had a special relationship with this company dating from the time he officially left Kure in 1966. IHI had taken over National Bulk's Kure operation nearly intact. Ludwig had immediately become its biggest customer, and IHI his chief shipbuilder. The company's president, Dr. Hasashi Shinto, had previously been employed by D.K. as an executive at Kure, and there is strong circumstantial evidence, but no overt proof, that Ludwig still has a financial interest, possibly a controlling one, in IHI. In any case, this company and its technology were soon to play an important role in Ludwig's tree-plantation project in Brazil.

As of 1973, D.K., much to his disgust, was having to depend largely on human labor to grow his Gmelinas. An engineer by training and temperament, he much preferred machines to men. Humans were unreliable and had far too many needs. With a machine, you only had to give it a little fuel and maintenance occasionally and it would perform faithfully and uncomplainingly until it wore out. It didn't ask for food, shelter, clothing, or higher wages, and had no wife and family to support. It was necessary to have *some* human employees, of course — people who were highly skilled and loyal, who could stand the heat and stay in the kitchen, doing a consistently good job year after year. These people would be paid more or less according to their worth.

But the mass of men were dirt under Ludwig's feet. It had wounded him to have to bring the machines home from Jari and replace them with manual labor. He never bothered to hide his contempt for the lower-class workers brought in to do the hard physical labor at Jari, and he treated them no better than he had to.

The gatos he had hired had experienced no trouble rounding up two thousand laborers in the slums of Belém. Unemployment was very high in such areas of Brazil, and the rumor of a job — any job — was enough to attract a crowd. Most of the workers had little idea of what they were signing up for. All they were told was that they were going into the interior to cut brush, and that they would receive the Brazilian minimum wage of $1.60 a day. They expected that. Nothing in their lives had given them reason to hope for more. On the other hand, they didn't know until later that their transportation and the gatos' fees would be taken out of their salary — about 20 percent — and that another 20 percent would be used to pay for their meager food at Monte Dourado, where the only place to buy anything was at Ludwig's stores.

These stores were stocked mainly with food, clothes, and hardware. Of the food, starches (mainly rice grown at Jarilandia) were relatively cheap, meat and vegetables were expensive. When the men were out on the job cutting brush in the jungle, meat would be hauled out in garbage trucks and was often rank before it reached them.

Ludwig's managers and technical staff had a relatively decent standard of living and received reasonable wages. Neat rows of Con-Tech houses were being erected for these privileged employees in Monte Dourado. The field hands had to sleep at jungle camps, in unprotected hammocks slung between trees. Living conditions were barely tolerable. Still, they couldn't very well leave. The gatos, to whom they still owed money for their transportation, were watching to make sure they didn't. Also, by the time they had been there a few weeks, they were usually in debt to the company stores, and Ludwig's ruthless security staff (mainly ex-military men) was there to track them down.

Escape was nearly impossible. The only ways back to the cities were to fly (not a likely possibility), go down the Amazon by canoe (they could easily be spotted from the air), or try hacking their way through 250 miles of jungle, where they would almost certainly be pursued and caught, or die on the journey.

Protest was equally futile. There was no one to complain to who wasn't in Ludwig's employ. No one — not even Brazilian government officials — came into Jari without D.K.'s personal consent. Any worker who had a gripe soon learned to keep it to himself if he didn't want a beating. The only real way out was to get sick and die, which quite a few of the laborers did. A doctor who worked at the Jari tree farm during 1971, when some 2000 people, permanent and seasonal, were living there, later reported that he had treated 1224 cases of malaria and another 2161 cases of dysentery and diarrhea that year. A small hospital was constructed at Monte Dourado, but it had few beds and almost no equipment.

This abysmal situation had not changed much by February 1973, when the new Brazilian president, Emelio Médici, came to Jari for an official visit. Presumably he had Ludwig's permission to do so. He and D.K. enjoyed a friendly relationship. (It is likely that the billionaire was in Monte Dourado at the time to greet him.)

The precise purpose of the visit remains an enigma. With Médici was a small delegation of bankers and other businessmen from Rio and São Paulo, so it may have been a business trip for investment purposes. Or perhaps Médici had heard the rumors that Ludwig was smuggling gold and precious stones out of the country and running a slave-labor operation at Jari and wanted to assure himself that none of these reports was true.

A key factor, though, was that a number of journalists from Brazilian newspapers who *had* heard the rumors hitched a ride with the presidential party so that they could see for themselves what this wealthy foreigner's mysterious "state within a state" was really like.

It didn't take them long to find something to write about. As the visitors were being driven along the jungle road from the airport to Monte Dourado, they encountered a group of workers carrying a crude banner made of toweling suspended between two sticks. On the banner had been painted the words in Portuguese for WE WANT OUR FREEDOM!

Accounts of this episode would differ from paper to paper. Newspapers known to have close ties to the Brazilian government reported that only two workers were involved and that, as Clayton Posey (the head of Jari's welcoming committee) later explained, such complaints were "normal," and the laborers were "always insisting on better work conditions than those previously agreed upon." Besides, he added after supposedly questioning them, the demonstrators only wanted the freedom to play cards.

More independent newspapers printed a different story. The protesting workers, they said, had numbered over a hundred and had been "impeded" by Posey and Ludwig's security men from talking to the president and his party. Some reporters got the impression that the protesters wanted a lot more than the right to play cards.

Whatever the case, both the visitors and the Jari staff were highly embarrassed by the incident, and, on returning home, Médici, to save face, ordered an investigation into working conditions at the plantation. Not that the probe accomplished much; it concluded with a timid suggestion that perhaps Mr. Ludwig should think about upgrading facilities at Jari to make the workers' lot a bit easier. But at least the protective governmental barrier around the project had been punctured. Some journalists no longer felt obliged to treat Ludwig and his ventures as being immune from criticism.

Unlike the U.S. media, which generally have handled the billionaire with kid gloves, some of the Brazilian press, having taken a potshot at D.K. and gotten away with it, were emboldened to take others. For his part, Ludwig remained his usual belligerent self toward all media representatives who weren't downright worshipful.

Once, while visiting the governor of a state in which he had projects, the billionaire was snapped in conversation with that executive by an official photographer. Ludwig turned and scowled, and immediately ordered that the negative be ripped from the camera and burned before his eyes. The trembling governor had it done.

Another time, as he was walking out of a similar meeting toward a waiting car, a reporter from a Brazilian daily yelled at him in English, "Mr. Ludwig, what do you have to say to the Brazilian people?"

D.K. stopped and, fixing the presumptuous one with a stony stare, rasped, "I do not have anything to say to the Brazilian people. I do not have anything to say to anybody. I do not give press interviews. To hell with you. I'm busy."

Such incidents, reported in Brazilian papers, did little to improve Ludwig's image. The damage was compounded when it was announced in 1974 that Ludwig was deeding Jari to a cancer research foundation he had set up in Switzerland. Many Brazilian businessmen had allowed themselves to hope that the aging billionaire, as he neared death, would let local investors in on what they foresaw as a successful venture. When they realized this was not going to happen — that Ludwig even at his death did not intend to turn Jari over to Brazil — many who had previously supported the venture became opponents of it. Heretofore, only the suppressed left had been against Jari. Now there were military leaders and businessmen beginning to believe that, where nationalization was concerned, former President Goulart might have had a point.

By 1976, several government agencies were starting to wonder aloud at the tax breaks and other favors D.K. was getting. Members of the board of governors of SUDAM (Superintendency for Development of the Amazon) questioned the wisdom of continuing such practices. "How," asked one member, "can we justify tax exemptions for a company that doesn't even have headquarters in Brazil?"

Another, who was also governor of Amapá Territory, stated that Jari needed supervision by Brazilian officials to determine whether or not it was really of benefit to the country. "And I ask myself," he added, "whether the government *can* supervise an enterprise of this size."

Just when it appeared that SUDAM might decide to hold Ludwig's feet to the fire, intervention came, and from none other than General Ernesto Geisel, who had succeeded Médici as president of Brazil in 1974.

Geisel and Ludwig had known each other for years. The general, while head of Brazil's state-owned oil monopoly PETROBRAS, had helped D.K. land a deal to haul the country's petroleum. (It was a Ludwig policy to become chummy with the leaders of nations where he had business activities. As Allen Cameron, a National Bulk executive who often acted as D.K.'s emissary in foreign operations, once put it, "We never play politics, but we always make a point of getting acquainted with the premier and finance minister.") It was helpful to have Geisel in a position to intercede with recalcitrant bureaucrats and make sure that Ludwig got his usual tax breaks.

During the late 1960s and early seventies, the United States had gotten a black eye in the world press for its support of dictatorships that regularly used imprisonment, murder, and torture (along with U.S. arms and dollars) to suppress dissent. The Carter administration attempted to reverse this bad publicity by using U.S. influence to promote more humanitarian policies through diplomatic and economic pressures.

As a result of this shift in policy, a number of rulers started sliding toward ruin. The Shah of Iran, the Greek colonels, General Anastasio Somoza — all these could be considered casualties of the new human rights policies. Other authoritarian leaders, getting the message of the Carter administration, began falling into line and relaxing some of their harsher methods of dealing with dissenters. President Geisel was one who took the hint. Under pressure from the U.S. State Department, he permitted the rise of what would be known as "Abertura" — an aperture, or window, opening on democracy. It was not freedom in a true sense, but it was much better than what had prevailed in Brazil since April 1964. Some political rights were restored to enemies of the regime, and press censorship, which had already been loosening slightly, was relaxed still further. (Censorship of television programming, however, remained in place, the rationale being that only about 10 percent of the population were well enough educated to read the papers intelligently, but nearly everybody in the country watched TV.)

For many U.S.–based corporations in Brazil, and particularly for Ludwig, Abertura was bad news. D.K. had been able to enjoy empire status at Jari only because he had the firm backing of the Brazilian government. Now even Geisel was being quoted in the newspapers as saying that, much as he liked Ludwig, it was obvious that the U.S. billionaire didn't give a hoot about Brazilian laws.

D.K. didn't need trouble with the Brazilian government; he was having difficulties enough at Jari without that. Many of the problems had to do with cash flow. For more than a decade Ludwig had been pouring money into the Amazon project with very little return. Only the mines were producing income. The tree and rice plantations had not yet begun to pay their way. Much of this, of course, had been anticipated. Ludwig had known that it would be at least six or seven years before he would have wood pulp and lumber for sale. He had budgeted about $350 million to spend on Jari before it started giving him a return.

But too many things had not gone according to schedule. He had already spent nearly twice as much as he had budgeted, and the tree farm was still years behind schedule. Several factors were responsible — flooding, soil problems — but, characteristically, Ludwig blamed his underlings. By the time Jari was a dozen years old, he had hired and fired twenty-four project managers — an average of one every six months — along with scads of lower-ranking employees.

313

Several of the former managers later hinted that the boss may have
been a major part of the problem. One indicated that D.K. tended
to leap before he looked: "Mr. Ludwig always goes from idea to
execution. That's how he does everything. It was hit or miss."

Another felt much of the overspending was caused by Ludwig's
habit of constantly changing his mind. "The budget was an empty
thing," this frustrated former manager recalled. "It changed
monthly. One visit from Ludwig, and there'd go another $50 million
in another direction. He'd say, 'Build five hundred workers' houses
here.' . . . 'Put a road in there.' . . . If a manager complained, Ludwig
would snap, 'You worry about getting the place built, I'll worry
about the money.'"

Some observers attributed Jari's financial problems to the death of
William W. Wagner in 1970. Since the mid-1930s, they felt, it was
Wagner who had kept D.K.'s complex empire together and running
relatively smoothly. The two men had functioned as a team, as even
the imperious Ludwig acknowledged to a *Business Week* interviewer
in 1963: "I spend my time putting projects together and then I let
Mr. Wagner find the money. That's his job."

In reality, Wagner's job was much more. He and D.K. operated
as partners in everything except stock ownership. As Ludwig told the
same interviewer, "Wagner and I virtually are interchangeable. All
major decisions must pass across the desks of one of us. The present
organization permits either of us to step in on any decision, at any
time, at any level we choose."

The shrewd National Bulk vice-president had also been the only
one able to rein in his mercurial boss without raising his dander.
When the billionaire bought a villa on Uruguay's Rio de la Plata,
with the idea of establishing a giant tanker depot nearby, Wagner had
quietly and tactfully talked him out of the project as a bad investment. And when D.K. jumped into the Amazon with both feet,
Wagner had assured worried National Bulk lieutenants, "It's just an
innocent hobby. It'll pass."

But Wagner had passed instead, and his unexpected death left a
void no one else could fill. One astute observer later said, "Jari went
hell-bent when Wagner died."

To plug the gap, D.K. elevated John Notter to be his second-in-
command. Notter, born in Switzerland, was a bright young banker-
accountant who had worked his way up through the Ludwig organi-

zation from a California savings and loan to the presidency of American-Hawaiian Steamship before coming to National Bulk as a vice-president. He was a good money manager, careful, cautious, and conservative — qualities D.K. appreciated in an employee even if he didn't possess them himself.

But Notter lacked Wagner's long experience, money-finding abilities, and skill in handling the obstreperous billionaire. Furthermore, he had never thought Jari a good idea and had been tactless enough to tell Ludwig so. All these points would work against him when D.K. sent him out to locate investment capital to help keep Jari afloat.

Even having to scout for additional funds outside the organization was a defeat for Ludwig, who had earlier stated defiantly, "As long as I'm alive, no one will own a piece of Jari but myself." But mounting costs had forced him to change his mind, and it was now Notter's job to find the money to keep the bills paid. The young banker first went to Prudential Life, which, as an institutional investor, had put up much of the funding to build Westlake Village. But the insurance firm considered Jari too soft an investment to become a piece of the rock, and Notter had to look elsewhere.

He went to major oil companies and pulp-and-paper firms. At each, he again drew a blank. After sending their own experts down to look over the project, these corporations were doubtful that Jari could ever make money. "It was nothing but jungle," said one oil executive on his return. "That he could ever put a modern industrial complex in there just boggled our minds."

Why, many were asking, was one of the richest men in the world having to go begging for money? There were several reasons. One was that most of his wealth was tied up in other projects. (By 1974 he had already started selling off some of his properties, dumping the Xanadu Princess on the semicomatose Hughes for $15 million and selling off his International Housing operation to E. P. Taylor, a wealthy Canadian, for an undisclosed sum.) Another reason was that he was already far over budget and simply did not want to commit more of his own money toward a project that was looking ever less promising. A third reason — and a major one — was the 1974 collapse of the tanker market resulting from OPEC's show of strength. Ludwig had made most of his billions in oil-related activities. Now he was not only making less than before; it was costing him more in fuel expenses to keep his tankers and such projects as Jari in operation.

By 1976 D.K. was starting to sell off his Australian mining ventures, letting British Petroleum buy a 50 percent share of his Clutha Development Pty. coal interests for $202.5 million. (BP picked up the other half in 1979 for a similar amount.) In 1978 he sold ARCO a smaller coal venture, S & M Fox Pty., for another $20 million. In 1977, he sold to Christina Onassis, daughter and heir of his late hated, envied rival, a supertanker he had built but had no charter for. Christina got the *Universe Frontier* for the bargain price of $27 million (about half what it would have sold for before the tanker market collapsed) and promptly renamed it the *Aristotle Onassis,* which may have struck Ludwig as a choice bit of irony.

Even with these added millions from the sale of his properties, D.K. was still coming up short. Unable to raise investment money through Notter's scouting expeditions, he finally had to take the route of smaller entrepreneurs and go to the bank for a loan. He had borrowed $150 million from Chase Manhattan in 1972 to help finance Jari. Now, five years later, he went back for more. Chase was able, by forming a consortium with several other big banks, to come up with $400 million, one of the largest loans ever made to a private investor.

The money was crucial. Ludwig had to get his hands on enough cash to keep Jari going until he could start marketing pulpwood to pay back the years of capital outlay. When he first came to the Amazon, he had figured that Jari would be earning money by 1975 or 1976. Now, at the end of 1977, pulp production was still more than a year away, owing to the series of delays caused by floods, managerial problems, the switch from mechanization to manpower, the replacement of some of the Gmelinas by pines, and the various other problems. And Ludwig still had to accomplish the most important and spectacular part of the entire Jari operation — building a giant pulp-factory complex in Japan and transporting it halfway around the world to the Amazon jungle.

Back in the mid-1950s, D.K. had come up with a solution to the problem of how to carry out industrial development in remote third world countries: build floating factories and tow them by water to isolated spots. All you had to do then was find a power source to run them and bring people in to operate them, and you could turn almost any wilderness area into a thriving industrial center within a short time — as long as there was access to navigable water.

Potential uses for the floating factory idea were numerous. Desalinization plants for desert countries were one possibility. But the probability of a world shortage of pulp and lumber had occurred to him at about the same time, and he had determined to test the idea by putting huge pulpwood plants in the midst of a jungle.

D.K. started building the first of his floating factories in 1976 at the IHI yard in Kure. The project would help make up for the ULCC contracts he had had to cancel earlier. Initial estimates of cost were pegged at $240 million, which again, since Ludwig was having cash flow problems, had to be borrowed.

It is a measure of the billionaire's continuing influence in Japan that, despite his having officially pulled out of Kure a decade earlier, he was able to get the Japanese Export-Import Bank to lend him the entire amount. Ordinarily, the Ex-Im Bank made loans only to Japanese businessmen, but D.K. could still pull strings when he needed to. He did, however, have to get Brazil's National Development Bank to guarantee $175 million of the loan package, which took more string pulling in the Geisel regime.

Accelerating costs of the project during construction drove the price up another $29 million, which Ludwig was able to borrow from Lloyd's Bank of London. These loans, plus the ones from Chase, meant that, over ten years' time, D.K. had borrowed some $819 million to fund Jari. And this amount was in addition to what he had put in from his personal hoard.

Some observers, noting the hundreds of millions Ludwig had poured into the project, doubted whether he ever intended to recoup his investment. Jari, they speculated, might be the aged billionaire's great monument and gift to the world — an attempt to use his wealth for the benefit of mankind by showing that unproductive jungle could be turned into productive farmland if anyone was willing to spend the money to make it happen. According to this view, D.K. was donating his wealth to bring a dream to reality.

Nonsense, said the *Fortune* writer Gwen Kinkead. Ludwig had never done anything in his life except as a means to make money, and Jari was no exception. He had fully planned on living a very long time — this was why he had become a health food advocate — and was initially counting on a 30 percent return on his Amazon investments during his life. By 1980, as he had figured it, his floating factory would be producing fifteen hundred tons of pulp per day, and the tree plantation was to be supplying thousands more feet of lumber, all of which added up to an income of $300 million a year. By 1984, with newsprint and plywood operations added to the pulp and lumber activities, Jari was to yield twelve thousand tons of marketable wood per day.

If these figures are accepted, it is clear that D.K.'s Amazon venture was intended to be not a monument nor a humanitarian gesture but a profitable commercial operation. And as of 1977, Ludwig still had hopes of turning it into one. But events were turning against him, and both his political and financial positions were steadily getting weaker.

In February 1978 Brazil was due to have a new president. Geisel was stepping down and had hand-picked as his successor General João Baptista de Oliveira Figueiredo. As the candidate of the country's ruling ARENA Party, Figueiredo was a shoo-in, since other parties were able to mount only token opposition. But to many Brazilians, including a large number of high-ranking military men, the choice of Figueiredo was repugnant. At a time when nationalistic feeling was rising, the candidate was widely considered a tool of multinational corporations.

One Army officer, General Hugo de Andrade Abreu, who had served as an adviser to Geisel, was particularly affronted. He wrote an evaluation of Figueiredo to the effect that the man was unfit to be president, and when Geisel chose him anyway, Andrade Abreu resigned in protest and circulated his report among his fellow officers.

In the evaluation were several serious charges — accusations that the chief architect of Figueiredo's campaign, General Golbery do Couto e Silva, was an embezzler who regularly accepted bribes from transnational companies, and that two of Figueiredo's strongest and most influential supporters — the National Savings Bank chairman, Humberto Esmeraldo Barreto, and Geisel's personal secretary, Major Heitor Aquino — were regularly and secretly receiving large payments from Daniel K. Ludwig.

The charges were never answered or investigated. Andrade Abreu, despite his high military rank, was clapped in jail for his temerity, and Figueiredo, as expected, was easily elected. He held office as

Brazil's chief executive until March 14, 1985, but the accusations hung over him like a cloud, and he had to be careful, particularly where Ludwig was concerned. Given these circumstances, many military leaders and government officials felt relatively free to criticize Jari and its wealthy, arrogant owner.

Undaunted, D.K. pressed ahead with construction of his floating factories. Two such structures were being assembled at Kure — the pulp plant and an attachable power plant to generate the energy that would run the pulping operation. Twenty Japanese factories, plus numerous other industries in the United States, Europe, and Asia, were manufacturing components for the two plants, which in appearance were enough alike to be twins. Each was nearly 250 yards in length — as long as two and a half football fields or three city blocks — and nearly twenty stories tall. Each weighed thirty thousand metric tons — sixty-six million pounds — and was being constructed on a bargelike hull, complete with storm-resistant braces, for transport over the oceans.

In function, though, and in interior design, the two buildings were very different. The power plant was designed to burn wood — 2000 tons a day, 540,000 cubic meters a year — and convert the heat into 55,000 kilowatts of electricity, enough not only to run the pulp plant but to supply all of Jari's current and future needs for power. Fueling the plant with wood rather than fossil fuels was calculated to save Ludwig between $8 and $10 million a year, and he was planning to burn native jungle trees rather than the commercially valuable Gmelinas and pines.

The pulp plant was based on Finnish plans, Finland having outstripped the rest of the world in innovative technology for producing cellulose from pulpwood. The plant Ludwig was building would be able to crush 4000 cubic meters of pulpwood each day into 750 metric tons of cellulose, which could be processed into bleached kraft paper. A day's finished product could then be hauled to market in a Ludwig vessel and sold for $300,000. That would be nearly $110 million a year if the plant ran every day at full capacity.

These were only the first two plants D.K. was planning to install at Jari. Later, if all went well, he intended to add a newsprint plant and a plywood factory, which would require another 250,000 acres of trees, as much again as he presently had under cultivation.

As final assembly of the two massive plants was going on at Kure, crews of workers at Jari were preparing a place to put them. At a tiny settlement called Munguba — near the kaolin strip mine and some fifteen miles down the Jari from Monte Dourado — crews of workers were constructing a large lagoon. Once it was finished, thirty-seven hundred long pilings — each made of exceptionally hard, rot-resistant massaranduba wood — would be driven into the soft, alluvial soil of its bottom to create a platform for the factories to rest upon. Once they arrived and were put in place, they would not sink, as some of the heavy machines Ludwig had sent to the Amazon had done previously.

In January 1978, the two floating factories were ready to go. Their journey would take them 15,500 miles, more than half the circumference of the globe. If this wasn't the shortest route, it was the cheapest available. The Panama Canal was too narrow to accommodate the giant structures, and the Suez had just raised its rates to a level D.K. felt was uneconomical.

Since the factories were going a longer route, timing was all important. The heavy winds and high seas around the Cape of Good Hope, at Africa's southern tip, had been the bane of mariners for hundreds of years. It was risky enough sailing ships into that weather. Taking two floating factories around would be worse.

Using the best weather data available, Ludwig's meteorologists calculated that during the latter part of March there would be a two-week lull in the normally rough conditions that plague the cape. Accordingly, they planned to launch the first of the seagoing skyscrapers six weeks earlier.

On February 1, 1978, under clear skies, the power plant began its long voyage. Towed by one powerful tugboat and steered by two others alongside to sternward, the massive, rectangular factory headed south out of Kure. Passing east of Taiwan and the Philippines, the flotilla turned southwest through the Macassar Straits off Borneo. Cutting between Sumatra and Java, it steered due west across the Indian Ocean on a course for Africa.

Passing north of Madagascar, the little fleet swung southwest again, following the coast of the continent past Mozambique and around the Union of South Africa. Despite the careful forecasting, the factory and its escorts now ran into heavy seas, which slowed its progress by several days. But the plant's solid steel construction held up under the weather and nothing was lost except time.

Eventually the convoy steamed past Cape Town and set a straight course northwest for the mouth of the Amazon. Arriving a few weeks later at Belém, it headed upriver, reached the Jari, and turned north, snaking its way through that narrow, winding stream until it reached Munguba on April 28.

The arrival of the power plant at Jari, though it was expected by the workers, was a shock to other residents along the river. According to *National Geographic,* one young mestizo who had been fishing in the muddy waters looked up, saw the strange sight, and frantically paddled his dugout canoe home, yelling to his mother, "There's a city coming up the river!"

Once at Munguba, the giant factory was pulled to the mouth of the holding lagoon by tug, then dragged in by means of lines attached to bulldozers. The lagoon's entrance was then diked, which raised the water level and allowed the building to be maneuvered over the sunken pilings. All this was done as quickly as possible, and there was reason for haste. The pulp plant had set out from Kure on February 10, nine days behind its sister, but had met better weather around the cape and was now less than a week behind. Ludwig's managers felt it imperative to get the first plant set into place before the second arrived. The Old Man would come down and give them holy hell if they didn't.

For three days and nights, driven on by shouting managers, sweating and cursing in the humid heat, the workers tugged and pushed and pulled the sixty-six-million-pound monster into precise position over the sunken pilings. The slightest puff of wind against the building's side was enough to make it drift off center, a movement the crews tried to prevent by hauling on the webbed lines radiating out from the plant to the shores of the lagoon.

Finally, as they held it where they wanted it, like some giant prehistoric beast that, captured, still threatens to break loose and wreak havoc, water was pumped, a little at a time, into the hollow steel hull that had borne the factory over three oceans. As the hull filled, it sank gradually lower and lower, the men all the while keeping the lines taut, until at last the huge structure came to rest squarely on the foundation of pilings, after which the dammed-up water behind the dikes was released into the river, leaving the plant sitting stolidly on firm, if somewhat muddy, ground.

Placement had been so accurate that bolt holes drilled into the hull in Japan were lined up to within three-eighths of an inch of those on the stationary fittings of the base. "When the bolt holes aligned," the construction manager, Thomas Connor, recalled later, "we were jubilant. But we were just too tired to celebrate."

There was precious little time to rest, though. The pulp plant would be arriving the next day, and the same procedure would have to be done all over again.

Within a week it was finished. The crews were almost dead with exhaustion. The two massive plants were now sitting side by side in the midst of the Brazilian jungle, waiting to be linked together and made operational. And Ludwig had another impressive first. These were the largest industrial plants ever to be moved across water.

Once again D.K. had flown in the face of the doubters and obstacles and done the seemingly impossible — an engineering feat few men would have even conceived, much less carried out. In the process, he had convincingly demonstrated that raw materials do not have to be transported from undeveloped regions to industrial centers to be made usable.

Taking the factories to the wilderness has other advantages. When the supply of resources dries up, or the operation is no longer profitable, the industrial plants can simply be refloated and moved somewhere else. This portable feature may also be cost-saving in other ways. Should a host country's political situation change, and the new leaders decide to nationalize industry, an entrepreneur can simply pick up his factory and move out, with no great loss of investment.

Having made these points to a skeptical world, Ludwig still had something else to prove: that these floating factories of his could be made to work profitably and efficiently. Only one phase of the operation had been completed, and no matter how impressive that was, he was still losing hundreds of thousands of dollars every day the plants weren't running.

To make the pulp mill operational in the fastest possible time [wrote the author-producer Vivienne King in a script, "Mr. Ludwig's Tropical Dreamland," for public television's "NOVA"], Ludwig gathered together a team of experts from around the world. In the green helmets, Brazilian engineers, recruited from the south. They would be trained to run the mill once it was fully on stream. In white, Japanese engineers from IHI, who had designed and built the plant. In blue, engineers from Finland, experts in pulp manufacture. And in orange, the rest of the world. A curious international team assembled under the Amazon sun by one man.

This colorful assemblage scurried busily around inside the two plants for months, getting everything ready for a startup date in January 1979. Outside, the Brazilian laborers were cutting many thousands of native trees, dragging them in to be sawed into usable lengths at an on-site sawmill, then stacking them in huge piles by the power plant, whence powerful forklifts, each capable of picking up a sixty-ton "bite," came to get wood for feeding the plant's insatiable furnaces. On the opposite side of the complex, other loggers were piling equally high stacks of Gmelina to be pulped into cellulose for the manufacture of kraft bags, wrapping paper, and cardboard boxes. Ludwig's dream, toward which he had been working and scheming, ordering and spending, for some twenty years, was finally about to be realized. Or was it?

Such was the magnitude of this industrial complex in the midst of the jungle that even its privacy-mad owner seemed uncharacteristically eager to show it off, perhaps to silence his detractors, perhaps to put a good face on Jari for public relations and financial reasons. Whatever the motives, for the first time in his career D.K. invited selected representatives of the world press for a firsthand look at the no-longer-floating factories.

He himself did not show up to play host, but Jari administrators and Brazilian officials were on hand to give journalists and other guests a guided tour around the factories, all the while explaining what a great miracle Ludwig had brought to pass.

All this PR work paid off. In the United States, for example, several national magazines and a number of newspapers ran favorable articles on Jari and the floating factories. *Time,* in its September 10, 1979, issue, published a three-page piece dismissing the earlier rumors about gold smuggling and slave labor as "wild charges" and praising D.K. for his foresight and organizational ability. Two months later, Warren Hoge of the *New York Times* wrote another upbeat article, U.S. MAGNATE, ONCE ASSAILED, IS HAILED FOR AMAZON PROJECT. Pointing to Jari as the wave of the future in Amazon development, Hoge quoted scientists, Brazilian bureaucrats, newspaper editorial writers, all of whom voiced the opinion that the pulpwood project was an excellent model for other industries to follow in opening up third world resources.

Why hadn't this been pointed out before? A Jari official had a ready answer: "Mr. Ludwig didn't have time to polish his image, and he never rose to the bait when he was being criticized. But now a hell of a lot of people are having to eat crow over this thing."

Hoge quoted one such crow eater, Dr. Gary Hartshorn, a forestry expert who, according to the article, had arrived at Munguba as a skeptic and left ten days later "marveling at the foresight and verve of Daniel K. Ludwig in conceiving and developing Jari." Asked to comment on a statement that Brazil could use fifty more such projects, Hartshorn had replied that the notion "no longer is that farfetched."

Reporters on a tour of Munguba were given publicity handouts, including a Brazilian newspaper editorial that read, in part: "The Jari project deserves total support. It is to be hoped that Daniel Ludwig and the Brazilian government will engage in an objective dialogue excluding all radicalism in order to establish directives for the continuation of this remarkable social and economic undertaking."

All of this was a carefully calculated effort to win media and public support for a venture that, up to now, had been the target of much rumor and criticism. As if to remove any remaining doubts, D.K. himself broke his long silence and invited Loren McIntyre of *National Geographic* for breakfast and an interview at his Beverly Hills estate.

Suitably flattered, McIntyre responded with another glowing article, complete with numerous color photographs, making the billionaire and his Amazon venture look exemplary. If development had to come to the Amazon, the *Geographic* essay implied, Ludwig's method was probably the best way to go about it.

Not everyone was taken in by the publicity effort. Some Brazilian newspapermen, recalling the days of the Médici visit, refused to accept the official version and continued to write that Jari was not as wonderful as it was being painted. One environmentally conscious journalist, after visiting Munguba, wrote that the twin factories were severely polluting the region's air and water. The power plant's stacks, he said, were belching black smoke into the atmosphere, and the pulp plant was dumping 20 percent of its untreated, acidic chemical wastes directly into the Jari River. Because of Ludwig's status, he added, Brazilian officials were unable to monitor the site for environmental damage.

A feature article in another Rio newspaper pointed out that two slum towns had grown up across the river from Monte Dourado and Munguba. Called Beiradão (Big Place Alongside) and Beiradinho (Little Place Alongside), these villages had started as collections of rude huts built by laborers for whom Ludwig had not provided housing. They had grown in size as sleazy merchants and traders, prostitutes, gamblers, bootleggers, drug dealers, and others — all attracted by the money the plantation laborers were willing to spend as a way of relaxing from the hard conditions of the ten-and-a-half-hour workdays at Jari — swarmed to the area to get their hands on what the writer estimated to be 60 percent of the workers' wages.

The reports of pollution and the dismal conditions under which most of the Jari laborers lived added fuel to the fire that was spreading among Brazilian intellectuals. Theirs was a hot anger at D.K. as a grasping plutocrat who was robbing the country of its natural heritage.

> For many Brazilians [noted the U.S. anthropologist Shelton Davis], Ludwig's project has become a symbol of everything that is wrong with the military government's program to open up and develop the Amazon. . . . Unfortunately, many foreign observers have failed to understand the depths of the Brazilian public's concern for the political, social and environmental consequences of projects such as Jari. Rather, they have been mesmerized by the technological scale of Ludwig's effort and continue to accept [his exploiting of the Amazon] uncritically.

In July 1979, at the annual meeting of the Brazilian Society for the Progress of Science, the anger exploded. As part of Ludwig's new public relations program, Jari's forestry manager, Charles Briscoe, was appearing in a panel discussion titled "Agricultural Uses of the Amazon." As Briscoe began to wax eloquent about the glories of the tree plantation, other delegates jumped to their feet to interrupt and contradict. And as the moderator frantically rapped with his gavel for order, the assembly of scientists began chanting in unison: *"A Amazonia é nossa!"* (The Amazon is ours!) and *"Fora Ludwig!"* (Ludwig, get out!).

Briscoe was booed off the stage amid shouted charges that Jari was a creation of the big banks, and at the end of the conference, the delegates, representing the ten-thousand-member scientific organization, passed a resolution condemning the military government's support of multinational projects and blasting Ludwig and other foreign speculators for destroying the Amazon's ecosystem, exploiting the local Indians and mestizos, and robbing Brazil of the benefits of national development.

Back at Jari, despite Briscoe's claims to the contrary, things were no better. Now that the pulp plant was on stream and producing, it was growing painfully more apparent that the tree plantation was not going to yield enough pulpwood to keep the operation going at full capacity.

D.K. had had ample warning, but had chosen to ignore the evidence, basing his faith in the Gmelina mostly on the early experimental plantings in Panama and elsewhere. According to those findings, Gmelinas could be expected, under prime conditions, to produce annually thirty-five cubic meters of wood per hectare for each year of growth.

In 1977, when Ludwig had been scrounging around for funds to keep the project going until the pulp plant could arrive, potential investors insisted Jari should be independently evaluated by the World Bank. The bank had sent down its own team of experts, who estimated that projected Gmelina growth would be only half what Ludwig expected. D.K. had refused to believe the figures. His own foresters were still predicting far cheerier numbers, and he preferred to believe those. What he failed to realize was that his foresters, trying to protect their own jobs, were telling him what they knew he wanted to hear. To get the higher estimates, they were taking the best yields on the plantation and passing them off as averages.

Left to himself, Ludwig might have kept pouring all the money he could raise into Jari, as he had been doing for years. But reality finally intruded. Chase Manhattan would not let him have the $400 million loan package until he got his management problems straightened out. His going through two project chiefs a year smacked too much of irresponsibility to make the bankers comfortable about advancing money even to the world's richest man.

Eventually, D.K. gave in to Chase Manhattan's conditions and hired a management consulting firm, Cresap, McCormick & Paget, to get things back on track. After a thorough evaluation, CM&P handed the billionaire a set of recommendations. They included:

1. *Selling off the rice plantation.* After an encouraging start, yields had fallen off and by 1979 were about a third below target levels. Less than 25 percent of the originally projected acreage was now under cultivation, costs had doubled, and the rice operation was presently losing $8 to $10 million dollars a year. (After firing his rice manager, D.K. started talking ARCO chairman Robert Anderson into buying him out.)
2. *Handing over the reins of management.* In CM&P's opinion, the continual bickering between D.K. and his project chiefs, and the frequent hirings and firings, were costly and counterproductive. The consultants recommended that an executive board be appointed to manage Jari. (Ludwig responded by choosing two retired Olinkraft officials, plus his own National Bulk vice-president, William Fisher, Jr., to serve on the board. Henceforth, Jari managers would report directly to this group, not to D.K.)
3. *Paring costs.* At the tree farm, as at the rice plantation, expenditures had been soaring at the same time production was shrinking. The price of fuel to run the big trucks D.K. had shipped down to haul the Gmelinas had climbed steeply since the OPEC crisis of 1973–1974. Now it appeared that the trucks themselves were unnecessarily large for harvesting the scrawnier-than-expected trees. With wood production about half what it should be, the cost of production was twice what D.K.'s accountants had earlier predicted. It was also twice as much as the average U.S. pulp producer was paying. For 1979, the wood and rice plantations together would take in $70 million from sales. For the same year, Ludwig would spend $110 million in operating costs, another $50 million in construction, and loan repayments of $60 million, for a total outlay of $220 million, $150 million of which was loss. In 1980, sales would rise to $90 million, and the operating deficit would be cut drastically to $10 million (largely by halting the rice operation and laying off several thousand workers), but there was $20 million in construction outlays and $64 million in debt payments, meaning that Jari was still deep in the red. (In an effort to cut costs still further, D.K. even allowed outside merchants to come in and run concessions he

had previously guarded jealously. Brazilian merchants were, for the first time, allowed to open stores and run taxi services in Monte Dourado.)

Despite the economy measures, the prognosis was still bleak. The chief reason surfaced during a meeting at which the new executive board called Clayton Posey and his foresters on the carpet and demanded real figures, not the ones they had been giving D.K. "The board," one participant recalled, "was hearing two different stories, and, by God, it wanted the truth."

After a bitter, heated exchange, the facts emerged. Over the next five years, the foresters confessed, Jari would face a pulpwood shortage of at least 10 percent, probably more. A third more wood than originally projected, and more than was presently under cultivation, was needed to keep the plant running at capacity. Native trees were now being cut and mixed in with the Gmelinas at a ratio of about 1:4 to produce enough Jaripulp to fulfill contracts. ("This move," *Fortune* remarked, "after a decade spent burning most of the native forest and spending millions on an imported species, surpasses irony.")

For nearly two decades, Ludwig had remained stubbornly committed to the dream that his tree was the answer to the global wood shortage. Now, when a board member came to report the grim truth — that his foresters had been lying and the Gmelina was falling far short of expectations — the old man took the news hard. "My God!" he croaked. "You've cut my throat with a rusty knife!"

To make matters worse — much worse — D.K.'s problems with the Brazilian government and people were reaching the critical stage. Charges and countercharges were flying back and forth. "A Amazonia é nossa" and "Fora Ludwig" were starting to appear as graffiti on walls in Rio.

Brazilian social agencies were insisting that Ludwig provide at least a minimum of human services to Jari laborers and their families. Ludwig replied that if Brazil wanted the workers to have these services, the government could pay for them; he couldn't afford to.

Ludwig blamed the Brazilians for obstructing Jari. For years, he charged, Brazil had refused to let him build hydroelectric dams for energy to process his bauxite deposits into aluminum. Now, when he was trying to sell those deposits to Alcoa, the government was blocking that move, too.

Government agencies, he claimed, had also stymied his attempt to bring a newsprint plant from Japan to Jari, even though Brazil was currently importing two thirds of its newsprint. Eventually the government had given ground, but only on the condition the plant be built in Brazil. "We had a balance-of-payments problem," Finance Minister Mario Simonsen later explained, "and it made no sense to give a guarantee on an import. I gave Mr. Ludwig a choice: either import a mill *without* a guarantee, or buy 70 percent here *with* a guarantee."

Ludwig had balked at these conditions. He wanted to give the business to IHI, not some Brazilian company over which he had no control. But now there was another reason. He had just learned that he didn't have enough wood at Jari to supply the pulp plant, much less a newsprint plant.

In order to get more acreage to cut, D.K. said he had originally bought much more land than he had claimed earlier: not three and a half million acres but *nine* million; not an area the size of Connecticut but one larger than Connecticut, Massachusetts, and Rhode Island *combined!*

Officials at Brazil's Land Colonizing Office dismissed such claims as "crazy." One claim, they said, would give Ludwig ownership of a stretch of the Atlantic Ocean if allowed. Word started floating around the agencies that D.K., now in his eighties, had become senile and could not be reasoned with. At one meeting with agency officials, a bureaucrat recalled, Ludwig, in the midst of serious negotiations, had distracted the other participants by calmly pulling bananas out of his briefcase and eating them.

Senile or not, the billionaire was determined to get more forest land, even if Brazil did not give him clear title to it. In the middle of 1980 he ordered his laborers into an area under dispute to cut native trees for the power plant. One day the workers were met by Brazilian soldiers, who ordered them off the land and would not let them remove the trees they had already cut.

This was the last straw. On August 5, 1980, Ludwig dictated a seventeen-page letter to President Figueiredo's chief of staff (the man who had been the architect of the military regime set up in 1964), General Golbery do Couto e Silva. In this epistle, D.K. gave his terms: either Brazil must pick up the $6-million-a-year tab for Jari's social services and settle Ludwig's land claims in his favor, or he would stop the forestry project and throw several thousand people out of work.

"If the Government cannot satisfy our legitimate pleas for assistance," the billionaire wrote, "I am seriously considering either paralyzing our operations or selling our paper mill to any third parties, including the Government, who would be interested in continuing operations."

In plain language, this meant: "Bail me out or buy me out."

Ludwig went on to attack eleven different Brazilian government agencies for impeding his operations and saddling him with "infrastructures" twice as large as he needed to support the existing operation. By the end of 1979, he added, he had personally invested $625 million in Jari, $75 million of which had gone to pay for these infrastructures.

Accusing the government of responsibility for the results of his own bad judgment and bad management was a typical Ludwig ploy, intended to bully the country into compliance with his wishes. To emphasize the threat, he specified the steps by which he would suspend activities (naturally cutting the least profitable projects first): "I will begin by stopping the forestry operations and the cellulose mill while I try to continue with the activities dealing with kaolin, bauxite and the sawmill. Naturally, this will be a last resort because it will mean leaving extremely valuable equipment and facilities unprotected and making them no longer productive. However, it is absolutely clear to me that this is the only path I can follow."

Official reactions to the ultimatum were mixed. Neither Golbery do Couto e Silva nor President Figueiredo could afford to take a strong public stand in Ludwig's favor. General Andrade Abreu's charges were still too fresh in some minds to risk their being aired again. Planning Minister Delfim Netto, who, like his predecessor in the office, Roberto Campos, had always been a vocal defender of D.K., predictably leaped in with an offer of aid: "The time has come when Ludwig should stop being treated like a foreign body in this country. We will give him the support he needs to guarantee the project."

Other officials, however, were much less enthusiastic. Jari's problems, said Industry and Commerce Minister Camillo Penna, were due more to poor management than to bureaucratic hindrance, and it would be folly to cave in to Ludwig's demands. The Colonizing Office was also holding firm. It was willing to grant clear title to only 1.4 million acres of Jari land, less than half what Ludwig had originally been conceded to have bought, and only 15.5 percent of what he was now claiming.

Other critics brought forth new ammunition. Congressman Modesto da Silveira, after a fact-finding trip to Zürich, came back to report, in a book entitled *Ludwig: Imperador do Jari,* that the billionaire's Swiss cancer research foundation, to which he had deeded the Amazon projects, was less a charitable institution than a tax dodge and "a front for strange, secret business deals."

An editorialist for the Rio newspaper *Journal do Brasil* put the issue bluntly: "The Brazilian political system hasn't yet invented a way by which society can refuse to fund these megalomanias. But the Brazilian political system should have no difficulty, acting through Congress and aided by a free press, in barring the Federal Government from bailing Mr. Ludwig out of his own business collapses."

Even some elements of the military were now openly attacking D.K.'s venture. A manifesto by an Amazonian defense committee declared the project to be "a revolting challenge to the nation." And in Rio, a popular stage play titled *Jari: The Country of Mr. Ludwig* had audiences hooting at D.K. and his state within a state.

In January of 1981, while Brazilian officials were arguing among themselves about how to respond to Ludwig's ultimatum, a tragedy occurred at Jari; some took it to be an omen. A rickety, overloaded wooden ferry carrying project workers' wives and children out of Monte Dourado hit a sandbar in the river and sank. About half the passengers managed to swim or wade to safety, but 120 bodies were recovered from the muddy waters and as many as a hundred more were presumed trapped at the bottom in the sunken vessel.

It was becoming apparent that the entire project was sinking as well. Of fourteen hundred engineers who had been on Jari's staff a year earlier, a mere hundred now remained. The tree plantation's Forestry Research Department had, until recently, boasted a staff of fifty. Only thirteen were left. The Gmelinas were no longer being pruned, and the planting of new pine and experimental eucalyptus seedlings had been halted. Machete-wielding laborers no longer patrolled the rows, hacking back undergrowth and spraying pesticides. The native jungle was starting to come back unhindered.

The herds of water buffalo and cattle were being slaughtered, their carcasses shipped out to foreign markets. The rice plantation was already abandoned. A new town of 365 concrete houses just built by Ludwig's Con-Tech crews stood empty and abandoned. The executive board had decided against spending the money to supply it with electricity.

In May of 1981, D.K. formally put Jari up for sale. Many Brazilian officials were elated. Said Admiral Roberto Gama e Silva, director of national security for the Upper Amazon, "I am going to uncork a bottle of champagne when Jari is sold."

But it wasn't to be that easy. What Ludwig had on his hands was a huge green elephant that nobody else wanted. As one Brazilian newspaper sympathized editorially, "The real point is that the rational economic development of the Amazon wasn't a good deal for Daniel Ludwig, and when a deal isn't good for Daniel Ludwig it's hard to imagine anyone else sinking that kind of money into the same spot."

By best available estimates, D.K. had sunk some $863 million into Jari and was still showing debts of another $180 million, for a total outlay of well over $1 billion. There were no good guesses as to how much he had taken out in sales of kaolin, bauxite, rice, meat, wood pulp, and other products, but it was a safe bet that he had lost a large part of his investment.

The official story was that Ludwig was giving up the project because of failing health, and reports were leaked that illness was confining him to his Manhattan penthouse. Some observers speculated that he was just sick of losing money at Jari, a notion Project Manager Howard King seemed to confirm in answering a reporter's question: "Mr. Ludwig is exasperated with this project. It's a long way from his dream. Now we're in a retreat situation."

Somebody, of course, had to clean up the mess, and, predictably, the Brazilian government would be called on to do so. Figueiredo and Delfim Netto, fighting a rearguard action against other officials, congressmen, and citizens who opposed a bailout, first appropriated $35 million in stopgap funds to keep Jari from total collapse while a more permanent solution was being worked out.

This wasn't nearly enough. In the fall of 1981, a $40 million loan installment was due, and Ludwig was saying he simply wasn't going to pay it. This time it was D.K.'s friend and long-time partner A. T. A. Antunes who came to the rescue. In exchange for the kaolin operation, said Antunes, he would pay the loan installment and keep Jari out of bankruptcy.

The offer was not charity. The kaolin project had been the only venture at Jari to make money consistently, and Antunes could count on recovering his investment within a few years and reaping large profits thereafter.

For the rest, Brazil was left holding the bag. The debts to banks in Japan and London for loans to build the power and pulp plants were now around $260 million, with another installment coming up in January of 1982. Since Brazil's National Development Bank had underwritten most of this amount, the country had little choice but to pay. Ludwig had originally purchased Jari for $3 million. Now Brazil was having to pay upward of a hundred times that amount to get it back.

Delfim Netto, Antunes, Ludwig's Brazilian lawyer, and a host of other financial and legal experts worked feverishly to hammer out an agreement that would let D.K. exit more or less gracefully and keep Jari out of receivership. In its final form, the deal, which covered the next thirty-five years, looked like this:

The government-owned Bank of Brazil would pledge $180 million toward paying off Ludwig's debts. Antunes's $40 million would get him the kaolin operation. Some $69 million more would be raised from private Brazilian sources — banks, insurance companies, industrial groups — with twenty-three contributors each kicking in $3 million. This amount, nearly $300 million, would retire Jari's liabilities and keep things running on a shoestring until the project could begin to pay off.

In return, Universe Tankships (now officially owned by Ludwig's Swiss cancer foundation) would hand over its Jari stock — currently valued, by some rather inflated calculations, at $480 million — to a newly created holding corporation, Companhia do Jari, Ltda., jointly owned by the Bank of Brazil, Antunes, and representatives of the other companies.

Even so, there was still a chance, albeit remote, that Ludwig and his heirs could still receive profits from Jari. Written into the agreement was a clause stipulating that if the project started showing a profit in this period, neither D.K. nor his foundation would receive anything for five years, but, starting in 1987, would get 5 percent of dividends over the next ten years, 4 percent in the decade 1997–2006, and 3 percent over the remaining fifteen years of the contract.

Once all the details of the agreement had been worked out, Delfim Netto got on the phone and started twisting arms to get the twenty-three private companies to ante up their $3 million each. Not that the companies were apt to refuse; they were too closely tied to multinational interests and the Figueiredo regime to show recalcitrance. The president of one such firm, South America Insurance Company, when asked why he had agreed to put $3 million of his corporation's investment funds into such a risky proposition, replied that Delfim Netto had told him to regard it as "a service to the nation." Another executive, the head of Atlantica Boavista Life Insurance Group, said he had signed up "out of obligation. The government thinks it's necessary — that I have to do it — and so I'll do it. I didn't spend ten seconds reading the proposal. I accepted, and that was that."

Thus, company after company fell into line, dutifully contributing $3 million as Delfim Netto passed the hat to pay off Ludwig's debts and let him get out of Jari with some dignity. It had been a bad experience for nearly everyone concerned. Ludwig had seen his dream shattered and his fortune considerably diminished. Most of the thirty thousand people who had once lived and worked at Jari had been left homeless and jobless. Brazil had lost heavily, both in money and environment. No one except a few optimists believed Jari had much of a chance to recover sufficiently to pay back the bailout money, much less show a profit. And several hundred thousand acres of native rain forest that had been destroyed appeared unlikely to grow back to their former size and diversity.

At this writing, the future of Jari is still uncertain. Neither the Brazilian embassy nor the U.S. State Department, when contacted recently, acknowledged having any information about what is currently going on there. But a Cousteau Society expedition to the region in 1983 reported that the pulp plant was still in operation, to the detriment of the environment. Jari, like its predecessor, Fordlandia, seems destined to endure as a costly, destructive example of a rich man's egocentric attempt to make nature conform to human demands.

# Nineteen

# "A Gray Old Wolf
# and a Lean"

Ludwig's failure in Brazil was only one of several reversals of fortune in his vast financial empire. His shipping enterprises weren't doing all that well either.

During the late sixties to mid-1970s, after finishing the giant Bantry tankers for Gulf Oil, Ludwig continued to build large ships. None so large as the Bantry class, to be sure, but still very big vessels.

Between 1969 and 1971, D.K., using the IHI shipyard at Kure, built three 160,000-ton bulk carriers: the *Universe Aztec, Universe Patriot* and *Universe Kure.* These he followed with a series of 265,000-ton tankers: *Universe Pioneer* (1972), *Universe Burmah* (1973), *Universe Explorer, Universe Mariner, Universe Ranger* (all 1974), *Universe Sentinel, Universe Monitor* (both 1975), and *Universe Frontier* (1976).

He had planned to use all or most of these vessels in an ambitious transshipment operation arranged with Britain's Burmah Oil. The scheme was very similar to what he had put together with Whiteford of Gulf Oil in Ireland's Bantry Bay. Burmah Oil would construct a large terminal and transshipment facility on Grand Bahama island east of Freeport. Ludwig's huge tankers, and other ships, would bring oil from the Persian Gulf to the Bahamas, where it could be offloaded and transferred to smaller vessels that could haul it to refineries in Philadelphia, Delaware, and elsewhere on the East Coast. The ports at these refineries were not deep enough to accommodate the ships Ludwig and the Greeks were currently building, but at least Arab oil could be hauled for most of its journey on the economical ultra-large crude carriers and only a short distance on smaller, less economical ships from the Gulf and Burmah Oil terminals to European and American oil refineries.

Having a stake in the Bantry Bay and Grand Bahama transshipment facilities would give Ludwig a share of the profits from much of the oil being carried from the Middle East to Western Europe and the eastern United States, which, in the early 1970s, was a considerable amount. But again, things did not go exactly as planned.

Burmah built its Grand Bahama terminal and created a new corporation, Burmah Oil Tankers (registered in Bermuda), to operate it. Elias Kulukundis, a member of a prominent Greek shipping family and a one-time adviser to Onassis, was brought in to run the new company. Like Ludwig, Kulukundis had gotten his first job in shipping with a firm of ship chandlers. Now he was chartering ships from D.K. Two of these vessels were the 265,000-ton *Universe Burmah* and *Universe Explorer*. (Another tanker Kulukundis chartered was from a company with the fitting name of Hoccus Poccus, Ltd.)

Burmah Oil Tankers had problems from the outset. The transshipment facility was not operational as early as expected. Also, the U.S. demand for crude in the early seventies turned out to be less than anticipated, which caused several of BOT's tankers to sit idle at anchorage just off Grand Bahama for extended stretches of time. Tied to this was the fact that most of the major U.S. oil companies that had been expected to hire the ships to haul their oil did not sign up. Only Shell made a strong commitment to use the Grand Bahama facility, and this contract would utilize only one sixth of the terminal's capacity.

Even so, Kulukundis was able to show a profit for a while. The first year of operations, 1970, he earned Burmah Oil $800,000 in profits. The next year this improved to $2 million. BOT's profits climbed to $6 million in 1972, then jumped to $43 million for 1973, when the facility began to hit its stride. But then came the Arab oil embargo, and things slowed to a virtual halt. By the end of 1974, losses were approaching $35 million.

Part of the problem was the escalating chartering fees. In 1970, Burmah had estimated that the requisite number of tankers could be chartered for $8.5 million, but by 1974 these fees (many of them paid to Ludwig) were \$40 million. Burmah Oil Tankers and its parent company were in trouble. The British company started hauling its oil to Antwerp, not Freeport, aboard tankers chartered from a Japanese company, not Ludwig's ships. A letter of resignation was brought over in early 1975 for Kulukundis to sign as a condition for Burmah's being able to borrow bailout money from the Bank of England. He had no choice but to sign.

So the Grand Bahama oil transshipment facility Ludwig had placed such high hopes on turned into a fizzle, just as the Bantry Bay venture would do a little later. Much of the failure resulted from the inability of even the oil cartel, powerful as it was and is, to control all the factors that govern the petroleum market, particularly in the volatile Middle East. One outbreak of hostilities in the area can change the whole structure of supply and demand. Ludwig, a gambler, had placed his faith in big ships, which, he had long maintained, are more economical for hauling oil as long as demand remains steady or keeps rising. Over the long haul, the gamble had paid off, mainly because, as an integral part of the cartel, he was playing with house odds. But even the house loses occasionally, as it did in the OPEC struggles of the early 1970s (in control if not in money).

But the wheel of fortune keeps turning, and if matters did not work out in one area, they had a way of compensating in another. For some time, the forces controlling gambling in the Bahamas had been trying to get casinos accepted in the eastern part of the United States. In 1976 — the year of the American bicentennial — they finally succeeded. Atlantic City, New Jersey, became the center of legalized casino gambling on the East Coast.

James Crosby of Resorts International was the man who made it happen. Resorts, with the help of Intertel, had spared no effort to "clean up" casino gambling and get the visible mob presence out of it in the Bahamas. And with lots of help from powerful political allies, it organized an expensive campaign to "sell" gambling to the people of New Jersey. By promising to resurrect the declining old resort town of Atlantic City, it finally got its way and was given a year's head start to come in and set up gambling operations before other casinos — several of them branches of existing Las Vegas operations — could build their own casino-hotels.

Once Resorts opened the door in Atlantic City, gambling took off like a rocket. Within a few years, casino-hotels came to dominate the skyline above the famed Boardwalk in the city where the game of Monopoly was born decades earlier. Harrah's, Caesars Palace, the Golden Nugget, Bally's, the Tropicana, Claridge's, the Sands — all trooped in and set up to keep Resorts International company and make Atlantic City the new gambling capital of the world.

And where does Ludwig fit into the picture? It would be naïve to assume that he did not have a large hand in bringing gambling to Atlantic City, just as it would be naïve to accept the 1967 *Life* magazine interpretation that Wallace Groves, after letting Ludwig build hotels and housing around the proposed casino in Bahamia, could deny him ownership of the casino itself. The most reasonable assumption, given the evidence, is that Ludwig was the shadowy figure behind James Crosby, just as he seems to have been behind Groves and I. Gordon Mosvold. It seems equally reasonable to assume that D.K. had considerable professional help from the Lansky organization in carrying out the feat of getting gambling accepted in the eastern United States. The Mafia is a very real and powerful entity in the Garden State. "New Jersey mob" springs to the lips as easily as "Florida orange juice" or "California sunshine." It is impossible to imagine casino gambling coming to Atlantic City unless the mob wanted it there. But an organization without any obvious mob connections had to make it happen. And that was probably the function of James Crosby's Resorts International, which, directly or indirectly, was also Daniel Ludwig's Resorts International.

But whatever profits he was making from gambling were probably more than offset by his Brazilian losses. His worldwide empire, though still intact, was considerably diminished after he sold off many of his holdings for cash to pour into Jari. How much had he really lost?

One can best find an answer by looking again at the brochure National Bulk had prepared nearly a decade earlier, in 1973–1974, to impress potential clients with the company's breadth and versatility. This thirty-six-page document is interesting not only for the look it gives at D.K.'s multifarious ventures but also as evidence that he was willing to draw partway open the veil of secrecy customarily surrounding his operations and put many of his projects on display.

Though it was not intended for general perusal, the National Bulk brochure did give prospective customers a broad view of what Ludwig acknowledged as his accomplishments. The list was impressive, revealing the extent to which D.K. had by this time become a gigantic one-man multinational. On pages two and three, the brochure offered three separate views of the globe. One featured the Americas, another Europe, Africa, and the Mideast, and a third the Far East and Australia. Above and below these three worlds were the names of specific countries where Ludwig-owned operations existed.

From the brochure, and by interpolating facts about certain other countries where he is known to have had holdings, one can form an approximation of D.K.'s global activities — at least those which are visible. As of 1974 his world empire looked like this:

### Australia

The brochure lists agriculture, mining, office towers, real estate, financial services, and shipping. Known enterprises include Ocean Shores (the three-thousand-acre recreation community north of Sydney), a large cattle ranch, a mining company (Clutha Development Pty., Ltd.) operating coal, iron, and bauxite mines, the Greater Pacific Building (an office tower housing Ludwig-owned insurance companies and other financial service corporations).

### The Bahamas

The brochure mentions financial services, hotels, and real estate. Ludwig is known to have dredged the harbor at Freeport and to have operated limestone and cement plants here. The extent of his operations on Grand Bahama and perhaps elsewhere in the islands is unknown, but there is reason to suspect much greater involvement than the brochure suggests.

### Bermuda

The brochure mentions financial services and hotels. Two of the Princess chain hotels are here, and Ludwig had his West African Marine Insurance Company headquartered here, too. Universe Tankships and Sea Tankers were also located here for a while.

### Brazil

The brochure mentions agriculture, mining, and housing. Ludwig's operations at the time were extensive, not only at Jari but elsewhere in the country.

### British Honduras

The brochure mentions farming, but does not give details.

### Canada

The brochure mentions only agriculture. At various times, though, Ludwig seems to have been engaged in mining and oil-drilling ventures here. One source indicates that his Princess hotel chain operated one or more hotels here. (Could the Bayshore Inn, where Hughes spent a few months between stays in Nicaragua, have been a Ludwig hotel?)

### Cayman Islands

No mention in the brochure, but Ludwig is known to have recruited many of his seamen from these islands. Evidence points toward his having established offshore banking activities here as well.

### Costa Rica

Ludwig's International Housing, Ltd., in 1974 had a substantial minority interest in Monarca de Costa Rica, a construction company that was building six hundred housing units.

### Ethiopia

D.K. is known to have had a potash-mining operation here in the 1960s.

### France

The brochure refers to financial services. This probably means the Paris branch of European American Securities, a merchant-bank operation Ludwig started in the early 1970s to manage real estate investment, mergers, acquisitions, and other services for wealthy individual and corporate clients. Other European American offices were in New York, Los Angeles, London, Zürich, Sydney, Hong Kong, and Tokyo. Some sources have indicated that Ludwig owned millions of dollars worth of real estate in several of the Common Market countries, but specific holdings are difficult to determine.

### Great Britain

The brochure lists financial services, shipping, and real estate. He is also known to have been active in oil activities in Bantry Bay off the Irish coast and at Cromarty Firth in Scotland, where he was planning to establish a refinery.

### Greece

London sources indicate that D.K. established a refinery in Greece, which is likely, since another source indicates that some of his idle tankers were tied up and awaiting business at a Greek port.

### Hong Kong

The brochure lists both financial services (probably European American Securities) and manufacturing, without specifying what is being produced.

### Iceland

Ludwig is listed as forming a joint venture with a local contractor to build a thousand houses by the Con-Tech process.

### India

D.K. is known to have dredged the Hooghly River in order to export iron ore from mines in the interior of the country.

### Indonesia

Brochure: Petroleum and gas, refining and mining exploration, are mentioned.

### Japan

Ludwig's Japanese interests are extensive. The brochure lists only shipping, but it is likely that he has a financial interest in the world's largest shipbuilding company, Ishikawajima-Harima, which took over his operations at Kure when his lease expired. Given his long history of carrying iron and other ores to Japan, it would not be surprising if he holds stock in the country's steel and other mineral industries.

### Liberia

The brochure makes no mention of any activities here, but D.K. is known to have based several of his shipping companies, including Universe Tankships and Sea Tankers, here and to have put most of his fleet under Liberian registry. He also maintains a bank in Monrovia.

### Malaysia

The brochure suggests that D.K. is carrying on exploratory mining operations here for interested clients.

### Mexico

The brochure lists hotels and housing. Ludwig's giant solar salt plant had just been sold, but he is also known to have maintained agricultural experimental stations here.

### Nicaragua

The brochure lists housing, and Ludwig is known to have gone into a joint venture construction project with General Anastasio Somoza Debayle to reap profits from rebuilding Managua after the 1973 earthquake. His friendship with Somoza predates this, however, and it can be guessed that he had other business interests in the country before that time. A pertinent question is whether he was an owner or operator of Managua's Intercontinental Hotel, where Howard Hughes resided for a time.

### Panama

The brochure mentions only agriculture, but D.K. is known earlier to have been involved in operating several of his flag-of-convenience shipping companies from here and to have established a refinery and petrochemical complex on the eastern coast. He also built housing developments using the Con-Tech system.

### Singapore

Shipping is listed in the brochure.

### South Korea

The brochure lists shipping, and D.K. seems to have a bulk-transfer offloading operation there.

### Switzerland

The brochure lists financial services. The extent to which Ludwig is involved in Swiss banking can only be guessed at, given the country's secrecy laws about banking. One source indicates that Ludwig owns a substantial minority share of Crédit Suisse–First Boston. D.K. also maintains his cancer research foundation here and has placed his foreign assets under its ownership.

### Taiwan

The brochure lists shipping.

### Union of South Africa

Housing and mining are listed in the brochure, which adds, "The International Housing division of Somerset Mining, another National Bulk Carriers affiliate, is building a large number of town houses in Johannesburg, and proposals have been made for the construction of low-cost housing there as well." The brochure also indicates that Somerset Mining has located sizable coal reserves, but has not yet found a local market for them.

### Venezuela

The brochure lists only agriculture and dredging, but D.K. is known to have had extensive projects here dating back to the early 1950s, including mining and oil wells. He was also engaged in several building projects in urban areas: luxury homes, a shopping center, low-income housing.

### West Germany

The brochure mentions shipping. Ludwig is also known to have had part interest in an oil refinery near Hamburg.

### Yugoslavia

The brochure refers to shipping activities.

### United States

Here the brochure lists financial services, hotels, housing, mining, office towers, and shipping. The lists of projects in each of these categories, of course, would themselves be extensive.

This roster of Ludwig's holdings and activities around the globe, though extensive, is by no means exhaustive. We know, for example, that he was involved in projects in other parts of the world: the Mideast, where he was shipping oil out of several producing countries; Africa, where he had earlier engaged in ventures in Nigeria and other countries not mentioned in the brochure; Uruguay, where he had purchased a villa. There are almost certainly other countries that could also be included. Ludwig's empire has always been in flux, never stable for very long. Buying and selling, getting and spending, starting projects and sometimes abandoning them — Ludwig made acquisitions and divestitures that reveal a pattern as restless and kinetic as the man himself. Even if they were not frequently cloaked in secrecy, keeping track of them would be a difficult enough task.

After Jari, though, the task becomes somewhat easier, because D.K. had sold off many of his earlier holdings, either to raise money for keeping his Amazon enterprises afloat or for other reasons. International Housing, the foreign branch of his Con-Tech construction system, was gone, sold to E. P. Taylor. His Australian mining ventures were gone, sold to oil companies. His Princess hotels were gone, sold to a British conglomerate. European-American Securities was gone, sold to a Bank of America executive. A number of his ships were gone as well, including the giant Bantry-class tankers, either scrapped or sold to rivals like Stavros Niarchos and Christina Onassis. And now Jari — the green jewel in his crown of empire — was also gone, sunk in a morass of debts and false hopes.

Even so, Ludwig was hardly a pauper. Although *Fortune,* trying to calculate the effects of the loss of Jari on D.K.'s wealth, had estimated it would reduce his assets from several billion to a few hundred million, the fall seems not to have been nearly so far. In 1983, *Forbes,* which annually compiles a list of America's richest four hundred people, said that, though Ludwig was no longer to be considered the richest man in the world — that title having been conferred on Gordon Getty — he was still probably the third richest, with a "net worth believed to . . . exceed $2 billion." In 1984 the magazine demoted him well down the list to being a "half-billionaire," but only because he had put an estimated three quarters of his assets — $1.5 billion — under the direct ownership of his Swiss foundation and had relinquished control over them. *Forbes* left him in 1985 in about the same position he occupied in 1984. Just how accurate is the *Forbes* estimate? That's not easy to say. An editor at the magazine, when asked, admitted that Ludwig's fortune was one of the most difficult to keep tabs on. But he did little to dispel the mystery, saying he could reveal nothing about how *Forbes* arrived at its figure, nor could he give out any names of sources for the information on which the estimate is based.

It is safe to say that the aged billionaire, since leaving Jari, has not remained idle. Even as he was closing down his Amazon operations in 1981, he was putting together proposals that had the potential of recouping some of his lost wealth. If things were dark, they weren't hopeless. The Brazilian situation had fallen to pieces, but D.K. now had a close friend in the White House. With Ronald Reagan in Washington, Ludwig could safely bring his ventures back home. The United States was gearing up to become, once again, the land of opportunity for entrepreneurs.

One opportunity was in the exploitation of America's vast coal reserves, which, since World War II, had been largely lying idle. In the postwar period, coal had given way to petroleum as the world's prime energy source. There were several reasons for this. Less clean-burning than oil, coal, particularly the high-sulfur types, is a major source of air pollution, releasing large quantities of sulfur dioxide into the atmosphere during combustion. Also, it is much more expensive than oil to get out of the ground. When petroleum is in plentiful supply, coal cannot compete with it economically as a source of energy fuel. There are certain industrial processes, though, including steelmaking, that require coal, so there is still a small but steady market for it. And in times of oil shortages, it is available in quantity as a fairly cheap alternative fuel.

Around 1960, Ludwig, looking for other cargoes as the oil market tapered off following the Suez-crisis boom of 1956–1957, had started looking at the possibilities of shipping U.S. coal to Japan. Toward this end he had bought up a West Virginia coal-mining enterprise, Superior Pocahontas, with the idea of exploiting Appalachian reserves for export. The costs of extraction and transportation, however, precluded big profits, and in 1964 he sold the coal company to Allied Chemical and invested instead in Australian and South African reserves much closer to Japan. Not only would this reduce his transportation costs; it would also lower the cost of labor, since he would not have the United Mine Workers to contend with.

Even so, things did not work out as planned. As the oil market picked up again, mining South African coal was not profitable, and though D.K. did ship some Australian coal to Japan, it did not prove a big moneymaker for him. Eventually — in 1976 — he started selling off his Australian coal-mining operation, Clutha Development Pty., to British Petroleum as a way of raising cash to sustain Jari. But that year, Democratic presidential candidate Jimmy Carter campaigned on a platform that included a plank calling for the revival of America's coal industry as an alternative to petroleum and nuclear fuels. Hearing this, oil companies suddenly began buying up U.S. coal reserves and mining companies.

It is not recorded whether Ludwig bought back into U.S. coal himself, but he had long since learned not to put all his investment eggs in one basket, and even with the cartel controlling oil, political factors in the volatile Mideast and elsewhere frequently destabilized the petroleum market. (The major oil companies had learned the same lesson, and had ploughed many of their "obscene profits" of the mid-1970s into buying up all potential alternative energy sources — not only coal and nuclear, but also companies specializing in fuel-cell technology, solar and geothermal power, synthetic fuels, and the like — in an effort to keep all bases covered even as they strove to reassert control lost by the rise of OPEC and the entry of various other developing nations into oil production.)

During Carter's years as president, the expected switch from oil to coal by U.S. industries and utilities did not take place. Instead of an oil shortage, there was an oil glut. The oil companies, straining to keep petroleum prices in some sort of equilibrium, were also stuck with millions of tons of coal they couldn't sell on the domestic market. The answer was to export it to Western Europe and Japan — to countries that had no adequate supplies of fossil fuel of any kind.

This is where Ludwig found his opportunity. He had the ships — numerous large bulk carriers able to carry oil, coal, or ore — and many of them were sitting idle as oil supply exceeded demand. If he could set up an operation to ship coal out of the eastern United States to Europe and the Far East, he could put these vessels back to work and recoup some of the money he had lost in the Amazon.

Exporting coal was a project the United States government should have been interested in. Since the country had largely exhausted many of its other mineral resources in the years during and following World War II, it had few commodities left to export besides food. The balance-of-trade deficit was starting to tilt dangerously toward making the U.S. a debtor nation; new markets had to be found for American products. Further, the plans of the Soviet Union to open a natural gas pipeline into Western Europe raised the specter of having America's NATO allies become energy-dependent on the Russians. Pushing European factories to use American coal instead of Soviet natural gas was one way of countering this.

Before large-scale U.S. coal export could become a reality, though, certain problems had to be worked out. One was economic. Even though America had the largest coal reserves in the world, it was still at a disadvantage, because it was farther from potential customer countries than were Australia and South Africa, both rival coal exporters. Transportation costs from U.S. ports, therefore, were prohibitively high. Added to production costs, they threatened to price American coal out of the global market.

Transport costs could be cut considerably by shipping the coal in larger vessels such as Ludwig's bulk carriers, but here too there were problems. America's East Coast port facilities, most of them having been built at least half a century ago, were unable to accommodate such deep-drafted vessels. Ports like New York, Boston, Philadelphia, Baltimore, and Charleston had shipping channels only forty feet deep or less. (Norfolk, built to handle warships, was the only exception; it had greater harbor depth but ships of more than forty-six-and-a-half-foot draft could not enter because of the Chesapeake Bay Bridge Tunnel.) But a coal-hauling ship the size of Ludwig's bulk carriers might, fully loaded, sink fifty-five feet or more below the water line.

When Ludwig had encountered a similar problem on the Orinoco in the early 1950s, he had gone into the dredging business, converting old tankers into oceangoing dredges able to dig deep channels and harbors in existing waterways. But dredging was not the best answer for America's Atlantic ports. With rivers and ocean currents constantly bringing in new loads of silt and sand, the expensive process would have to be done too frequently to be cost-effective.

D.K. and other supertanker owners had run into this difficulty in transporting oil to East Coast refineries. The solution then had been lightering. A large tanker coming from the Middle East to, say, Philadelphia would stop in deep water some miles from port and offload part of its cargo onto a smaller ship called a lightering vessel. This allowed the larger tanker to become buoyant enough to raise its draft to forty feet or less and navigate into port without scraping bottom.

Something like this in reverse, Ludwig felt, could be used to export coal. A 160,000-ton bulk carrier could take on part of a load of coal in Philadelphia, sail south into Delaware Bay to a deep-water channel located about halfway down (where tankers were already being lightered) near Big Stone Beach, and rendezvous with a coal-bearing barge to "top off," filling its cargo hold to capacity before heading for a foreign port.

Better yet, both the bulk carrier and the barge could meet at a large "mother ship" stationed in the anchorage area, and this vessel could, by means of a conveyor system and grab buckets, transfer the barge's coal to the bulk carrier. Ludwig had just the vessel in mind for his mother ship — the *Cedros,* a 171,000-ton bulk carrier built at Kure in 1966 and designed primarily as a self-unloading salt hauler but versatile enough to carry oil, coal, or ore as well. Built to carry bulk salt from his giant evaporation plant on Baja, she was named for Cedros Island, where the salt was loaded for export after its production at nearby Black Warrior Lagoon. After selling the salt operation to Mitsubishi, Ludwig had kept the hauling contract, but now the *Cedros* was finally unemployed and looking for something else to do.

D.K. planned to anchor her at the lightering area in Delaware Bay — the only sheltered deep-water transfer point on the eastern seaboard — and convert her to coal loading. Her own hold could be filled with coal, which she could use to supplement what she was moving from barge to bulk carrier by means of conveyor.

The scheme promised to be quite profitable. Ludwig planned to charge coal exporters $4.50 per ton to use the mother ship. If he handled an estimated ten million tons per year, this process would yield an annual revenue of $45 million. He would also charter out several of his other bulk carriers to the coal companies, offering them rates of around $9.00 to $10.00 per ton. For the coal exporters, this would represent a saving of around $6.00 per ton over the rate they were currently paying to haul coal in ships roughly half the size of Ludwig's bulk carriers.

So far so good. Of course, now that Ludwig was operating in U.S. waters, he would have to deal with various levels of government. But D.K. didn't anticipate any real problems; the new policy in Washington was to lessen government interference with business.

An initial step was to get the U.S. Coast Guard to enlarge the anchorage area off Big Stone Beach in Delaware to make room for the proposed coal-transfer operation. The Coast Guard proved cooperative, not only agreeing to the enlargement but even issuing the required public notice about the move without mentioning why it was being done. At the state level, D.K. sent his representatives to meet with Delaware legislators and present the proposal, simultaneously contacting officials of the state's Department of Natural Resources and Environmental Control to get the proper permits.

A possible barrier was Delaware's Coastal Zone Act, a law passed under the administration of former Governor Russell Peterson (later head of the Council on Environmental Quality, the Office of Technology Assessment — a congressional agency — and the National Audubon Society). This 1971 act — passed to head off a Shell Oil attempt to establish a refinery complex on Delaware Bay — banned heavy industry and offshore bulk-transfer facilities along the Delaware coast and was vigorously defended by local environmentalists and by the fishing and tourist industries.

Delaware officials, however, were promoting industrial development despite the Coastal Zone Act, and the current governor, Pierre S. (Pete) du Pont, heir to a chemicals fortune, was in favor of Ludwig's project. The governor may even have had a vested interest, since the Du Pont Company, in which he was a large stockholder, had recently, in one of the biggest deals of all time, bought up Conoco (Continental Oil Company). Conoco in turn owned, through its Consolidation Coal Company, vast reserves of Appalachian coal.

In this favorable climate, everything seemed to be going Ludwig's way. Then, abruptly and for no apparent reason, he stopped pushing for the coal-transfer project. In October of 1982, a spokesman for Universe Tankships said the plan had been placed on a back burner, awaiting an upturn in the world coal market. Another reason may have been that certain other potential coal shippers seeking the business had dragged out an old Maritime Administration rule, stating that coal exported from the United States must be carried in American-flag vessels. Nearly all Ludwig's ships were still under flag-of-convenience registry.

Into the vacuum stepped Elias Kulukundis, the Greek shipper who had gone in with D.K. on the aborted Burmah Oil transshipment facility at Grand Bahama. Kulukundis had recently bought up twenty-seven acres of dockside property in Philadelphia and was planning to start his own coal-exporting operation in Delaware Bay, similar to but simpler than the one Ludwig had proposed. In view of their earlier association, it is possible that Ludwig still had a hand in the Kulukundis project. But the Greek soon lost interest, leaving the field open to a small outfit called Coastal Barge, Inc., which has ties to Norfolk-Southern Railway. There may also be ties to Ludwig. The officers of Coastal Barge — a man named Henry Dowd and his two sons, Patrick and Robert — were three of those mentioned in the lawyers' interrogatories in the *International Bank v. Price Waterhouse* suit over the fraudulent sale of Mercantile Bank.

At this writing the issue of the Delaware Bay coal-transfer operation is still being fought in the federal court system between the Dowds and Norfolk-Southern on the one side and a coalition of state and county governments, environmental organizations, and fishing interests on the other. Coastal Barge and its backers are maintaining that the Delaware Coastal Zone Act unnecessarily restricts interstate commerce by banning such activities as the proposed coal port, and the state and environmentalists hold that the act is constitutional and does not *unnecessarily* restrict trade but simply bans methods of shipping that are potentially damaging to the ecosystem.

Recently the U.S. Departments of Justice and Commerce stepped into the suit on the side of the coal interests. Some environmentalists feel that the Reagan administration has a vested interest in seeing legal obstacles to full-scale coal export broken down. Also, the Maritime Administration has a stake in the case, since it lent Coastal Barge and related interests amounts of money in the tens of millions to construct two special self-unloading barges with which to carry out barge-to-ship transfer of coal. Unless the project goes through, Maritime may be left with an uncollectible loan.

Whether or not Ludwig still has any financial interest in the coal-transfer operation is not clear. Seemingly, he has dropped out of the competition, though that is by no means certain. But it is worth noting that he did set in motion a chain of events that may result in the loss to Delaware — the state that has provided a low-cost haven for many of his corporations for over more than half a century — of the law that protects its coastline from harmful industrial development.

At the time he was busy putting together a coal-shipping facility for the eastern United States, Ludwig was also active in the West, where he was still wheeling and dealing in savings and loan institutions. Owning S & Ls was a good way to maximize profits and at the same time get substantial tax write-offs.

As he finished developing Westlake Village, D.K. began selling off his California S & Ls, investing the money in similar businesses elsewhere. In 1973, for example, he used the proceeds of some Los Angeles thrift sales to buy American Savings and Loan, which had numerous branches in Utah and Hawaii. In 1976, he acquired Arizona's Southwest Savings & Loan, and in 1978 he bought Home Savings, a Texas thrift with twenty-one branches. During 1980 and 1981, he picked up two more Arizona S & Ls, which he merged with Southwest, and added another pair in Oregon — Willamette and Fred Meyer Savings & Loan.

By the fall of 1981, having sold off all his California thrifts (the last being Westdale, which he had acquired in 1972 and let go to an Oakland corporation in 1980), he had bought eight more — with numerous branches and combined assets of around $4 billion — in six other western states. He was the ninth largest holder of thrift institutions in the United States.

Atypically for Ludwig, he owned all these companies under his own name, this because federal regulations prohibit corporations from owning S & Ls across state lines but allow individuals to own where they please. *Business Week,* surveying D.K.'s collection of thrifts, remarked:

> Federal regulations do require that S & Ls in separate states owned by an individual be operated independently. But Ludwig has partly circumvented this requirement by buying thrifts in states that have reciprocity agreements with each other on S & L branching. His flagship, American Savings & Loan Assn. in Salt Lake City, has been operating in Hawaii as well. In fact, it is the largest S & L in both Hawaii and Utah. And by virtue of an agreement between Utah and Oregon, American is in the process of consolidating Ludwig's recently

acquired Oregon S & Ls into a new division, pushing its total assets near the $2 billion mark.

Given D.K.'s advanced age (he was then eighty-three) and the near collapse of his Brazilian empire, *Business Week* was led to wonder what the billionaire intended to do with his S & L holdings. The magazine noted that in June of 1981 Ludwig had signed an agreement with the Baldwin-United Corporation whereby he would pay it a $70 million fee, and the company would buy, or find a buyer for, his entire S & L collection at a guaranteed 175 percent of book value at time of sale, plus an amount that might be as much as $74 million, any time between 1984 and 1993 that D.K. decided to sell out.

Morley P. Thompson, a whiz-kid financier who headed Baldwin-United at the time, was quoted as saying of the deal, "We got $70 million, and he's bought himself an insurance policy." As for Ludwig, he was reported by *Fortune* to have called up a friend immediately after signing the contract and said, "I've just made a deal with the smartest man in America!"

Considering D.K.'s high regard for his own mental abilities, this was quite an accolade. Just who was Morley P. Thompson, and what had he done to deserve such lavish praise from the world's richest man?

Thompson had started out modestly enough around 1950, selling pianos door to door for his employer, the D. H. Baldwin Company, a Cincinnati-based firm that had been making keyboard instruments for nearly a century. Glib and handsome, he was a super-salesman, and within a few years he had worked his way up to a vice-presidency. From that position, he was able to talk the company into diversifying by buying the Central Bank of Denver. This move proved so profitable that Thompson was soon elevated to the presidency of Baldwin, where he led the company on a shopping spree of acquisitions. When it bought up the United Corporation, a closed-end investment company, in 1978, the piano company became Baldwin-United, a conglomerate with a string of banks, insurance companies, an S & L, and a number of other ventures under its umbrella. B-U soon branched into another area: trading stamps.

During the 1960s and early seventies, grocery chains and many other businesses went through the great trading-stamp war, vying with one another for customers by giving away with purchases little stamps that could be pasted in booklets and later redeemed for merchandise. After an extended flurry, the stamp craze eventually faded, and most merchants gave them up as a way of attracting trade. But for Morley Thompson they were still pure gold. The reason? They represented an enormous amount of "float" money.

Float capital is money you can use temporarily before you have to pay it out. A marketer would sell trading stamps directly to a merchant for a price. The merchant would then hand out the stamps over a period of time to his customers, who would paste them in books. Eventually many of the stamps would get turned in — redeemed — at a local stamp store for merchandise. But the average span between the time a merchant bought the stamps and the time they were redeemed at a stamp store was about eighteen months. The stamp marketer, in other words, had roughly a year and a half to play with the money before he gave anything back for it. A sharp investor with millions of dollars in available cash can turn a lot of profit over eighteen months.

Looking at this potential, Morley Thompson saw a new meaning to the old adage "Time is money" and had Baldwin-United buy up the nation's two largest trading-stamp firms, Sperry and Hutchinson, maker of S & H Green Stamps, and the Top Value line, then owned by a Kroger grocery chain subsidiary. These two acquisitions represented nearly three fourths of the trading-stamp business.

At about the same time, Thompson, looking for other kinds of float money, committed B-U to spend $1.2 billion in the purchase of MGIC Corporation (known in the trade as "Magic"), the largest insurer of home mortgages in the United States. Here was another mother lode of float capital. Home buyers, when they make their mortgage payments, normally include their taxes and insurance in each monthly payment. But a company like MGIC had to pass the taxes on to the appropriate government agency only once every six months. In the interim it could use this interest-free money for its own investments.

Daniel Ludwig, who was something of an expert himself at using other people's money to get rich, obviously appreciated the skills of Morley Thompson in pulling venture capital out of a hat without paying interest or taxes on it. He was so impressed, in fact, that he was willing to gamble $70 million that the bright young B-U president could produce the goods if and when D.K. decided to sell off his S & Ls.

As for Thompson, he was only too glad to get the opportunity to land a chain of thrift institutions that were proven moneymakers, shaped by the hand of a master. He was also happy to get a commitment of $70 million in hard cash, for, to tell the truth, Thompson had spread himself, and Baldwin-United, very thin by grabbing up potentially profitable companies. During the last few months of 1981 alone, he had invested more than $1.5 billion in S & H and MGIC, most of it borrowed from a consortium of large lenders headed by Chemical Bank (which had given Ludwig his start nearly half a century earlier).

Now a large part of that debt, made on a short-term basis, was coming due, and Thompson was beginning to run into problems. He had planned to loot MGIC of assets to get some quick cash, but had been stopped by the state of Wisconsin before he could carry out his scheme. He also had to pay off $5.2 million in debentures being held by a Tennessee bank. The IRS and regulators in several states began taking a closer look at his activities, and the financial genius Morley P. Thompson and his Baldwin-United were suddenly way out on a long limb.

In March of 1983 Thompson met with bank officials to ask for postponement of a $682 million debt payment for a month. In April he was back to ask for another extension until mid-July. Chemical and the other members of the consortium reluctantly agreed, but insisted on sending their auditors in for a close look at B-U's books. By late April the auditors had found enough to force Thompson's resignation. Now it was a matter of the company's trying to tread water and stave off bankruptcy.

On July 8, 1983, in a delayed financial statement, Baldwin-United reported a first-quarter loss of $617 million — the fourth worst single-quarter loss in U.S. corporate history. The company was found to be paying out more in loan interest than it was earning. Cash had to be found somewhere immediately.

To avoid total collapse, B-U sold off five of its companies to E. F. Hutton (soon to have its own difficulties as a result of manipulating float capital) and yelled "Help!" to Daniel Ludwig. D.K. responded by prepaying a promissory note for $77.5 million he had given for his S & L "insurance policy." He had not paid Thompson the

$70 million, had merely given him paper to hold as security. Once the note was called in, Ludwig did come through, with interest added on. But it was too little too late. In September, Baldwin-United filed for bankruptcy and reorganization under Chapter 11, still owing more than $1 billion to creditor banks and another $3 billion to policyholders of its insurance division.

Just what Ludwig got for his $70 million (plus interest) is questionable. Certainly he had misjudged the situation and perhaps Thompson's intelligence. It can be debated whether Morley Thompson was not as smart as he thought he was or else too smart for his own good. But a Wall Street banker had summed it up perfectly when the Baldwin-United wizard was still at the top of the roller-coaster, saying to an acquaintance: "Look, Thompson's smarter than you and me. If he's doing anything wrong, we won't know until it's too late."

Whatever other effects it may have had (and the repercussions were considerable), the collapse of Baldwin-United left Daniel Ludwig without a place to dump his savings and loan institutions should he decide to sell them. With that option closed, he looked around for other opportunities. He soon found one.

In April of 1985, Jersey City officials announced that they had just signed an agreement with Ludwig allowing him to develop a hundred-acre tract along the city's blighted Hudson River waterfront by building office towers and apartment complexes.

The project, estimated to cost $700 million, is being handled by a new Ludwig company, A-S-H Management Corporation. The letters stand for American, Southwest, and Home Savings — his three large S & L companies headquartered in western states. A-S-H Management, however, has its offices near National Bulk's on the Avenue of the Americas in mid-Manhattan. From there it's just a ride down the avenue to Canal Street and then through the Holland Tunnel to Jersey City.

The area to be developed, Harsimus Cove, is almost directly across the Hudson River from the World Trade Center and that part of lower Manhattan where Ludwig got his start in shipping some sixty years ago. It is presently a dingy, dismal area — a terminal depot where rail lines, trucks, and ships have converged for most of this century to exchange cargoes.

Ludwig, as one of several developers renovating the Jersey City waterfront, plans to erect, after ripping up the tracks and upgrading utility service, some fifteen hundred town house and apartment units and five office towers containing 750,000 square feet of space for sale or lease.

Plans call for the land to be developed in seven stages, the first being the construction of some 180 apartment units in two-to-five-story town houses on the southernmost part of the property. These apartments will be expensive. Ludwig is hoping to attract yuppies willing to pay high prices for the advantages of living close to New York and having a view of the famed Manhattan skyline just across the river.

A lot of work must be done before construction can start. About half the land — the forty-six acres owned by the city — is presently submerged, which means that D.K. will have to dredge and fill in order to give himself something to build upon. Another quarter of the land is crisscrossed with railroad tracks. Conrail sold him this parcel as is. The remaining quarter, previously owned by a trucking firm and a realty company, had to be condemned as blighted area by the city and fought through the courts before it could be freed.

Ludwig, rather than receding into retirement and letting his organization handle all the details, is taking a personal interest in the Harsimus Cove project. He went to Jersey City to sign the initial contract with Mayor Gerald McCann and allowed himself to be photographed for the occasion. The *New York Times* mistakenly labeled the picture the first one the aged billionaire had permitted to be taken of himself in nearly twenty years. (He has permitted several photos during the 1980s.)

Jersey City officials, having made the initial announcement, are reluctant to give out more information about the project, A-S-H Management, or its secretive owner. They have, however, outlined some of the other proposed stages. The second phase includes a twenty-five-story condominium tower with a pool and raised parking deck. There will also be a thirty-five-story waterfront high-rise, or, if opposition to such a tall building develops among local residents, a series of low-rise condos instead. Phases three and four will be mid-rise residential buildings toward the west; and phase five, even farther west, features an eighteen-story office tower with 365,000 feet of commercial space.

Some other major building projects to be undertaken in Jersey City over the next decade will use federal funds, but a city spokesman said Ludwig's Harsimus Cove project is being constructed entirely through private financing, which means either that D.K. still has plenty of available capital to draw on or that his credit is still good despite the Jari disaster and other setbacks. Presumably much of the construction money will come directly from his savings and loan institutions. Even so, it's a big gamble, and one he could easily lose if the economy or the building industry takes a hard tumble.

Conventional wisdom has it that Ludwig will not be around to see the project brought to completion eight to ten years from now, but the voices saying this are the ones that have for the last two decades proclaimed that D.K. was finally winding down his affairs and calling it quits. Each time they said it, he confounded their predictions and bounced back with a new project.

American billionaires are a notoriously long-lived bunch. Knowing they can't take it with them, they seem collectively determined to hang on to it as long as possible, and most have taken steps to ensure their own longevity. John D. Rockefeller's answer was mother's milk. Ludwig's seems to be buttermilk and bananas. Only Howard Hughes, his body wasted by drugs and neglect, did not make it into advanced age, but even he reached his allotted threescore and ten. So it is folly to predict how much longer D.K. can go on.

What will happen when he finally dies? Undoubtedly the massive corporate organization he built will continue to function for a while, but no one can tell how it will fare without his hand on the helm. Over the past few decades, a cadre of senior management people have risen to the top, where they handle most of the detail work. Among these, William E. Fisher, Jr., F. E. Kahl, F. C. Hess, J. A. Fish, F. J. Joyce, Ronald Sun, and a few others have the most responsibility and power within the Ludwig hierarchy. Little is known about these men. They seem to have almost no identity outside the organization, and they have all been with D.K. a long time. It can be assumed that they do their work well and don't make waves or question the Old Man's authority. Unless they were efficient and subservient, he would not have kept them around so long. John Notter, who in the early 1970s was the rising star in the National Bulk organization, had the temerity to disagree with Ludwig over the wisdom of the Jari investments. He is no longer on the team.

And what about Ludwig's wealth? As we have seen, most of it, including all of his known foreign holdings, has already been placed under the ownership of his Swiss cancer research foundation. The remainder — conservatively estimated at half a billion by *Forbes* — will probably end up in the control of a similar organization, the Virginia and Daniel Ludwig Foundation, Inc., based in New York.

This foundation, like the one in Zürich, was set up by Ludwig ostensibly to distribute money for cancer research. In reality, considering the vast wealth of its founder, it is an extremely modest affair. D.K. established it about a quarter century ago with a few hundred shares of stock he had purchased in a handful of companies: Mobil Oil, General Motors, Gulf Oil, TRW, Illinois Power, General Telephone & Electronics, and First Interstate Bancorp. According to a foundation report, he acquired those stocks in the spring of 1961 for a total price of around $26,500. In recent times, their collective market value has doubled, and they yield dividend income of around $3500 annually. This amount is customarily distributed to two recipients: New York City's Presbyterian Hospital ($2000 per year) and the Jackson Laboratory of Bar Harbor, Maine ($1500). As far as is known, this $3500 yearly donation from the foundation's stock dividends represents the billionaire's only contributions to charitable causes in the United States.

The New York foundation is governed by a board of directors headed by D.K.'s wife, G. Virginia Ludwig, as honorary chairman. The directors are divided into two groups. Class A members are the officers: D.K., president; Virginia, vice-president; and William E. Fisher, Jr., F. E. Kahl, and Ronald Sun, respectively, secretary, treasurer, and assistant treasurer.

Of the four Class B members, two — George Jenkins and R. Palmer Baker, Jr. — have no other known connection to the Ludwigs. But Malcolm McLean, D.K.'s rival and then partner in roll-on-roll-off shipping, and James R. Kerr, long-time head of AVCO, are identifiable. (Kerr was president during Ludwig's two three-year terms as an AVCO director, during which time the formerly stable aviation company, diversifying into financial services, land development, and other activities that National Bulk was also currently pursuing, staged a dizzying climb, followed by an even more dizzying fall into near bankruptcy — AVCO stock plummeted from $65 per share to $2.00 in a short period — before changing course and pulling out of its nosedive.)

Less is known about D.K.'s Swiss foundation. When Brazilian Congressman Modesto da Silveira went over to investigate it a few years back, he found that the Ludwig Institute for Cancer Research in Zürich was housed in a small, unprepossessing building that gave no hint of the wealth controlled there. The institute, Silveira learned, had fifty shares of stock, thirty-nine of which (78 percent) were in Ludwig's own name. At that time, John Notter, himself of Swiss descent, had six of the other shares, and the remaining five were split equally among four men — Herbert Brownell, Dr. Adolph E. Kemmerer, Dr. Hugo E. Frey, and John F. Barry — and the Swiss government. Of the men holding one share each, only the name of Brownell — U.S. attorney general under President Eisenhower and a long-time friend of Ludwig's — is easily recognizable.

Silveira was apparently unable to learn from available records how much money D.K.'s Swiss institute actually distributes for cancer research, but if the charitable giving of the New York foundation is any clue, the amount is probably not large. In all likelihood, what Ludwig saves by vesting ownership of his vast financial empire in nonprofit organizations far outweighs any donations those foundations may make to charity.

Yet their very existence makes D.K. — to those who have no reason to suspect the contrary — seem a philanthropist using his wealth for the betterment of humankind. At its 1980 graduation ceremonies, Johns Hopkins University of Baltimore saw fit to bestow on Daniel Ludwig — who never had more than eight years of formal schooling — an honorary doctorate. Despite his notorious hatred of publicity, D.K. did attend the ceremony and allowed himself to be photographed standing beside Leonard Bernstein, both of them decked out in academic regalia. In receiving the degree, Ludwig, sitting among thousands of graduates, faculty, and guests, heard himself lauded in these terms:

> Self-made man, innovator, entrepreneur, you are an industrialist of global vision.
>
> With foresight, you created one of the world's largest private shipping fleets and revolutionized the way ships are built and financed. Akin in spirit and action to the founding benefactor of this University, you have diversified your interests among many enterprises, aware always of the long-range needs of mankind.
>
> At a time in life when most men think of retirement, you began the

monumental task of converting a vast tract in the Amazon jungle into productive land — thereby adding to the world's resources and providing a livelihood for the people of that region. That venture has been described as "capitalism in the epic sense." Nor have you forgotten the virtue of charity. Among other acts, you have established and endowed a cancer research institute in Switzerland.

Daniel Keith Ludwig, in recognition of your extraordinary accomplishments in all you have undertaken, The Johns Hopkins University is proud to confer upon you the degree of Doctor of Humane Letters, *honoris causa.*

One has to wonder how Ludwig felt at the Johns Hopkins ceremony, listening to himself being praised, knowing full well that, only ten months earlier, another group of academicians at the annual conference of the Brazilian Society for the Progress of Science had hooted his forestry manager off the stage and broken up the meeting with cries of "The Amazon is ours!" and "Ludwig, go home!"

Knowing what we know of this mysterious capitalist, we must guess that he felt he was getting his just recognition at last, and that he regarded the Brazilian scientists as benighted nuisances. But could he ever admit to himself that he had been wrong from the start about the Amazon's potential for growing an alien tree? Or that those who had said it couldn't be done had been right all along?

Probably not. It is likely that D.K. will always insist on his prerogative to experiment and make mistakes, even horribly expensive ones, in the name of progress and for the pursuit of wealth. After all, his gambles have paid off — for him at least — more than they've lost, and he is still, if not *the* richest, at least *one* of the world's richest men.

How, then, do we assess his career? No matter what colors we use for his portrait, we must paint him on a large scale — much larger than life. There can be no question that he has had a very powerful impact on his time, far greater than the influence of many better-known entrepreneurs. Because he has lived, the world is a different place from what it would have been otherwise. A recent National Bulk brochure boasts that Ludwig's ships have moved an estimated *billion tons* — two trillion pounds! — of cargo from one part of the globe to another. That's roughly four tons of material for every man, woman, and child in the United States.

Most of this has been in the form of crude oil and its refined products, iron ore, salt, bauxite, kaolin, cement, limestone, coal, grain, and molasses. Much of it, of course, would have been shipped by someone else if Ludwig hadn't shipped it. But some of the things D.K. has done — the Jari project is a conspicuous example — would almost certainly not have been attempted by anyone else. He is in this respect a loner, a one-of-a-kind individualist, perhaps the last of the great empire-building capitalists.

Looked at from another angle, he is not nearly so much a loner as he is usually portrayed. A study of his career turns up quite a number of close associations and friendships, mostly with business acquaintances, to be sure, but enough to put him in a category quite apart from the paranoid Howard Hughes. It is much more accurate to regard D.K. not as *re*clusive but *ex*clusive. He sees only those few people he wants to see and avoids everyone else. Certainly he does not seem possessed of an abundance of social graces. He detests small talk, and at parties, it is said, he tends to withdraw into a corner with a few other male guests and discuss business. As a host he can be downright rude. Once, according to *Time* magazine, "he insulted a fading Hollywood star who came to dinner, and showed no remorse when she departed in tears."

Yet he has long made it a point to socialize at least occasionally with people of wealth, fame, or power — top executives of major banks, oil companies, and other corporations; celebrities like Clark Gable and Art Linkletter; heads of state like Richard Nixon, Haile Selassie, General Somoza, and Ronald Reagan; other top political figures such as George E. Allen and Herbert Brownell. Much of Ludwig's reputation as a recluse stems from the fact that most of the people he sees socially or professionally don't talk about him to outsiders, especially media representatives. This conspiracy of silence, more than any other single factor, has enabled him to retain his aura of mystery all these years. Whether the silence is based on respect, fear, or other causes is difficult to determine. D.K. is said to have kept some employees on his payroll long after they stopped working for him in order to make sure they kept their mouths closed.

But though it is true that Ludwig has taken great pains to shield his private life and business dealings from unwanted publicity, it is also true — particularly in later years — that he has sought recognition for his achievements, at least among those he wants to impress. The brochures National Bulk prepares to hand out to prospective clients are filled with self-praise and frequent references to the company's having built the world's largest this-or-that. Underlying the puffery is a tone of Ozymandias-like arrogance. "Anything you can do, I can do bigger and better," Ludwig seems to be saying. "Look on *my* works, ye mighty, and despair."

Certainly there has always been an economic motive behind D.K.'s continual upscaling — a desire to keep a jump ahead of the competition, to do it cheaper by doing it bigger. But there has always been something else as well — a compulsive one-upmanship driving him on to succeed at what lesser men consider impossible.

We can attribute it, if we like, to his childhood influences: a grandfather who was himself an empire builder of sorts; an early obsession with money; the wrenching experience of being torn away from home, mother, and classmates by his restless, authoritarian — and unscrupulous — father. We can postulate a deep insecurity based on a combination of those factors and perhaps others we have no way of knowing about.

We can add to the portrait a clever, mechanically inventive mind committed to the principle of getting the maximum utility and profit from the minimum expenditure of time, space, energy, and money. Plus an ambition that seemingly knows no limits. Plus a decided preference for deeds over words, machines over men. Plus a high degree of ruthlessness.

All of this, and luck, adds up to a man who is going to be successful and innovative. It does not, however, give us the person who for years held the title "richest man on earth." For that, we need one more ingredient, which we can call "the corporate exponent."

What this means is that Ludwig, along with a number of other nineteenth- and twentieth-century entrepreneurs, has been able to multiply his individual abilities exponentially by adroit use of the corporation as a legal, political, and financial device.

In jurisprudence, a corporation is considered a person. It is not. It is a machine, and, like other machines, it is constructed to do a job. The job of a corporate machine is to make money, and its success is measured in terms of how efficiently it does so. Being a machine, a corporation has no value system, no conscience. It neither knows nor cares whether — or what — it creates or destroys. Decisions about how it is to be used are left to its human owners.

Like many other complex machines, the corporation is largely a creation of the Industrial Revolution; it is a means for harnessing energy more effectively to do greater amounts of work. A man driving a bulldozer can move many times as much earth or push down more trees than a man using a simple, primitive tool such as a shovel or an ax.

But multiplying the power to do work can serve for good or ill. The danger comes when the machine's human owners ignore the destructive effects it is having on the world while performing its task — either because they have become so fascinated by its efficiency that they can think of nothing else, or because they are so eager to further their own ends that they care nothing for the harm they wreak on anyone or anything else. When this happens, the owners of the machine become as machines or monsters themselves, wielding enormous power to destroy.

For the sake of analogy, let's suppose that, instead of a half-drowned, waterlogged Lemuel Gulliver, a shipload of cunning, fully armed pirates had landed on the coast of Lilliput in Jonathan Swift's famous tale. Gulliver, in the original version, was able to get along nicely with his diminutive hosts because he was courteous and considerate of their needs and limitations, and was willing to help them against their enemies. But a gang of rapacious pirates, each the size of Gulliver but without his benevolence, would be able to subdue and dominate the Lilliputians, then live among them as enormous, bullying parasites.

Such, in essence, is the case with many modern corporations. Treated as persons by the law, which grants them the freedoms and privileges guaranteed to individuals, they use their size and power to dominate and control the society they inhabit. Not all corporations, of course, are piratical titans; some are useful, well-intentioned Gullivers. But those which *are* pirates generally find nothing to stand in their way — not the law, not the people, not even the corporate Gullivers.

The situation is not new. In a book called *The True American,* published in 1840, a political writer named Joseph Coe wrote the following warning to his fellow citizens:

The people must constantly remember that the great foe of American liberty is a wealthy aristocracy. It has been and ever will be, from time to time, the duty of the state and national governments to check, by legal enactments, *the influence and power of overgrown moneyed corporations;* and it is the solemn duty of the people to protect and sustain them in such enactments.

The great contest that has been waged for many years past, and now divides the people of this country, is a controversy between the real democracy on the one hand, and an aristocracy of wealth on the other. [Italics added.]

Some seventy years later, Owen Wister, author of *The Virginian* and a close friend of trustbusting President Theodore Roosevelt, wrote that the main thing the American Revolution had accomplished was to exchange the divine right of kings for the divine right of corporations. This was the period during which John D. Rockefeller was bragging that corporate combination and control of the marketplace had ended individualism and free enterprise once and for all.

The rise of Daniel Ludwig, then, has to be viewed in this context. By building layer upon layer of corporate entities, he has multiplied his own abilities and ways of making money many times over. And, on the corporate level at least, he has belied his reputation as a lone wolf in favor of being a team player, making his own operations fit neatly with those of giant oil, steel, and other interests for the purpose of mutual profits. On this level, he has never been a maverick — never once kicked over the traces, as Onassis did in making a separate deal with the king of Saudi Arabia to get an oil-hauling concession for himself.

When D.K. has rebelled, he has done so against government — against paying taxes, obeying regulations, allowing inspections. He has taken many of his operations outside the United States in order to avoid high taxation and high wages, and has sought — and gained — empire status in a number of countries that allowed him to operate outside and above the law. At the same time, he has remained in the United States as a citizen, using its conveniences and enjoying its protection, even sitting as a participant to help determine government policies as (1) an adviser to the Maritime Administration on oil and maritime matters; (2) a member of the Military Petroleum Advisory Board of the Department of Defense; (3) a member of the Advisory Board of the National Petroleum Council; and (4) a member of the Commission of the American Merchant Marine Institute.

In many respects, Daniel Ludwig's life and career have mirrored America's history in the twentieth century: his small-town boyhood; his first steps toward prosperity during World War I; his lost innocence in the Jazz Age; his financial struggles during the Great Depression; his recovery in the late thirties; his wartime contributions and profiteering; his postwar expansion throughout the world and the tremendous wealth that came as a result — all these mark him as a man very much attuned to the national experience.

Yet he can also be viewed as the antithesis of what America is supposed to stand for: privilege and exclusiveness in place of equality and democracy; miserliness instead of generosity; exploitation in lieu of aid. If he represents many of the qualities that have made the American nation great — hard work, ingenuity, thrift, imagination, organizational ability, technological achievement — he also personifies many of its worst qualities — greed, secretiveness, ruthlessness, insensitivity, arrogance, and an ever-ready willingness to put his own desires above all other considerations — country, humanity, and the natural world.

SOURCES

NOTES

INDEX

# Sources

## Newspapers

(United States) *Bergen County* (N.J.) *Record, Boston Globe, Journal of Commerce, Miami Herald, Miami News, New York Times, Parade* Sunday Supplement, *San Francisco Chronicle, Wall Street Journal, Washington Post, Wilmington* (Del.) *Morning News,* (Wilmington, Del.) *Sunday News-Journal.*

(United Kingdom) *Guardian, Daily Telegraph, Sunday Telegraph, Times, Sunday Times.*

(Bahamas) *Freeport News.*

(Brazil) *Jornal do Brasil, O Estado de São Paulo.*

## Magazines

*Americas, Brazilian Trends, Business Week, Financial World, Forbes, Fortune, Garden, Interciencia, Journal of Contemporary Asia, Life, Multinational Monitor, National Geographic, Newsweek, New York, Penthouse, Playboy, Rolling Stone, Saturday Evening Post, Saturday Review, Sundance, Time, U.S. News & World Report.*

## Newsletters

*Washington Report on the Hemisphere.*

## Files

Materials from the files of the Anthropology Resource Center, Boston, Massachusetts, and *Multinational Monitor,* Washington, D.C.

## Reference Works

*Congressional Record, Current Biography, Facts on File, Lloyd's Register of American Yachts, Lloyd's Register of Shipping, Record of the American Bureau of Shipping, Tanker Directory of the World, USCG List of Merchant Vessels of the United States, Who's Who in America.*

## Services

Tanker Advisory Service, New York City.

## Court Cases

*Detroit Fidelity & Surety v. U.S., Hoover et al. v. Allen et al., International Bank v. Price Waterhouse, U.S. v. Patten et al.*

## Interviews

With historians, librarians, Chamber of Commerce officials in the South Haven, Michigan, area; with the editor of the *Freeport* (Bahamas) *News;* with planning officials in Jersey City, N.J.; with Brazilian embassy officials; with former staff members of the Senate Select Committee on Multinationals (chaired by Senator Frank Church, 1974); with staff aides of Senator Joseph Biden, ranking Democrat on the Senate Judiciary Committee; with writers for business and other periodicals.

## Government Records

Corporation records, Department of State, State of Delaware, Dover, Del.; Shipping records pertaining to Ludwig companies, Maritime Administration, Department of Transportation, Washington, D.C.; State Department Records, National Archives, Washington, D.C.; U.S. Circuit Court records, Federal Repository, Bayonne, N.J.; U.S. Census Records, National Archives, Washington, D.C.

## Family Records

Material on the life and family of Charles Palman Ludwig, Sr., obtained through the courtesy of R. W. Appleyard, South Haven, Michigan.

## Books

Arruda, Marcos; Herbet de Souza; and Carlos Alfonso. *The Multinational Corporations and Brazil.* Toronto: Brazilian Studies, Latin American Research Unit, 1976.

Barlett, Donald L., and James B. Steele. *Empire: The Life, Legend and Madness of Howard Hughes.* New York: Norton, 1979.

Barnet, Richard J., and Ronald E. Müller. *Global Reach: The Power of the Multinational Corporations.* New York: Simon & Schuster, 1974.

Blair, John M. *The Control of Oil.* New York: Pantheon Books, 1976.

Brashler, William. *The Don: The Life and Death of Sam Giancana.* New York: Harper & Row, 1977.

Coombs, Charles: *Tankers: Giants of the Sea.* New York: Morrow, 1979.

Da Silveira, Modesto. *Ludwig: Imperador do Brasil.* Rio de Janeiro: Civilizacão Brasileira, 1981.

Drosnin, Michael. *Citizen Hughes.* New York: Holt, Rinehart & Winston, 1985.

Eisenhower, Dwight D. *Waging Peace: The White House Years, 1956–1961.* Garden City: Doubleday, 1965.

Gunther, Max. *The Very, Very Rich and How They Got That Way.* Chicago: Playboy Press, 1972.

Higham, Charles. *American Swastika.* Garden City: Doubleday, 1985.

————. *Trading With the Enemy: An Exposé of the Nazi-American Money Plot, 1933–1949.* New York: Delacorte, 1983.

Hutchinson, Robert M. *Vesco.* New York: Praeger, 1974.

Ickes, Harold. *The Secret Diary of Harold Ickes: The First Thousand Days, 1933–1936.* New York: Simon & Schuster, 1953.

Kefauver, Estes. *Crime in America.* Garden City: Doubleday, 1951.

Lamott, Kenneth. *The Moneymakers.* Boston: Little, Brown, 1969.

Lilly, Doris. *Those Fabulous Greeks: Onassis, Niarchos and Livanos.* New York: Cowles, 1970.

Lundberg, Ferdinand. *The Rich and the Super-Rich.* New York: Lyle Stuart, 1968.

————. *The Rockefeller Syndrome.* Secaucus, N.J.: Lyle Stuart, 1975.

Mahon, Gigi. *The Company That Bought the Boardwalk.* New York: Random House, 1980.

Marchetti, Victor, and John D. Marks. *The CIA and the Cult of Intelligence.* New York: Knopf, 1974.

Messick, Hank. *Lansky.* New York: Putnam's, 1971.

————. *Secret File.* New York: Putnam's, 1969.

Moldea, Dan E. *The Hoffa Wars: Teamsters, Rebels, Politicians and the Mob.* New York: Paddington Press, 1978.

Mosley, Leonard. *Dulles: A Biography of Eleanor, Allen, and John Foster Dulles and Their Family Network.* New York: Dial Press/James Wade, 1978.

Roosevelt, Elliot, with Joseph P. Lash (eds.). *FDR: His Personal Letters, 1928–1945.* New York: Duell, Sloan & Pearce, 1950.

Schlesinger, Arthur M., Jr. *Robert Kennedy and His Times.* New York: Ballantine Books, 1979.

Servadio, Gaia. *Mafioso: A History of the Mafia From Its Origins to the Present.* New York: Stein and Day, 1976.

Summers, Anthony. *Conspiracy.* New York: McGraw-Hill, 1980.

Teresa, Vincent, with Thomas C. Renner. *My Life in the Mafia.* New York: Doubleday, 1973.

Thompson, Jacqueline. *The Very Rich Book.* New York: Morrow, 1981.

Tobias, Andrew. *Fire and Ice: The Story of Charles Revson — The Man Who Built the Revlon Empire.* New York: Morrow, 1976.

Tully, Andrew. *CIA: The Inside Story.* New York: Morrow, 1962.

Waller, Leslie. *The Swiss Bank Connection.* New York: New American Library, 1972.

Wolf, George, with Joseph DiMona. *Frank Costello: Prime Minister of the Underworld.* New York: Morrow, 1974.

## *Articles*

Adde, Leo, "$40-Million Plant 'Certain' For S. Dade," *Miami Herald,* November 18, 1961.

"Alien-Flag Ships Free of U.S. Curbs," *New York Times,* November 19, 1960.

"Allied Chemical Acquires West Virginia Coal Mine," *Wall Street Journal,* November 17, 1964.

"American-Hawaiian Suspends Dividends; Announces Plans to Build a New Fleet," *New York Times,* June 24, 1955.

Amory, Cleveland, "Why the Rich Hide," *Parade* Sunday Supplement, October 17, 1982.

"Anatomy of a Failure," *Newsweek,* January 25, 1982.

Anderson, Alan, "Farming the Amazon: The Devastation Technique," *Saturday Review,* September 30, 1972.

Anderson, Jack, "Washington Merry-Go-Round: Secretive Pair," *Washington Post,* January 14, 1974.

———, "Washington Merry-Go-Round: Somoza's Millions," *San Francisco Chronicle,* September 5, 1978.

"Asia: Pilgrims in the East and West," *Newsweek,* November 8, 1954.

"The Bahamas: A Little Bit Independent," *Time,* January 24, 1964.

"Bank of America Officer Leaves to Buy Company," *New York Times,* December 27, 1982.

Bender, Marylin, "D. K. Ludwig: The Man and the Money," *New York Times,* May 2, 1976.

"The Biggest Tankers," *Time,* October 14, 1957.

"Billionaire Ludwig's Brazilian Gamble," *Time,* September 10, 1979.

"A Billionaire's Jungle Empire," *Washington Post,* April 12, 1973.

"A Billionaire's S & L Collection," *Business Week,* September 28, 1981.

Blundy, David, "After Getty, Who Is the World's Richest Man?" *Sunday Times* (London), June 13, 1976.

"Bonanza in the Bahamas," *Newsweek,* October 26, 1964.

"Brazil: A Billion-Dollar Dream Goes on the Block," *Business Week,* January 25, 1982.

"Brazilian Group Completes Purchase of Ludwig Venture," *Wall Street Journal,* January 26, 1982.

"Brazil: Ludwig's Project Flops," *Multinational Monitor,* May 1981.

"Brazil's Fitful Abertura," *Washington Report on the Hemisphere,* November 2, 1982.

Briscoe, C. B., "Intensive Management of Forest Plantations in Northern Brazil," unpublished paper by chief of forestry at Jari, circa 1970s.

"Britain: Lonrho Joins Ludwig in Its Hunt for Growth," *Business Week,* April 21, 1980.

Brooke, Jim, "Billionaire's Dream Founders in Amazon Jungle," *Washington Post,* May 31, 1981.

"Business Diary," *Times* (London), January 12, 1978.

"Business Diary," *Times* (London), October 31, 1980.

Campbell, Kenneth, "Metro Rezones South Dade Land to Restrict Future Development," *Miami Herald,* January 29, 1981.

"The Case for Seadade, as Presented by Preston Bird," *Miami Herald,* August 2, 1962.

"A Chill Wind Nips Island Hotels," *Business Week,* April 3, 1971.

"Christina Onassis Buys Supertanker from D. K. Ludwig," *Wall Street Journal,* February 22, 1977.

"Cinerama Drops Talks on Selling Stock Block to Unit of National Bulk," *Wall Street Journal,* June 7, 1971.

"Cinerama Plans to Sell Large Block of Stock to National Bulk Unit," *Wall Street Journal,* May 19, 1971.

Conway, Barbara, "The Link with Lonrho," *Sunday Telegraph* (London), February 27, 1980.

"Daniel Keith Ludwig," *Current Biography 1979.*

"Daniel K. Ludwig Is Elected a Director of Union Oil Co.," *Wall Street Journal*, July 30, 1963.

"Daniel K. Ludwig: Top Man in Tankers," *U.S. News & World Report*, October 11, 1957.

"Daniel Ludwig's Floating Factory," *Time*, June 19, 1978.

Davidson, Bill, "The Mafia: Shadow of Evil on an Island in the Sun," *Saturday Evening Post*, February 25, 1967.

Davis, Shelton, "Ludwig's Castle Built on Sand," *Multinational Monitor*, May 1980.

————, "Mr. Ludwig Comes Out of Hiding in Brazil," unpublished article from files of Anthropology Resource Center, Boston, Mass., circa 1980.

"Delafield & Delafield Is Penalized by SEC over Stock Violations," *Wall Street Journal*, December 27, 1968.

"D. K. Ludwig Plans to Harvest a Jungle," *Business Week*, July 31, 1971.

Einstein, Paul, "Refinery Pumps Hope into Dade," *Miami Herald*, November 18, 1961.

————, "Seadade Attacked by U.S. Agencies," *Miami Herald*, December 21, 1962.

"End of a Billion-Dollar Dream," *Time*, January 25, 1982, p. 59.

"Ex-Wife Sues Tycoon Ludwig for $10 Million," *San Francisco Chronicle*, January 27, 1978.

"The Face of an Unknown Multi-Millionaire," *Telegraph* Sunday Magazine, February 27, 1980.

Fearnside, Philip M., and Judy M. Rankin, "Jari and Development in the Brazilian Amazon," *Interciencia*, May–June 1980.

"55,000-Ton Ship for Oil or Ore, World's Largest, on First Trip," *New York Times*, November 28, 1955.

"The Fight for the Amazon," *Newsweek*, January 25, 1982.

"Final Pleas Heard in Suit to Prevent Picketing of Vessel," *New York Times*, November 29, 1960.

"Financiers to Back Brokerage House," *New York Times*, July 30, 1966.

Flanagan, Richard, "The Richest Man in America Walks to Work," *New York*, November 28, 1977.

"Floating Assets," *Sunday Times* (London), May 7, 1978.

"A Floating Warehouse to Speed Coal Exports," *Business Week*, November 16, 1981.

"The Forbes Four Hundred," *Forbes*, Fall 1983.

"The Forbes Four Hundred," *Forbes*, Fall 1984.

"*Fortune* Reports on Millionaires," *New York Times*, April 29, 1968.

Friedlander, Paul J. C., "Acapulco's Brand New 'Aztec Pyramid,'" *New York Times*, December 12, 1979.

373

Gall, Norman, "Ludwig's Amazon Empire," *Forbes,* May 14, 1979.

Gemmill, Henry, "Shipbuilding Champ: Rocket Rise of Japan's Yards Gets Lots of Its Steam from Americans," *Wall Street Journal,* May 20, 1957.

"General Host Unit Buys Solar Salt Co. for Cash," *Wall Street Journal,* September 12, 1972.

Gerth, Jeff, "Nixon and the Mafia," *Sundance,* Spring 1972.

"Giant Development Eyed in South Dade," *Miami Herald,* June 8, 1959.

"Government Loses in Court," *New York Times,* July 13, 1955.

Greene, Juanita, "How Much Industry? Dade Must Decide," *Miami Herald,* December 21, 1962.

———, "Waterfront Protection Beginning," *Miami Herald,* November 25, 1979.

"Gulf Orders Six Huge Tankers," *New York Times,* April 27, 1966.

"Here Come Supertrees," *Newsweek,* November 24, 1980.

Hinckle, Warren, and William W. Turner, "The Mystery of 544 Camp Street," *Penthouse,* October, 1981.

Hoge, Warren, "Ludwig May Cut Brazil Project," *New York Times,* October 16, 1980.

———, "$1 Billion Venture in Amazon Is Given Up by U.S. Financier," *New York Times,* January 15, 1982.

———, "U.S. Magnate, Once Assailed, Is Hailed for Amazon Project," *New York Times,* November 30, 1979.

Hougan, Jim, "The Plot to Wreck the Golden Greek," *Playboy,* September, 1978.

"How the Amazon Defeated an American Millionaire," *Times* (London), January 26, 1982.

"Industrialist Clears $46 Million on Sale of Union Oil Stock," *New York Times,* February 13, 1965.

"Investment Filing Is Sought by SEC," *New York Times,* November 13, 1958.

James, Lewis, "The Billion-Dollar Dream of America's Richest Man," *Sunday Telegraph* (London), September 9, 1979.

"Japan: Ambush for Yoshida," *Newsweek,* November 22, 1954.

"Japan: Out — Or What?" *Newsweek,* December 6, 1954.

"Japan: Tempest at Teatime," *Newsweek,* September 27, 1954.

"Japan: The Atomic Fisherman," *Newsweek,* October 4, 1954.

"Japan: The Twin Blade of Crisis," *Newsweek,* November 29, 1954.

"Jari: Improved Utilization of Tropical Forests Silviculture in Plantation Development," unpublished paper presented at a University of Wisconsin forestry workshop, May 1978.

Kandell, Jonathan, "The Expanding Empire of a Quiet Tycoon," *New York Times,* May 2, 1976.

Karmin, Monroe W., and Stanley Penn, "Las Vegas East: U.S. Gamblers Prosper in Bahamas with Help from Island Officials," *Wall Street Journal,* October 5, 1966.

"Killing of Indians Charged in Brazil," *New York Times,* March 21, 1968.

Kinkead, Gwen, "Trouble in D. K. Ludwig's Jungle," *Fortune,* April 20, 1981.

Kohn, Howard, "The Hughes-Nixon-Lansky Connection: The Secret Alliances of the CIA from World War II to Watergate," *Rolling Stone,* May 20, 1976.

"Largest Ore Ship Sails," *New York Times,* January 31, 1955.

"The Last Billionaires," *Fortune,* November, 1976.

Lee, John M., "Queen Helps Gulf Oil Open Wales Refinery," *New York Times,* August 12, 1968.

"Letter Scuttles Ship Stock Boom," *New York Times,* January 24, 1956.

"Line Chides I.C.C. on Rate Policies," *New York Times,* April 17, 1960.

"Line Renames Chief," *New York Times,* March 18, 1958.

"Line Will Build Ten Trailer Ships," *New York Times,* August 27, 1955.

"Lonrho May Have Deals with Ludwig," *Daily Telegraph* (London), October 16, 1981.

"Lonrho Takes £36m Stake in U.S. Hotel Group," *Times* (London), September 1, 1979.

Lucoff, Morton, "Court Backs Rejection of South Dade Project," *Miami News,* February 20, 1982.

"Ludwig, Daniel K.," *Who's Who in America, 1978–79.*

"Ludwig: No Profit on a Plate," *Sunday Telegraph* (London), September 9, 1979.

"Ludwig Concern to Pay $13.2 Million for Coal Interests in Australia," *Wall Street Journal,* February 24, 1965.

"Ludwig King's Inn Hotel Opens," *Freeport News,* January 29, 1965.

"Ludwig Raises Offer," *New York Times,* June 11, 1968.

"Ludwig's Jari Dream Turns Sour," *Daily Telegraph* (London), September 27, 1981.

"The Man Who's the World's Richest Now," *San Francisco Chronicle,* July 2, 1976.

"March On, Bahamaland," *Newsweek,* July 16, 1973.

McDowell, Edwin, "The Amazon: A New Search for El Dorado," *New York Times Magazine,* November 22, 1981.

McGrath, Anne, "Resorts' Action Hints at Sale of 1 Casino," *Wilmington* (Del.) *Morning News,* October 16, 1985.

McIntyre, Loren, "Jari: A Billion-Dollar Gamble," *National Geographic,* May 1980.

"Meet Daniel Ludwig, the New 'World's Richest,'" *Boston Globe,* July 2, 1976.

Meyer, Phil, "New Ordinance in Nine Months Is Dade's Goal," *Miami Herald,* January 12, 1962.

"Mr. Ludwig's Tropical Dreamland," *NOVA* (a public television program script), circa 1980.

"Mitsubishi Buys Salt Firm in Mexico for $20 Million," *Wall Street Journal,* April 11, 1973.

"Molding a Future for the Amazon Basin," *San Francisco Chronicle,* August 11, 1978.

Morrow, Edward A., "Union Faces Fight with Big Ship Line," *New York Times,* October 28, 1960.

Murphy, Richard C., Neal Shapiro, William Vogel, and Charles Eilers, "Amazon: River of the Future," a Cousteau Society Teachers' Guide (for use with a film of the same title), Atlanta, 1983.

"National Bulk Carriers, Conoco to Build Refinery in Panama," *Wall Street Journal,* February 22, 1960.

"National Bulk Carriers Plans Iron-Ore Venture," *Wall Street Journal,* May 17, 1968.

"National Bulk Carriers Proposes $230 Million Oil Refinery in Scotland," *Wall Street Journal,* December 13, 1972.

"National Bulk Carriers Unit Plans $40 Million Oil Refinery in Florida," *Wall Street Journal,* November 24, 1961.

"National Bulk Pulls Out of Joint Australian Project," *Wall Street Journal,* July 15, 1969.

"The New Argonauts," *Time,* August 6, 1956.

"Once a Sailor . . ." *New York Times,* December 6, 1958.

"On the Crest of the Sea," *Newsweek,* October 14, 1957.

"Orders All to Jail in Volstead Cases," *New York Times,* December 16, 1922.

"Ore Ship Pickets Upheld by Court," *New York Times,* December 16, 1960.

Oulahan, Richard, and William Lambert, "The Scandal in the Bahamas," *Life,* February 3, 1967.

Penn, Stanley, "Mary Carter Paint Co. Plans to Take Over Gambling Permit, Casino in British Bahamas," *Wall Street Journal,* June 14, 1967.

————, "Mary Carter Paint Stock Breezes High with Casino, Calypso of Paradise Island," *Wall Street Journal,* January 19, 1968.

Penn, Stanley, and Monroe Karmin, "Kingdom in the Sun: Tough-Willed American Turns a Bahamas Island into Thriving Enterprise," *Wall Street Journal,* October 19, 1966.

"Personality: A Golden Touch with Capital," *New York Times,* April 18, 1965.

Peterson, Charles, "Who Is America's Richest Man?" *Boston Globe,* August 1, 1976.

"Picketing of Ships Is Scored in Dissent," *New York Times,* December 12, 1960.

"Pickets in Mix-Up; Ore Ship Unloads," *New York Times,* December 20, 1960.

"Plea Is Allowed in Picketing Case," *New York Times,* November 16, 1960.

"Pot Shots," *Time,* February 13, 1984.

"The Private Amazon Kingdom of Mr. Daniel K. Ludwig," *Times* (London), February 27, 1980.

"Proxy Solicitor Asks Liquidation," *New York Times,* April 29, 1958.

"Pulp Plant Will Float on Amazon," *Journal of Commerce,* December 31, 1976.

"Raid on Gorini's Nets $50,000 Rum," *New York Times,* July 29, 1922.

"Retraction," *Rolling Stone,* April 28, 1983.

"The Richest Men in America," *Newsweek,* August 2, 1976.

Roberts, John G., "The Lockheed-Japan-Watergate Connection," *Journal of Contemporary Asia,* Spring 1976.

"A Rough Road Ahead for the Newest Nation," *U.S. News & World Report,* November 26, 1973.

Saunders, Dero A., "The Wide Oceans of D. K. Ludwig," *Fortune,* May, 1957.

"Seadade Port Called Vital to Dade Economy," *Miami Herald,* November 19, 1962.

"Sea Union Declares 3 Crews Organized," *New York Times,* December 3, 1960.

"Sea Union Hearing Put Off by N.L.R.B.," *New York Times,* December 10, 1960.

Seglem, Lee, "N.J. Panel Renews Resorts' License," *Wilmington* (Del.) *Morning News,* February 27, 1985.

"Seize British Ship, $200,000 in Liquor," *New York Times,* August 13, 1922.

"$700M Complex in Jersey City," *Bergen County* (N.J.) *Record,* April 14, 1985.

"A $700 Million Plan for Jersey City's Shore," *New York Times,* May 12, 1985.

"The Shepherd & His Lambs," *Time,* January 19, 1968.

"Ship Jobs Drop, Institute Says," *New York Times,* March 14, 1960.

"Ship-Pickets' Ban Voided by Court," *New York Times,* April 19, 1961.

"Shipping Concern Protests Pickets," *New York Times,* October 29, 1960.

"Shipping Events: Merger in Japan," *New York Times,* September 13, 1967.

"A Shipping King Comes Ashore," *Business Week,* November 23, 1963.

"Skipper Accused of Plot to Run Rum," *New York Times,* August 17, 1922.

"Small Change for a Billionaire," *Business Week,* March 21, 1977.

"Some Trading in Mary Carter Paint Stock by Outsiders Is Subject of Inquiry by SEC," *Wall Street Journal,* June 25, 1968.

Steif, William, "Al Capone Is Name Used to Lure Tourists to Island; St. Pierre Revels in Prohibition Days That Brought Gangsters There," (Wilmington, Del.) *Sunday News-Journal,* October 14, 1985.

"Tanker King Who Shuns Crown," *Business Week,* March 16, 1957.

"Tanker's Loss to Mean Unusually Heavy Bill to U.S. Ship Insurers," *Wall Street Journal,* December 14, 1960.

"Texaco Buys Control of Refinery in Panama," *Wall Street Journal,* September 1, 1971.

"This Man Ludwig," *Time,* August 2, 1963.

Thompson, Jacqueline, "The Ten Richest Americans: Who They Are, What They Do, and How They Got Their Money," *Financial World,* September 15, 1978.

"Three Banks Defy Order to Return Funds to Lebanon Branch Here," *New York Times,* October 19, 1966.

"Tiny, Ludwig and the House of Frazer," *Sunday Telegraph* (London), September 2, 1979.

"Twilight of a Tycoon," *Time,* November 30, 1970.

"$250,000 in Liquors Seized with 3 Ships," *New York Times,* July 28, 1922.

"276,000-Ton Tanker Begun by Japanese," *New York Times,* October 8, 1967.

"2-Way Cargo Ship Now Major Boon," *New York Times,* September 18, 1955.

"Tycoon Loses Millions in Amazon Pulp Plant," *Boston Globe,* April 2, 1981.

"Union Protests to Labor Board," *New York Times,* November 10, 1960.

"Unlocking Amazonia," *Americas,* April, 1980.

"Vesco Redux," *Time,* September 19, 1983.

Wade, Robert, "N.J. Still at Odds on Casino Gamble," *Wilmington* (Del.) *Morning News,* May 23, 1983.

———, "Resorts Int'l Defends Itself in N.J. Casino License Probe," (Wilmington, Del.) *Sunday News-Journal,* February 17, 1985.

Wardlow, Jean, "The Big Refinery Debate: What Your Neighbors Say," *Miami Herald,* June 8, 1962.

Weitzel, Pete, "Seadade Refinery Killed," *Miami Herald,* June 12, 1964.

"We Say Yes to Seadade," *Miami Herald* editorial, March 19, 1963.

"When Giants Marry," *Fortune,* October 8, 1979.

"Williams Brothers Co., National Bulk Propose Pipeline Across Panama," *Wall Street Journal,* April 3, 1969.

Wolfe, Laurie, "Daniel K. Ludwig: Global Businessman," unpublished paper from files of Anthropology Resource Center, Boston, Mass., circa 1980.

# Notes

## 1. The Richest Man Alive

*New York* magazine photographer episode: This is from Richard Flanagan's article "The Richest Man in America Walks to Work" (*New York,* November 28, 1977, pp. 56–58). I have taken the liberty of putting into the mind of Morris Warman, the waiting photographer, information gleaned from other sources: "The New Argonauts" (*Time,* August 6, 1956, pp. 55 ff); "Tanker King Who Shuns Crown" (*Business Week,* March 16, 1957, pp. 105–108); Dero Saunders's article "The Wide Oceans of D. K. Ludwig" (*Fortune,* May, 1957, pp. 171 ff); "A Shipping King Comes Ashore" (*Business Week,* November 23, 1963, pp. 88–97). Much of the material about Onassis, Niarchos, and Livanos is from Doris Lilly's *Those Fabulous Greeks* (N.Y.: Cowles, 1970) and *Time*'s "New Argonauts" piece. Facts about the Mideast War are from contemporary news accounts.

Shipping data: I am indebted to Lennie Thomas of the Maritime Administration for his explanation of gross, net, and deadweight tonnage. Other information is from *Lloyd's Register of Shipping* and *Lloyd's Register of American Yachts.*

## 2. South Haven

The town's history: Information about South Haven's past comes from histories of the area and from telephone conversations with local journalists, historians, reference librarians, and Chamber of Commerce officials.

Charles Palman Ludwig and family: A short, fragmentary family history, evidently written for genealogical purposes, was supplied by R.W. Appleyard, historian of the South Haven area. He also furnished a copy of the *South Haven Sentinel* letter and an old photo of the *Mary Ludwig.* Quotes in the text about C. P. Ludwig and his family are from the family history.

Daniel F. Ludwig and family: The citation from the *South Haven Directory* was supplied by an area librarian. Other information has been excerpted from U.S. Census records in the National Archives.

D. K. Ludwig's boyhood: The only details available are those given by Ludwig himself to Dero Saunders for the 1957 *Fortune* article.

Psychological analysis of the rich: Taken from Max Gunther's *The Very, Very Rich and How They Got That Way* (Chicago: Playboy Press, 1972).

The *Lusitania* episode: From the account in Colin Simpson's *The Sinking of the Lusitania* (London: Longman's, 1972).

Woodrow Wilson and Prohibition: Information from numerous books on the Wilson presidency and the Prohibition era.

*Idlewylde* purchase: From Saunders interview.

## 3. The Mosher *Incident*

The liquor war: This summary has been put together from Richard Hammer's *"Playboy*'s History of Organized Crime, Part II: Chicago and the Prohibition Years"* (September, 1973, pp. 145 ff) and from other books and articles about the Prohibition era.

Frank Costello and St. Pierre: See George Wolf, with Joseph DiMona, *Frank Costello: Prime Minister of the Underworld* (New York: Morrow, 1974).

Al Capone and St. Pierre: See William Steif, "Al Capone Is Name Used to Lure Tourists to Island; St. Pierre Revels in Prohibition Days That Brought Gangsters There" (Wilmington, Del. *Sunday News-Journal,* October 14, 1985, p. A4F). A South Haven area reference librarian recounted to the author in a telephone interview that Capone maintained a hideout and branch base of operations in South Haven during his reign as king of Chicago bootlegging.

The one-league versus four-league limit: This argument is spelled out clearly in documents in the *Mosher* file in the State Department records at the National Archives.

The *Mosher* capture: See "$250,000 in Liquors Seized with 3 Ships" (*New York Times,* July 28, 1922, p. 3). See also documents in the *Mosher* file referred to above and in the *Mosher* case record of New York's Eastern District Federal Court, stored in the federal repository, Bayonne, N.J.

Captain Gilbert's capture: See "Skipper Accused of Plot to Run Rum" (*New York Times,* August 17, 1922, p. 17).

Charles Evans Hughes: Hughes's involvement in the *Mosher* case, his correspondence with Mabel Walker Willebrandt, Sir Auckland Geddes, and others, are all detailed in the National Archives' *Mosher* file, which also contains the court decisions concerning the episode. Details of Hughes's meeting with President Harding and the other Cabinet members are in State Department files in the National Archives.

### 4. *The* Ulysses *Imbroglio*

Ludwig's early years in oil transportation: Many of the details of D.K.'s career between 1923 and 1930 come from the *Fortune* interview. Other details are from Maritime files and shipping records in the Department of Transportation library.

21 West Street: The office D.K. set up in Manhattan for American Tankers was less than half a mile — a ten-minute walk — from both 28 South Street (where the Ludwigs, according to grand jury testimony in the *Mosher* case, maintained an apartment) and 150 Broadway (where Ludwig and Gilbert had their Globe Line offices). This proximity is further evidence that the Daniel Ludwig of the *Mosher* crew and the Daniel Ludwig of American Tankers Corporation were the same person.

The David C. Reid Company: The nature of this company is obscure. Though it was supposedly a shipper and importer, the only record of it found in Maritime files is in connection with Ludwig.

The *Dannedaike* and the *Overbrook:* Saunders does not mention these in his *Fortune* article, but both appear in U.S. shipping records as vessels owned briefly by American Tankers Corporation in the mid-1920s.

Ludwig's first wife: The statements of the elderly caller identifying himself as a former friend of Ludwig's were relayed to the author by the South Haven Chamber of Commerce official who received the call. Other information about Gladys Madeline Ludwig is from "Ex-Wife Sues Tycoon Ludwig for $10 Million" (*San Francisco Chronicle,* January 27, 1978) and "Twilight of a Tycoon" (*Time,* November 30, 1970, p. 77).

American Steamship Corporation: The information is from its charter and annual reports in Delaware corporation files and from Maritime records, File 501-12.

He always preferred doing business with friends: In the *Fortune* article, Saunders quotes D.K. as saying: "I like to do business with friends. Why the hell should I deal with somebody who isn't my friend?"

Robert W. Malone: Malone's relationship with Ludwig is based on Maritime records from the mid-1920s through the mid-1940s. His earlier career has been pieced together from *New York Times* articles. His activities on behalf of United Dry Dock were reported in the *Congressional Record* during 1935 in connection with the Senate Munitions Committee's investigation into bid rigging and influence peddling in the granting of government shipbuilding contract awards.

*Ulysses* purchase and renovation loans: See memo in American Tanker Corporation file from Construction Loan Committee to U.S. Shipping Board, dated October 21, 1929, Maritime Administration records (501-12).

Default on the *Ulysses* construction loan: From extensive correspondence in Maritime files between the Shipping Board and Ludwig and Malone during the early 1930s, a period in which Ludwig was desperately trying to hang on to the ship and stave off board efforts to foreclose (File 501-12).

Secretary of Commerce Daniel Roper: See mentions of Roper in *The Secret Diary of Harold Ickes* (New York: Simon & Schuster, 1953) and *FDR: His Personal Letters* (New York: Duell, Sloan & Pearce, 1950).

Ludwig's oil-hauling contract with the fascist government of Italy: This is revealed in a letter from Ludwig to the Shipping Board dated October 29, 1935, in Maritime's American Tanker Corporation file. Another Ludwig letter, dated November 1, confirms that the charter was being handled through the David C. Reid Company. Peacock's letters to Johnson and his scrawled memo after receiving the call from Roosevelt are in the same file.

Roosevelt's policy toward the Mussolini government: See *FDR Letters.*

Richard Washburn Child: See Mussolini's autobiography.

Emperor Haile Selassie's visit with Ludwig: Mentioned in "Twilight of a Tycoon" (*Time,* November 30, 1970, p. 77).

Dern's letter to Roper: Dated January 3, 1936, in Maritime's Amtankers file.

Pending sale of *Jay:* In a letter from Ludwig to Shipping Board dated April 15, 1936, in Maritime's Amtankers file.

Transford, Tankers Oceanic, National Petroleum Transport, and American Petroleum Transport Corporations: Charters and records of these companies are found in Delaware corporation records. The ships they owned are listed in shipping records at the Department of Transportation library.

National Bulk Carriers: Its charter is also in Delaware corporation records. Its purpose is set forth in correspondence between Ludwig and the Shipping Board, found in Maritime's files (905-1-32).

## 5. The Rockefeller Connection

Phoenix Steamship Corporation: Its existence is documented in Delaware corporation records and in correspondence between Ludwig and the Shipping Board and Maritime Commission (see File 309-44).

The *Webster* and *Adams:* Present-day Maritime officials are unable to account for the fact that records of the sale of these two ships to Ludwig are missing.

John D. Rockefeller: The sketch of his career in oil has been pieced together from several biographies.

The Achnacarry Agreement and the oil cartel: This information has been compiled from John M. Blair's *The Control of Oil* (New York: Pantheon, 1976) and from conversations with staff members of the Senate Multinationals Committee (The Church Committee), which, during 1974, investigated abuses in the oil industry following the 1973 Arab boycott.

Ginger Ludwig: D.K.'s second wife is mentioned in *Time*'s "Twilight of a Tycoon" and in other articles. Her name also appears as a director of several of her husband's corporations, including the Swiss and U.S. cancer research foundations.

Daniel F. Ludwig's disappearance: See Delaware corporation records, which show that after 1938 Daniel F. Ludwig's name did not appear as an officer or director of any of the companies he had previously been associated with. Vital statistics records of Connecticut, where he was last reported living, did not turn up evidence that he had died.

## 6. *D.K. Welshes on a Deal*

FDR's abolishing of the Shipping Board: This is recounted in news stories of the time and is detailed in Maritime's records. The president's disillusionment with Secretary Roper is apparent in his letters and in Ickes's diary.

Malone's letter to Knight: Dated January 20, 1937, it is in Maritime's Amtankers file. Bidding for the *Invincible* and other ships is described in the National Bulk Carriers file at Maritime (905-1-32), as is Ludwig's action on the purchase agreement for the *Invincible*.

The Phoenix loan: The Chemical Bank loan officer's anecdote is in Saunders's *Fortune* article.

The Neutrality Acts and flag-of-convenience shipping: The material is to be found in histories of the period. The Neutrality Acts appear to have been enacted because of the failed boycott of oil and other vital materials to Italy. FDR's efforts to get around the Neutrality Acts in order to ship oil to Britain resulted in a windfall to oil companies and shippers.

Carl Farbach: The efforts of the Maritime Commission's general counsel to prevent Ludwig's reneging on the *Invincible* are detailed in the National Bulk file at Maritime (905-1-32).

## 7. *The War Years*

American and British industrialists with Nazi leanings: Charles Higham, in his books *Trading With the Enemy* (New York: Delacorte, 1983) and *American Swastika* (Garden City: Doubleday, 1985), has described the activities of these companies.

Welding Shipyard: Ludwig's shipyard activities, and his fight with Maritime over upgrading crew's quarters, are detailed in Welding and National Bulk files at Maritime (503-60, 905-1-32, 610-58, 302-5-60).

*Time* quote: November 30, 1977, p. 30.

Lamott quote: From *The Moneymakers* (Boston: Little, Brown, 1969, pp. 33–34).

Livanos anecdote: Quoted from Lilly, *Those Fabulous Greeks* (New York: Cowles, 1970).

Ludwig's shipbuilding innovations: Taken mostly from Saunders's *Fortune* article.

His wartime shipping activities: These are available in the files of D.K.'s various companies at Maritime (see files note above and 302-5-157).

Welding Shipyard officers and directors: Listed in Delaware corporation records.

Maritime corruption: Senator Aiken's charges are set forth in the *Congressional Record.*

The Ludwigs in Darien: See "Twilight of a Tycoon" (*Time,* November 30, 1970, p. 77) and Gunther, p. 184.

## 8. The Maritime Scandals

Ludwig's postwar surplus ship deals: These are documented in Maritime's files on National Bulk Carriers and other Ludwig-owned companies (905-1-32, 302-5-157).

Standard Oil of New Jersey's wartime petroleum shipments to Nazi Germany: See Higham, *Trading With the Enemy.* As to Onassis, it is a matter of record that Nazi U-boats operating in the Western Hemisphere used the waters just off Argentina for staging areas and refueling depots. See Jim Hougan's "The Plot to Wreck the Golden Greek" (*Playboy,* September 1978, pp. 94 ff).

Ludwig's Panamanian companies: D.K. notified Maritime that he was setting up these corporations and transferring some of his U.S.-flag fleet to them. The notifications are in Maritime's files (905-1-32).

Ludwig's secret deal with the Navy: Documents in the National Bulk file at Maritime show how D.K. was able to get around Maritime regulations with the Navy's cooperation and send out his supertankers under foreign flags without first putting them under the U.S. flag. If anyone at Maritime caught on to what was happening, the file records give no hint of it (905-1-32).

The Maritime investigations: Most of the material in this section is from the *Congressional Record* and from *Facts on File,* as well as from newspaper accounts. Ludwig's part in the scandal has been pieced together from Maritime's files, though neither he nor his companies are mentioned by name in the transcripts of the congressional hearings.

## 9. Going Japanese

Senator Brewster's letter: This was reported in the *Congressional Record* for 1949.

## 10. Grand Bahama Island

The Bahama Islands: This brief historical glimpse has been drawn from a variety of sources. The comment by the "native" was made to me during a stay in Freeport.

Wallace Groves: Groves's early history has been pieced together from contemporary newspaper accounts of his career and trial. His later adventures in the Bahamas are based on accounts of Bahamas gambling in the *Wall Street Journal, Life, Saturday Evening Post, New York Times*, etc., during 1966–67.

Sands and the Bay Street Boys: These facts are also in the aforementioned exposés of Bahamian gambling in U.S. periodicals and in testimony given to the Royal Commission of Inquiry.

The founding of Freeport: The account is taken from the sources just mentioned.

Charles R. Allen, Jr.: See his biography in the *"Forbes* List of the 400 Richest Americans."

Dredging of Freeport Harbor: Documentation of Ludwig's construction and operation of dredges at this time is in Maritime's files.

Sir Charles Hayward and the Grand Bahama Port Authority: This is from the gambling exposé stories and the Royal Commission of Inquiry testimony.

Ludwig's plans for a Grand Bahama shipyard and lime plant: This story, based on the Earl of Ranfurly's premature press release, appeared in the *New York Times.*

Con-Tech: This method of construction, for which Ludwig apparently owned the patents, is detailed in the National Bulk Carriers' brochure issued around 1974. Surprisingly, no stories about this method seem to have appeared anywhere, even though, at the time the brochure came out, Ludwig had 100,000 housing units completed or under construction, in addition to hotels and stores.

Exportadora de Sal: Described in several of the early magazine stories about Ludwig.

The Panama refinery: Mentioned in several magazine and newspaper articles. The account of Ludwig's personally sounding the depths of the harbor at Colón is taken from *Business Week*'s "A Shipping King Comes Ashore" (November 23, 1963).

## *11. Seadade*

The Seadade development: This story drew almost no attention in the national media. Nearly all the information in this chapter has been gleaned from stories that appeared in the *Miami Herald* and *Miami News* from 1959 until recently.

## *12. American-Hawaiian*

American-Hawaiian's history: This has been compiled from Maritime's records (File QM11) and stories in the *New York Times.*

RORO and the Teamsters: Beck, who headed the West Coast Teamsters, seems to have been fond of taking bribes, as revealed in the transcripts of his trial.

Ludwig's control of American-Hawaiian Steamship Company: Some of this information came from *New York Times* articles, but most is from the American-Hawaiian files at Maritime (QM11).

The containership subsidy fight: Maritime's files contain the story of this struggle (QM11).

Loring R. Hoover: Hoover's losing battle to halt Ludwig's takeover of AHSS is revealed in Maritime's American-Hawaiian file (QM11) and in the court records of *Hoover et al. v. Allen et al.*

Albertson Ranch and Westlake Village: The information comes from a variety of sources, chief among them *Business Week*'s "A Shipping King Comes Ashore" (November 23, 1963, p. 92), Delaware corporation records, and National Bulk Carriers' brochure.

Union Oil deal: See the "Shipping King" article and *New York Times* stories covering the Union stock purchase and sale.

Frank Sinatra and *Robin and the 7 Hoods:* This information is from contemporary reviews of the movie.

Ludwig's control of Westlake area realty companies: See Delaware corporation records and *Business Week*'s "A Billionaire's S & L Collection" (September 28, 1981, p. 102).

Ludwig's Australian ventures: This comes mostly from National Bulk Carriers' brochure of the mid-1970s.

The longshoreman strike: Accounts of this were carried in New York and Philadelphia newspapers during the early 1960s.

Use of political influence to obtain government mortgage money: Letters documenting this are in Maritime's American-Hawaiian files (QM11), including the one from Donald Alexander to Hodges denying that pressure was involved in the decision to reject Ludwig's application.

Nuclear-powered containerships: From documents in Maritime's files (QM11).

The deal with Sea-Land: Also documented in Maritime's American-Hawaiian files (QM11). Various business periodicals reported the sale and the amounts involved.

## 13. Freeport

Meyer Lansky and Batista: Lansky's Havana connection has been documented in numerous books and articles.

Lou Chesler: Chesler's role has been explored in such investigative articles as Jeff Gerth's "Nixon and the Mafia" (*Sundance,* Spring 1972) and the Pulitzer Prize–winning series by Stanley Penn and Monroe Karmin in the *Wall Street Journal.*

Chesler's meeting with Lansky: Chesler himself, during testimony before the Royal Commission of Inquiry, gave details of this meeting.

Sands's manipulation of the Bahamas Executive Council: This also was in testimony before the Royal Commission, as reported in the *New York Times.*

The Seven Arts fiasco: These pieces are put together from news stories about the film industry at the time.

Ludwig's development of Bahamia: Derived from various sources including the *Freeport News,* the National Bulk brochure, several newspaper and magazine articles, and interviews with Freeport residents.

The Onassis precedent: The purchase of Monte Carlo by Onassis is detailed in Lilly's *Those Fabulous Greeks* and other sources.

## 14. Whiteford

Shipbuilding at Kure: From merchant shipping records in the Department of Commerce library.

W. H. Whiteford: The material is drawn from biographical sources, news articles, and testimony before congressional committees during the Watergate investigation.

The Whiteford-Ludwig Bantry tanker deal: For the tip that led to my learning of this episode, I am grateful to a Washington, D.C., attorney who served as counsel to one of the congressional committees investigating oil industry abuses during the 1974 oil crisis.

Ludwig's close ties with IHI: See "The Last Billionaires" (*Fortune,* November, 1976, p. 226).

Shearson, Hammill and Sellin, Forbes & Smith: Information about these brokerages was taken from stories in the *New York Times* during 1965–68.

The Bantry Bay tanker explosion and oil spill: As reported in *Facts on File* and *New York Times* stories.

Ludwig's scrapping and sale of the Bantry tankers: For this information I am grateful to Art McKenzie of the Tanker Advisory Service, New York City. I learned about the renaming of three of the ships from merchant shipping records at the Department of Commerce.

## 15. The Royal Commission of Inquiry

Pindling's New York press conference: As reported in the *New York Times.*

The Royal Commission hearings: Much of this is taken from a series of stories the *New York Times* ran on the hearings during 1967.

Allen Manus and Atlantic Acceptance Corporation: As reported in the *Wall Street Journal* and business periodicals.

Cohen and Lansburgh: These Miami Beach hotel men are mentioned in frequent articles on organized crime as associates of Meyer Lansky.

## 16. Hughes

Howard R. Hughes: Although I consulted many sources about Hughes's life and career, the two I most relied on are Don Barlett and Jim Steele's *Empire: The Life, Legend and Madness of Howard Hughes* (New York: Norton, 1979) and Michael Drosnin's *Citizen Hughes* (New York: Holt, Rinehart & Winston, 1985). Both books, quoting liberally from Hughes's own memos, give an intimate picture of the man, his thoughts, and his phobias, at least during certain periods of his life.

Robert A. Maheu: Both the Barlett-Steele and the Drosnin books deal in detail with the relationship between Hughes and Maheu.

Maheu's bribing of the Bay Street Boys: Told in *Empire,* p. 230.

Hughes's purchase of Vegas casino-hotels: Compiled from many sources.

The 1969 Hughes-Ludwig meeting: From "The Washington Merry-Go-Round," *Washington Post* (January 14, 1974, p. B11).

Hughes memo mentioning Crosby as a rival for Laxalt: *Citizen Hughes,* p. 112.

Hughes memo to Maheu about selling out and leaving Vegas: *Citizen Hughes,* p. 368.

Hughes memo on founding a new community: *Citizen Hughes,* p. 369.

Hughes memo on choice of Bahamas or Mexico; Ludwig's empire status in Freeport: *Citizen Hughes,* pp. 369–370.

"One tiger to each hill": *Citizen Hughes,* p. 371.

Hughes's blast at Maheu: Quoted in *Empire,* p. 473.

The Acapulco Princess grand opening: Travel editor Paul J. C. Friedlander wrote up the event in the *New York Times* (December 12, 1971, sec. X, p. 29). Ludwig's guest list for the three-day celebration is in Marylin Bender's "D. K. Ludwig: The Man and the Money" (*New York Times,* May 2, 1976, sec. III, pp. 1, 16). This demonstrates that Ludwig's friendship with both Somoza and Ronald Reagan dates back to at least 1971. Ludwig's no-explanation firing of the hotel's manager after the opening is told in William Flanagan's "The Richest Man in America Walks to Work" (*New York*, November 28, 1977, p. 56).

Somoza family ties to United States: A good summary is given on page 535 of *Facts on File* for 1979. Also see Jack Anderson's "Washington Merry-Go-Round" article "Somoza's Millions" (*San Francisco Chronicle*, September 5, 1978).

Somoza and Hughes: See Drosnin, pp. 432–433, and Barlett and Steele, pp. 475, 478, 486–488.

Hughes memo on Somoza gift: Quoted in Drosnin, p. 432.

Somoza's use of emergency aid following the earthquake: The Nicaraguan dictator's usurpation and abuse of aid moneys drew much notice in the world press. *Facts on File* is again a good source.

The Ludwig-Somoza joint venture: Mentioned in the Jack Anderson column, "Somoza's Millions," referred to above. Also described briefly in the National Bulk Carriers' brochure.

Hughes in Freeport: Despite the fact that Hughes is known to have gone to a Ludwig-owned hotel after leaving London, this has aroused remarkably little curiosity even on the part of Hughes biographers, who barely mention Ludwig in their works.

Hughes memo on purchase of Xanadu Princess: Quoted in Drosnin, p. 453.

Conversation between Jack Real and Dr. Thain: Quoted in Barlett and Steele, p. 21.

Shredding of Hughes's documents: Ibid., p. 24. Fenelon Richards has been identified by other sources as the Intertel agent who accompanied Thain to Acapulco.

## 17. Mercantile Bank

The founding of Mercantile: This information is taken from materials in the files of an undercover U.S. Treasury agent, since deceased, who spent many years in the Bahamas. It is obvious that much of the agent's information came directly from Bahamas corporation files.

Inge Gordon Mosvold: Mosvold is visible as the chief executive officer of Mercantile Bank in corporate records at Nassau. Ludwig is *not* visibly connected either to the bank or Mosvold, but it was the IRS agent's opinion, after many years of residence in the Bahamas, that Mosvold was a Ludwig representative there, in much the same way that, according to Leslie Waller, Wallace Groves was. It has been Ludwig's style of management to keep his various activities separate from one another, appointing over each a manager responsible directly to him.

The Mercantile Group: This sounds like the same sort of set-up Ludwig had put together as his Greater Pacific Group in Australia. (See the American-Hawaiian chapter.)

Paul L. E. Helliwell: During the Watergate investigations, Helliwell emerged as a lawyer tied both to Nixon and the mob. (See Gerth.) The Treasury agent said unequivocally of Helliwell: "He was . . . attorney for D. K. Ludwig and Disney's Florida attorney. He has been or is connected with the Castle Trust in the Bahamas and Caymans, the Mercantile Bank and its subsidiaries in the Bahamas and the Caymans, the First National Bank of Miami, the Bank of Perrine, and the Underwriters Bank Limited." Both First National and the Bank of Perrine were identified by Watergate investigators as being involved in illegal activities.

Bahamas banking: I have personally observed the proliferation of banks in Freeport. I never saw a single customer enter or leave any of them.

Land purchases around Disney World: Most of this material is from court records pertaining to the *International Bank v. Price Waterhouse* case in the Federal District Courthouse in Washington, D.C.

General George Olmsted and General Orval Cook: Biographical information about these men has been compiled from numerous sources, many of them *New York Times* articles.

International Bank's "virtual ownership" of Liberia: This statement is from the aforementioned undercover Treasury agent.

Olmsted and the dairy industry contributions to Nixon: Recounted in *Facts on File* during the Watergate hearings.

Olmsted as part of group seeking to take over Chessie Systems: From *Facts on File.*

Ludwig's attempt to buy into Cinerama: From two *Wall Street Journal* stories, dated May 19 and June 7, 1971.

Mosvold and the American Indian National Bank: From an article in the *Freeport News.*

Castle Bank and Mercantile Bank: The link is shown in Bahamas corporation records and in the undercover Treasury agent's files. Norm Casper's testimony was given to a Senate investigating committee.

Donald Alexander and the Castle Bank probe: Told by Howard Kohn in "The Hughes-Nixon-Lansky Connection" (*Rolling Stone,* May 20, 1976, p. 92).


## 18. *"Welcome to Brazil, Mr. Ludwig"*

A. T. A. Antunes: See Marcos Arruda et al., *The Multinational Corporations and Brazil.*

"Trees like rows of corn": Told by Ludwig to *National Geographic* writer Loren McIntyre.

Robin McGlown: From Arruda.

Amazon Indians and land policies: From an article on the Amazon in the London *Sunday Times Magazine* (June 18, 1978, pp. 39 ff).

Genocide policy of Brazilian government: Reported in *New York Times* stories and *Facts on File.*

Anthropologists' charges: Reported to the author by anthropologist Shelton Davis, who was at the meeting.

Absence of Indians at Jari: As noted in a study by Dominique Gallois, "Notícia Histórica Sobre os Indios do Rio Jari" (*A Questo da Terra,* 1981).

Ludwig's visit with Castelo Branco: Reported in Arruda.

"You would expect it only from a national government": Quoted in "D. K. Ludwig Plans to Harvest a Jungle" (*Business Week,* July 31, 1971, p. 34), also the source of the Campos quote.

Leading Brazilian agronomist: Quoted in Arruda.

Clayton Posey's advice: Quoted in Gwen Kinkead's "Trouble in D. K. Ludwig's Jungle" (*Fortune,* April 20, 1981, p. 106).

VERAGRO: Reported in Arruda.

Failure of Jari: See Kinkead.

General Hugo de Andrade Abreu: This is documented in *Facts on File.*

The floating pulp and power plants: From numerous sources, but *National Geographic,* with Ludwig's cooperation, gave the fullest account in an article by Loren McIntyre printed in May 1980.

Cresap, McCormick & Paget's recommendations: Summarized in Kinkead.

## 19. *"A Gray Old Wolf and a Lean"*

Ludwig's later shipbuilding: From merchant shipping records at the Department of Commerce.

The Burmah Oil transshipment facility: From the files of the undercover Treasury agent in the Bahamas, which also contain a brief sketch of Elias Kulukundis.

The National Bulk brochure: Citations are from a copy in my possession. There is no date of publication given, but certain events mentioned date it as being written around 1974.

Ludwig's proposed Delaware Bay coal-transfer operation: From copies of documents submitted by National Bulk Carriers to the Delaware legislators considering the project.

Savings and loan associations: See "A Billionaire's S & L Collection" (*Business Week,* September 28, 1981, p. 102).

Swiss banking practices: Compiled from various books and articles on the subject, including Leslie Waller's *The Swiss Bank Connection.*

A-S-H Management and the Jersey City project: Reported in Jersey City newspapers and the *New York Times.* Author's interview with Jersey City planning officials by phone about the project.

Ludwig's corporate organization: Compiled from Delaware corporation records, the National Bulk brochure, and newspaper articles.

The Ludwig foundations: Information about the New York–based foundation was obtained through a visit to the National Foundation Center, Washington, D.C. Information about the Swiss foundation comes from Modesto da Silveira's book *Ludwig: Imperador do Brasil* and such magazine articles as *Fortune*'s "Trouble in D. K. Ludwig's Jungle."

Ludwig's honorary doctorate: From a letter to the author from the Johns Hopkins University.

Ludwig's advisory positions: Listed in *Business Week*'s 1957 "Tanker King" article, repeated in *Current Biography.*

# Index

Acapulco, 262, 268–70
Acheson, Dean, 168
Achnacarry (Red Line) Agreement, 94–95, 160
Adonis, Joe, 237
Ahmanson, H. F. & Company, 216
Aiken, George, 125, 147–48
Albertson Ranch, 209, 210, 214–16
Alexander, Donald, 219, 220, 221, 280
Allen, Charles Robert, Jr., 188, 189, 214, 227, 229, 231, 237, 242, 259
Allen, George E., 178, 208, 359
Aluminum, Ludwig's plans for, 304–5, 327–28
Amazon rain forest project, 12–13, 14, 294–300, 312–13, 316–17; and Campos' initiatives, 286–87, 291; Ludwig's plans for, 290–91; size of, 295, 328; and Fordlandia, 298, 333; rice paddies in, 300–302, 326; cattle and agricultural operations in, 302–3; mining and planned hydroelectric operations in, 304–5, 327–28; laborers' conditions in, 307–10, 324, 327; public relations of, 310–12, 322–25, 327, 330; Ludwig's investment in, 312, 316, 331; financing sought for, 314–15; and floating factories, 315–16, 318–22, 325; consultants' report on, 325–26; difficulties of, 327–28, 330–32; and Ludwig's ultimatum, 328–30; ferry tragedy of, 330; final agreement on, 332–33; losses from, 337, 342, 344; and Ludwig self-doubt, 358
American-Hawaiian Steamship Company (AHSS), 6, 177–78, 203–4, 218, 222, 224; Ludwig gains control of, 204, 205–6; and

container ships, 205, 206–8, 218, 219–24; real estate ventures of, 208–10, 214–16, 218, 222; Notter heads, 314
American Petroleum Transport, 5, 85, 121, 123, 126, 127, 128
American Savings & Loan Association, 349
American Savings & Loan of Utah, 217
American Steamship Corporation (Amsteam), 61–62, 63, 67–69
American Tankers Corporation (Amtankers) of Delaware, 5, 73, 75, 84–85, 89, 105
American Tankers Corporation (Amtankers) of Massachusetts, 55–56, 57, 59, 60, 61, 63, 67, 68–73, 75–79, 80–82, 84, 104–5, 105, 122
*Amoco Cadiz,* 307
*Amtank,* 128
*Anahuac,* 54–55
Anastasia, Albert, 227
Anderson, Jack, 255–56
Anderson, Robert (ARCO chairman), 326
Anderson, Robert (Maritime Commission member), 148, 152
*Andrew Jackson,* 101, 102, 103
Antopol, Samuel D., 142
Antunes, Augusto Trajano de Azevedo, 287, 305–6, 332
ARAMCO, 160–61, 177
A-S-H Management Corporation, 353
Atlantic City, New Jersey, 336–37
Atlas Metals Corporation, 138
Auld, Robin, 248
Australia, 167–69, 217, 315, 338, 342, 344
AVCO (Aviation Corporation of America), 178, 356

Bacon, Sir Ranulph, 248–49, 250
Bahama Developers, Ltd., 232–33
Bahamas, 182–83, 186–87; as off-shore haven, 237–38; and Hughes, 257–60, 260–62, 265, 267–68. *See also* Grand Bahama Island
Bahamia, 233, 238, 249, 267, 275, 337
Bahamian Chemicals, Ltd., 191
Bahamian Shipyards, Ltd., 191
Baja California, salt extraction project in, 6, 193–94, 258, 346
Baker, R. Palmer, Jr., 356
Baker, Zedadok, 45, 47, 51
Ballantyne, Arthur A., 178
Bank of the Manhattan Company, 102–3
Bantry Bay terminal, 244–45, 246, 334, 335, 336
Barry, John F., 357
Batista, Fulgencio, 226
Bauxite, Ludwig's mining of, 304, 329
Bay of Pigs invasion, 272
Bechhold, Benno, 214
Beck, Dave, 205
BeLieu, Kenneth, 222, 223
Berkshire Industries, Inc., 217–18
Bermuda, Ludwig activities in, 6, 233–34, 338
Bernstein, Leonard, 357
Betts, Stuart, 62, 66, 72, 97, 122
Bird, Preston, 198, 201
Black Warrior (Guerrero Negro) Lagoon, 193–94, 258, 346
Bluhdorn, Charles, 277
Bootleggers, 31–37, 52, 53; and Bahamas, 35, 183; and law enforcement, 46; at end of Prohibition, 74; and Neutrality Act evasion, 108. *See also* Costello, Frank; *Marian Mosher*
Bounds, Joseph E., 242–43
Brazil, 284–86, 294, 305; and Ludwig's Amazon project, 291, 294–95, 304–5, 311, 327–30, 331–33 (*see also* Amazon rain forest project); Amazonia, conditions in, 292–94; VERAGRO projects in, 306; Ludwig's planned supertanker yard in, 306–7; Figueiredo's presidency in, 317–18; Ludwig activities in, 338
Brewster, Owen, 154
Bridges, Harry, 204, 205
Briscoe, Charles, 324–25
Britain: and Japanese peace treaty, 167–69; Ludwig activities in, 339
British Honduras, 338
Britten, Fred S., 64
Brockett, E. D., 244
Brownell, Herbert, 176, 357, 359

Brudner, Charles (Charlie Brud), 226, 230, 236
Bruno, Angelo, 237
Bulk carriers, 11, 85–86, 89
*Bulkcrude,* 127
*Bulkero,* 127
*Bulkfuel,* 127
*Bulklube,* 124
*Bulkoceanic,* 145
*Bulkoil,* 119–20, 125, 129, 130, 131, 132, 133, 136, 145
*Bulkpetrol,* 4, 145
*Bulkstar,* 145
*Bulktrader,* 145, 156, 159
Bunker, Ellsworth, 178
Burger, Warren, 176
Burmah Oil Tankers, 335–36

Caddy, Douglas, 277
*Caliche,* 85, 121, 125
Cameron, Allen, 311
Campos, Roberto, 286, 291, 295, 329
Canada: Hughes visit to, 266, 339; Ludwig activities in, 338–39
Capone, Al, 36
Cargo Despatch, Inc., 209
Caribbean basin, 181–82, 228. *See also* Cayman Islands; Grand Bahama Island
Carter, Jimmy, 344
Casper, Norman, 279
Castelo Branco, Humberto, 286, 291, 294, 305
Castle Bank, 279–81
Castro, Fidel, 226, 227, 285
Cattle raising, 171–73, 302–3, 306
Cayman Islands, 272, 277, 278–79, 290, 339
Cayman Islanders, 143, 181–82, 218
Cayship Investment Company, 271–72
*Cedros,* 194, 346
Celler, Emanuel, 220
Cellini, Dino and Eddie, 226, 230, 248
Cement, Bahamas plant for, 191–92
Central Industries, 195
Charity, Ludwig's contribution to, 356. *See also* Foundations
Chase Manhattan Bank, 315, 316, 325
Chesler, Lou, 227, 229, 230, 231, 231–32, 237, 249, 251
Child, Richard Washburn, 79–80
*Chiloil,* 85, 121, 125, 126
Churchill, Winston, 95, 113, 114
CIA, and Mercantile Bank, 282
Citricos de Chiriqui, S.A., 213–14
Clark, Joseph, 220
Clutha Development Pty., 315, 344
Coal, Ludwig activities in, 343–49

Cochrane, E. L., 159
Coe, Joseph, 361–62
Cohen, Samuel, 251–52, 274
Colonial Savings of the North, 216
Colonial Savings of the South, 216–17
Commonwealth, 174
Communism, 113, 155, 167–68
Compañia de Navigación Mandinga, S.A., 272
Cone, Hutchinson I., 70–71
Container ships, 205, 206–8, 218, 219–24
Con-Tech (concrete technology) housing, 192–93, 194, 214, 215, 232, 266, 304, 308, 339, 341, 342
Continental Oil Company (Conoco), 195
Cook, Orval, 276
Coppola, Trigger Mike, 227, 230
Cornfeld, Bernard, 232, 281
Cornwell, C. G., 132–33
Corporations, power of, 360–62
Costa Rica, 290, 339
Costello, Frank, 33–36, 41, 52, 151, 237
Courageous, 101, 102
Courtney, Max, 226, 230, 236
Cox (sailor on Marion Mosher), 38–40, 42, 44–45
Coyle, H. J., 178
Cresap, McCormick & Paget, 325–26
Crews' quarters, in Ludwig ships, 115–17
Cromarty Investments, Ltd., 282–83
Crosby, James, 252, 256, 260, 274, 277, 281, 336–37
Crowley, Elmer, 72
Cuba, 226, 285
Cummings, Homer S., 110

Dade County, Florida, 197–202
Dalitz, Moe, 254, 280
Danginn (yacht), 6, 7, 157–59, 193
Daniel Webster, 89–90, 97, 101, 119–20
Dannedaike, 57
Darien, Conn., Ludwig residence in, 6, 126
Daugherty, Harry M., 47, 49–50
Davidson, Frank J., 61
Davis, Chester, 254–55, 256, 261
Davis, Shelton, 324
Defiance, 101, 102, 103, 104, 105
Delaney, James, 220
Delaware: incorporation in, 61; coal-transfer operation offshore of, 346–47
Dern, George, 78, 83
Derounian, Steven, 220
DEVCO (Grand Bahama Development Corporation, Ltd.), 229, 231–32, 236, 237, 249, 250–51
Dewey, Thomas E., 175, 176

Dillon, Douglas, 219
Disney World, 273
Dizer, J. H., 37
Dourado, Rodolfo, 296
Dow Chemical, 194
Dowd, Henry, 281–82, 348
Dowd, Patrick, 282, 348
Dowd, Robert, 282, 348
Drake, George, 118
Drosnin, Michael, 256
Dulles, John Foster, 160, 161, 162, 163, 167–69, 179, 241–42
Dulles brothers, 176
du Pont, Pierre S. (Pete), 347
Duvalier, François (Papa Doc), 228

Eisenhower, Dwight D., 161, 175–76, 196, 199–200
Emden Tankschiffahrt-GmbH, 156
"Empire status," 235, 362
Engle, Clair, 220
Erdölwerke Frisia, A.G., 156
Ericson, R. A., 166
Ervin, Sam, 242, 243
Ethiopia, 83, 339
Exportadora de Sal, 194

Fairless, Benjamin, 241
Fall, Albert B., 65
Farbach, Carl, 109, 110, 111
Fearnside, Philip, 296
Ferrer, Juan, 296–97
Figueiredo, João Baptista de Oliveira, 317, 329, 331
Financial arrangements: "two-name paper," 9–10, 90, 97; in Ludwig's wartime operations, 124–25, 134
Financial General, Inc., 276
Fish, J. A., 355
Fisher, William E., Jr., 326, 355, 356
Fisher Brothers Construction Company, 208–9
Fitzgerald, F. Scott, 9, 34
Flagler, Henry, 197
Flag-of-convenience shipping, 107–8, 141–42; Ludwig in, 142–47, 152, 159, 348; right to picket, 219
Flegenheimer, Arthur (Dutch Schultz), 34, 53
Fleming, Philip, 152
Floating factories, 13, 315–16, 318–22, 325
Float money, 351
Forbes, Raymond, 245
Ford, Henry, 13, 16, 113, 298
Forestry, Ludwig's plans for, 287–90. See also Amazon rain forest project

Foundations, Ludwig money to, 14, 98, 310, 330, 332, 342, 356–57
France, Ludwig activities in, 339
Fred Meyer Savings & Loan, 349
Freeport. *See* Grand Bahama Island
Freeport Bunkering, 241, 242
Frey, Hugo E., 357
*Frisia,* 240

Gable, Clark, 7, 158, 193, 214, 359
Gable, Kay, 158–59, 214, 262
Gambling: and Lansky, 225–26; in Freeport, 226–32, 235–37, 247–48, 249; El Casino, 234, 235, 249; in Atlantic City, 336–37
Gatsby, Jay, and Ludwig, 9
Gay, Bill, 254–55, 256, 260, 261, 262, 269
Geddes, Sir Auckland, 45–51
Geisel, Ernesto, 217, 311, 312
General Agency Agreement, 120, 123, 130
General Dynamics, 221, 222
General Investment Corporation, 185
Genocide, upon Amazonian Indians, 293
Genovese, Vito, 33
*George Champion,* 240
Gerrity, John, 175
Getty, Gordon, 342
Getty, J. Paul, 2, 13, 135, 159
Gilbert, Mart, 38, 40, 41, 42, 43, 44, 46, 51
Gilpatric, Roswell, 220
Glastand, Karl, 272
Glenmoor Cattle Ranch Corporation, 214, 215
Global Seamen's Union, 218
Globe Steamship Line, 38, 39, 41, 42, 57
*Gmelina arborea,* 289–90, 296, 298, 300, 322, 325. *See also* Amazon rain forest project
Golden, James, 261, 262
"Golden Greeks," 3–4. *See also* Niarchos, Stavros; Onassis, Aristotle
Goldsmith, C. Gerald, 229
Gold smuggling, allegations of, 304, 309, 322
Gordon, Lincoln, 286
Gordon, Waxey, 53
Gottlieb, John O., 210
Goulart, João, 284–86, 290, 311
Grand Bahama Island, 183–84, 185–92; Ludwig's activities on, 182, 188–92, 195, 232–33, 234, 238–39, 259, 338; gambling on, 226–32, 235–37, 247–48, 249; royal commission of inquiry for, 248–49, 250–51; Hughes on, 258, 267–68; Mercantile Bank on, 271–77, 278–79, 281–82, 283; Ludwig's power on, 290; terminal planned for, 334–36
Grand Bahama Port Authority, Ltd., 189, 227, 237, 241

Great Britain. *See* Britain
Greater Pacific General, 217
Great Western Wine Company of Canada, 51
Greece, 339
Greenberg, Max, 53
Greene, Ralph C., 49
Greenspun, Hank, 260
Groff, Mary (Mrs. Charles P. Ludwig, grandmother of D.K.), 17–19, 20
Groves, Wallace, 183–89, 190, 191, 227, 229, 231, 236–38, 238–39, 248, 249, 250, 251, 259, 274, 337
Guerrero Negro (Black Warrior) Lagoon, 193–94, 258, 346
Gulf Oil Company, 190, 241–44, 246, 262
Gulick, James W., 220, 223
Gunther, Max, 24
Gushue, Jacob, 38, 45, 47, 51

Haile Selassie, 83, 359
Halfpenny, I. M., 119, 198
Hall, Leonard, 280
Hall, Marshall B., 55, 57, 60–61, 67, 70, 73, 75, 84
Hamilton, Marquess of, 232
*Hampton Roads,* 128, 130, 131, 132, 133, 136, 137
Hann, Elmer, 155–56, 162, 169, 173
Harding, Warren G., 46, 79, 93
*Harold H. Helm,* 240
Harsimus Cove, 353–55
Hartshorn, Gary, 323
Hato Vergareña, 172–73
Havenner, Franck R., 163
Hawaii, Ludwig office building in, 217
Hawaiian Freestone, Inc., 209
Hawaiian Realty, Inc., 208–9
Hawaiian Washington, Inc., 209
Hayward, Sir Charles, 189, 227, 229, 237, 242, 259, 281
Hayward, Jack, 281
Helliwell, Paul L. E., 272, 273–74, 275, 281
Hendrickson, John B., 119, 122
Herter, Christian, 241–42
Hess, F. C., 355
High Seas Tankships, 6
Hilles, Charles D., 64, 70
Hitler, Adolf, and western industrialists, 113, 114. *See also* Nazi Germany
Hodges, Luther, 207, 220
Hoge, Warren, 322–23
Holliday, Raymond, 256
Home Savings, 349
Honduras, 290
Hong Kong, 339
Hoover, Herbert, 63–64

Hoover, Loring Revere, 207–9, 218
Hotels, of Ludwig, 233, 234, 262, 269, 274, 338, 339, 340
Hougan, Jim, 175
Housing: Con-Tech innovation in, 192–93, 194, 214, 215 (see also Con-Tech housing); real estate activities, 208–10, 214–16, 217, 222, 232–34, 353–55
Hughes, Charles Evans, 45–51, 52
Hughes, Howard, 2, 13, 135, 253–57, 355, 359; on "empire status," 235; and Las Vegas, 254–55; and Ludwig, 255–56, 258–59, 262, 267; in Bahamas, 257–58, 260–62, 267–68; Nicaragua visits of, 262, 264–66, 340; Canadian trip by, 266, 339; London visit of, 266–67; Mexico trip by, 268–70; death of, 270
Hull, Cordell, 81
Hunt, E. Howard, 277
Hunt, H. L., 2
Hutton, E. F., 352
Hydroelectric power, and Ludwig's Brazilian plans, 304–5, 327–28
Hyman, Eliot, 229

Iceland, 339
Ickes, Harold, 78
Idlewylde (lake steamer), 29–30
Imperial Savings & Loan, 217
India, 340
Indonesia, 217, 340
Innovations by Ludwig: in shipbuilding, 117–19; Con-Tech housing, 192–93, 194, 214, 215
Inspectors, government, as absent from Norfolk shipyard, 134
Insurance companies, Ludwig's purchase of, 217
International Concrete Company, 192–93
International Housing, Ltd., 192–93, 266, 314, 342
International Tankers, S.A., 6, 142–43, 174
Intertel, 256, 261, 261–62, 266, 270, 336
Invincible, 101, 102–3, 103–4, 106, 107, 109–11, 115, 119
Irving, Clifford, 261
Isbrandtsen, Hans, 86
Italy, oil shipments to, 79–83

Jaffe, Richard, 279
James Otis, 60, 62, 66, 67, 68–70
Japan: shipbuilding competition from, 154; Ludwig shipbuilding in (at Kure), 155, 160, 162–70, 173, 179, 181, 188, 192, 240–41, 245, 290, 307, 334, 346; capitalist development of, 161–62; peace treaty on ship-

building in, 168–69; and newsprint plant, 328; Ludwig's activities in, 340
Jari Florestal e Agropecuária, Ltda., 296
Jari project. See Amazon rain forest project
Javits, Jacob, 220
Jenkins, George, 356
Jenkins, J. Caldwell, 68
Jersey City, Ludwig development in, 353–55
Jidda Agreement, 176–77
John Adams, 89–90, 97
John Hay, 60, 62, 66, 67, 68–70, 72, 75, 76, 77, 84, 90
Johns Hopkins University, Ludwig honorary degree from, 357–58
Johnson, J. M., 80–81
Johnson, Nicholas, 221, 223
Journapak Corporation, 208
Joyce, F. J., 355

Kahl, F. E., 355, 356
Kaiser, Henry J., 151
Kaolin, from Amazon, 305, 329, 332
Kaplan, A. I., 29–30, 42
Karmin, Monroe, 236–37, 250
Keith, William, 178
Kemmerer, Adolph E., 357
Kempton, James H., 172–73
Kennedy, Edward, 220
Kennedy, J. A., 178
Kennedy, Joseph, 52
Kerr, James R., 356
Kerkorian, Kirk, 256
Khashoggi, Adnan M., 267
King, F. F., 116
King, Howard, 331
King, John M., 281
King, Vivienne, 321
Kinkead, Gwen, 26, 316
Knight, Telfair, 101
Kodama, Yoshio, 179
Kroeger, Hal A., 178
Kulukundis, Elias, 335, 348
Kure, Japan: Ludwig shipyard in, 4, 6, 11, 155, 156, 163–70, 173, 179, 181, 191, 192, 194, 240–41, 245, 307, 334, 346; Ludwig's floating factories from, 316, 318–19

Lambert, William, 237
Lamott, Kenneth, 117
Land, Emory S., 104, 106, 109, 125, 148
Lansburgh, Morris, 202, 251–52, 274
Lansky, Jake, 226, 230, 248
Lansky, Meyer, 34, 52, 53, 202, 225–26, 227, 230, 236, 237, 248, 251, 259, 274, 279
Lansky organization, 337

Launching sideways, Ludwig's introduction of, 118
Laxalt, Paul, 256, 261
Leahy, Francis T., 55–56, 60–61, 70
Liberia, 6, 174, 240, 276, 282, 340
Liberty ships, 131–32, 137
Lightering vessels, 345–46
Lilien, Al, 53
Linkletter, Art, 359
Litton Industries, 207, 222, 224, 262
Livanos, Stavros, 3, 117
London, Hughes visits, 266–67
Lord, George de Forest, 86, 176n
Los Angeles area, Ludwig real estate development in, 209, 210, 214–16
Luciano, Charles (Lucky), 33, 52
Ludwig, Charles Palman, Sr. (grandfather of D.K.), 17–19, 20, 22
Ludwig, Daniel F. (father of D.K.), 17, 20, 22–24, 73–74, 98–99; and psychology of wealth, 25; and D.K.'s early career, 26; and *Mosher* incident, 38, 39–40, 41–43, 51; as D.K.'s backer, 84, 85, 86, 105, 121; and Rockefeller establishment, 96
Ludwig, Daniel Keith: personal and social life of, 12, 126–27, 359; birth of, 20; first petroleum hauling by, 54–55; back injury of, 56; first marriage of, 57–59, 74; second marriage of, 97–98 (*see also* Ludwig, G. Virginia); WWII gains of, 126, 130, 150; wealth of, 126, 342–43, 355–56; interviewer's impression of, 211–12; worldwide accomplishments of, 338–42; honorary degree to, 357–58; as empire-building gambler, 358, 359; impact of, 358–59; and corporate exponent, 360–62
Ludwig, Flora (mother of D.K.), 20, 23–24, 25
Ludwig, G. Virginia (Ginger) (wife of D.K.), 97–98, 126–27, 142, 157, 158–59, 356
Ludwig, Gladys Madeline (wife of D.K.), 58–59, 74, 97, 102
Ludwig, Patricia Margaret (daughter of D.K.), 58, 97
Ludwig & Gilbert, 39, 41, 57
Ludwig's Pier, 16, 17, 23
*Lusitania* incident, 27–28
Lynch, James J., 37, 40, 42, 43, 44–45, 53
Lynmar Company, Ltd., 282

Maas, Peter, 52
McCann, Gerald, 354
McCloy, John J., 243
McCormack, John (Congressman), 78
McCormick, Charles L., 119
McFarland, Carl, 110

McGlown, Robin, 290–91
McIntyre, Loren, 323
McKeown, J. A., 116
McLaney, Mike, 226
McLean, Malcolm, 207, 219–20, 222, 224, 356
McLean Industries, 206, 224
McNamara, Robert, 222
Maggadino, Steve, 237
Maheu, Robert A., 175–77, 254, 260–62
Malaysia, 217, 340
Malone, Robert W., 63–64, 65, 68, 70–71, 71–72, 73, 77–78, 81–82, 89, 96, 101, 103–4, 109, 122
Manus, Allen, 249
*Marian Mosher* (*Mosher* incident), 38–53, 54
Marine salvage, Ludwig's familiarity with, 109–10
Maritime Administration, 159, 181, 206–7, 219–24, 280, 347–48, 348, 362
Maritime Commission, 85, 100–101, 125, 147–49, 150–52; and Ludwig, 85–87, 89, 101–7, 108–11, 115–16, 129–30, 132–33, 136–39, 142–43, 144, 145–47, 149–50; and flag-of-convenience shipping, 107–8; and WSA, 120; and shipbuilders' role in scandal, 151; and U.S. shipbuilding, 152–53
Marshall, Lawrence C., 178
Maruzen Oil Co., Ltd., 212
Mary Carter Paint Company, 232–33, 252, 256, 281
Médici, Emelio, 309, 311, 323
Mercantile Bank, 271–77, 278–79, 281–82, 283
Mercantile Group, 272, 275
Merchant Marine Act (1936), 100–101
Merchant Ship Sales Act (1946), 131–32, 136
Messer, Alfred E., 25
Mexico: Hughes in, 268–70; and Ludwig, 290, 340 (*see also* Baja California)
Michaelides, Serge, 272
Miller, William, 220
Mills, Earl W., 152
Milluna company, 282
Moerman, Samuel H., 178, 205–6, 208–9, 221, 223
Molasses hauling, by Ludwig, 29–30
Monaco, and Onassis, 234–35, 257, 258
Moore, Mrs. Edward P., 127
Morgenthau, Robert, 247–48
Morse, Huntington, 103–4, 106, 108–9, 110, 115
Mortimer, Elias, 46
"Most favored treatment," for Ludwig by Maritime Commission, 138–39

Mosvold, I. Gordon, 272, 275–76, 277, 278, 282, 283, 337
Multinational corporation(s): Ludwig as, 172, 338; in Brazil, 284–85, 291, 295n, 305
Murchison, Clint, 277
Murder Incorporated, 34
Mussolini, Benito, 79–80, 88, 113, 114

NASA, and moon-rocket shipping, 219
*Nashbulk,* 128
National Bulk Carriers, 5, 86, 101, 102–6, 110–11, 115, 122, 123, 124, 127, 133–34; expansion through, 89; profits of, 121; stock distribution of, 126; and end of war, 128, 129–30; and transfer to Panama, 147; and Maritime Commission, 150; Nixon as attorney for, 176; and refueling station, 190; and Exportadora de Sal, 194; and Ahmanson, 216; and McLean, 224; shift from shipping by, 240; and Newport Industries, 277–78; brochures of, 337–42, 359–60
National Defense Act (1936), 104
National Petroleum Transport Company, 5, 85, 123, 138, 143
National Tankships, 5
Nazi Germany, Onassis/Niarchos oil-carrying for, 140–41
Negroponte, Catherine, 122
Netto, Delfim, 329, 331, 332, 333
Neutrality Acts, 107–8
Newport Industries, 277–78
Newsprint plant, and Amazon project, 328
New York City, Ludwig in, 29, 57, 84–85, 198
Niarchos, Stavros, 3–4; as free spender, 116, 117, 119; and Sud Americano de Vapores, 122; surplus ships to, 139–40; WWII activities of, 140–41; as Ludwig competitor, 141, 143, 144, 145, 157–58, 207; vs. Onassis, 174, 176–77, 235; supertankers by, 241; tankers sold to, 342
Nicaragua: Hughes visits, 262, 264–66, 340; U.S. intervention and rise of Somoza in, 263–64; earthquake aid diverted in, 266; Ludwig in, 290, 340
Nigeria, 290
Nixon, Richard, 175–77, 243, 272, 280, 359
Norfolk, Virginia, shipbuilding yards, 6, 10, 115, 118, 123–24. *See also* Sewalls Point yard
Noroton, Conn., Ludwig home in, 126–27
Notter, John, 313–14, 355, 357
Nuclear-fueled vessels, 221, 223–24

O'Brien, Leo, 220
O'Callaghan, Mike, 267

Oceanic Tankships, S.A., 5–6, 144, 174
O'Connell, John, 248
Offshore banking, 272–73
Oil industry, 91–95
Olmsted, George, 276–77, 281
Onassis, Aristotle, 3–4, 97, 174–75; as free spender, 117; and Sud Americano de Vapores, 122; surplus ships to, 139–40; WWII activities of, 140–41; as Ludwig competitor, 141, 143, 144, 145, 157–58, 207; Monaco bought by, 234–35; supertankers by, 241; Hughes on, 257, 258; as maverick, 362
Onassis, Christina, 315, 342
OPEC, 307, 314–15, 336, 344
Operation Haven, 279, 280
Orange growing, by Ludwig in Panama, 213–14
*Ore Chief,* 173
*Ore Convey,* 173
Ore hauling, Ludwig in, 170–71, 173–74, 177, 191, 192, 241
*Ore Mercury,* 219
*Ore Monarch,* 173, 218
*Ore Prince,* 173, 219
*Ore Titan,* 173
*Ore Transport,* 173
Ore Transport Company, 177
Orovitz, Max, 227, 229
Oulahan, Richard, 237
*Overbrook,* 57

Panama: Ludwig's activities in, 6, 174, 195–96, 213–14, 340–41; flag-of-convenience shipping in, 107–8, 141–42; Ludwig registers in, 142–47, 152; Mercantile Bank straws in, 282; Ludwig's power in, 290
Pan American Petroleum & Transport Corporation, 90–91, 95, 97, 101, 105, 119, 121, 134, 141
*Pan Carolina,* 119–20, 121, 125
*Pan Delaware,* 121, 130
*Pan Georgia,* 121, 125, 173
*Pan Massachusetts,* 120, 124, 129, 174
*Pan Pennsylvania,* 120–21, 124
*Pan Virginia,* 121, 125
Paradise Island, 252, 259, 261; Hughes on, 260–62, 265
Parental death, and wealthy men, 24–25
Parsons, Ralph M., 159
Patten, Frank, 39, 44, 53
Peacock, James Craig, 77, 78–79, 80, 81, 82, 84
Peloquin, Robert, 256, 268
Penn, Stanley, 236–37, 250
Peters, Dusty, 248

Peterson, Russell, 347
Petrochemical complex: of Ludwig in Panama, 195–96; South Florida plan for, 199–202
*Petrofuel,* 121, 124
*Petrokure,* 169
Pettipas, Joseph, 44, 45, 47
Philbin, J. Harry, 63
*Phoenix* (original), 56, 57, 60, 66, 67, 70, 72, 75, 76, 89, 103, 117, 121, 121–22, 139–40
*Phoenix* (second), 128
*Phoenix* (third), 170, 240
Phoenix Steamship Corporation, 89, 104–5, 121, 123
Pindling, Lynden O., 247, 259, 278
"Pittsburgh Connection," 241
Poe, F. Eugene, 272
Port Arthur, Texas, 25, 26, 136–37
Posey, Clayton, 300, 309–10, 327
Powell, Joseph W., 63
Princess International hotels, 269, 338, 339
Pritzger family, 281
Prohibition, 28–29, 31, 108, 183, 225; bootleggers during, 32–37, 52, 53, 74 *(see also Marian Mosher)*; and law enforcement, 46; end of, 74
Pulp mill. *See* Floating factories

Quinn, J. M., 132–33

Ranfurly, Earl of, 186, 189, 190–91
Rankin, Judy, 296
Reagan, Ronald, 159, 216, 262, 343, 359
Reagan administration, and coal export, 348
Real, Jack, 269–70
Real estate, Ludwig in, 208–210, 214–16, 217, 222, 232–34, 353–55
Reed, Red, 226
Refinery: of Ludwig in Panama, 195–96, 340–41; South Florida plan for, 199–202; in Greece, 339
Reid, David C., Company, 57, 72, 79, 81
Reinfeld, Joe, 53
Rice planting, by Ludwig, 300–302, 326, 331
Richards, Fenelon, 270
Richardson, J.A.W., 97, 122
Ritter, Frank, 226, 230, 236
Rockefeller, James S., 178
Rockefeller, John D., 2, 91–94, 162, 355, 362
Rockefeller establishment: and Ludwig, 90, 95–97, 99; and Nazi regime, 113; and Onassis/Niarchos, 141; and anti-Onassis campaign, 175–77
Roll-on-roll-off loading (RORO), 204–5. *See also* Container ships
Roosevelt, Franklin D.: and Mussolini, 79, 80; and oil shipments to Italy, 81, 82–83; shipping reorganization by, 100; and Neutrality Acts, 107–8, 141; and Nazism, 113, 114; and Bank of United States, 184; and Nicaragua, 263
Roosevelt, Franklin D., Jr., 220, 221
Roosevelt, James, 219, 220, 221
Roper, Daniel, 77, 78, 80, 83, 100
Rothstein, Arnold, 34
Ryan, H. R., 119

Sadlo, George, 226
*St. James,* 125
St. John, William B., 172
Sandino, Augusto Cesar, 263
Sands, Sir Stafford, 186–87, 226–27, 230, 236, 238, 242, 249, 250–51, 274
Santa Patricia Mining, Ltd., 305
Saud (king of Saudi Arabia), 7, 174
Saugatuck, Michigan, 23
Saunders, Dero, 7–9, 11–12, 20, 21, 29–30, 211
Savings and loan companies, Ludwig in, 216–17, 349–50, 353
Schapiro, Morris, 55, 109–10
Schlanbusch, John L., 272
Schober, Robert J., 73, 85, 126
Schultz, Dutch (Arthur Flegenheimer), 34, 53
Seadade Realty, Inc., 198–202, 203, 212, 272
Sea-Land Services, 206, 222, 224
*Sealane,* 173–74, 188, 190
Seatankers, Inc., 5, 174, 232
Security (Bahamas) Company, Ltd., 272
Sellin, Neil, 245
Sewalls Point yard, 124, 137, 155, 156, 159–60
Shearson, Hammill & Company, 245
Shelton, Turner, 262, 265
Shinto, Hasashi, 307
Shipbuilding: Ludwig's innovations in, 10, 117–19; by Charles Ludwig, Sr., 18–19; in Ludwig family, 21, 22; "bigger is better" as Ludwig motto in, 132, 173; to foreign yards, 152–53; in Germany and Japan, 154; Japanese, 168–69
Ship Sales Act, 137
Siegel, Benjamin (Bugsy), 34, 53, 225
*Silverpeak,* 138–39
Simonsen, Mario, 328
Simpson, Wallis Warfield, 183
Sinatra, Frank, 215
*Sinclair Petrolore,* 173
Singapore, 217, 341
Sirivich, William, 78
Slocum, B. E., 119

S & M Fox Pty., 315
Smith, C. Arnholt, 280
Smith, Clarence W., 119
Smith, F. Randall, 245
Smith, William W., 152
Solar Salt company, 194
Somoza Debayle, Anastasio, 262, 263–64, 266, 340, 359
South Africa, Ludwig in, 341
South Haven, Michigan, 9, 15–19, 20, 22–23, 58
South Korea, 341
Southwest Savings & Loan, 349
Spreckels, Adolph, 158
Stamford, Connecticut, 74, 99, 126
Stampados, D. G., 272
Standard Oil Company, 92–94, 140–41
Standard Oil of New Jersey, 93, 142–43, 146, 262
Steel: and Kure shipyard arrangements, 164, 165–67; Ludwig's Venezuelan project for, 170–73
Steinberg, Charles J., 53
Stinginess, of Ludwig, 116–17, 218
Sud Americano de Vapores, S.A., 122
Sun, Ronald, 355, 356
Sunrise Properties, Ltd., 233
Superior Pocahontas, 343
Supertankers, 4, 10; and Sewalls Point, 155; from Kure shipyard, 155, 156, 169–70, 240–41, 334; Grand Bahama facility planned for, 191, 192, 195; rivalry in, 241; Gulf Oil's order for, 244–45; Brazilian repair-yard proposed for, 306–7; Ludwig cancels plans for, 307; as gamble, 336
Surplus vessels: Ludwig acquires, 59–60, 130, 132, 136–38, 140; Ludwig attempts to acquire, 87; government cuts off sale of, 101; government sale of (post-WWII), 130, 131, 134; Onassis/Niarchos purchase of, 139–41
Switzerland: foundation in, 14, 310, 330, 332, 342, 356, 357; Ludwig enterprises in, 341
Symonette, Sir Roland, 186, 230, 236

Taft, Robert, 175
Taiwan, 217, 341
Tanker Service Agreement, 123, 128
Tankers Oceanic Corporation, 85, 121, 123, 126
Taylor, E. P., 232, 314, 342
Teagle, Walter, 93–94
Teamsters Union, 205, 251–52, 280
Terre Haute, 60, 62, 63, 66, 67
Thain, Wilbur, 269–70
Thompson, Morley P., 350–53

Thropp, Frank, 37, 38, 39, 43
Tisch, Lawrence, 277
Todd, Michael, 151
Tomkins, P. A., 272
Tomlison, William, 55
Trading stamps, 350–51
Trafficante, Santos, 237
Transford corporation, 85, 123
Transford II, 85, 107–8, 121
Transoil, 85, 121, 123, 125, 142–43
Triumph, 101, 102–3, 104, 105, 120
Truman, Harry S, 160–61
Turine, Charlie (the Blade), 230
"Two-name paper" arrangement, 9–10, 90, 97

Udall, Stewart, 200
Ugly Bahamians, The, 236
ULCC (ultra-large crude carrier), 307
Ulysses (original), 62–63, 65–87, 88, 90, 96, 105, 122, 139–40
Ulysses (second), 132, 137, 144
Union action, against Ludwig, 218–19
Union Oil Company, 212–13
United Dry Docks, 62, 63–65, 70, 72
Universe Admiral, 240
Universe Apollo, 241
Universe Aztec, 334
Universe Burmah, 334, 335
Universe Challenger, 240
Universe Commander, 240
Universe Daphne, 241
Universe Defiance, 240–41
Universe Explorer, 334, 335
Universe Frontier, 315, 334
Universe Iran, 246
Universe Ireland, 246
Universe Japan, 246
Universe Korea, 246
Universe Kure, 334
Universe Kuwait, 246
Universe Leader, 4, 240
Universe Mariner, 334
Universe Monitor, 334
Universe Patriot, 334
Universe Pioneer, 334
Universe Portugal, 246
Universe Ranger, 334
Universe Sentinel, 334
Universe Tankships, 5, 174, 218, 240, 305, 332
Uruguay, Ludwig's plan for, 313
U.S. Steel, 170–71, 173, 191

Venezuela: Ludwig's enterprises in, 6, 170–73, 173–74, 188, 195, 196, 302, 341; jaguar

hunting in, 9, 193; bribe to president of, 243; Ludwig's power in, 290
VERAGRO (Veredas Minas Agropecuária, Ltd.), 306
Vesco, Robert, 281
Vickery, Howard L., 104, 106, 116, 148, 152
*Virginia*, 119, 120, 121
Virginia and Daniel Ludwig Foundation, Inc., 356
VLCC (very large crude carrier), 307
Voetberg, Frances, 272
Volstead Act, 28–29, 31, 47
Voluntary Tanker Pool, 144

Wagner, William W., 6, 86, 313; as insider, 89–90; and "two-name paper," 97; as corporate officer, 122, 142, 198; in government dealings, 123, 129; as shareholder, 126; in interview, 212, 213; death of, 313
Waller, Leslie, 189, 259
Wang, Huang, 302
Warman, Morris, 1, 2–3, 13–14
Warren, Lindsay, 125
War Shipping Administration (WSA), 120, 123, 142, 149–50
Weaver, L. E., 116
Weber, William A., 131
Welding, Ludwig's introduction of, 117
Welding Shipyard, Inc., 10, 117, 119, 122, 124–25, 127, 128–29, 132, 134, 137, 145–46, 150, 160
Well, John W., 156
Wenner-Gren, Axel, 183

Western Operating Corporation, 86, 87, 88, 105, 122
West Germany, 154, 156, 341
Westlake Communications, 215
Westlake Village, 210, 214–16, 314, 349
Wharton, Joseph, 248
Whiteford, William H., 241–46
Whitney, John Hay, 277
*Wico*, 55
Wild, Claude, 243
Willamette Savings and Loan, 349
Willebrandt, Mabel Walker, 47–49, 50, 52
*William C. McTarnahan*, 121, 125
*William Penn*, 101, 102, 107, 108–9, 111, 115–16, 119, 121, 125
Windsor, Duke of, 183
Wister, Owen, 362
Wolfson, Mitchell, 201
Wolstencroft, Michael, 279
Working conditions: on Ludwig's ships, 115–17, 218; in Amazon project, 307–10, 324, 327
Wylie, Philip, 201
Wynkoop, Everett, 288–89

Xanadu Hotel, 234, 255, 267, 268, 314

Yoshida, Shigeru, 162, 163, 179–80, 181, 188, 192, 240
Yugoslavia, 341

Zizelman, Paul, 44–50
Zwillman, Abner (Longie), 53

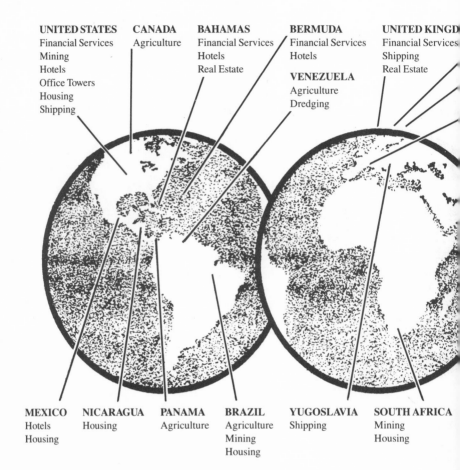

**UNITED STATES**
Financial Services
Mining
Hotels
Office Towers
Housing
Shipping

**CANADA**
Agriculture

**BAHAMAS**
Financial Services
Hotels
Real Estate

**BERMUDA**
Financial Services
Hotels

**VENEZUELA**
Agriculture
Dredging

**UNITED KINGD**
Financial Services
Shipping
Real Estate

**MEXICO**
Hotels
Housing

**NICARAGUA**
Housing

**PANAMA**
Agriculture

**BRAZIL**
Agriculture
Mining
Housing

**YUGOSLAVIA**
Shipping

**SOUTH AFRICA**
Mining
Housing